Coping with Life during the Thirty Years' War (1618–1648)

Studies in Central European Histories

Founding Editors

Thomas A. Brady and Roger Chickering

Edited by

David M. Luebke (*University of Oregon*)
Celia Applegate (*Vanderbilt University*)

Editorial Board

Steven Beller (*Washington, D.C.*)
Marc R. Forster (*Connecticut College*)
Atina Grossmann (*Columbia University*)
Peter Hayes (*Northwestern University*)
Susan Karant-Nunn (*University of Arizona*)
Mary Lindemann (*University of Miami*)
H. C. Erik Midelfort (*University of Virginia*)
David Sabean (*University of California, Los Angeles*)
Jonathan Sperber (*University of Missouri*)
Jan de Vries (*University of California, Berkeley*)

VOLUME 69

The titles published in this series are listed at *brill.com/sceh*

Coping with Life during the Thirty Years' War (1618–1648)

By

Sigrun Haude

BRILL

LEIDEN | BOSTON

Originally published in hardback in 2021.

This paperback contains corrections to minor inaccuracies of the hardback edition.

Cover illustration: Willem Cornelisz Duyster. The Marauders, 1630–35. Oil on panel, 36 × 50 cm. Paris, The Louvre.

All illustrations were created by Daniel Gladis.

The Library of Congress has cataloged the hardcover edition as follows:

Names: Haude, Sigrun, 1959– author.
Title: Coping with life during the Thirty Years' War (1618–1648) / by Sigrun Haude.
Description: Leiden ; Boston : Brill, [2021] | Series: Studies in Central European histories, 1547–1217 ; volume 69 | Includes bibliographical references and index.
Identifiers: LCCN 2021026762 (print) | LCCN 2021026763 (ebook) | ISBN 9789004466470 (hardback) | ISBN 9789004467385 (ebook)
Subjects: LCSH: Bavaria (Germany)—History—Maximilian I, 1597–1651. | Thirty Years' War, 1618–1648—Social aspects. | Bavaria (Germany)—Social conditions—17th century. | Germany—History—1618–1648.
Classification: LCC DD801.B373 H38 2021 (print) | LCC DD801.B373 (ebook) | DDC 940.2/4109433—dc23
LC record available at https://lccn.loc.gov/2021026762
LC ebook record available at https://lccn.loc.gov/2021026763

Typeface for the Latin, Greek, and Cyrillic scripts: "Brill". See and download: brill.com/brill-typeface.

ISSN 1547-1217
ISBN 978-90-04-69494-1 (paperback, 2024)
ISBN 978-90-04-46647-0 (hardback)
ISBN 978-90-04-46738-5 (e-book)

Copyright 2021 by Sigrun Haude. Published by Koninklijke Brill NV, Leiden, The Netherlands.
Koninklijke Brill NV incorporates the imprints Brill, Brill Nijhoff, Brill Hotei, Brill Schöningh, Brill Fink, Brill mentis, Vandenhoeck & Ruprecht, Böhlau Verlag and V&R Unipress.
Koninklijke Brill NV reserves the right to protect this publication against unauthorized use. Requests for re-use and/or translations must be addressed to Koninklijke Brill NV via brill.com or copyright.com.

This book is printed on acid-free paper and produced in a sustainable manner.

To My Family:
Gundula Haude-Ebbers
Manfred Ebbers
Ingo Haude
Marco Ebbers

And to the Loving Memory of
Elli and Gunter Haude

∴

Contents

Preface IX
List of Illustrations XIII
Abbreviations XIV

1 **Introduction: The Lay of the Land** 1
   1   Focus – Historiography – Methodology 1
   2   The Thirty Years' War, Abridged 8
   3   Places and Characters 16

2 **Experiences of War** 24
   1   Fear and Vulnerability 28
   2   Instability and Disruption 43
   3   Poverty – Hunger – Dearth 52
   4   Violence and Human Concern: World Views Turned Upside Down 56

3 **Governmental Support: Hopes, Measures, and Realities** 70
   1   Protection against Violence 70
       1.1 *Fortifications* 70
       1.2 *Troops* 74
       1.3 *Negotiations and Guidance* 80
   2   Stemming Deprivation and Disease 90
       2.1 *Poverty and Poor Relief* 90
       2.2 *Health and Disease* 100
   3   Averting Spiritual Harm and Promoting a Decent Life 113

4 **Coping with the Experiences of War** 123
   1   To Flee or Not to Flee 123
   2   News and Information 133
   3   Pragmatism, Resilience, and Initiative 149
   4   Connections, Communities, and Space 178
   5   Religion and Other Formative Forces 186
       5.1 *Official Religious Resources* 186
       5.2 *Responses to Official Religious Offerings* 207
       5.3 *Augmenting Official Religious Resources: Magic Practices* 211
   6   Lifting Up the Spirit 221

5 Conclusion: Life Beyond Devastation   232

Glossary   237
Bibliography   240
Index   289

Preface

It is a great privilege to work on a subject of which one never tires. Even after almost two decades of poring over texts, the Thirty Years' War has not lost any of its fascination for me. I first conceived of the topic during a conversation with Manfred Schulze, when we met over a glass of wine in Tübingen toward the end of my previous research project (focused on the Anabaptist Kingdom of Münster) and brainstormed about my next venture. These conversations seeded in me a desire to move from the Reformation's early stages to what is traditionally considered its last phase, the momentous Thirty Years' War. My curiosity about this conflict goes back to my childhood years when I tried to grasp its dimensions during history sessions at the Gymnasium. The fact that the war filled such a prominent space in the history curriculum underscores the enduring place it holds in the German consciousness. While interest in the war has traditionally been focused on its military and political players, I was drawn to the question of how people managed to survive – if they did – the seemingly unending war. This became the subject of my studies that has enthralled me ever since.

Passion for a project alone, however, is not enough to sustain oneself, and I have been very fortunate in the people and institutions who supported me generously and consistently throughout my long journey. Many colleagues offered invaluable advice, feedback, and encouragement over the years. The long list of cheerful and sage companions includes Jack Bernhardt, Tom and Kathy Brady, David Cressy, Ross Dickinson, Carlos Eire, Constantin Fasolt, Marc Forster, Michael Gross, Daniela Hacke, Karen Hagemann, Joel Harrington, Scott Hendrix, Reinhard Heydenreuter, Susan Karant-Nunn, Ethan Katz, Robert Kolb, Mary Lindemann, Ute Lotz-Heumann, Terry McIntosh, Hans Medick, Helga Meise, Cornelia Niekus Moore, Dorinda Outram, Geoffrey Parker, Ina Ulrike Paul, Beth Plummer, David Price, Helmut Puff, Jonathan Reid, Tom Robisheaux, Ulinka Rublack, Richard Schade (d. 2019), Ingo Schwab, Gerd Schwerhoff, Laura Stokes, Michael Stolleis (d. 2021), Ulrike Strasser, Mara Wade, Elisabeth Wåghäll Nivre, Peter Wallace, Merry Wiesner-Hanks, Gerhild Scholz Williams, Peter Wilson, Heide Wunder, and Charles Zika. Some of these colleagues and friends played leading roles as they encouraged and sustained me throughout this project. Ross Dickinson's early request for the film rights for this project cheered me no end. Several colleagues read early drafts of my manuscript and gave me crucial feedback. First among them is Tom Brady, whose incisive assessment of my initial draft set me on the right path. He also underscored the necessity of good maps by anticipating comments such as, "Franconia, where is that?" I am most appreciative of Peter Wilson's keen advice on an early chapter. Marc Forster's heartening appraisal and Jack Bernhardt's perceptive reading helped me make good choices in trimming the manuscript and fortifying my argumentation. And I am very grateful to the anonymous reviewers, whose excellent suggestions assisted me in tightening and bolstering my study.

During the course of this project, I spent extensive time at archives and research libraries and received generous assistance from their staff. The *Staatsarchiv Nürnberg* was a most welcoming place. Every time I visited the archive, its director, Gerhard Rechter (d. 2012), invited me to conversations about my work over a cup of coffee. Gerlinde Maushammer was a marvelous wellspring of information and support. The members of the *Nürnberger Archiv für Familienforschung* at the *Staatsarchiv* were enthusiastic supporters of my project. The team at the *Landeskirchliches Archiv der Evangelisch-Lutherischen Kirche in Bayern* (Nuremberg) helped me unearth crucial documents in their vaults. The archivists of Munich's *Stadtarchiv*, *Staatsarchiv*, *Hauptstaatsarchiv*, *Archiv des Erzbistums München und Freising*, and the *Staatsbibliothek* offered essential and ready support, as did the *Diozesanarchiv Augsburg*. The Herzog August Bibliothek with its superb and unparalleled collections became my anchor during the many years of researching and writing. There, I found rich material; an impressively knowledgeable and helpful staff; and an inspiring, international community of scholars, where I could test my findings. Jill Bepler, Volker Bauer, Andreas Herz, Christian Heitzmann, Christian Hogrefe, and Ulrike Gleixner of the HAB made sure that I found what I was looking for and readily engaged in eye-opening conversations about my project. I am most grateful for their unwavering and attentive assistance. And, finally, the history reference librarian, Sally Moffitt, of the Langsam Library at the University of Cincinnati, together with its incomparable Interlibrary Loan staff, furnished me with any material I needed and in record time. I am most grateful to these individuals and their institutions.

Several bodies generously funded my research trips and writing periods, none more so than the Taft Research Center at the University of Cincinnati. Taft not only provided substantial funding for summer research trips and conference travel to present my findings, but also awarded me a Center Fellowship, which allowed me to work on an early draft of this book, as well as a subvention for its publication. I received a three-month fellowship at the Herzog August Bibliothek in Wolfenbüttel, and the University Research Council (at UC) funded a summer research trip. The Department of History supported me both financially through its Von Rosenstiel Fund and general research subsidies, and by giving me time to write at crucial junctures during this process.

My colleagues in the University of Cincinnati's History Department provided me with the spiritual and thoughtful support that is so essential in our work, especially Gene and Dottie Lewis, Chris Phillips, Barbara Ramusack, Hilda Smith, and Willard Sunderland. Maura O'Connor – friend, colleague, and department head – never wavered in her faith in me and my work. My graduate students were a constant source of inspiration and support. Dan Gladis – with the judicious assistance of Susan Ryan – expertly created the relevant maps and tables that help us visualize the spatial dimensions of this study. Evan Johnson read a first draft of my bibliography.

I also had the benefit of many dedicated friends who lent me their essential services during the course of this project. Hildegard Zörkler with her regional expertise read an early version of the manuscript for local accuracy. Katharina Gerstenberger has not only been an unwavering friend throughout this long process, but she also went through the final manuscript with a fine-toothed comb in search of inconsistencies and mistakes, and helped me proofread the index. Anna Linders reviewed parts of my manuscript, gave me astute advice, and could not have been a better and more committed friend. My copyeditor, Cindy Carlton-Ford, made what could well have been a painful process a most agreeable and enriching one. We turned out to be a great team as we traded chapters, questions, and comments. Any remaining mistakes are, of course, mine. The editors at Brill were a pleasure to work with: David Luebke, the early modern series editor of Studies in Central European Histories, gave his crucial support and perceptive advice regarding my project; Wendel Scholma and Arjan van Dijk promptly and kindly responded to my many questions; and Theo Joppe ensured a smooth and expeditious production process.

Beyond friendly professional support, I was surrounded by many companions who cheered and rooted for me during my years of researching and writing. This would have been a lonely road, had it not been for a host of devotees, including Mike Bootes, Svea Braeunert, Prince Brown, Marian Budde, Linda Castell, Andrea Cheng (d. 2015), Angélique Droessaert-Robisheaux, Jean Dye, Hope Earls McSwigan, Janet and David Fedders, Udo Greinacher, Ellen Harrison, Robert Hater, Christina Hazlett, Yousef Hussein, Farihah Ibrahim, Beverly Jones, John Kessel, Marian McSwigan, Mary Sue Morrow, Susan Murtha, Tanja Nusser, Carolyn Reisinger, Ron Slone, Annalaurie Wattson Lamb, and Maria Zörkler. Through it all, my family sustained me in countless, fundamental ways. My siblings followed in our parents' footsteps and were always at my side mentally and spiritually during the ups and downs of this journey. They applauded my successes and stood by me during rough stretches. I dedicate my book to them.

A Note on Usages

All translations from German documents and secondary sources are mine, unless indicated otherwise. Most German names are rendered in their German spelling, including the use of "von" rather than "of," except for those cities and names which are commonly anglicized. Dates are usually rendered in Gregorian style, although some documents provide both the Julian and Gregorian forms of dates. I frequently use the word "confessional" or "confession," which in the early modern context means belonging to a religious community that is bound by, or "confesses to," a doctrinal statement (e.g., the Augsburg Confession of the Lutherans). Thus, in the early modern period, Lutheranism, Calvinism/Reformed Religion, and Roman Catholicism are referred to as "confessions," not denominations. The terms "evangelical" and "Evangelicals," too, have different connotations in the seventeenth century than they do nowadays: they indicate Protestants (both Lutherans and Calvinists/Reformed) and underline their strict adherence to the Gospel (*Evangelium*) in their perceived opposition to Roman Catholics (to whom I commonly refer as "Catholics"). Regarding the currency values around 1600, 1 thaler equaled 1 florin (or gulden) and 30 kreuzer (half a florin). Thus 1,000 thaler amounted to 1,500 florin. For further information on historical terms, please see the glossary.

Over the course of the last two decades, some of my work at various stages of its development has been published in articles. My study builds on these pieces, but none of the following chapters are reproductions of these articles. Some sections contain in revised form short segments that appeared in earlier publications, namely "The Experience of Disaster during the Thirty Years' War: Autobiographical Writings by Religious in Bavaria;" "The Experience of War"; "Female Religious Communities During the Thirty Years' War"; "Religion während des Dreißigjährigen Krieges (1618–1648)"; "The Thirty Years' War (1618–1648): Moving Bodies – Transforming Lives – Shifting Knowledge"; and "The World of the Siege in New Perspective: The Populace During the Thirty Years' War." Full references can be found in the bibliography.

Illustrations

Figures

1. Europe circa 1618   3
2. The Holy Roman Empire circa 1618   11
3. The path of Gustavus Adolphus and his troops in the south   13
4. Franconia   17
5. Bavaria and its administrative districts (*Rentämter*)   20
6. Eichstätt   29
7. Bamberg   31
8. Regensburg diocese   34
9. Ammersee region   36
10. Kitzingen and surrounding area   47
11. Greater Nuremberg   85
12. Munich and vicinity   95
13. Deaths vs. births in Nuremberg, 1618–1646   111

Table

1. Devastation in Munich's *Rentamt*: 1630 vs. 1636   98

Abbreviations

ÄA	Äußeres Archiv
AEM	Archiv des Erzbistum München und Freising
AKA	Ansbacher Kriegsakten
Akt.	Akten
AKTA	Ansbacher Kreistagsakten
ASHVMF	Archivaliensammlung des Historischen Vereins für Mittelfranken
BM	Bettelmandat
B&R	Bürgermeister und Rat
DA A	Diozesanarchiv Augsburg
Dk	Dekanat
DK	Dreißigjähriger Krieg
FA	Familienarchiv
fasc.	fascicle
GW	Gesundheitswesen
HAA	Hohenaschauer Archiv
HAB	Herzog August Bibliothek
HR	Hofrat
HRP	Hofratsprotokolle
HS	Handschriften
HSS	Handschriftensammlung
HStA M	Bayerisches Hauptstaatsarchiv München
HV	Historischer Verein
KB	Kurbayern
KHHA	Kirchen in der Herrschaft Hohenaschau
KL	Klosterliteralien
KR	Kammerrechnungen
KuO	Kirchen und Ortschaften
LAA	Landalmosenamt
LG	Landgebiet
LAELKB	Landeskirchliches Archiv der Evangelisch-Lutherischen Kirche in Bayern [in Nuremberg]
M	Mandate
MD	Markgräfliches Dekanat
Misc.	Miscellanea
MK	Markgräfliches Konsistorium
MS	Manuskriptensammlung

ABBREVIATIONS

Nbg	Nuremberg
NL	Nachlaß Lori
RA	Rentmeisteramt
Rep.	Repertorien
RK	Ratskanzlei
RL	Rentmeister-Literalien
RSP	Ratssitzungsprotokolle
Rst	Reichsstadt
SA M	Stadtarchiv München
SSS	Stadtschreiberserie
StA M	Staatsarchiv München
StA N	Staatsarchiv Nürnberg
StBM	Staatsbibliothek München
SV	Stadtverwaltung
URS	Unterrichterserie
VP	Visitationsprotokolle
Wfb.	Wolfenbüttel

CHAPTER 1

Introduction: The Lay of the Land

1   Focus – Historiography – Methodology

As the final chapter of the Reformation period, the Thirty Years' War is both a key event for understanding the history of the Reformation and a turning point in the evolution of modern Europe. Its destruction and tremendous toll on the population are its most well-known aspects. Until recently, its horrors were kept alive in German memory through folk songs and poems. The ruin during and following the conflict, however, was not just a product of the historical imagination of later generations. In the percentage category of world population loss for any war ever fought, the Thirty Years' War makes the "Top Ten List."[1] The event as a whole, then, certainly qualifies as a disaster in the modern sense, although, up close, experiences were more diverse.[2]

Two events in the recent past have brought the Thirty Years' War to the forefront of contemporary Europe: the 350th anniversary of the Peace of Westphalia in 1998 and the 400th anniversary of the outbreak of the war in 2018. Both celebrations occurred during uncertain and unsettling times in European history. In the late 1990s, Europe tried to come to terms with the fall of the Wall, the toppling of the Soviet Union, and the end of the Cold War, while also endeavoring to forge a new Europe around a common currency.[3] Twenty years later, Europe is straining under economic pressures, immigration issues, and political disunity, and is struggling once again to determine its direction. At this juncture, when its future as an integrated political and economic unit is under assault, Europe is remembering the beginning of the Thirty Years' War four hundred years ago. Besides its impact on the future of the Holy Roman Empire and Europe, the war continues to serve as a touchstone for examining

---

1   "Population Control, Marauder Style," *The New York Times*, 6 November 2011. The list is headed by Genghis Khan in the thirteenth century, when 11.1 percent of the world population was lost, as opposed to the Thirty Years' War with 1.4 percent of world population loss.
2   Scholars of disasters have pointed out that catastrophes are not by nature disastrous but are defined as such depending on their impact on humans – and, one might add, the environment. While contemporaries did not use the word "disaster" or *Katastrophe* in our modern sense (they understood it to mean "change" or "alteration"), many of them experienced the war as catastrophic. For a discussion of the use and meaning of *Katastrophe*, see François Walter, *Katastrophen*, 16–21.
3   The euro was introduced virtually in 1999 and in 2002 with notes and coins.

the accelerating and retarding conditions of conflict, as it did for previous generations of historians.[4]

Much has been written about the motives and origins of the conflict.[5] Scholars are still debating whether the 1555 settlement made the Thirty Years' War inevitable, what role religion played in instigating and sustaining the war, whether its occurrence was part and parcel of the larger wave of wars taking place in Europe, what the war was about, and what constituted the significance of the Peace of Westphalia for the future of the Holy Roman Empire and Europe as a whole. On some of these issues, historians have reached a degree of consensus; on others, the debate continues. A major shift in the war's assessment concerns the question whether one can draw a straight line from 1555 to 1618, i.e., whether the Peace of Augsburg set up the later conflict. While earlier scholarship had stressed the shortcomings of the 1555 settlement, which presumably heightened the Holy Roman Empire's fragmentation by adding religious to political divisions, historians more recently have drawn attention to the impressive longevity of the treaty – a remarkable 63 years – and to the concerted efforts on both sides to make the Peace work.[6] In this important shift of historical perspective, the outbreak of the war is not regarded as inevitable, but largely as a result of failings among the Habsburgs and of dynastic quarreling. Moreover, it emphasizes the importance of personalities over structures if conditions are right.

While cognizant of the almost inseparable entanglement of religion and politics in the early modern period, most historians are agreed that religion or confession was by and large a contributing rather than a decisive factor in the outbreak of the war.[7] Moreover, confession played a much diminished role during the second half of the war. Historians have also underlined the difference between propaganda and reality. While political players found it useful to rally people around their cause through starkly confessional language, their tactic on the ground was generally more sensitive to practical concerns. Indeed, most of the territorial princes engaged in the war were driven by interests relating to their dynastic claims, such as expansion of their power and territory, rather than by overarching political objectives.

---

4   Earlier in the twentieth century, in *Thirty Years War*, Cicely V. Wedgwood elucidated the lessons of the war as she interpreted them on the eve of World War II.
5   Most recently, Geoff Mortimer in *The Origins of the Thirty Years War*.
6   See especially Wilson, *Thirty Years War*; Brady, *German Histories*; and Medick and Marschke, eds., *Experiencing the Thirty Years War*.
7   Wilson, *Thirty Years War*, 9; Wilson, "Role of Religion."

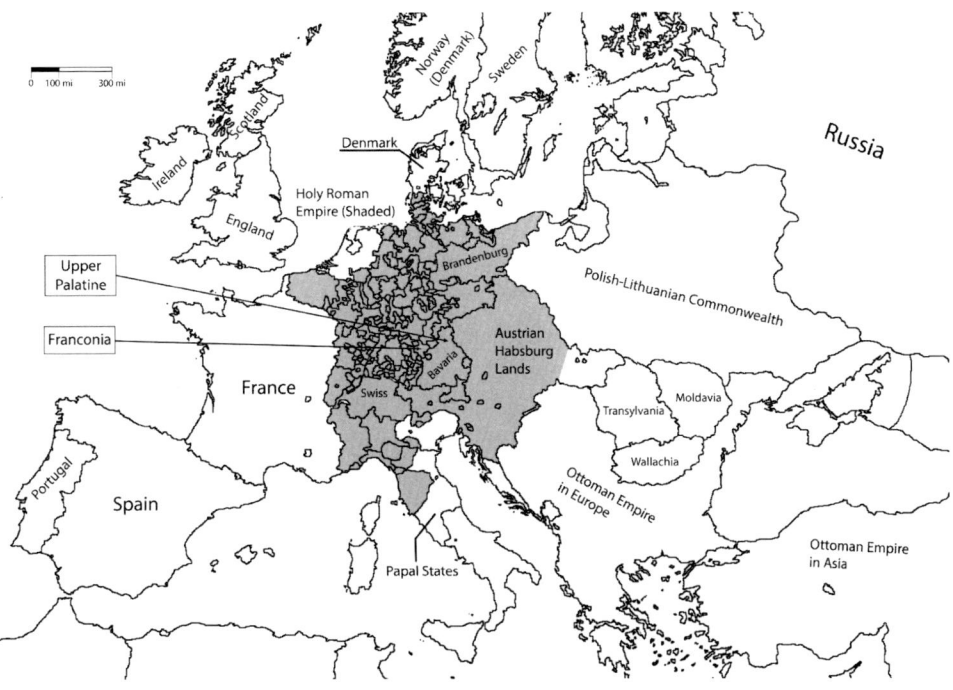

FIGURE 1   Europe circa 1618

Still, the involvement of other European powers in the conflict points to larger issues at stake. The debate over the war's broader political significance remains in flux, with the most intriguing thesis advanced by Johannes Burkhardt, according to whom the war represented a *Staatsbildungskrieg*, rather than a *Staatenkrieg* (a war about how a state is formed and constructed rather than a war between states) and was fought over who would rule Europe.[8] In this view, the French, Habsburg, and Swedish (Gothic) visions of empire, in which each power aspired to supreme rule over Europe, eventually gave way to the compromise of a "summitless pyramid," with a number of powers existing "side by side with equal entitlement."[9]

In the same way as the inevitability of the war has come under scrutiny and criticism, so has the assessment of its resolution in the Peace of Westphalia. Earlier scholarship evaluated the settlement in mostly negative terms as reverting to antiquated patterns that perpetuated its political and religious

---

8 See Burkhardt, *Der Dreißigjährige Krieg*; "Summitless Pyramid"; and "Worum ging es im Dreißigjährigen Krieg?"
9 Burkhardt, "Summitless Pyramid," 58.

fragmentation and arrested Germany's development, while nation states were blossoming elsewhere. More recent studies have highlighted both the rearward- and forward-looking qualities of the treaties, and have assessed them decidedly more positively. During a time when nation states have lost their cachet, Germany's political path now looks more like shrewd federalism than obstinate particularism. Moreover, legal scholars have underscored the path-breaking legal dimensions of the Peace of Westphalia. Echoing Burkhardt, Heinhard Steiger contends that "the treaties of Münster and Osnabrück attained their epochal significance because for the first time they had succeeded by means of modern international law to make peace between equal powers within Europe without creating a summit hierarchy – thus laying the first foundations of the international law of treaties in the European order for the next 150 years."[10]

The 1998 anniversary also occurred in the wake of new impetus in the historical profession. Stimulated by a series of cultural turns, ever more historians embraced micro history, historical anthropology, and the history of everyday life. These approaches have had a decisive impact on studies of war, which broadened their investigations to include everyday experiences of life during wartime.[11] Chief among these are the works of Hans Medick, Benigna von Krusenstjern, and Geoff Mortimer.[12] The new concentration on experience also prompted the creation of a *Sonderforschungsbereich* (Special Research Branch, SFB 437) at the University of Tübingen with experiences of war as its focus.[13] The heightened interest around the anniversary furthermore engendered copious publications of wartime accounts found in local archives, which illuminate the heart-breaking misery that many contemporaries experienced. Military leaders and their strategies, in contrast, for the most part have taken a backseat.[14]

This study is greatly indebted to the methods of historical anthropology, and departs from earlier panoramic views of the conflict, in which deaths and damages are tallied up into dizzying numbers, to focus on more local occurrences and a range of witnesses of the Thirty Years' War. It illuminates the

---

10 Steiger, "Concrete Peace," 440.
11 Lüdtke, ed., *History of Everyday Life*; Medick, "Mikro-Historie." On cultural turns, see Doris Bachmann-Medick, *Cultural Turns*, now in an updated English translation.
12 Krusenstjern and Medick, eds., *Zwischen Alltag und Katastrophe*; Mortimer, *Eyewitness Accounts*; Mortimer, *Eyewitness Accounts*.
13 SFB 437 existed from 1999 until 2008 and focused on early modern and modern experiences of war. Matthias Asche and Anton Schindling published the first results of this project in *Das Strafgericht Gottes*, a collected volume on the Thirty Years' War.
14 There are a few exceptions, such as Mortimer's *Wallenstein*, which places the military leader in the larger context of the war.

war up close – life in and out of crisis – or what Hans Medick and Benigna von Krusenstjern have called an existence between everyday life and disaster (*zwischen Alltag und Katastrophe*). In the process of tracing contemporaries' actions, the discussion engages with various other areas of historical study, among them the history of communication, news, and media in the seventeenth century; of home and exile; of the emotions; of poverty and poor relief; and of health and epidemic diseases. One especially prominent theme is the importance of space.

Why another book on the Thirty Years' War? Countless hours of reading contemporary testimonies have convinced me of the need for a study that reflects a broader range of experiences and reactions than histories of this conflict typically offer. While the war brought devastation and trauma to much of the population, the narrative of utter ruin has been all-pervasive. Historians readily acknowledge that some areas suffered less than others, and that certain locales on the geographic margins capitalized on the war effort and came out as economic, social, and cultural winners. Hamburg, situated at the outskirts of the military action, profited substantially from the war.[15] Conversely, territories lying in the corridor of troop movement likely faced the greatest amount of destruction. But here, too, a hidden-away valley might escape the carnage.[16] The more complex dynamics of interaction in the war zones, however, has rarely been addressed. Against a largely uniform perception of the war as wholly devastating, this study seeks to expand our view of the war to include not only its – albeit predominantly – destructive power, but also its intermittent positive encounters. Furthermore, even in areas where the war raged, we find not only despair, but resilience, pragmatism, and surprising ingenuity. Life during the Thirty Years' War was not a homogenous vale of gloom and doom, but a multifaceted story that is often heartbreaking, yet, at times, also uplifting.

My work thus contributes to a recent trend in scholarship that tries to move early modern European studies beyond straightforward narratives of conflict and tension, and heeds, instead, the gray zones and patterns of coexistence and cooperation as well. For the Holy Roman Empire, scholars have focused particularly on cities and territories, where different confessions existed and where these communities had to find ways to live together.[17] The Thirty Years'

---

15   Knauer and Tode, eds., *Krieg vor den Toren*.
16   Unterammergau in Bavaria, for example, was touched by neither war nor pestilence, even though Bavaria in general was hit hard by the war. SA M, HV MS 151/1–2, vol. 1, 91.
17   See, for example, Bahlcke et al., eds., *Konfessionelle Pluralität*; François, *Unsichtbare Grenze*; Greyerz et al., eds., *Interkonfessionalität*; Kaplan, *Divided by Faith*; Louthan et al., eds., *Diversity and Dissent*; Luebke, *Hometown Religion*; Luebke and Lindemann, eds., *Mixed Matches*; Luria, *Sacred Boundaries*; Pietsch and Stollberg-Rilinger, eds.,

War has rarely been considered in this regard – perhaps because it stands as the conflict par excellence. Peter Wilson and Johannes Burkhardt have noted efforts at political negotiations and compromise that continued throughout the war, efforts that were drowned out by the noise of the more belligerent contestants.[18] But on the local level, too, this horrendous war has more to offer than tales of conflict. The continuous movement of people brought together communities of different faiths in countless places throughout the empire, which affords a particularly fruitful and instructive lens onto issues of coexistence in a confessionally divided society.

At its core, this study explores how people coped with this long war; on what resources they drew to survive violence, hunger, loss, and disease; and how they tried to make sense of a conflict that appeared ever more meaningless as the war dragged on. This discussion is preceded by two chapters that situate contemporaries' responses to the war and make us appreciate their significance. The first (Chapter 2) centers on experiences: how did people experience a war of such magnitude, length, and severity with its disastrous repercussions, such as inflation, famine, disease, destruction, violence, and displacement? These questions are not easy to answer since, beneath a general sense of suffering, contemporary experiences varied considerably. As Günther Franz noted long ago, the protracted conflict did not have an evenly devastating impact on the Holy Roman Empire.[19] Geographic variation often also meant chronological divergence. Some territories felt the brunt of the war early on; for others, it came ten or more years into the conflict. Even the official end point of the war – 1648 – does not apply everywhere, since in some regions troops were not retired until years later, when they were finally paid. This study pays close attention to the uneven and diverse ways of experiencing the war. It begins by tracing the experiences of several people in their communities: they ranged from fear, uncertainty, and instability, to exile, homelessness, disorder, and disruption. I argue that all these experiences were rooted in a deep sense of vulnerability and lack of protection.

Konfessionelle Ambiguität; Safley, ed., *Companion to Multiconfessionalism*; Spohnholz, "Multiconfessional Celebration"; *Tactics of Toleration*; and Warmbrunn, *Zwei Konfessionen in einer Stadt*.

18 Wilson, *Thirty Years War*, and Burkhardt, *Krieg der Kriege*.

19 Franz, *Der Dreißigjährige Krieg*. Many of Franz's findings still stand, even though he has received criticism. See Behringer, "Von Krieg zu Krieg," and Theibault, "Demography." Some correctives to Franz's study and numbers are offered by Christian Pfister in *Bevölkerungsgeschichte* and Quentin Outram in "Socio-Economic Relations." A summary of the results of regional studies can be found in Wilson, *Thirty Years War*, 786–95.

This leads directly into the second part (Chapter 3) of the investigation: what were the day's political realities and how did governments try to help their subjects? What could the populace expect from their lords? How did authorities attempt to protect their subjects against violent attacks, material losses, poverty, and epidemic diseases occasioned or accelerated by the war? As one disaster followed the next or intersected with one another, did governments even have any room to maneuver? This section discusses efforts at physical protection, poor relief, and disease control. It exposes the social and political dynamics between subjects and local, middling, and central authorities that are particularly discernable during this time of crisis. I argue that, despite earnest efforts, authorities could rarely help, and that this lack of assistance and protection eventually led to a loss of confidence by the populace in their governments. When authorities no longer could be relied upon to hold up their end of the bargain (protection), as their subjects held up theirs (service) under ever more trying circumstances, people lost faith in their governments. Worse, when their own troops appeared to behave more appallingly than those of their enemies, this experience shook the foundations of their understanding of the world. As a consequence, survival depended largely on the actions of the subjects.

How, then, could safety be attained? How did people try to help themselves in the face of widespread government inability? How did they attempt to counter the war's chaos? The final and most expansive section (Chapter 4) seeks to answer these questions. In tracing flights and negotiations, courageous acts and furtive moves, spiritual aids and practical resources, this focal chapter exposes a populace that confronted the challenges of war in creative, sometimes desperate, but often ingenious ways.

The arc of the investigation, thus, moves from experience to governmental action to people's responses in the face of the war's trials. In the local, scaled down perspective foregrounded in this study, the rich vignettes of contemporaries afford us glimpses into the devastation and trauma the war brought to so many, but they also demonstrate that people were not solely helpless victims overrun by the war. They showed remarkable agency and initiative in stemming the war's negative consequences. While the movement of people unleashed by the war precipitated violent confrontations, at times, it also led to more amicable encounters.

The analysis rests heavily on archival material – a good portion of it little known – and, as such, necessitates geographic restrictions for much of its investigation. The regions in and around modern-day Bavaria serve as geographic focus. These southeast lands include Franconia with Nuremberg, the margraviate Brandenburg-Ansbach, various bishoprics in Franconia, the duchy of Bavaria with Munich, and the Upper Palatinate. This diverse assortment of regions and cities lends itself profitably to comparisons of Protestants and Catholics, imperial and court city, as well as city and countryside. The majority of sources come from archives in Munich, Nuremberg, Augsburg, and the Herzog August Bibliothek in Wolfenbüttel, and span a wide range of genres, including council minutes, health and financial records, newspapers, recording calendars, pamphlets and broadsheets, correspondence, diaries, chronicles, songs, sermons, poems, and visitation style records. The focus on the southeast German lands brings with it a chronological concentration on the period after 1630, since Bavaria did not become the center of the action until Sweden entered the war (1630). These mid- to later stages of the conflict provide further comparative angles between the heated early 1630s and late 1640s and the less belligerent but nevertheless challenging period in between.

Many years ago, when I started my research into *Lebensbewältigung*, i.e., coping with and surviving this long war, archivists could not point me to a specific assortment of sources. Munich's *Hauptstaatsarchiv* had a sizable inventory for documents on the Thirty Years' War, but these comprised materials on military battles, sieges, contracts, and correspondence between military commanders; there were few, if any, pieces on how people dealt with the war. The same was true for Nuremberg's *Staatsarchiv*, although in both places archivists thought creatively about ways to unlock this aspect of the past. During one sabbatical and many subsequent summers, I worked through stack after stack of archival records – secular and ecclesiastical – in search of insights on how contemporaries tried to survive. Because of this circuitous journey, the selection of documents did not proceed as systematically as one might expect in terms of an even geographic or chronological spread, but instead yielded a rich chorus of voices. A range of published autobiographical accounts from the regions round out this documentary base. Because of the intense time for Bavaria and Franconia during the Swedish Intervention, many documents focus on the early 1630s, but repeatedly accounts move beyond this time frame.

2 The Thirty Years' War, Abridged

The following sketch of the Thirty Years' War offers a rough outline to help position the political and military developments underlying our exploration.[20]

---

20   In place of a long list of studies on the war's political and military history and its major players, I will limit myself to Peter Wilson's recent *Thirty Years War* – a scholarly masterwork that illuminates not only crucial aspects of the military event, but also places it in the larger history of the Holy Roman Empire.

The heated decades of the Reformation ended with the Religious Peace of Augsburg (1555), in which Lutheranism (but not the Reformed religion, sometimes also called Calvinism) was acknowledged as a legitimate confession alongside Catholicism. The formula "whoever rules a region can decide its religion (*cuius regio eius religio*)" came to describe the mode by which a territory's lord could choose the religion (Roman Catholicism or Lutheranism) for his or her region. The Augsburg compromise was viewed as a preliminary settlement, whose religious stipulations would be addressed again at a future meeting, at which religious unity would once more be established.

Over the next decades, the 1555 peace agreement proved remarkably resilient and functioned as the foundation upon which conflicts in the empire were settled, and neither the expansion of the Reformed religion/Calvinism nor disputes over the ecclesiastical imperial estates derailed the equilibrium in the empire. Around the turn of the century, however, the Habsburgs were distracted with internal affairs and weakened by the financially ruinous involvement in the Long Turkish War (1593–1606). During this political vacuum, extremists gained ground. In 1608 the Reformed Palatinate founded the Protestant Union, and Catholic Bavaria followed in 1609 by establishing the Catholic League. Peter Wilson nevertheless underlines that, "despite these ominous developments, support for the Augsburg settlement remained strong among moderate Catholics and most Lutherans, and there was no inevitable slide towards war."[21] The antagonistic rhetoric, however, rose, especially around the Lutheran Jubilee celebrations of 1617 just prior to the outbreak of war.[22]

In 1617 the militant among the Catholics managed to get Archduke Ferdinand (1578–1637), who was sure to impose strict Catholicism upon a hitherto religiously fairly heterogeneous Bohemia, elected as Bohemian king and future emperor. The radical (Reformed) opposition responded by throwing two (Catholic) Habsburg officials and their secretary out the window of Prague castle, which came to be known as the (second) Defenestration of Prague (23 May 1618). The "rebels" (so called by their opposition) deposed Ferdinand and offered the Bohemian crown to Frederick V (1596–1632), elector of the Palatinate and champion of the Reformed religion. Neither faction in this dispute, as Peter Wilson has emphasized, represented the majority of their religious party, whose members were more moderate and wanted "to advance their faith by pragmatic and peaceful means." Indeed, this situation escalated

---

21   Wilson, *Holy Roman Empire*, 124.
22   Burkhardt, *Der Dreißigjährige Krieg*, 128–43. Taking Martin Luther's Nailing of the 95 Theses as its point of reference, this celebration marked the centennial of the Reformation.

into a war because of "the failure to contain successive crises," not because of a general predisposition toward war.[23]

Frederick's acceptance of the Bohemian crown in 1619 placed him in opposition to the Austrian Habsburgs, and soon other forces aligned themselves with one side or the other. Bavaria and the Spanish Habsburgs joined the emperor, while the Dutch, English, and French supported the Bohemian "rebels" and the Palatinate. The reasons for these alignments were not exclusively informed by confessional rationales, but also by larger strategic thinking. In November 1620, forces on the imperial side faced Frederick and his allies at the White Mountain outside Prague and pulled off a resounding victory. Against his expectations, Frederick had little support from his allies, neither from the Protestant Union nor from England.[24] Some 27,000 men of the Catholic League under General Johann Tserclaes, Count of Tilly (1559–1632), swiftly defeated the Bohemian army of roughly 15,000 men. Duke Maximilian of Bavaria (r. 1598–1651) played a large part in this victory, which gained him the Upper Palatinate and the electoral title from 1623 onward.[25] The Bohemian rebels, many of them nobles, lost their land and possessions, and Frederick his electorship, while the Palatinate and Heidelberg were overrun by enemy troops. Frederick became henceforth known as the "Winter King," since he ruled for only one winter (1619–1620).

Between the Battle at the White Mountain and Denmark's intervention in 1625, the hyperinflation of 1622 and 1623 had a powerful impact on the empire. The financial fallout of the military confrontation, the previous involvement in the Long Turkish War, the continued maintenance of armies, and crop failures in 1621 and 1622 precipitated an economic crisis, which states tried to manage by minting debased coins (the so-called *Kipper und Wipper* period). Only drastic imperial measures were able to curb the inflation. The subsequent entry of Denmark into the war in 1625 on the side of the Protestants did not change the dominance of the Catholics. The Danish king, Christian IV (r. 1588–1648), plunged into the war because of dynastic and political rather than religious goals, among them greater control over Lower Saxony and a desire to get there ahead of Sweden.[26] He, too, however, was decisively defeated because he faced

---

23   Wilson, *Holy Roman Empire*, 124–25.
24   Bohemia had not been a member of the original treaty in 1608 and was thus excluded from support by the Union. Frederick was married to Elizabeth Stuart, daughter of King James I of England (r. 1603–1625), but this marital bond did not translate into military support.
25   The electoral title initially pertained only to Maximilian, not to later generations. The duke of Bavaria received the electoral title through transfer from the Palatinate, which lost its electorship. At the Peace of Westphalia (1648), Bavaria's temporary electorship was made permanent, and an eighth electorship for the Palatinate was added to the seven existing ones.
26   Wilson, *Thirty Years War*, 387–88.

THE LAY OF THE LAND

not only the Catholic League army under Tilly, but also a new formidable imperial army led by Albrecht Wenzel Eusebius von Wallenstein (Waldstein) (1583–1634). Tilly's and Wallenstein's armies quickly asserted supremacy over the north German lands and parts of Denmark, forcing Christian to make peace with the emperor in 1629 (Peace of Lübeck).[27]

FIGURE 2   The Holy Roman Empire circa 1618

---

27 Christian's holdings were reduced to his pre-war territories, and he had to agree not to involve himself again in imperial affairs.

That same year, the advantageous position of the Catholic party prompted Emperor Ferdinand II to release the Edict of Restitution (1629), which demanded that all Catholic church property taken by the Protestants since 1552 be returned (i.e., the Peace of Passau was taken as the normative year or *Normaljahr*). There is general agreement – among contemporaries, including Catholics, and later historians – that, with this document, Ferdinand overplayed his hand. The strict interpretation of the Peace of Augsburg in favor of the Catholics made people wonder whether there were any limits to Ferdinand's designs. The emperor's uncompromising stance alienated the moderates among both Lutherans and Catholics, and snubbed the Calvinists, since it demanded their categorical exclusion from the terms of Augsburg's peace treaty. Yet, even in this volatile situation, moderates led by Electoral Saxony and Brandenburg continued to negotiate for a compromise that would be acceptable to Lutherans and Catholics, one that would overcome even the Lutheran-Calvinist divide. Five years later, a similar compromise was fashioned with the Peace of Prague (1635).

In 1630, under pressure from the electors, the emperor dismissed Wallenstein, who, to their minds, had become too powerful with his huge army. That same year, Gustavus Adolphus (r. 1611–1632) landed on the Baltic coast (at Usedom off Pomerania) and inaugurated the Swedish phase of the war, which reset the political realities in the empire. The motives for Sweden's entry into the war have been much debated. Without denying the king's own deep religiosity, historians nowadays are by and large agreed that, contrary to Swedish and Lutheran propaganda, Gustavus did not enter the war to save the Protestants from imperial and thus Catholic annexation. Rather, he was driven by a desire for security and by his own political ambitions.[28]

In order to procure soldiers and funds, the Swedish king needed the support of the empire's Protestant estates, but many princes and cities were reluctant to surrender their intermediate position and side with a largely unknown political actor; however, Gustavus Adolphus did not accept neutrality. The princes' cautious stance began to change when imperials besieged and (accidentally) burned down the city of Magdeburg in May 1631, leaving about 20,000 dead. The event became a defining moment in the perception of the war and its parties. At that point the electors of Brandenburg and Saxony

---

28 Sweden had just emerged from the Polish-Swedish War (1626–1629) as the dominant power in the eastern Baltic Sea. Gustavus Adolphus was concerned about the strong imperial presence in the northern German territories close to his domain. Johannes Burkhardt also posits that the king had designs for a Swedish (Gothic) empire (Burkhardt, "Summitless Pyramid," 58).

THE LAY OF THE LAND

joined the Swedish king. On 17 September 1631, their combined forces (over 40,000) fought the Catholic allies (over 30,000) at Breitenfeld (a small village about five miles northwest of Leipzig) and carried off a decisive victory – the first for the Protestant party. With the Catholic forces weakened, Wallenstein was recalled as commander-in-chief of the imperial army in December 1631, while, after Tilly's death (30 April 1632), Maximilian assumed leadership over Bavaria's troops (with the assistance of Johann von Aldringen, 1588–1634).

Gustavus Adolphus next moved the war to the German South. In early 1632, his second-in-command, the Swedish-Finish count, Gustav Horn (1592–1657), attacked Bamberg, but Tilly, who hurried there from Nördlingen with some 22,000 men, was able, after fierce fighting, to retake the city. Meanwhile, the Swedish king marched from Mainz to Nuremberg and on to capture

FIGURE 3   The path of Gustavus Adolphus and his troops in the south

Donauwörth, and then to Munich. On his way, his army crossed the river Lech, which was a considerable feat, and in April 1632, at the Battle of Rain, defeated and mortally wounded Tilly (who died two weeks later). Augsburg surrendered, but reinforced Ingolstadt held. Frustrated, Gustavus Adolphus took aim at Munich, devastating Bavaria's South on his way. On 17 May 1632, the city fathers turned Munich over to the Swedish king; meanwhile, Maximilian had already withdrawn.

After Wallenstein had been recalled, he managed quickly to raise a large army and faced Gustavus Adolphus at the *Alte Veste* (Old Fortress), a derelict castle on a wooded hill outside of Nuremberg. Both sides camped in the vicinity for several weeks before they joined the battle in early September 1632. The size of armies had grown from a median 20,000 at the beginning of the war to, in the case of Wallenstein's and Gustavus' armies, over 100,000 during the late 1620s and early 1630s.[29] It is difficult to give exact numbers for the armies facing each other at the *Alte Veste*, but likely estimates run to about 56,000 for the Swedish and allied forces, and about 70,000 for the imperial and Bavarian troops.[30] In the end, it was the total exhaustion of the countryside and its inability to feed the troops that compelled Gustavus Adolphus to force the battle at the *Alte Veste*, which did not end decisively for either side. Afterwards, first the Swedish king and then Wallenstein, the commander of the imperial troops, moved their armies elsewhere since they would have starved in Franconia.[31]

When Gustavus Adolphus could not score a victory, he pulled out after sustaining huge losses not only from fighting but also from disease. While the Swedish king removed his men to Swabia, Wallenstein's army – much less decimated but suffering from sickness as well – went north, and on their way they devastated Franconia and Thuringia. Realizing that Wallenstein was headed for the king's ally Upper Saxony, Gustavus Adolphus raced north and attacked Wallenstein at Lützen (southwest of Leipzig) on 16 November 1632. Even though the Swedish army was victorious, Gustavus Adolphus died on the battlefield. Protestant broadsheets following his death glorified him as a religious hero, who continued to look on and protect from heaven. As one broadsheet announced: "The Swede still lives (*Der Schwede lebt noch*)!" The Swedish command then passed to Adolphus' lord chancellor, Axel Oxenstierna (1583–1654), who occupied himself with the negotiations and logistics of the war, but he did

---

29 Frauenholz, *Heerwesen*, 1:36–37.
30 Mummenhoff, *Altnürnberg*, 18–21.
31 For the logistics of supplying troops and the business of war, see van Creveld, *Supplying War*, and Parrott, *Business of War*.

not fight in the field. Generals Horn and Bernhard of Saxe-Weimar became his commanders-in-chief.

The next couple of years brought further significant developments. In February 1634, Wallenstein, who after the loss at Lützen had increasingly become a suspect figure, was condemned by a secret imperial tribunal and assassinated by his own advisors. The plague hit the German lands with force in 1634 and severely decimated a population that had already been weakened by hunger in large parts of the country. Finally, on 6 September 1634 during the Battle of Nördlingen, the imperial allies dealt the Swedish-Protestants a severe blow. The Protestant coalition collapsed, the Catholic alliance was exhausted, and much of the country was devastated, which prompted the German players, led by Saxony's elector, John George I (r. 1611–1656), and Emperor Ferdinand II, to pursue peace talks in earnest. The result was the Peace of Prague (30 May 1635), which suspended the 1629 Edict of Restitution and set 1627 as the normative year (this allowed the Lutherans to retain many more church lands than the previous date of 1552). The agreement, however, was not satisfactory to Sweden or France.[32] Fighting thus continued after France, under Cardinal Armand-Jean du Plessis de Richelieu (1585–1642), openly entered the war in 1635 on the Swedish side.[33]

Negotiations for a lasting peace began once more in earnest in 1643, with hundreds of diplomats convening in the Westphalian cities of Münster and Osnabrück (both of which had been declared neutral). After five years of dialogues, on 24 October 1648, the two sides agreed on two treaties (one signed in Münster by the Catholic constituents; the other in Osnabrück by the Protestants), which collectively came to be known as the Peace of Westphalia. This treaty established an international settlement that regulated claims of and relations between the major countries of Europe, and revised the constitution of the empire.[34] It reaffirmed the Peace of Augsburg (1555) as well as the princes' privileges, but set the normative year at 1624 and recognized Calvinists alongside Lutherans. *Friedensreiter* (heralds of peace) rode

---

32 France so far had not sent troops but had supported the Swedish-Protestant effort with funds since 1625.

33 Against an earlier assumption that the war had now deteriorated into an out-of-control slaughter, Peter Wilson argues that the empire experienced the full impact of that alliance only from 1642, once France and Sweden had coordinated their strategies and focused "on forcing a succession of pro-imperial principalities into neutrality. The war was channeled into fewer areas, but fought with desperate intensity, contributing to the lasting impression of all-destructive fury" (Wilson, *Holy Roman Empire*, 127, and more extensively in his *Thirty Years War*).

34 Notably, one international player, the papacy, never accepted the Peace.

throughout the country to proclaim the Peace, and cities staged fireworks to celebrate the war's end. Still, peace did not come immediately to all German territories, since the troops withdrew only after they were paid.

3   Places and Characters

The political, economic, social, and religious conditions in the southeast German regions were quite disparate on the eve of the Thirty Years' War. Franconia as a geographic unit came into existence in the sixteenth century. It became one of the initially six, then ten, imperial circles created to maintain order in the empire. With five imperial cities (Nuremberg, Rothenburg, Windsheim, Schweinfurt, and Weißenburg), three bishoprics (Würzburg, Bamberg, and Eichstätt), the margraviate Brandenburg-Ansbach, and numerous smaller territories held by imperial knights, Franconia lacked the jurisdictional unity of Bavaria's dukedom. In the Franconian circle, the weightiest political player was the imperial city of Nuremberg with its city council. Personalities and dynasties played a role among the councilors, but none as prominent as Maximilian I in the Bavarian circle.

As an imperial city, Nuremberg's only overlord was the emperor. In effect, the city was ruled by patrician families, from whose ranks came the members of the small council (*Kleiner Rat*), Nuremberg's most important governing instrument. Only eight of its 42 seats were occupied by master artisans, and their right to participation was limited. All governmental decisions lay in the hands of this small governing body. In addition, from 1525 onward it was overlord of the church in its large territory. While the office of the burgomaster rotated every 28 days between pairs taken from thirteen "young" and thirteen "old" lords of the council, the state affairs were conducted by seven old burgomasters, the "old lords" (*Herren Älteren, Septemvirat*, or *Geheimer Rat*). Three of these "old lords" were elected as "captains" (*Hauptmänner*) to oversee military affairs. Besides the small council, Nuremberg had a large council (*Großer Rat*) of some 300 to 500 merchants and master artisans called "the nominated" (*Genannte*). They were chosen by the small council, and their function was purely advisory and representative. After the council blocked the path upward into the patriciate in the early 1520s, Nuremberg was essentially ruled by an oligarchy.[35] Nuremberg's territory was divided into districts (*Pflegämter*), each

---

35   Bog, *Bäuerliche Wirtschaft*, 318; Porzelt, *Pest in Nürnberg*, 33; Reicke, *Geschichte der Reichsstadt Nürnberg*, 260–64.

THE LAY OF THE LAND 17

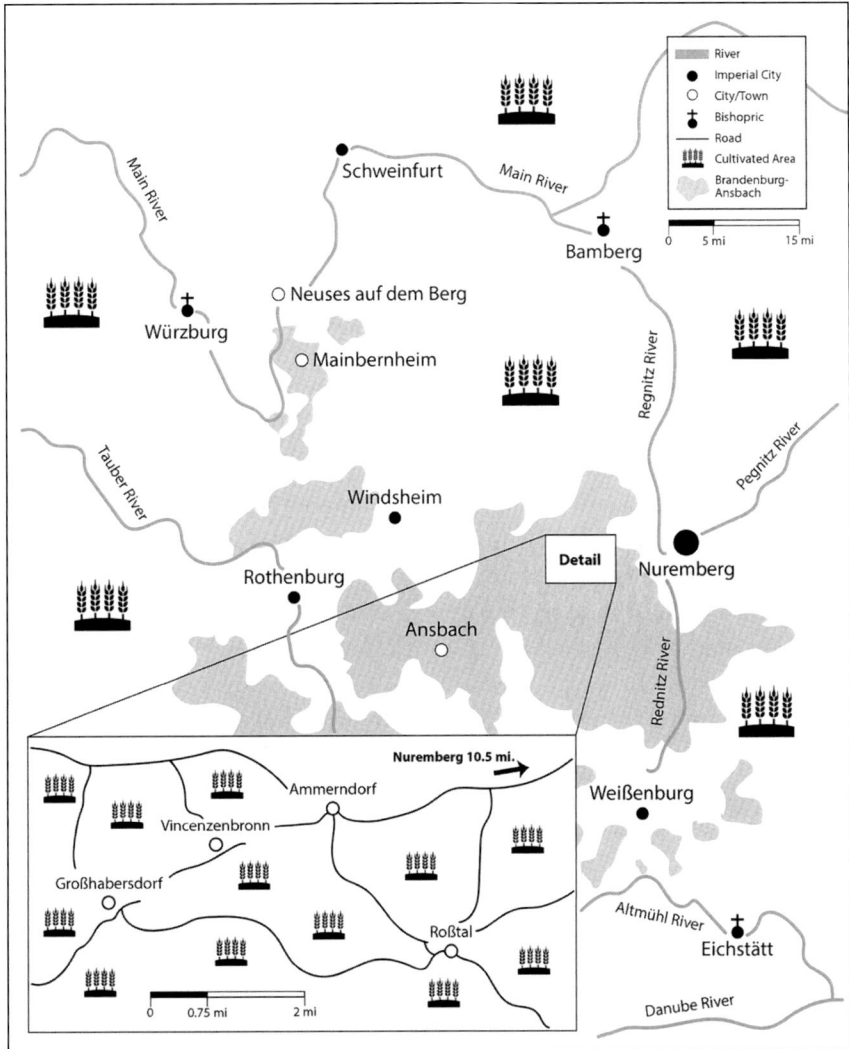

FIGURE 4   Franconia

governed by a district administrator (*Landpfleger*), who was answerable to the city's district office (*Landpflegeamt*). Lowest in this chain of command were the heads of the villages (*Dorfhauptleute*).[36]

---

36   Porzelt, *Pest in Nürnberg*, 146.

From the beginning of the sixteenth century, Nuremberg owned the largest territory of any city in the empire (25 sq mi or 65 km^2). Around the start of the Thirty Years' War, its population had risen to about 45,000.[37] Its earlier ascension to becoming a leading power in Franconia and the empire led to animosity with the margraves in Ansbach.[38] Even though Nuremberg had always sought to avoid irrevocably alienating the emperor, it had adopted the Lutheran Reformation in the 1520s, but had refrained from joining the Schmalkaldic League.[39] In the following decades it continued its diplomatic position. When, during the early 1600s, tensions between Protestants and Catholics intensified, leading to the formation of two opposing alliances (the Protestant Union in 1608 and the Catholic League in 1609), Nuremberg initially kept its distance. The imperial city finally joined the Union in 1609 under pressure from the Protestant princes and from its own subjects, but only under the condition that the alliance would not act against the emperor. In 1621 in the wake of the Bohemian War (1618–20), the imperial cities, led by Nuremberg, left the Union, which subsequently dissolved itself.[40]

When, in 1632, Gustavus Adolphus chose Nuremberg as his military base, he forced the council's hand by threatening that, if the magistrates did not join him, he would move against the city with "fire and sword."[41] Caught between the demands of the emperor and those of the Swedish king, Nuremberg decided to support the Protestant forces, albeit in a diplomatically complicated way. Franconia's other imperial cities looked toward Nuremberg for support or when weighty decisions needed to be made, and usually followed its example.

To the west of Nuremberg lay the margraviate Brandenburg-Ansbach. Its rivalry with Nuremberg had been temporarily mitigated by a common

---

[37] The size of Nuremberg's population is not easy to establish, since its council rarely initiated censuses, and there are no tax lists. In 1622, 10,069 households were registered in the city. With four to five persons per household, the number of inhabitants most likely lay between 40,000 and 50,000 (Porzelt, *Pest in Nürnberg*, 34–35).

[38] Spindler, *Handbuch*, 3:195–96.

[39] The Schmalkaldic League was a defensive Protestant alliance formed in 1531 to defend itself against the enforcement of the 1530 Augsburg Recess that mandated Protestants return to Catholicism.

[40] See Emil Reicke's comment in his *Geschichte der Reichsstadt Nürnberg*, 958: "The politics of the imperial city during the (Thirty Years' War) was the old timid one that we know well from the turmoil of the Reformation period: utmost preservation of neutrality, caution and circumspection toward both sides to avoid open rupture with either of the belligerent parties, submissiveness toward the winner, but, most of all, as long as possible humble concessions toward the emperor."

[41] StA N, ASHVMF, HS 219, 224^r.

commitment to the Brandenburg-Nuremberg (Lutheran) church ordinance of 1533.[42] Especially with the legalization of the Augsburg Confession after 1555, the margraves promoted a reform program aimed at greater spiritual and disciplinary oversight. Over the next decades, the margraves developed a hierarchical structure for their churches, in which parishes were organized into twelve chapters (*Dekanate*), which were headed by a central institution, the consistory.[43] After some toying in his territory with ideas of Philip Melanchthon, Margrave Georg Friedrich (r. 1556–1603) committed himself firmly to the Book of Concord (1580) and to "pure" Lutheranism. When Georg Friedrich died childless in 1603, Brandenburg's territories were divided between the two younger brothers of Brandenburg's elector, Joachim Friedrich (r. 1598–1608), in Berlin. The margraviate Ansbach went to Joachim Ernst (r. 1603–1625) and the margraviate Kulmbach-Bayreuth to his older brother Christian (r. 1603–1655). Even though in 1613 the Berlin-Hohenzollern line opted for Reformed Protestantism under Elector Johann Sigismund (r. 1608–1619), the Franconian margraviates held firmly to orthodox Lutheranism.[44] As general of the Protestant Union army, Joachim Ernst was intricately involved in the war's early phase. When he died in 1625 not even 42 years of age, his wife, Sophia (born Countess von Solms-Laubach, 1594–1651), together with her cousin Count Friedrich von Solms-Rödelheim (1574–1649), ruled for fourteen years as regent for her children, until her son, Albrecht (r. 1639–1667), took the reins.[45]

Besides the sizable Protestant territories of Nuremberg and Brandenburg-Ansbach (and Kulmbach-Bayreuth), the Catholic bishoprics Bamberg, Würzburg, and Eichstätt, not to mention the imperial knights, added to the political and religious complexity in Franconia. Still, as Max Spindler points out, the Franconian circle constituted an "integrated economic sphere" and formed an "economic union" with Bavaria and Swabia.[46]

---

42 Rudersdorf, "Brandenburg-Ansbach," 12.
43 These were Crailsheim, Cadolzburg, Gunzenhausen, Wassertrüdingen, Feuchtwangen, Schwabach, Uffenheim, Kitzingen, Leutershausen, and Wülzburg. The capital Ansbach was exempt. In 1565 Neustadt an der Aisch and Baierdorf were added as chapters (Rudersdorf, "Brandenburg-Ansbach," 23).
44 Rudersdorf, "Brandenburg-Ansbach," 24–28. Johann Sigismund became also officially Duke of Prussia in 1618.
45 Spindler, *Handbuch*, 3:225; Wittmann, *Sophia*, 10–11, 23. Sophia's oldest son, Friedrich, died in 1634 at the Battle of Nördlingen.
46 Spindler, *Handbuch*, 3:213.

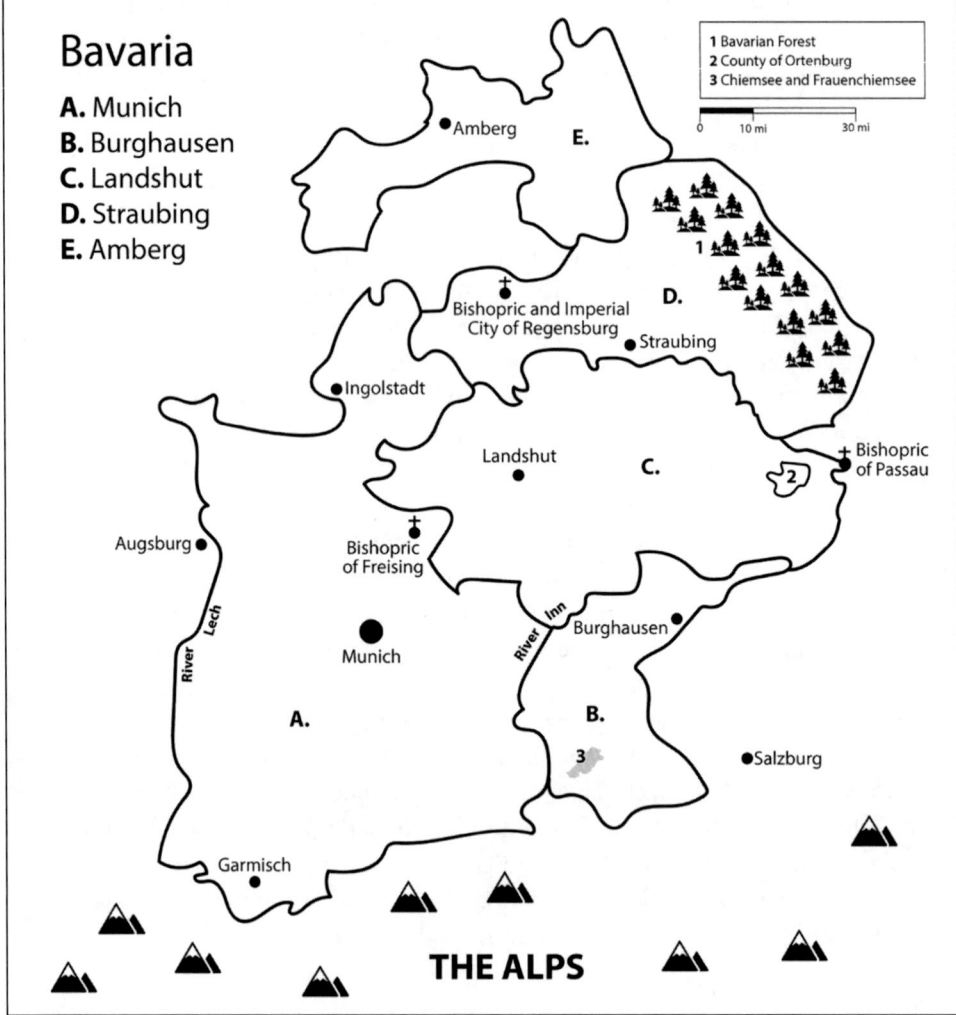

FIGURE 5 Bavaria and its administrative districts (*Rentämter*)

In contrast to the complex political territory of Franconia, the duchy of Bavaria was much more homogenous. After the unification of Lower Bavaria (Bavaria-Landshut) and Upper Bavaria (Bavaria-Munich) following the Landshut War of Succession (1504–1505), the duchy became a largely unified state governed centrally from Munich.[47] It stretched from the river Lech in the West to the Inn Viertel in the East (which is today part of Upper Austria) and to the Alps in the South, with about 900,000 inhabitants around 1600. During

---

47 The primogeniture ruling of 8 July 1506 assured a stable succession.

the early seventeenth century, Bavaria was divided into four, and from 1628 five, administrative districts or *Rentämter* (Munich, Burghausen, Landshut, Straubing, and then Amberg). These territories were each in the hands of an administrator, or *Rentmeister*, who thus held one of the most crucial offices in the princely government. By the time of Maximilian, the *Rentmeister*'s responsibilities included finances as well as law and order.[48] They were also the right hands of the territorial lord. Every few years, Maximilian ordered his *Rentmeister* to visit each town and village under their jurisdiction and report on the state of their officers, the local administration of justice, accounts, tax payments, and the local economy (*Pollizeywesen*).[49] Besides the *Rentämter*, which reflected the old division before the unification, the duchy included several enclaves that were only answerable to the emperor, especially the imperial city of Regensburg, the bishoprics of Freising and Regensburg, and the county of Ortenburg.

The leading political personality in Bavaria and beyond was Maximilian, whose character, religion, and understanding of his role as *Landesvater* (father of the country) informed his actions. He ruled his territory for over half a century – including the entire period of the Thirty Years' War – and attempted to guide his subjects during an unusually tumultuous time. The duke, who from 1623 was also elector of Bavaria, stands out as the most powerful amid his Bavarian predecessors and successors. None of his peers was as successful as Maximilian in consolidating princely power. Robert Bireley called him "the most significant prince of the Counter Reformation in the Empire," and noted that contemporaries compared him to Philip II of Spain (r. 1556–1598).[50] Scholars have noted his political and dynastic ambitions, and his extensive program of social and religious disciplining, while the other side to this policy, his profound concern for social justice and fairness, has rarely drawn attention.[51] It is widely acknowledged that the Bavarian ruler was intensely religious, but opinions are divided with regard to which motives – whether religious or political (imperial, state, or dynastic) – primarily drove Maximilian. Against the many

---

48 See Heydenreuter, *Der Landesherrliche Hofrat*, 50–52.
49 This term referred to issues pertaining to the local economy, such as weights and measures as well as the quality and price of meat, bread, and beer.
50 Bireley, *Maximilian*, 7. Immler even describes him as the first absolutist prince in "Maximilian I," 203.
51 Among the most important studies on Maximilian are: Albrecht, *Maximilian I.*; Glaser, ed., *Um Glauben und Reich*; Heydenreuter, *Der Landesherrliche Hofrat*; Immler, "Maximilian I"; Kraus, *Maximilian der Erste*; Pfister, *Kurfürst Maximilian*; Zimmermann, "Territorium und Konfession"; and the articles in the *Sonderband* of the *Zeitschrift für Bayerische Landesgeschichte* 65/1. For a discussion of his social justice program, see Haude, "Social Control and Social Justice."

who believe the major force behind this deeply religious man was his concern for Bavaria and the Wittelsbach dynasty, Bireley has argued Maximilian's first objective was religious, namely the restoration of Catholicism in the empire.[52] The prince's life was clearly framed by prayer and devotion – he spent about three hours a day praying and searching his conscience, and, unbeknownst to most of his contemporaries, he wore a scourge and hair shirt under his clothes.[53]

Maximilian's attitude and strategies toward the Protestants changed over the course of the war. He had been intransigent during the war's first decade and a half, but during the early 1630s, after Bavaria felt the heat of the war at the hands of the Swedes, the elector became more conciliatory. These shifts in standpoint roughly coincided with a change in confessors: the rigid Adam Contzen, S. J., died in 1636 and the more temperate Johannes Vervaux (1586–1661) stepped in. Bireley, however, makes a convincing case that Maximilian was not a pawn of his Jesuit confessors, but chose these men from outside Bavaria based on a similarity in attitudes.[54] Still, it is also true that Contzen, if anything, reinforced Maximilian's intransigent style. The elector's change in position and choice of a new confessor were most likely motivated by the fateful events during the early 1630s when peace increasingly became the more desirable goal.

No matter what the interpretation of leading motive, scholars are agreed that Maximilian was not a man with his head in the clouds. When his father abdicated in Maximilian's favor in 1598, the future ruler of Bavaria (he had already been co-regent since 1595) had a much better grasp of the country's needs than his predecessor ever possessed. His father left him empty coffers, and Maximilian made it one of his first priorities to build up the treasury. He was convinced that money was the source of power, and thus he initiated a thorough financial reform. His success in this area ensured that he was in a financially strong position at the beginning of the war. Besides his religious fervor, Maximilian was politically ambitious, curbing the power of Bavaria's territorial estates at home and becoming one of the most important political players during the first half of the Thirty Years' War.[55] He was a key member of the Catholic camp before and during the first phase of the war, and, as chief commander of the allied Bavarian and League forces, he secured the victory for

---

52 Bireley, *Maximilian*, 104; see also Bireley, *Jesuits*.
53 Bireley, *Maximilian*, 15.
54 Bireley, *Maximilian*, 221 and 227. Bireley advocates a more differentiated view with regard to the Jesuits' influence on Maximilian (and Ferdinand II) and argues that the Jesuits were not a monolithic group but made up of moderates and zealots.
55 Bireley, *Maximilian*, 17.

the emperor and the Catholics over the Protestants in the Battle of the White Mountain near Prague (8 November 1620).

Maximilian represents not only a deeply religious, financially astute, and politically powerful prince during the Thirty Years' War, but also a sovereign who elevated governmental oversight to a whole new level. Famous for his incessant orders and mandates, he tried to regulate seemingly every aspect of his subjects' lives in his desire to establish a pious, morally disciplined, and economically prospering society.[56] He also tried to exert control over his court city, Munich, but, as Reinhard Heydenreuter has shown and as the discussion below will highlight, he and Munich's city council were frequently at odds over issues of policy and actions.[57]

These are the geographic and chronological parameters of the study with its basic outline of the actions and players. We will now first turn to contemporaries' experiences during the war.

---

56   A look at his predecessors' and successors' practices shows that Maximilian stood out in his proliferation of mandates and ordinances. See Helmuth Stahleder's *Chronik* for Bavarian princes' pronouncements during the early modern period. Most of Maximilian's decrees show his hand-written comments in the margins, which means that he involved himself actively and relentlessly in every facet of his territory's administration. Bireley calls Maximilian a "born bureaucrat." *Maximilian*, 17. To what extent these measures and demands were met with compliance is another matter that will be explored further in Chapter 3.

57   Heydenreuter, "Magistrat."

CHAPTER 2

Experiences of War

The Thirty Years' War tends to evoke rather uniform and one-dimensional images of ruin and destruction. This almost reflexive impression is not surprising since the conflict wrought staggering devastation and suffering. On the local level, however, encounters with the war proved to be remarkably diverse. Contemporaries' experiences and responses to the war delineate a more colorful and often more perplexing spectrum than an unvarying story line of destruction can capture. We are by now well aware that certain areas suffered more than others, and the southeast German lands belong to those that were hit severely, but local conditions and personal situations also led to unique and inconsistent experiences. Reported incidents of care and concern show that people did not experience only violence. Despite this more complicated reality that upends both past and present images of the Thirty Years' War as solely destructive, people were united by a deep sense of vulnerability.

The lenses through which this section approaches contemporaries' experiences are personal accounts. These offer glimpses of the war up close and help us understand how people encountered the war, how they responded to it, and how they tried to make sense of it. Historians have debated intensely both the subject of experience and the terminology of sources that might provide access to it. Is it possible to recover or know anything about how early modern people experienced certain events or situations?[1]

Major shifts in thinking have occurred particularly regarding approaches to "autobiography."[2] Early modern autobiographical writings have long been

---

1   Münch, *Erfahrung*; Brändle et al., "Texte zwischen Erfahrung und Diskurs." Joan Scott calls upon scholars "to historicize experience," and warns that if one holds the evidence of experience to be "transparent" and "uncontestable," one merely "reproduces rather than contests given ideological systems …" ("Evidence of Experience," 777–78, 790). While scholars in the 1990s, such as Scott, expressed concern about essentialism and constructivism, Kaspar von Greyerz sees most studies now situated somewhere in the "middle ground between pure constructivism and the evidence of experience offered by their sources" ("Ego-Documents," 276).
2   The terminology in terms of documents that narrate something about the self varies from autobiographical accounts, testimonies about or to oneself (*Selbstzeugnisse*), ego-documents, self-narratives, personal accounts, or any variation of the above. James S. Amelang describes autobiographical texts as "any literary form that expresses lived experience from a first person point of view" (*"Vox populi,"* 33). See also Kaspar von Greyerz's assessment of autobiographical sources (in this case, autobiographies and diaries) in "Religion in the Life of

the stepchildren of literary scholars as well as historians, but for diametrically opposed reasons. While historians have often bemoaned these writings' lack of objective data and have questioned their representativeness, their colleagues in German literature have faulted the texts for not being subjective and individual enough.[3] In the first half of the seventeenth century, however, the lines between the literary forms of autobiographies, diaries, and other chronological accounts were fluid.[4] "Autobiographical" texts, unlike their post-Enlightenment counterparts, focused little on self-reflection or the construction of an individual personality. Instead of confidently arranging one's personal history from hindsight, these texts frequently listed events or experiences chronologically, without explanatory connections or transitions.[5] Often the author stepped back, while he or she recounted events of the day and other facets of life around him or her.[6] Early modern German autobiographies until the end of the seventeenth century, therefore, narrated personal facts in their external rather than internal contexts.[7]

More recently researchers have turned former problems into promising assets. Literary scholars have pointed out the danger of making Goethe the benchmark for all autobiographies. Prominently, women scholars have underlined the gendered – that is, masculine – typography of autobiography, which has also led to a movement away from Goethe as yardstick.[8] Historians, on the other hand, have increasingly highlighted the communal dimension of the experience expressed in personal accounts: "personal narratives, both in reproducing and in creating discourse, are deeply embedded in a collective

---

German and Swiss Autobiographers," and von Krusenstjern, "Was sind Selbstzeugnisse?" as well as the special issue of *German History* 28 that is dedicated to ego-documents.

3 Among literary scholars, "autobiography" used to be associated with modernity and a sense of "self" that they saw first fully expressed in the works of Johann Wolfgang Goethe.
4 Von Greyerz, *Vorsehungsglaube*, 16.
5 With the adoption of such a serial structure, many seventeenth-century "autobiographies" were still indebted to the medieval recording tradition (Schiewek, "Zur Manifestation des Individuellen," 893).
6 See Stephan Pastenaci's pithy comment: "The reading of Early-Modern High German autobiographies is – superficially regarded – certainly no pleasure due to the heterogeneity of the texts. Intimate, personal matters alternate with impersonal reports of events; civic anecdotes and biographies of other personalities are described in great detail. Private letters alternate with full accounts of contemporary documents. Facts dominate over reflection" ("Probleme der Edition," 11).
7 Amelang, "*Vox populi*," 33.
8 See Gabriele Jancke and Claudia Ulbrich's introduction to and the articles in their collection, *Vom Individuum zur Person*. See also Daniela Hacke's introduction to *Frauen in der Stadt*; Davies et al., eds., *Autobiography by Women*; and Kormann, "Heterologe Subjektivität."

context."⁹ In other words, early modern personal narratives offer more than one singular viewpoint; in observing the society and culture in which these persons lived, they tell us something about their larger community. Indeed, scholars have gone one step further by underlining that any narrative, whether early modern or modern, is created within a social context and reflects the relational nature of humans, and thus, by necessity – consciously or subconsciously, positively or negatively – references this framework.¹⁰ Kaspar von Greyerz consequently finds the term "ego-documents" inadequate in capturing the broader implications of autobiographical accounts precisely because they go well beyond the "ego."¹¹

With these developments in mind, the seventeenth century has become a rich field for mining these narratives. The personal accounts, around which the following analysis is built, strongly reflect the communal dimension of their setting, but they also show a wider variety of characteristics than typically attributed to early modern autobiographical narratives. As we will soon see, the diary of the Augustinian prioress, Clara Staiger, for example, is in character very close to the medieval serial structure of a chronicle, where descriptions of chores, religious rituals, hardships, finances, the weather, etc. follow one another with no interpretive frame. Other narratives, like those of the Benedictine abbots Maurus Friesenegger and Veit Höser, however, provide much more than the usual series of personal facts in their external contexts: their extensive, sometimes funny, often rhetorically gripping comments, explanations, musings, and occasional dramatizations point in the direction of modern autobiographies. And the narrative of the Dominican nun Maria Anna Junius offers a spellbinding story rather than a detached chronicle of chores and events. Seventeenth-century autobiographical accounts, then, spanned a broad range of characteristics and reflect the markings of a transitional period in the genre.

The vivid accounts and graphic images of personal and official records convey the relentless devastation in the German lands and beyond. The

---

9   Von Greyerz, "Ego-Documents," 276. See also Mary Fulbrook and Ulinka Rublack's comment: "one does not have to follow down a post-modernist route to realize the significance of the fact that no account of the self can be produced which is not constructed in terms of social discourses: that the very concepts people use to describe themselves, the ways in which they choose to structure and to account for their past lives, the values, norms, and common-sense explanations to which they appeal in providing meaning to their narratives, are intrinsically products of the times through which they have lived." ("In Relation," 267). Jancke and Ulbrich also emphasize the author's embeddedness in his or her social context (*Vom Individuum zur Person*).
10 See, e.g., Fulbrook and Rublack, "In Relation," 263–72.
11 For this and a discussion of the history of the term, see von Greyerz, "Ego-Documents."

forcefulness of their combined testimony suggests a homogenous experience of loss, destruction, and desperation. A sense of utter ruin does indeed pervade most documents, but beneath this profound reality lies a more complex and variegated web of experiences that was shaped by multiple factors. It is widely known that the greatest number of deaths did not result from the battles themselves but from the repercussions of war, such as forced contributions, inflation, famine, disease, pestilence, plundering, and violence. These effects were more intensely felt along the paths of troop movement than in areas further removed from the army routes. Thus the war did not hit every region equally. The war's uneven visitation on the populace is only part of the explanation for the diversity in experiences. Other aspects played a role as well, among them one's gender, social and occupational group, personality, upbringing, networks, whether one lived in the city or the countryside, and sheer luck.

This chapter offers windows on the breadth and depth of contemporaries' experiences by looking closely at a selection of personal accounts written by male and female members of a variety of religious orders. At a time when literacy was still largely confined to the upper and upper-middle classes, some of the most prolific recorders of the days' events could be found among the *religiosi*, members of religious orders. Their position encouraged and sometimes demanded a daily record, and a good part of these works survived due to the preservation by their orders. It is important to remember our earlier discussion of the communal dimension these texts offer. The writings of those in religious orders go far beyond presenting an insular view of a nun or monk; rather, they provide the reader with astonishing perspectives on the monastic community and the world beyond the convent walls. In other words, these accounts are testimonies of the time, not just of a single individual. The writings by male and female religious will then be placed in the context of other contemporary narratives. Parish ministers also frequently left diary-style accounts in addition to general parish records, as did some nobles and government officials and even the occasional artisan and soldier.[12]

Most of the texts under review come from regions in and around modern-day Bavaria , which suffered severely under the war. Many focus on the period traditionally termed the Swedish Intervention – between Gustavus Adolphus' landing on the Baltic in 1630 and the Peace of Prague in 1635. As the southern regions became the scene of military action, troop movement, and stationing,

---

12   Benigna von Krusenstjern's *Selbstzeugnisse der Zeit des Dreißigjährigen Krieges* broadened our access to a host of narrative accounts and provides an invaluable tool by locating 240 testimonies on the Thirty Years' War, often published in obscure, nineteenth-century regional journals.

authors frequently expressed their horrendous experiences with surprising attention to nuances.

In trying to identify experiences through these narrative accounts, one has to keep in mind that many authors at some point in their testimony state the impossibility of articulating what happened to them. On one hand, writing down occurrences was a means of coming to terms with the events. Placing one's thoughts outside oneself on paper could perhaps alleviate the heavy burden. On the other hand, authors continuously pushed against the limits of language since some of their experiences could not be put into words. They repeatedly broke off in the middle of a painful description and declared they were unable to narrate the full extent of the outrage. Words could not convey, nor human understanding grasp the true magnitude of horror and pain. Such utterances reflect both the constraints and the power of language. Writing down the details of an ordeal meant having to endure the suffering all over again. There was, then, a fine line between easing the burden of one's experience and being overwhelmed by it anew. Amazingly, however, despite these declarations, authors expressed vividly a range of experiences. The following discussion explores those that are conveyed most prevalently. Even though the analysis divides these experiences into distinct sections, many of them overlap and cannot properly be separated.

1 Fear and Vulnerability

Authors voiced one experience above all – fear.[13] Its paramount presence, however, should not be taken for uniformity of experience. A close look at the autobiographical accounts under review reveals a broad range of manifestations. Fear was expressed as both a communal and an individual experience, which changed over time and according to the proximity to danger. We hear from nuns and monks in various locales and situations – some inside, others outside city walls; some in the line of troop movement, others off the beaten track.

---

[13] On fear, see Bouwsma, "Anxiety and the Formation of Early Modern Culture"; Naphy and Roberts, eds., *Fear in Early Modern Society*; and Tuan, *Landscapes of Fear*. More specifically on fear and the Thirty Years' War, see Bähr, *Furcht und Furchtlosigkeit*, especially Chapter 5.2. For Bähr, fear is closely connected with the fear of God: "God punished with fear to call toward the fear of God …" (376). My own analysis does not deny the fear of God but highlights a broader spectrum of expressions of fear.

EXPERIENCES OF WAR 29

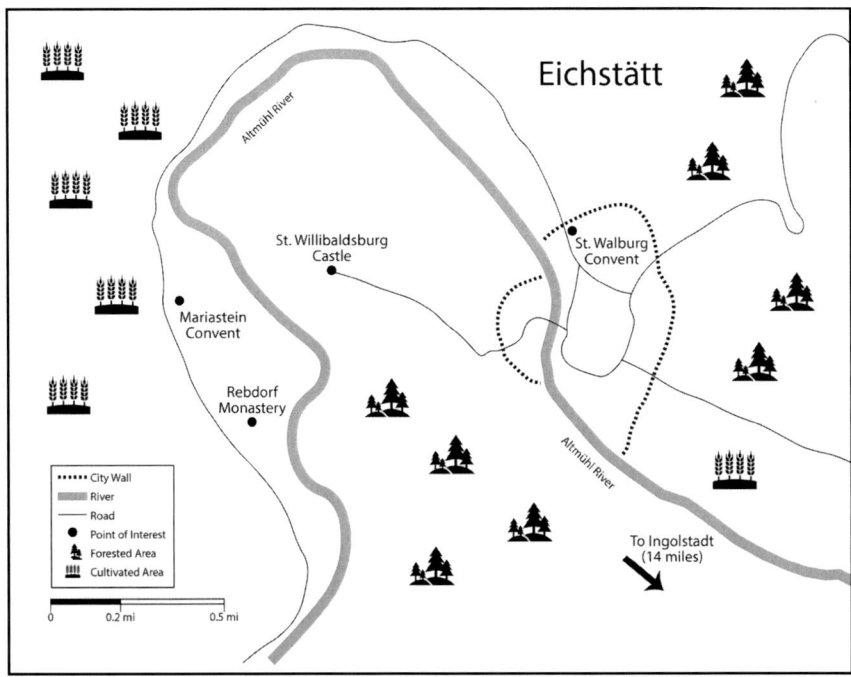

FIGURE 6   Eichstätt

The Augustinian convent Mariastein lay about 40 miles south of Nuremberg outside Eichstätt's city walls. Situated on the Altmühl River in close proximity to the Augustinian canons of Rebdorf, who functioned as the nuns' guardians, the convent was in good financial and disciplinary shape prior to the war. Both noble and bourgeois women belonged to the religious community.[14] In the early 1630s Mariastein became repeatedly the target of destruction whenever troops crossed their territory. The diary-style *Verzaichnus* of its prioress, Clara Staiger (1588–1656), offers a minute record of the convent's day-to-day happenings with occasional comments, and gives the reader insight into her personal experiences and reactions to the war, as well as the larger context of her convent and the world around them in war times.[15] Catharina Staiger came from a middle-class family in Schongau, quite a distance away from Eichstätt, but her family had close ties to the cloister: her aunt, Clara I (r. 1592–1605), had been

---

14   Wallner, *Clara Staiger*, 9–10.
15   *Klara Staigers Tagebuch*, 326. Entries start in earnest in 1632 with the attack of the Swedes. Staiger's notes are interrupted from 1645 until August 1646, when she was gravely ill and could not continue her writing.

prioress when the younger woman entered the cloister of the Augustinian canonesses in 1599 at the age of ten and joined the ranks of the canonesses six years later. In 1632 Catharina followed her aunt as Prioress Clara II.[16]

Over the course of her diary, from the early 1630s until the end of the war, Staiger describes communal experiences of fear – those of her own convent, other nuns, peasants, citizens, and political and religious leaders – as well as her own personal dread. In her diary, she moves between the more prevalent "we" (most often in the dialectal *mir* rather than *wir*) and the "I" (*ich*). When the Swedes marched into Eichstätt's territory in April 1633, the sisters fled to the castle, St. Willibaldsburg, high above the city. The castle, however, quickly became the enemy's target, and during its ten-day bombardment the nuns were terrified. Worse, their fright was exacerbated by watching from their post in the stronghold the way the troops ransacked their cloister.[17] When the Eichstätters succumbed, the officials' subsequent negotiations of an accord could not quiet the sisters' fears. While the clergy was supposed to be spared and the soldiers promised a free departure, those men and women who had sought refuge at the castle were to remain until their value was estimated for ransom: "It is impossible to describe what fear and distress was among us because everybody was afraid for her life and honor. Some wanted to flee to Ingolstadt, some to St. Walburg, others to our cloister."[18] Besides this shared experience, Staiger also discloses something of her own personal anxiety. As these events were unfolding, the prioress felt a deadly fright that threatened to overcome her: "I am so deeply afraid that I thought I would lose my body and my life, yes even my sanity (*vernunfft*) since no one knows the outcome [of the siege]."[19] Evidently, more than death itself, Staiger dreaded losing control of her mind. This concern beyond the body – that the horrific experiences of the war might trigger the loss of one's sanity – is also reflected in other writings that contain reports of melancholy and sometimes suicide because of distress over the war.[20]

Their encounter with war during the first half of the 1630s made the prioress and her nuns shrink back in horror at the mere mention of troops approaching.[21] Importantly, even an accord which was supposed to protect

---

16 Staiger's father was a merchant. Besides her aunt, two of her cousins were members of the convent (Wallner, *Clara Staiger*, 10; Nolting, *Sprachgebrauch*, 77–78).
17 *Klara Staigers Tagebuch*, 82.
18 *Klara Staigers Tagebuch*, 83 (13 May 1633). St. Walburg was a Benedictine convent inside Eichstätt's walls, with which the Augustinian nuns had close relations.
19 *Klara Staigers Tagebuch*, 83.
20 On suicide, see Kästner, *Tödliche Geschichte(n)*.
21 See also Imhof, *Die verlorenen Welten*, 95–96 and 100–101, for a discussion of the traumatization of a local population and the difference between concrete fear and latent anxiety.

EXPERIENCES OF WAR 31

the religious could not impart a sense of safety. The continuous attacks wore Staiger down and brought her to the limit of what she could endure. While she suffered anxiety of varying intensity, by the end of the war, the experiences had so depleted her that the fear was almost unbearable.

On the other side of Nuremberg, about forty miles to its north just outside Bamberg, lay the Dominican convent Heiliggrab (also: Heiligengrab). Much like the Augustinian convent Mariastein, Heiliggrab was located in the line of troop movement and lacked the protection of city walls. Its steward, Maria Anna Junius (ca. 1605–1675), left behind a *Kurze verzeignuß* (Short Account),

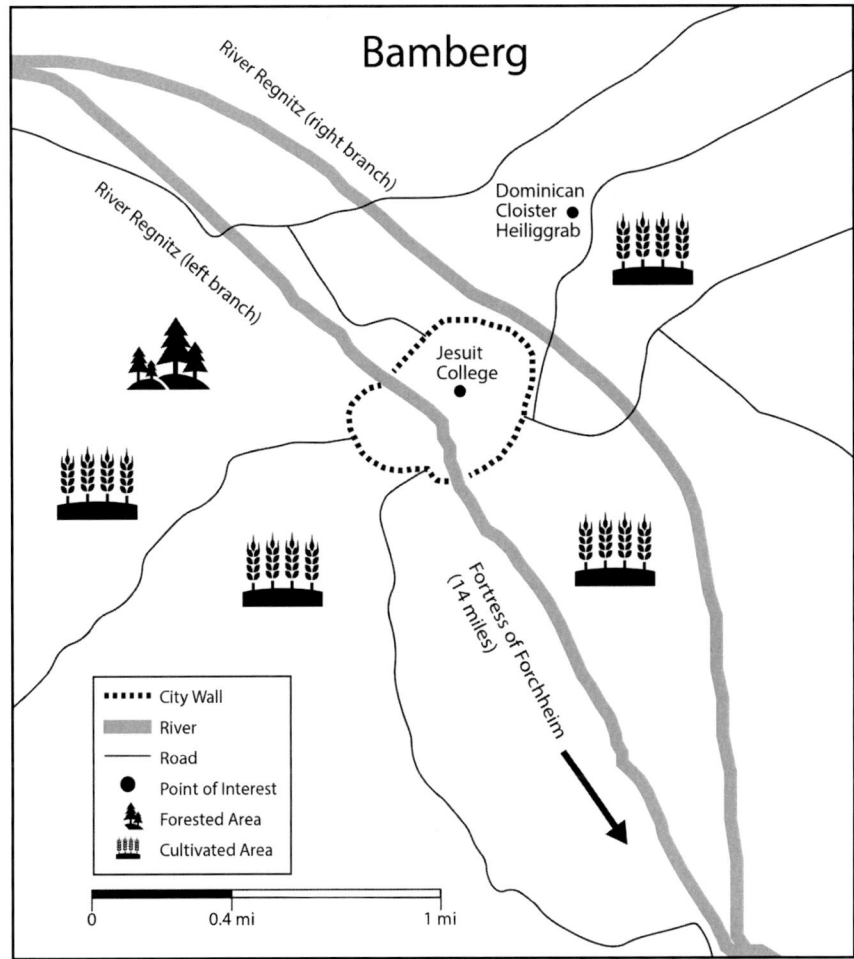

FIGURE 7   Bamberg

which provides fascinating insight into the nuns' experiences during the years from 1631 to 1634.[22] The daughter of Johannes Junius, burgomaster and councilor of Bamberg, she began her writing in 1631 (although her recordings go back to 1622), the year of her entrance into the cloister, and include brief notes on the city's preoccupation with witchcraft, which claimed the lives of both her parents in 1628. Her account follows the days and months of the years, but, unlike Clara Staiger, she rarely talks about the cloister's finances or the daily routines. Rather, Junius captivates the reader with stories of the sisters' plight and how they managed to overcome the war's challenges, and so her testimony is more consciously constructed than Staiger's.

Junius conveys the nuns' fear so viscerally that one can almost feel it. Her *Kurze verzeignuß* delivers the riveting story of how this Augustinian convent managed to survive the difficult years of Swedish occupation. As soon as news of the approaching Swedes reached the nuns in 1631, they made preparations and sent for secular clothes to flee at the first sign of danger, even though they had no idea where they might go.[23] The city itself was in enormous upheaval "because of the great fear."[24] If imagining what might happen had terrified them, their neighbors' concrete reports about the enemies' destruction of villages and their assault on religious men and women nearby lent fresh fuel to their anxiety. When *Newe Zeitungen* daily reported new atrocities, their fear commenced in earnest.[25] Junius ended her notes for 1631:

> Thus we concluded this year with great terror, fear, fright, and misery because the entire time that [the commotion] lasted we were constantly extremely frightened, which I am unable to describe. And everyone who reads this can easily surmise what we as feeble women, who were located so far outside [the city walls], endured. During this time we rarely slept at night because of our great fright. Moreover, they threatened Bamberg that they would deal with it worse than they did with Würzburg, which happened.[26]

---

22   Hümmer, ed., "Bamberg im Schweden-Kriege." We do not know when Junius was born. She probably became the cloister's steward around 1630 and eventually its prioress, since she is listed as such when she died (Nolting, *Sprachgebrauch*, 76–77).

23   During the war, the clergy regularly disguised themselves by wearing secular clothes. For further discussion of this point, see Section 4 below and Chapter 4.

24   Hümmer, ed., "Bamberg im Schweden-Kriege," 52:15.

25   Hümmer, ed., "Bamberg im Schweden-Kriege," 52:17, 19.

26   Hümmer, ed., "Bamberg im Schweden-Kriege," 52:23–24. On the commotion: some subterfuge occurred between Swedish and allied soldiers, and the citizens feared that it would all come to light and they would be the victims.

EXPERIENCES OF WAR							33

Time and again, Junius tells the reader of their tremendous fear and then of its further intensification; indeed, she often underlines that she is unable to fully articulate their fright. Her persistent references to fear may make one wonder whether she expressed real experiences or used the sentiment as a mere figure of speech, an exclamation point to add drama to her narrative. They may well have been figures of speech, but there was nothing "mere" about them. Scholars have debated how experience can be expressed, and Joan Scott has asserted its discursive dimension.[27] In response to Scott, Claudia Jarzebowski has insisted that experience is conveyed not only through language. The experience of violence, she argues, manifests itself physically and is retained in the body's memory, which provides a space beyond language.[28]

I suggest the anticipation of violence is also expressed physically, as is evident in Junius' account and in other testimonies below. Junius' repeated utterances of fear, her listing of synonyms for terror, and her periodic statements that their anxiety escalated to ever higher levels of intensity represent her way of expressing an experience that transcended the words she possessed. She may have lacked the vocabulary and psychological ability to communicate their experience, but her repeated, continuous cues form an image, and their crescendo recreates for the reader the reality the nuns encountered during the early 1630s, namely, a convent that saw itself exposed, unprotected, and forced to endure the enemy's frightening presence.

Articulations of terror were not restricted to testimonies of women. About 83 miles to the southeast of Nuremberg, in the Regensburg diocese, Abbot Veit (Vitus) Höser (1577–1634), too, described the fear in and all around him. A renowned reformer of the Benedictine abbey Oberalteich (in Bogen near Straubing) and a virtuoso of the word, Höser chronicled the Swedish advance on their region in 1633 and 1634 that eventually forced the brethren to leave their monastery. With great rhetorical skill, he recalled the fear he experienced himself and that he observed among his neighbors: "Who could describe the terror, fear, and dread of the horrified and stricken burghers? The silent screams of the women and children, their weeping and wailing, their moaning, their choking fear, their wild speech, and how they are thrown out of their own homes ..."[29] Like Junius', Höser's testimony is more constructed than Staiger's. He heightens the perception of fear by enumerating its synonyms.

---

27   Scott, "Evidence of Experience," 793. Scott also stresses that our reading needs to be alert to the words' multiple – even contradictory – meanings.
28   Jarzebowski, "Gewalt und Erfahrung," 206–7.
29   Sigl, *Veit Hösers Kriegstagebuch*, 103 (24 November 1633). The Latin original can be found in the Staatsbibliothek Munich (Clm 1326, "Viti Hoeseri Abbatis ..."). This is the third volume of Höser's three-volume work entitled "Monomonastikon." I counter-checked

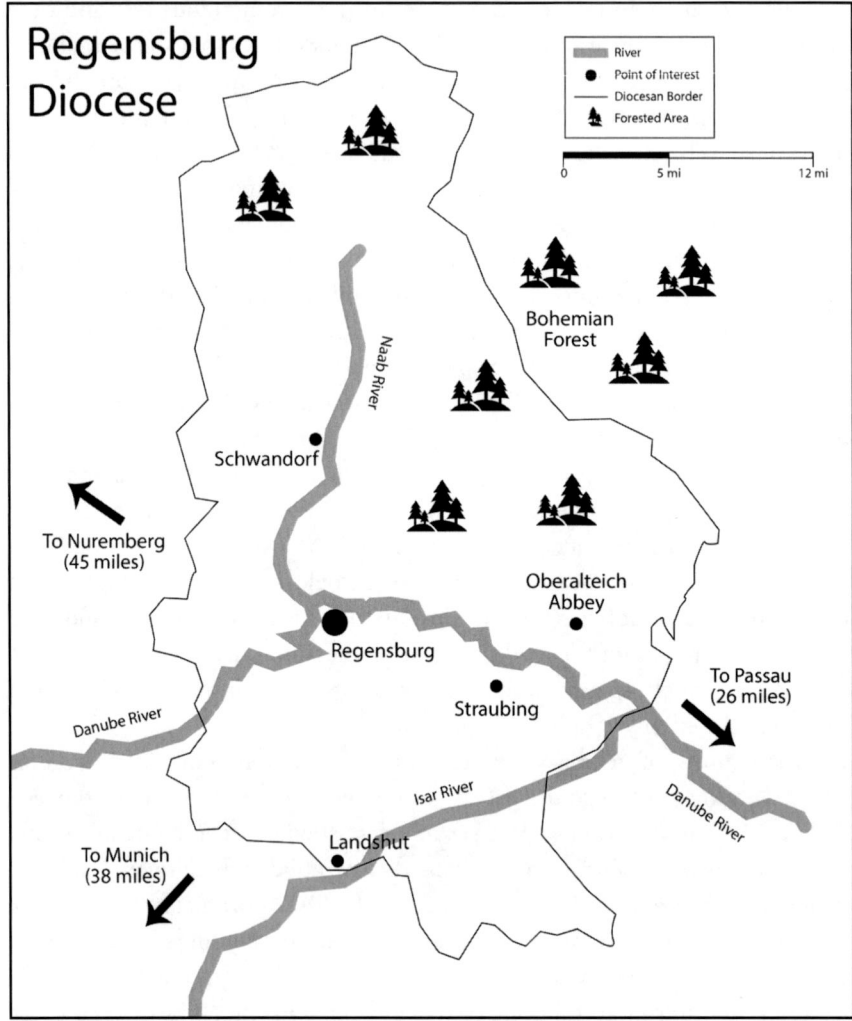

FIGURE 8   Regensburg diocese

While he particularly mentions women and children in his observations, his account soon turns to the fear among his own community. Over the next couple of weeks, sightings of Swedes caused the brethren to rush restlessly from one place to the next. With deep psychological insight Höser communicates the effects of terror: "Already pierced by the arrows of fear and the sheer imagination of horror, and bleeding like wounded game, we immediately disappear

---

several pertinent passages between Sigl's German translation and the Latin original and found the translation to be to the point.

into the thicket since we do not know what trap the enemy has set. With the night's terror still in our bones, we return alone one after another to the charcoal hut."[30] Not only concrete events, Höser implies, but the anticipation of disaster produced fear of a kind that was equally debilitating. This dread, whether real or imagined, penetrated the body, "settled" there, and, like a bleeding wound, affected and dominated the entire body.

Not surprisingly, chronicles and diaries of *religiosi*, whose monasteries lay in the thick of military action or in the line of troop movement and thus had intimate knowledge of the war, are filled with references to the great fright they experienced as soon as they heard news or rumors about an approaching army or a negative turn of military events nearby. The converse – distance from the war – however, did not necessarily induce calm. The *Geschicht Buech* of Maria Magdalena Haidenbucher, abbess of the Benedictine abbey of Frauenwörth on the island of Lake Chiemsee in Upper Bavaria (also called Frauenchiemsee), shows that even when sisters were situated farther from military action and troop movement, they were not free from fear. In many ways they had a much easier lot than the nuns of Mariastein, for example. Although the war eventually took all the Frauenwörthers' financial resources, the nuns did not experience the continuous dearth and the nearly constant threat to their survival that other sisters did. Nor did they lie in the line of action, since for most of the war they witnessed its horrors from afar. The war, nevertheless, came to the sisters in the form of the many refugees they took in.

The *fear* of harm, then, could be almost as debilitating as the harm itself. Nor did the continuance and longevity of the disaster make the fear less traumatic or less visceral, and a lull in the action did not necessarily bestow calm. Over the years, Staiger's convent Mariastein by Eichstätt was repeatedly looted and then burned down. After one of the nuns' many flights, Staiger returned home saying: "Right now we live in good peace in our cloister but not without great anxiety and fear."[31] While looting became a common occurrence over the years, its familiarity did not reduce the panic. For Staiger, there was little that could ease her fear, and, indeed, proclamations of alarm over the uncertainty of the roads, the safety of her nuns, and their endangered livelihood permeate her diary. Her words indicate that even a reprieve from military action and plundering could not quiet her dread of further misery.

30   Sigl, *Veit Hösers Kriegstagebuch*, 132 (12 December 1633).
31   *Klara Staigers Tagebuch*, 66.

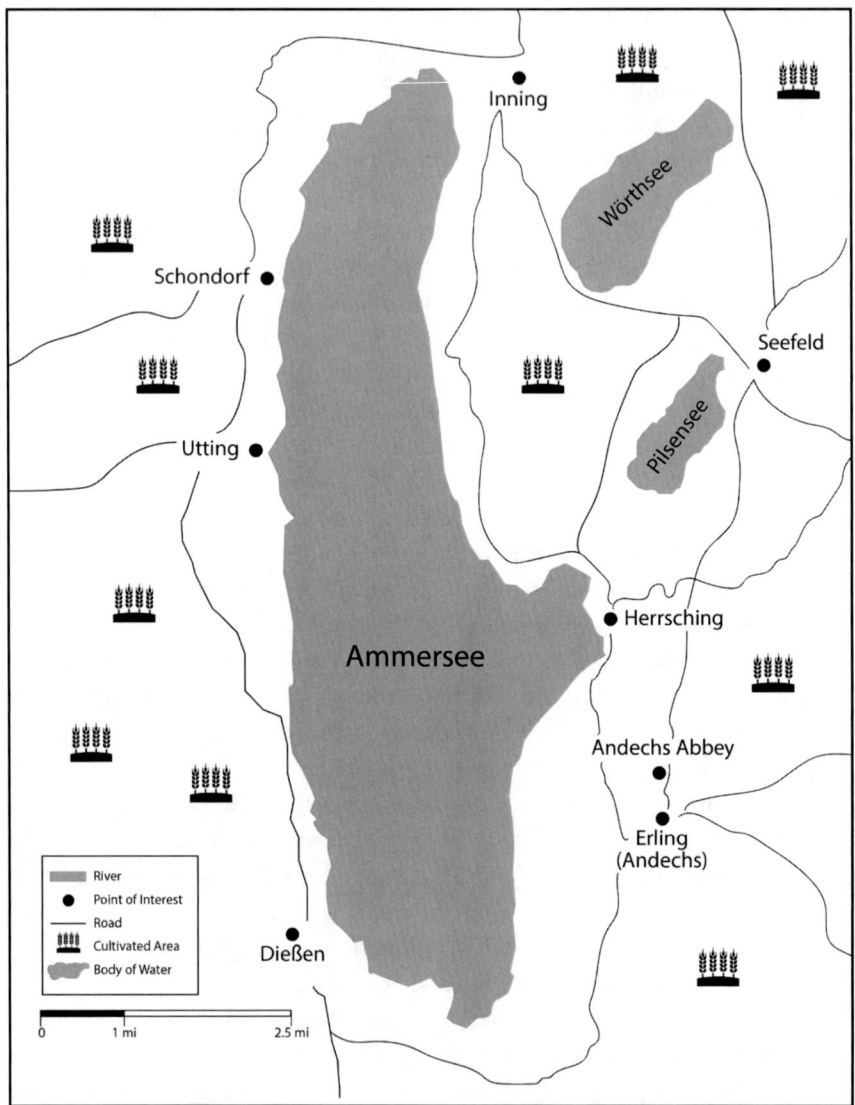

FIGURE 9   Ammersee region

Maurus Friesenegger (1590–1655), of the Benedictine abbey Andechs on the Ammersee southwest of Munich, agreed that a calmer period did not quiet the fear.[32] A professed monk at Andechs since 1614, Friesenegger was vicar of the parish Erling from 1627 until 1638, while at the same time advancing from

32   Friesenegger, *Tagebuch*, 37 (1633).

sub prior to prior and eventually to abbot in 1640. Born as the son of a baker in Dießen on the Ammersee, he became an erudite religious leader of Andechs.³³ His is one of the more balanced accounts of the war that gives evenhanded consideration to both Catholics and Protestants, peasants and soldiers. Standing back, he comments – sometimes in an almost detached, sometimes in an ironic or sarcastic way – on the events of his day. His astute assessment of the war and his sense of humor pervade the pages.

Friesenegger frequently points out that his monastery was spared the kind of misery other religious houses experienced and that he saw in the village or on his flights to Tegernsee and Munich or further afield. But the abbey's relative good fortune did not alleviate its inhabitants' anxiety. The war's continuous threat of violence and ruin may have led to a certain dulling of the senses. In his *Tagebuch*, Friesenegger suggests as much when he concludes: "So we end this year [1638] again in fear, and terror! Maybe [this year was] even more terrifying, if we were not almost used to every kind of evil."³⁴ Later, however, Friesenegger indicates that the last years of the war were no easier to bear, and were perhaps even worse. Particularly during the peace negotiations of the mid-1640s, the news of further attacks and the prospect of destruction shocked the abbot, who used unusually strong language to reflect the thwarted hopes that came with renewed attacks during the peace talks. When in 1646 the rural militia was once again recruited and the monks were ordered to prepare for flight, the "command almost knocked us to the floor." These are strong words from a man who was known for his mild manner, deep piety, and learned leadership.³⁵

For Friesenegger's Benedictine colleague, Veit Höser, in the Regensburg diocese, experiencing terror and disruption over and over did not make the experiences less frightening either: "For me, who had encountered such things many times, this is no longer a novelty, and yet I am nevertheless horrified because the angry assaults of the enemy repeat themselves so often and

---

33   Friesenegger, *Tagebuch*, 8–10. Friesenegger worked steadily to promote the Benedictine university in Salzburg. His "Tagebuch von Erling," based on a longer, two-volume Latin version, which he shortened and translated into German, is not a day-to-day record but rather a year-by-year summary of his observations, which he composed later. The Latin original, "Ephemerides Andecenses … (1627–1649)," can be found in Augsburg's diocesan archive (HS 108). The years 1633 and 1634 take up the most pages in this diary. The purpose of the shorter, vernacular text is unclear. Editor Willibald Mathäser suggests that it may have been intended for the benefit of novices or as reading material for the abbey's guests.

34   Friesenegger, *Tagebuch*, 111.

35   Friesenegger, *Tagebuch*, 137. The abbot wore a penitential robe at all times (Friesenegger, 8–10).

unannounced."³⁶ As abbot and renowned Catholic reformer, Höser presented a sought-after target, which was underlined by the fact the Swedes put the price of 60 thaler on his head.³⁷ When, after many close calls, they cornered him in a house where he had taken refuge, Höser relates his reaction: "Instantly I break out in cold sweat. I know that one moment can decide over life and death, that I am in danger of losing my liberty. Where to go in this emergency?" While he moved into the darkest, uppermost corner of the house, the raiders hacked their way through every room.

> I am right next to the robbers and hear everything; I listen to the tiniest sound and in my hideout keep as silent as a mouse, petrified, a living image. Only trembling with fear, I await the outcome. I barely dare to breathe. I would have dearly liked to silence the beat of my heart that almost burst with fear, but as long as the enemies were near me and my hideout, I could not even slow, let alone stop, the beat.³⁸

While Höser may have added some dramatic notes to his narrative, it is nevertheless plain that, for these witnesses, one more attack or raid was not "more of the same," but that each tested the limits of what one could bear.

Besides these intense and visceral expressions of fear, some authors show more restraint. The chronicle of Bamberg's Jesuit College, for example, whose writer is unknown, correlates closely with the record of Bamberg's Dominican Maria Anna Junius in terms of its description of events, but in the Jesuit record fear appears less front and center.³⁹ The Jesuit writer chronicles fear among the populace around him, since they were kept in constant terror through military skirmishes and frequent fires in the surrounding villages.⁴⁰ Rarely, if ever, however, does he describe himself as frightened, which may be in part because, other than the fear of God, he may not have considered fear fitting comportment for *religiosi*.⁴¹ Instead, the chronicler creates distance between the reality

---

36 Sigl, *Veit Hösers Kriegstagebuch*, 147 (19 December 1633).
37 The reason for the price on Höser's head is not explained but may have something to do with the fact that, if he were caught, the Swedes could extract a much larger sum for ransom.
38 Sigl, *Veit Hösers Kriegstagebuch*, 147–48 (19 December 1633).
39 *Jesuitenchronik* "Historia Collegii S. J. Bambergensis," trans. and published in excerpts by Weber, *Bamberg im dreißigjährigen Krieg*.
40 *Jesuitenchronik* in Weber, *Bamberg im dreißigjährigen Krieg*, 27–29.
41 Melchior von Straubing, friar of the Capuchin monastery in Landshut and chronicler of his congregation's experiences during the Swedish attack in 1634, does not portray the friars in the grip of fear and terror either. While at the outset he casts the war as God's deserved punishment for humanity's sins, he describes his religious community as one

of fear and his personal experience by framing it as something objective outside of oneself, not as a force that permeates everything: "Such clamor of weapons, such fright, always face to face with the enemy as it were, lasted day and night. The anxiety made life grueling and nights sleepless." The author does not exempt himself from fear but depersonalizes the feeling instead of highlighting its viscerality.[42]

The narratives tell us about both the collective experiences of fear among the religious communities and its more individual manifestations. One such aspect concerns the matter of leadership and the dread this office engendered. The leaders of religious communities, especially of female convents, suffered their own kind of fear that came with the enormous responsibility for their charges and with the need to make life-or-death decisions during the volatile times of the military conflict. And yet, these women and men needed to keep their fear to themselves because those in their care relied on their strength and leadership during this crisis. Some may have had a small circle of experienced nuns and monks to confer with, but most accounts – generally written by the leaders themselves, sometimes by a recorder or second-in-command of the community – highlight their loneliness as they tried to be steady and intrepid leaders to their subordinates.[43]

From the testimonies of the *religiosi*, we also learn how other contemporaries in the world around them fared: in the villages, towns, and cities as well as among different social groups, generations, and genders. Their observations of various people and their experiences of vulnerability are echoed in other personal narratives as well as in official reports of local and regional administrators who describe panicked flights, especially of peasants.[44] Countrymen were particularly exposed to attacks by armies and the violence of marauders. If they managed to flee into a nearby city or forest, they invariably lost whatever they left behind. Enemy and "friendly" troops destroyed their crops,

---

that knows itself secure and safe in God's hand and untroubled by earthly concerns (StBM, Cgm 2943, 2ʳ). The manuscript appears to be a copy since it is noted on the cover that the original can be found in the archive of Schärding. On the "right" kind of fear, i.e., the fear of God, which takes away all other fears, see Bähr, *Furcht und Furchtlosigkeit*, 376.

42 *Jesuitenchronik* in Weber, *Bamberg im dreißigjährigen Krieg*, 29–30. One might also argue that, as a *Historia*, the document is closer to a more impersonal chronicle, but the author does talk about "our" brothers, which again underscores the hybridity of the genre during this era.

43 *Klara Staigers Tagebuch*, 88, 90, 130. See also the chronicler of Augsburg's Dominican convent St. Katharina, who underlined the taxing demands of leadership (DA A, HS 97, 2ʳ). The abbess of the Poor Clares at Munich's Angerkloster, Catharina Bernardina Graff, expressed the weight of leadership similarly (Zwingler, *Klarissenkloster*, 1063).

44 E.g., HStA M, DK, Akt. 323, 22ʳ; StA N, ASHVMF, HS 219, 210ʳ.

demanded increasingly astronomical payments, and robbed them of the seeds that might have ensured a better future. Citizens were less exposed to such ravages than the peasants, since they lived in walled communities that provided some protection – and, in the case of select cities such as Nuremberg, state of the art fortifications. But the cities' more secure nature was a mixed blessing for its inhabitants. Once frightened subjects sought refuge in these more fortified places, their new shelters frequently turned into uncontrollable hazards. Cities were not equipped to accommodate hundreds or thousands of peasants and others complete with their belongings and farm animals. Some refugees were able to rent a room in a burgher's house, but the rest had to contend with the streets. The almost inevitable results of invasions from the countryside were price increases, hunger, and epidemics. These consequences are palpable in the diary of Hans Heberle, a shoemaker in a village near Ulm, who, over a period of eighteen years (1631–1648), fled twenty-eight times into Ulm. During his third flight he noted: "There is distress and misery, starvation and death. There we lay on top of each other in great wretchedness. Then price increase and hunger broke in on us, after these the evil disease, pestilence. Many hundreds of people died during this year, 1634."[45] Heberle lost his second son as well as three of his sisters and a brother on this flight.

Pastors, the spiritual guides of the villagers, regularly suffered an even more dire fate than that of the peasants, who were at least able to pool their resources to defend themselves and their livelihood. More conspicuous than their parishioners, ministers were often singled out by raiding parties as lucrative targets or taken hostage. Their parish houses afforded not even the little protection that a monastery might provide. With the dwindling population, their living was endangered since the parishioners could no longer pay their pastors. As a result, and because of their diminishing numbers, pastors often had to serve several parishes, which involved considerable travel on treacherous roads. They were also expected to hold out and serve the parish rather than flee to safety. And when the enemy took over their territory, they typically lost their job and either had to convert or move to a region of their own confession. The ministers' lot was grim indeed, as was that of their wives and children.

Both the ministers' superiors and parishioners turned to them during times of crisis. In Ansbach's territory southwest of Nuremberg, for example, the consistory and deans demanded that pastors be an example and guide to the disoriented parishioners. They were to tend to their flock no matter what the danger – be it soldiers or pestilence. The lists of ministers who died during the war are a telling testimony of how many tried to persevere, but the war

---

45   Zillhardt, ed., *Der Dreißigjährige Krieg*, 152.

also took a tremendous emotional and spiritual toll on them. Both ministers and deans repeatedly asked for a transfer to a quieter, less dangerous parish.[46] Some exhibit a seemingly unshakable trust in God, such as the Lutheran pastor Bartholomæus Dietwar of Kitzingen in the margraviate Brandenburg-Ansbach (Franconia), who chronicled exiles, material loss, and the death of several of his children, while thanking God for his mercy. Others, however, were less sanguine, as an example from Miehlen, Nassau illustrates. There, Pastor Plebanus often did not know how to go on. The deserted villages, the dead who were eaten by dogs since there was no one to bury them, the lack of salary, and his exile created in him "a deep melancholy, sadness, and depression (*Schwermut*)." The fact that thirty-three parishes around him were without a minister may well have made him feel as if he were fighting a losing battle.[47] Catholic ministers were in a situation comparable to their Protestant counterparts. During the Swedish intervention, Stephan Mayer in Unteregg, Windelheim, had to flee ten times and hide out for long periods of time without being able to live in the parsonage. When he was arrested, he did not admit to being a minister because "they treated the ministers very severely."[48]

The lack of protection could be especially traumatic for women. The violence perpetrated upon females found its literally most striking expression in their rape.[49] In contrast to rape in day-to-day life, war presents somewhat different circumstances in which to consider this crime. The violation of women constitutes a common feature of war from antiquity to the present. Commentators throughout the ages regarded rape in war as "inevitable."[50] War was brutal in general, but soldiers violating men's wives, children, and mothers manifested ruthlessly and graphically who had the power. Rape typically entailed a loss of honor, and scholars have argued about whether it was the honor of the woman or that of her husband that was lost.[51] In the context of war, such neat distinctions disappeared. Furthermore, the quick assumption that a woman's rape

---

46   Kroner, *Langenzenn*, 52–53.
47   Heymach, "Aufzeichnungen des Pfarrers Plebanus von Miehlen," 269.
48   Mayer, "Kurze Aufzeichnungen," 29.
49   On rape see Brownmiller, *Against Our Will*, esp. 23–34; Cubero, *La femme et le soldat*; Dane, *"Zeter und Mordio"*, esp. 186–97; Loetz, *Sexualisierte Gewalt*; Ruff, *Violence*, 140–47; Vigarello, *History of Rape*; and Walker, "Sexual Violence and Rape."
50   Brownmiller, *Against Our Will*, 23. Brownmiller is referencing a comment by World War II General George Patton, Jr. The Dutch jurist Hugo Grotius (1583–1645) wrote that while "civilized nations 'do not allow rape,' … some 'judge [it] admissible' during times of war" (Vigarello, *History of Rape*, 15, quoting from Grotius' 1625 *De Jure Belli ac Pacis*).
51   Walker, "Sexual Violence and Rape," 437. Against most historians, Garthine Walker argues with reference to the German criminal law code of the *Carolina* (1532) that the stolen honor was that of the woman, not the husband.

by a soldier sent a clear message to the subjugated reveals itself as problematic when one considers the differences in the military over time. During the Thirty Years' War, the opponents had some colorful contingents from all over Europe, but natives still made up a sizable part of the armies.[52] When the soldier comes from the next village, it muddies the oppositional picture of soldiers and civilians and disrupts the "clear message" we usually associate with rape during war.

The context of war also realigned another reality: while, outside of wartime, raped women were often not believed and sometimes even faulted for provoking sexual aggression, this was generally not the case during a military conflict.[53] As noted above, everyone expected this to be true and saw it as part of war's reality. Peter Hagendorf, who left behind a diary of his journeys as a soldier, describes his taking of women as part of an army person's everyday life.[54] Importantly, he provides no specifics about these acts, which underlines that, while ready access to women is taken for granted, rape is never an approved behavior – not even in war.[55]

Contemporary accounts are full of references to soldiers raping women. Scholars have noted the silences around rape, and this is evident in our sources as well. The women religious never openly speak about being raped, nor do they mention the term. Even the male protectors talk about it in indirect terms. They voice their fear of "something worse" than losing their lives and gratefully note that the enemy left them their "honor." Or they relate news about the violent experiences of others: the Dominican nun Junius, for example, mentions the news of violence against brothers and sisters nearby.[56] The women religious address sexual violation only haltingly, hesitantly, and indirectly, as through a veil. For them, virginity was essential, and thus sexual violation was even more traumatic than any other physical assault since their purity was central to their calling. And although women did not have to shoulder the blame for being raped, it still carried a stigma. It is therefore not surprising that the references to sexual violence are largely surrounded by a hushed silence.

---

52 On recruitment and conscription, see Tallett, *War and Society*, 69–104.
53 Walker, "Sexual Violence and Rape," 435, references a case in Württemberg to the contrary. There, an unmarried, pregnant woman claiming to have been raped by soldiers was punished nonetheless because the authorities took her for a liar. This occurred in 1646 toward the end of the war.
54 Peters, ed., *Ein Söldnerleben*.
55 Brownmiller, *Against Our Will*, 33. Brownmiller calls rape "unmentionable" under any circumstances.
56 Hümmer, ed., "Bamberg im Schweden-Kriege," 52:17.

Whether it was the fear of harm or loss of life or dispossession or the very intimate violation of rape, all of the dreads and terrors articulated in contemporary accounts were rooted in a deep sense of vulnerability. The realization or perception that nothing stood between oneself and the war's violence was expressed in countless ways.

2   Instability and Disruption

Contemporaries frequently reacted to the threat of violence by fleeing, which may have led to a measure of security for some, but more often it brought about varying degrees of instability. For many religious communities, flight was a recurring reality; it involved difficult, dangerous journeys to more distant, unfamiliar locations and typically entailed a separation of their group. Their lives – formerly routine and fairly predictable – became anything but. For most, their flights led to temporary exile, not permanent emigration.[57] While this undoubtedly was the hope of those in exile, there was no certainty of the outcome nor any knowledge of how many more times they would have to flee. People described their experience as "going into misery" (*ins Elend gehen*). This standard phrase, found throughout narratives of lay and clerical men and women, implied having to leave one's place for a region that was not home. This strange land could be a distant county or a foreign country, but it could also be as close as the nearby forest, the next city, or, in the case of many members of religious orders, another monastery or convent. In short, it was an area beyond the immediate boundaries of one's home. The expression has its roots in the middle-high German word "ellende" (old-high German: *alilanti/ elilenti*) and connotes an alien country (*Fremde*), banishment (*Verbannung*), exile, as well as the notion of suffering and desolation.[58] Early modern narratives continue the conceptual association between exile, misery, and hardship.

If leaving one's home was experienced as alienating and stressful, how much more disturbing must it have been for monks and nuns who lived in

---

57   Among the burgeoning literature on exile and migration, see especially Asche et al., eds., *Krieg, Militär und Migration*; Bahlcke, ed., *Glaubensflüchtlinge*; Briegel and Frühwald, eds., *Erfahrung der Fremde*; Evelein, ed., *Exiles Traveling*; Koopmann, "Exil als geistige Lebensform"; and Krauss, "Heimat."

58   Eberhardt, "Exil im Mittelalter," 15; and *Deutsches Wörterbuch von Jacob und Wilhelm Grimm*, 3:406: ("Elend" – "*exilium, captivitas, miseria ...*" 1) "urbedeutung dieses schönen, vom heimweh eingegebenen wortes ist das wohnen im ausland, in der fremde" ("original meaning of this beautiful word that is evoked by homesickness is the dwelling abroad, in foreign lands").

enclosure? Still more traumatic were flights for the Benedictines. The Council of Trent (1545–1563) had stipulated enclosure, especially for all female orders. While this recent measure had been internalized to varying degrees by religious houses, for the Benedictines the rule of *stabilitas loci* (stability of place) was foundational from the order's beginning in the sixth century.[59] Having to leave their enclosed space, in which they had resided most of their lives, was a traumatic experience. The Benedictine abbot, Veit Höser, captures these elements perfectly:

> Tomorrow I must commence my journey into misery, into exile. I have to pronounce the word again: exile, misery, banishment, because I have to leave my *Heimat*, depart from our monastic settlements, desert the house where I took my vows, where I swore lifelong faithfulness to my cloister and *stabilitas*. Now I must abandon my brothers and sons who are dearest to me on earth…. Misery, I say, because I depart in the tattered gown of a homeless foreigner, poor, needy, and miserable and without any brotherly comfort. Banishment because I have been FORCED to leave home and live among strangers. It is hard but I must bear it calmly, with composure.[60]

Even before Höser "despaired of hope that he might find an undisturbed residence here in this region [of Oberalteich]" and before he decided "to wander far away," he recounts volatility and aimlessness as central hallmarks of his present life. Incessantly he moved up and down dangerous mountain paths and across icy stretches from one hideout to the next – from the abbey's provostry, properties, and outposts to huts tucked away in the impenetrable Bavarian Forest and a rocky ledge shrouded in clouds – and then back again to survey his abbey:

> Thus I wandered constantly, waveringly without aim, and nowhere did I find a minute of peace because the daily and nightly, irregular, sudden, and unpredictable attacks and persecutions of the Weimar horsemen and soldiers did not leave me a single corner where I could have rested with any feeling of security or even taken a short respite, let alone used it as a hiding place. O good God, how often during the course of a day or

---

59   Among some religious, enclosure became a contested issue. See Strasser, *State of Virginity*.
60   Sigl, *Veit Hösers Kriegstagebuch*, 152 (capitalization in the original).

night was I forced to get up from bed, prayer, or work, after I just started something, to flee helter-skelter? How often was I discouraged by the terror of the Swedes? And still I see no end.[61]

Aimlessness and restlessness, however, characterized not only his life but that of the people he encountered on his flights as well. In shelters there was a continuous coming and going. Wandering refugees warmed themselves for a while at a campfire to dispel the wintry cold but then left again. They changed places constantly and moved from one hiding place in the wilderness to the next, since they did not know where to find safety.[62] Even in the most inhospitable places, Höser and his companions regularly came across wandering people. Eventually they trudged back to the provostry:

> [We were] trembling of fear. Our heart raced when we entered. In fearful expectation we ate our evening soup and stayed overnight without finding peace. With fear and anxiety we anticipated dawn. The lords and barons of Neuhaus and Au fled to us who were refugees ourselves. The former had crawled out of his hiding place in a cavern which he could no longer endure. The latter wandered aimlessly for weeks since the Swedes had robbed him of his *Heimat* and everything else. Countless people from the countryside of all ages were there who could not find safety anywhere.[63]

Höser provides close-ups of what leaving one's home meant for the populace around him. While many *religiosi* and political leaders had the chance to prepare for their flight, the broader populace was often caught off guard. After the Swedish troops had overthrown Neuburg on the Danube, Abensberg, and Kelheim and were advancing on Regensburg while committing countless atrocities, the people were so horrified that they left their "Heimat" and "sought their salvation in flight."[64] The Benedictine abbot describes with great sensitivity the suffering of the refugees he encountered, and he is cognizant of their burden: "No one can see the daily and night-long treks of refugees passing before his eyes without the deepest pity."[65] He highlights the suddenness of the assault that made any planning impossible. People had to vacate their

---

61 Sigl, *Veit Hösers Kriegstagebuch*, 145, 149.
62 Sigl, *Veit Hösers Kriegstagebuch*, 136.
63 Sigl, *Veit Hösers Kriegstagebuch*, 137.
64 Sigl, *Veit Hösers Kriegstagebuch*, 84.
65 Sigl, *Veit Hösers Kriegstagebuch*, 93.

homes at once and had to abandon family, friends, and possessions: "Without hesitating for a second and without a glance back they had to leave for the unknown and start a miserable life [i.e., a life away from home]." Helplessly, Höser watched as parents and children were torn apart and everyone, whether elderly, half-naked, injured, or crippled, wandered aimlessly among strangers. War became the great equalizer: "They who previously had plenty were now forced to go begging." The paths of nobles, clergy in disguise, and commoners crossed as they were filling up the houses and every last hiding place of the area.[66] Their sense of vulnerability, thus, was closely linked to the experience of instability and uncertainty during the war.

The experiences from the world of the *religiosi* are echoed in narratives of other contemporaries and reflect a similar sense of vulnerability, instability, and the changeability of life. The Lutheran pastor Bartholomæus Dietwar highlights the unpredictability of life during the war. Dietwar chronicled his experiences and those of his colleagues in Kitzingen in the margraviate Brandenburg-Ansbach, Franconia. Barely twelve miles southeast of Catholic Würzburg, Kitzingen faced both the quartering of troops and the repeated takeover by a power of another religious confession. When the town fell to the bishop of Würzburg in January 1629, the evangelical pastors had either to convert or leave and lose their jobs. Dietwar decided to depart, and other evangelical ministers were eventually chased out of the city as well.[67] While Dietwar took over the parish of Höchstadt, the Swedes drove the bishop and his men out of Franconia. The recently installed Catholic ministers fled Kitzingen, and the evangelical pastors returned. Even though the Lutheran ministers were again in control of their parishes, they then had to contend with troops in their territory, since the Swedish and imperial forces had converged on nearby Nuremberg. Ministers were robbed on their journeys to their parishes, and plundering was endemic. In 1634 Kitzingen fell again to the Catholics. This time the Evangelicals were promised that they could retain their religion, but before long Lutheran sermons were again forbidden, and the evangelical ministers were pushed out of their homes. On 9 April 1635, Dietwar went once more into exile.[68] Incessant change represented the only constant.

---

66   Sigl, *Veit Hösers Kriegstagebuch*, 94–96.
67   LAELKB, MD Uffenheim, Akt. 95:22–39. Dietwar's account for the year 1629 is particularly long (29–44), whereas he spends only one page on most other years. Dietwar's chronicle has been edited and published by Volkmar Wirth (Bartholomäus Dietwar, *Leben eines evangelischen Pfarrers*), although Wirth's is not a precise rendering of the original. Dietwar's chronicle also has poignant and valuable drawings in the margins, such as death masks of his dead children and images of comets.
68   LAELKB, MD Uffenheim, Akt. 95:59–63, 78–82, 93.

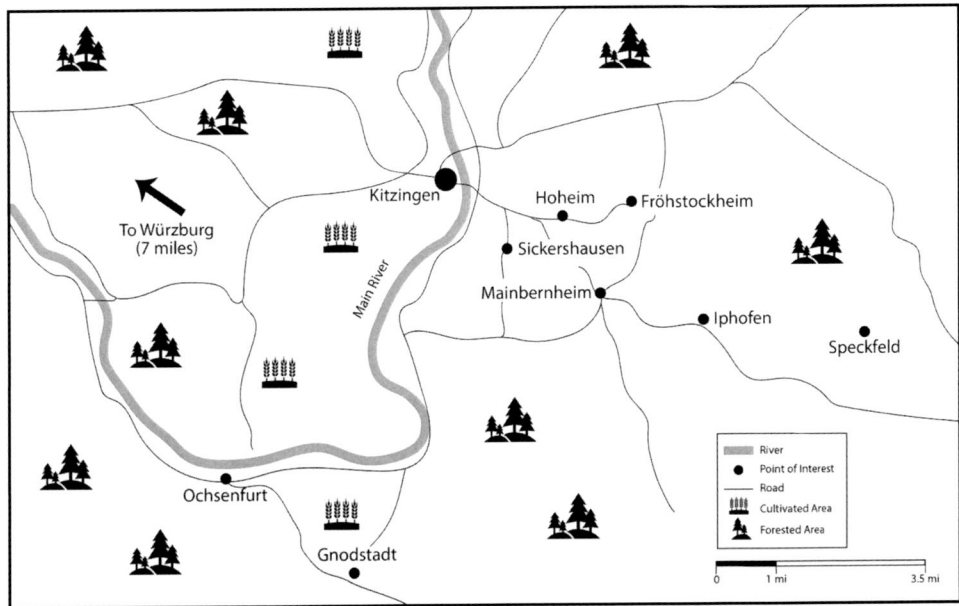

FIGURE 10   Kitzingen and surrounding area

Soldiers, too, experienced the changeability of fate during the war. Even though they were often the ones perpetrating violence and destruction, their lot was not an enviable one. Much of their aggression was prompted by the fact that they were paid insufficiently, infrequently, or not at all. Cities tried to bar their gates against them, and maltreated peasants often paid marauding soldiers back atrocity for atrocity. In his journal, the soldier Peter Hagendorf continually underlines the volatility of a soldier's life: one day was feast, the next famine.[69]

The testimonies of *religiosi* convey another traumatic aspect of the flights: the breaking up of their community. Members of convents who were forced to flee usually left behind a few to ensure the continued viability of their economy, while a larger group sought refuge. Those who remained fled only when the enemy was all but upon them. When, toward the end of the war, Prioress Staiger followed their guardian's order and fled with her nuns, she suffered agonizing fear for those who had stayed behind at Mariastein: "The concern for my twenty sisters in the cloister made me so anxious that I did not know how I felt. I dragged myself up the mountain [to St. Willibald's Castle] and thought I could not stop myself from falling down…. I was then carried and guided

---

69   Peters, ed., *Ein Söldnerleben*.

rather than that I walked myself."[70] Not only was *she* afraid for the lives of those who had remained to look after the cloister and do the baking, washing, and other necessary chores; she was also aware, as she noted during an earlier assault, that *they* were extremely frightened – "more so ... than they could ever tell us."[71] Having to suffer such fear, her words suggest, leaves an indelible mark upon one's life, one that was shared by many but could not be communicated.

The war's plundering and violence and the frequent dislocations could disrupt and separate a community for years.[72] Moreover, flights caused both mental and physical suffering. The Benedictine convent Hohenwart south of Ingolstadt is a case in point of the hardships associated with exile and separation.[73] For them, the unrest started in 1631 following the destruction of Magdeburg (20 May 1631) and the Swedes' advance into the southern German lands. The nuns first fled to nearby Pfaffenhofen (April 1632), but travelled to more distant places during their next flight (in mid-October 1632). The refugees endured many adversities on their travels and were not always welcome. At Landshut they had to wait a long time before they were admitted into the city, and then no one wanted to give them housing. When they reached the Benedictine monastery St. Veit in Neumarkt some 20 miles southeast of Landshut, they received a friendlier welcome, but other monastic groups used such safe havens as well, so these must have been crowded spaces. The fact that monasteries in still viable locales could typically take in only a handful of people and for only a limited time highlights the reality of separation and continued movement for many monastic communities. Frauenchiemsee, which took in an unprecedented number of women religious, was an exception. Not surprisingly, the records are full of gratitude for this refuge and for Abbess Haidenbucher's willingness to open her doors to the exiled, but Frauenchiemsee eventually also reached its limits.

If the nuns who decided to flee experienced much distress, those who stayed behind at the cloister were often in a worse situation. We hear harrowing stories of the remnants who upheld the cloister's economy during these volatile

---

70 *Klara Staigers Tagebuch*, 316 (31 March 1648).
71 *Klara Staigers Tagebuch*, 51 (1632).
72 The Benedictine convent under Abbess Agnes von Neuegg in Holzen by Donauwörth in Augsburg's diocese offers a vivid example of this reality. HStA M, KL, fasc. 739/59, 1^r–2^v (1639). The Dominican convent of Altenhohenau southeast of Munich (near Wasserburg) is another example of a community that had to flee repeatedly and experienced frequent separation of their group (HStA M, KL, fasc. 13/1a, 8^r–15^v).
73 StBM, HS, Cgm 5727, 57–58. See also Reischl, ed., *Hohenwarter Klosterchronik*. The chronicle of the Benedictine convent was written by a female member of the convent, probably the prioress or another woman officer, most likely, however, not by the abbess.

EXPERIENCES OF WAR 49

and dangerous times. When most of the Benedictine nuns at Hohenwart fled in 1632, two sisters, Magdalena Fürleger and Ursula Dienstorfer, remained at the convent. As the chronicler underlines, the two stayed behind of their own volition (*gerne*) since they – mistakenly – believed only the Croats were approaching, not the Swedes.[74] The abbess told Dienstorfer: "I am not ordering you to stay; but if you do, I will not be displeased."[75] Thus, Ursula Dienstorfer was not easily frightened. At seventy, age may have been a factor for avoiding the exertions of the journey, but older nuns were often among those who held the fort at home, in part because the convent leader could rely on their greater experience.[76] Testimonies also note that younger nuns tended to be more afraid and had to be taken to safety earlier than the rest.[77] And yet, the experiences during the Swedish assault turned Ursula Dienstorfer from a spirited into a timid and terrified woman.

After the other nuns had fled, the two sisters stayed in the convent during the day but at night went to their *Markt* (i.e., market town), most likely for greater protection.[78] The next day, Friday, the Swedes came and wreaked havoc on the market town. On Saturday, a quiet day, the parish buried the dead. Sunday started calmly enough with a mass, but then the Swedes suddenly stormed the market. The nuns' deacon and their father confessor quickly hid underneath the bath's floorboards – one face-up, the other face-down. The Swedes struck the floor three times with their axes, but the two men remained mute and motionless. After the enemy left, the men crawled out of hiding and fled. The market, however, was ruined, including the items the sisters had brought there for safekeeping.[79]

We do not hear what happened to Madgalena Fürleger, but experiences with the Swedish attackers transformed Ursula Dienstorfer. She left the market that same evening, although she was so afraid she could barely walk. Two neighbors accompanied her to Thierheim, where she sat down in a garden, but

---

74 Neither the term "Croats" nor "Swedes" should be taken literally. "Croats" (*Kroaten, Crabaten*) was used as a collective term for irregular light cavalry from east and southeast Europe. The Croats were allies of the Catholic armies. "Swedes" typically did not refer to the Swedish nationality but more often to members of the Protestant coalition. On Croats, see Ebermeier, *Landshut*, 17.
75 StBM, HS, Cgm 5727, 55.
76 See, for example, the Püttrich cloister in Munich, where, in 1632, their mother superior took 27 sisters to the Tyrol and left 14 of the older nuns behind. HStA M, KL, fasc. 423/1, 100^r.
77 See, for example, Klara Staiger's diary.
78 The term "Markt" is particularly prevalent in Bavaria. It connotes not simply an economic trading center but something akin to a village or town.
79 StBM, HS, Cgm 5727, 55–56 (14–17 October 1632).

when she thought she saw riders in the distance, she got up again and fled – this time alone – to Tegernbach, where Hans Fähn offered to keep her overnight. Fortunately, two of her fellow sisters, Walburga Frumm and Margretha Zächin, arrived and accompanied her to Pfaffenhofen, but Ursula was too distressed to eat or drink anything all day. Finally, late at night, after she had a drink of beer at a brewer's house, she was able to eat something. There was a coming and going in the city and at the inn, and at 1 a.m. over 400 people left Pfaffenhofen for Freising, the nuns among them. They reached Freising around noon the next day – "poor Ursula" so tired she sat down in front of a house. Dienstorfer and her two fellow nuns looked so miserable that people pitied them, but apparently not enough to give them lodging for the night. The nuns begged one Herrn von Weischenstöffen to take them just for a night since they were so tired and hungry, but he refused. Finally, Walburga Frumm managed to organize housing with the city's "learned" minister, Andre Sedlmayr, who also fed them. When, in the morning, the news came that the Swedes had left Hohenwart, her two companions returned to the cloister, but Ursula Dienstorfer – "over seventy years old and full of fear" – stayed with the minister. She remained there for four weeks and then went to the Benedictine monastery Scheyern. After Andree Andlezausser came and told her that "one would like to have her back at home, and nothing would happen to her anymore because they had a *Salva Guardia*; she should no longer be frightened," Ursula Dienstorfer finally went home.[80]

This story offers a rare glimpse of the psychologically debilitating power of war. Its brutal reality could turn an experienced nun into a dazed and terrified shadow of herself, who was unable to move, eat, or drink and was indeed so paralyzed with fear that, even after the Swedes had left and her fellow sisters had returned, she could not bring herself to trust in the safety of her old home.

Not all who stayed behind had such harrowing experiences as Ursula Dienstorfer, but for most life hardly continued as before once their community separated and a large contingent went into exile. These stay-at-home nuns and monks faced disruption in their familiar spaces that were distinct from those encountered by the refugees but just as real. Almost always they took in sisters and brothers from other convents and orders, which not only necessitated a reorganization of their home but could lead to friction over religious lifestyle. The split of their own group weighed heavily on them, and some felt left behind and exposed.

Even though Munich's Angerkloster of the Poor Clares was not destroyed during the war, the twelve sisters who kept the convent going experienced

---

80 StBM, HS, Cgm 5727, 58–60.

EXPERIENCES OF WAR   51

great challenges.⁸¹ In her letter to Anna Catharina Frölich, who had taken the other sisters to Tölz, Constantia Grindl describes the disorientation that the sisters' departure caused among the remnant in Munich and offers a moving narrative of the home community's state:

> I imagine that I have to say all the time: wonder, wonder above wonder that the sisters of the Anger should no longer be here. Believe me we pity you so severely that we often cannot sleep half or all of the night. Yes, we cannot remain on our straw mattress when we consider that you have to sleep on hard floors. I think that I must carry all my pillows and bedding on my back toward you. You have already brought many tears to our eyes.⁸²

Whereas here Grindl states that she can hardly believe the others are gone, a few paragraphs later it seems to her as if the sisters had left a hundred years ago. Without them, the convent is so large that they get lost in it, and Grindl exclaims that she "cannot live without them." The sister is torn between conflicting sentiments: although she sympathizes with the sisters who have to endure deprivations and suffer exile, there is also a trace of reproach at the absent sisters for having abandoned them. She describes herself and her small group as "orphaned" and "left behind." For good measure, Grindl adds that "everyone" is glad the cloister has not been deserted entirely and that some of the nuns remained.⁸³ Her fellow sister, Anastasia, comments similarly: "with regard to us poor orphans, I cannot express in words what fear and sorrow are among us. We are simply without protection (*vogelfrei*).... We need nothing more than to prepare for the blessed end."⁸⁴

The sisters' exchange also conveys how overburdened the smaller group was in trying to run the convent's economy at home all by themselves. It meant hard work and chores that many were either unused or not trained to do. Keys and vital documents could not be found because suddenly a crucial

---

81 Besides three reports/chronicles of the abbess and the convent recorder, we also have some of the correspondence between the exiled sisters and those who stayed or went home – a most rare and fortunate circumstance. Zwingler, *Klarissenkloster*, summarizes several of these letters and provides a selection of them in her study. For the larger original correspondences, see HStA M, KL 393/1831.
82 Zwingler, *Klarissenkloster*, 1058 (# 14), 10–15 April 1632.
83 Zwingler, *Klarissenkloster*, 1059–60. "Everyone" is most likely the subjects and agents on their grounds.
84 Zwingler, *Klarissenkloster*, 983 (# 2/3), 3 May 1632.

layer of their operation was gone.[85] Some had no regrets about having stayed behind, but others became heavy at heart. Sister Anastasia had initially fled but had not gone all the way to the Tyrol and had returned from Tölz to the Angerkloster. Eventually, however, she regretted having done so. For her, being a nun meant being quiet in her cell with God: "O my dear heart, it is a pleasure above all pleasures for the one who can serve God in her cell in silence."[86] Instead, she had to take on tasks she had neither wanted nor was trained to do, and be involved in the business of running the economy. The sisters and their remaining *Patres* also had to navigate the messy business of forced contributions. When Gustavus Adolphus took Munich, the Angerkloster was supposed to contribute two horses and a cart to the Swedes. Anastasia exclaimed: "Help us God through pure prayer that they do not take all of our horses. One almost wants to die because of all the misery – when one [hardship] is over, another surfaces."[87]

If exile led to a form of disequilibrium – a *Gleichgewichtsstörung* in the words of the twentieth-century exile Stefan Zweig, the experience of a reconfigured home also tested one's sense of identity.[88] Space is an important dimension in these experiences.[89] Some nuns were carted off to new places, but for those who stayed behind, the landscape of the place they called home changed as well, not only because of the potentially real destruction of their convent, but also due to the shifts in the home community once a large contingent of the sisters had left. "Home" needed to be constructed anew in accordance with the altered situation. Some adjusted and rallied; others become disoriented – and so were not unlike their exiled sisters. To some extent, then, space eluded the nuns' control.

3 Poverty – Hunger – Dearth

The war led to dearth and poverty on an unprecedented scale. Besides a slow increase in the impoverished layer of society over the course of the sixteenth and early seventeenth centuries, there were famines caused by inflation and bad harvests, as in 1626 when price increases and starvation followed bitterly

---

85   Zwingler, *Klarissenkloster*, 988.
86   Zwingler, *Klarissenkloster*, 989 (# 2/12) and 983, fn. 58.
87   Zwingler, *Klarissenkloster*, 1072 (# 20), 2 July 1632.
88   Zweig, "Die Welt von Gestern," 468.
89   On the spacial turn, see Bachmann-Medick, *Cultural Turns*; Fisher and Mennel, "Introduction"; Schlögel, *Im Raume lesen wir die Zeit*.

cold weather.⁹⁰ Such an occurrence was not uncommon during this period that has been termed "Little Ice Age," in which summers became shorter, wetter, and colder.⁹¹ But besides these cyclical factors, the war with its destruction, extortions, inflation, and displacement accelerated the forces driving poverty and deprivation, and thus brought these experiences to the doorstep of most contemporaries. For the southeast German lands, shortages of food and other necessities became a common infliction during the Swedish intervention in the 1630s. Clara Staiger describes the great destitution during July 1634, when many people starved to death. Because of the enormous scarcity, people "cut off before its time the little that was on the fields, and dried, ground, and baked it. [The nuns] were not able to preserve anything from the poor people, the birds, and the mice."⁹² More often than not, troops trekking through their region were the sources of deprivation, as when the Hungarian king – the future emperor Ferdinand III who was on his way to what became the battle of Nördlingen – arrived with his army of 40,000, in addition to thousands of officers, princes, and other dignitaries, not to mention the troops' train. After four days of soldiers passing, "there was such a dearth that no one could lay their hands on meat, wine, beer, bread, or other provisions. Quite a few would have given a reichsthaler or his horse for a loaf of bread – if someone would have bought it from him."⁹³ Whether by violence and exorbitant demands of the troops or regular contribution payments, the war drove people into poverty, and this poverty engulfed not only the chronically poor, but also those who in the past had not experienced deprivation.

In early spring 1635 Staiger offers a panorama of the great need everywhere. Their former caretaker brought distressing news about Speyer's takeover and destruction by enemy troops: "He also spoke of such famine that at several places [people] crushed, ground, and baked the bones of the dead." A day later, two women brought a half-dead twelve-year-old girl, a peasant whom they had pulled out of the Altmühl River, to the nuns. Despite the sisters' care and warm soup, the girl died during the night. Rumors of cannibalism circulated. A messenger from Swabia reported the famine was so great there that "one

---

90 *Klara Staigers Tagebuch*, 46. The prime example of out-of-control inflation is the so-called *Kipper* and *Wipper* period during the early 1620s.

91 Of the authors discussed here, Friesenegger records most consistently the weather patterns and their often adverse effects on the harvest. On climate change, see Behringer et al., eds., *Kulturelle Konsequenzen der "Kleinen Eiszeit"*; Glaser, *Klimageschichte Mitteleuropas*; Lehmann, "Frömmigkeitsgeschichtliche Auswirkungen"; Parker, *Global Crisis*; and Schenk, ed., *Katastrophen*.

92 *Klara Staigers Tagebuch*, 143.

93 *Klara Staigers Tagebuch*, 145 (11 August 1634).

woman had already eaten five children. Also another woman had eaten her dead husband and had dug up two more [bodies]."[94] Whether these far from rare reports of cannibalism are true or not, they add to the sense of extreme deprivation.

Unable to collect interest on their endowments, the Mariasteiner nuns had to rely almost entirely on begging to sustain themselves. In contrast, the Benedictine Veit Höser of Oberalteich in Regensburg's diocese rarely mentions suffering hunger, although toward the end of his narrative he vividly describes the hunger and dearth in the countryside. Instead, the abbot underlines time and again how rich the abbey and its holdings were, and that, if the enemy knew how to curb his appetite, the abbey could have supported his army for a winter and longer.[95] Many religious communities were well off or at least in good financial standing when the war began, but, by late 1633, circumstances had changed for most, yet apparently not for Oberalteich. While Staiger slaved to secure a single horse, Höser had several dozen at his disposal and directed some of them to safer places. Oberalteich was rich not only in provisions but also in properties, to which Höser could flee.

Andechs was also well off, but in Maurus Friesenegger's observations, hungry soldiers and starving subjects keep reappearing. Since the abbey lay in the line of troop movement and became the repeated refuge for up to a thousand residents from surrounding locales, it was caught up in the general deprivation. The Benedictine describes the multiple scourges on their village, Erling, where he was vicar until 1638. Destitution was everywhere, not only among the peasants but also the soldiers, who were starving to death since their supplies from Munich were delayed: "Among those [soldiers], who just had died the night before, there were two, who, before they starved to death, had taken bites of their arms and gnawed at their fingers." At the same time, the soldiers went after the peasants and claimed that what had been owned by the peasants now belonged to the soldiers. Friesenegger intervened and organized 1,600 loaves of bread, but soon the next crisis arose. When their own soldiers went after the cloister's pigs, the monks asked the officers in their quarters for help. Although this initiative ended badly for the soldiers, the officers swiftly demanded animals to feed their soldiers. The peasants, however, preferred to slaughter their own animals – even though they were essential to their future survival – rather than lose them to the army: "When the peasants thus saw that it was truly arranged to take everything from them and to consign them to starvation, they slaughtered the few animals that were left and therewith wanted to quench

---

94   *Klara Staigers Tagebuch*, 174 (31 March 1635).
95   Sigl, *Veit Hösers Kriegstagebuch*, 124–25.

their own hunger rather than that of the soldiers."⁹⁶ The soldiers in turn stole the peasants' loads of bread and grain on the latter's return from Munich, notwithstanding that, according to Friesenegger, their subjects had not had bread for five days. It is clear, then, that during times of extreme deprivation both peasants and soldiers suffered severely. While peasants were often more vulnerable, soldiers experienced their own share of dearth.

After these taxing confrontations with troops and their extortions, the abbey of Andechs faced a difficult and lean spring. Particularly disastrous for the future was the fact that many farmers could not till their fields because of a lack of seeds and horses. Friesenegger notes, however, that the cloister was able to cultivate its land. The crisis continued, and May saw more people leaving for the Tyrol or young men joining the army. Many simply died. Harvest time did eventually come to Erling, but Friesenegger describes the heart-breaking scenes, "how naked, and from hunger emaciated humans work to take down their grain without horses, carts, and other instruments that go with this kind of work, and with what great struggles they carry it home, and, once home, not knowing how they should store it since some have no house and others no roof."⁹⁷ Thus, even though the fields' yield was finally plentiful, people lacked the means to use it adequately.

Hard on the heels of the widespread hunger followed pestilence. The Benedictine opined that this was one more way for God to bring humans to the right path – first war and hunger, now pestilence – but after this brief reference to the Divine, Friesenegger returns to his astute observations of the epidemic's more mundane realities and its repercussions. Here, as throughout his account, he shows a tendency toward balance rather than drama and exaggeration. Friesenegger notes when the year ended better than expected or when a month was quiet, and he differentiates between different levels of need and crisis. At the end of 1634, after an intense wave of epidemic and damage from the armies in the nearby winter quarters, he records that Augsburg suffered the greatest famine. In Erling, however, "no one any longer died of hunger, but people generally lived in the greatest poverty." The hardships continued into the next year and were exacerbated by the severe cold. Friesenegger, himself a vicar to the village, remarks that not only the parishioners but also their pastors were forced to leave their parishes and seek their bread elsewhere. The Vicar General had revealed that four hundred parishes in Augsburg's diocese were without pastors – either because they had died or moved away. Conversely, the parishes had also lost most of their parishioners: some parishes had declined

---

96   Friesenegger, *Tagebuch*, 66–67 (1634).
97   Friesenegger, *Tagebuch*, 74–75, 85 (1634).

from 1,000 to 20 or 30 "souls." Want was all around, and Friesenegger, too, circulates rumors of cannibalism for Augsburg.[98]

The steward of the Poor Clares in Munich, Friedinger, also communicates the dire state of both the Poor Clares' cloister and their peasants. Besides relating to the exiled sisters the general sense of economic depletion, he describes concrete examples of individuals who lacked clothes on their backs and were needier than the poor in front of the church.[99] Sister Anastasia, part of the remnant who kept the Angerkloster going, echoes Friedinger's words; indeed, she is unable to put into words the desolation of the impoverished peasants around Munich: "I cannot express it … I would have to write you day and night how there is misery and want everywhere in the countryside. [The Swedes] have just burned down and devastated everything around the city."[100]

The references to hunger and destitution engendered by the war and its consequences are legion in these and other contemporary accounts. Especially during the early 1630s and toward the end of the war, many towns and villages around Franconia and Old Bavaria suffered severe food shortages, ruining not only the citizens and peasants in the countryside but also the soldiers who starved for lack of provisions.

4   Violence and Human Concern: World Views Turned Upside Down

Despite the fact that soldiers usually chose their armies with little concern for religious alignment, the opponents in this war ostensibly belonged to different confessions, and part of the violence was fueled by religious antagonism. Narratives speak of the damage to religious objects and spaces, such as churches, cloisters, and chapels. While, from a practical point of view, it made sense to stable horses in a church, this utilitarian move could also imply, and was certainly perceived as, a confessional insult. Even though the confiscation of costly liturgical paraphernalia could serve a monetary purpose, the willful destruction of saints' statues, crucifixes, reliquaries, and organs attests to religious violence toward the opponent.[101]

---

98   Friesenegger, *Tagebuch*, 91–92 (1634). Notably he designates it as a rumor and renders it in brackets: "[One says that they have even eaten the flesh of children and humans.]"
99   Zwingler, *Klarissenkloster*, 969–71.
100 Zwingler, *Klarissenkloster*, 985 (16 June 1632). While Gustavus Adolphus had made sure that Munich was not ransacked, the surrounding countryside suffered severely under his troops.
101 See, e.g., *Jesuitenchronik* in Weber, *Bamberg im dreißigjährigen Krieg*, 22–23.

Religious antagonism was directed not only at objects and spaces, but also at people. When the nuns of Munich's Angerkloster fled their cloister, they had to endure humiliations at the hands of the populace: "There were secular people everywhere, some had pity [on the women religious], others made fun of us. There was one wicked woman who wished us every evil and said we would not escape the enemy anyway."[102] To counteract the prejudices against the Jesuits, their rector in Bamberg followed one pater's advice to offer the enemy "everything he demanded so that one did not give opportunity to those who charged in a hateful manner that the Jesuits were warmongers but did not ever want to contribute any aid."[103] The chronicler of Bamberg's Jesuit College also reported on the fate of other orders and the cruel treatment of several Catholic pastors, who were tortured for religious reasons.[104] He pointed out that such atrocities were not only perpetrated by common soldiers but also by noblemen. Members of religious orders as well as ministers and their congregations experienced confessionally motivated violence. The fact that the religious travelled in secular clothes as a matter of course shows their fear of repercussions against them if their status were evident. When Abbot Veit Höser hid from the enemy in the uppermost corner of a house, he took off his golden cross with its relics so that, should the enemy find him, they would take him for a layman.[105]

The destruction and violence inflicted upon the populace were real and extensive, as was the religious antagonism, both of which are prevalent themes in contemporary accounts. Many monasteries became targets of violence, and their residents were frequently killed, taken for ransom, or scattered. The relationship between the involved parties, however, is more complex than a first glance might suggest. For example, Colonel Wilhelm Lohausen, the commander of the Swedes and a Calvinist, both rebuked Bamberg's Jesuits and emerged as their protector. While he openly discussed the common (negative) opinion regarding the Jesuits and reprimanded them for their double-talk, "he took the college under his protection and subsequently guarded it in such a way that he proved to be a father and guardian, not an enemy."[106] This

---

102   Zwingler, *Klarissenkloster*, 1063 (# 16).
103   *Jesuitenchronik* in Weber, *Bamberg im dreißigjährigen Krieg*, 32.
104   *Jesuitenchronik* in Weber, *Bamberg im dreißigjährigen Krieg*, 37–39.
105   Sigl, *Veit Hösers Kriegstagebuch*, 148 (19 December 1633).
106   *Jesuitenchronik* in Weber, *Bamberg im dreißigjährigen Krieg*, 42–43. The Jesuits were criticized not only by the Protestants but also by the Catholics because they faulted the Jesuits for the outbreak of the war. Wilhelm von Kalcheim (or Kalkum and other spellings of this town by Düsseldorf), called Lohausen (1584–1640), is a fascinating character, who directed his interests toward both the military and the arts. He served in several armies, lost his right leg in 1610, and studied Latin, mathematics, and fortress construction for four years, while moving up in his military career. After being imprisoned for a year and a half

military man and humanist did not fit easily into the category of a ruthless enemy. Instead of brash animosity, Lohausen commonly displayed fair judgment, curiosity, and care toward those who were ostensibly his enemy.

Generally, the armies' cruelty toward the populace is plainly evident in the *religiosi*'s observations and in the damage reports of the district administrators, and several of the authors discussed above render their experiences with the enemy entirely in this vein. Others, like the Jesuit chronicler, narrate not only the opponents' violence, but also their occasional care and concern for the victims. The Benedictine abbot, Veit Höser, represents one of the former. His gripping account is suffused with portrayals of the barbarity of the *Weimarers* (the army of Bernhard of Saxe-Weimar) and other enemies. When he describes the treks of refugees before his eyes, he exclaims:

> These are exactly the consequences of this Weimarish and barbaric tyranny, which knows no forbearance of rank or honor, or, to be precise, if they know such forbearance, they do not want [to exercise] it. Because the soldiers of the Weimarers spread the word among the populace and boasted: HE [Bernhard] had the power and the right to rob any citizen of Bavaria, to destroy his existence, even to kill, slaughter, and banish him.[107]

Höser highlights not only the enemy's inhuman and barbaric behavior, but also his excessive and gratuitous violence toward religious objects. The Weimarers desecrated the cloister's church by using it as a stable, while plundering, destroying, or profaning the altars, holy relics, and other sacred objects and sites. They even disturbed the peace of the dead by opening the tombs: "In short, to defile and destroy all and everything was the order of the day."[108]

---

by the imperials, he became a member of the *Fruchtbringende Gesellschaft* ("Fruitbearing Society," the first German language society) in 1629 and was known as "Der Feste" (*the firm or resolute one*). Lohausen published not only on geometry and fortress architecture, but, in line with the intentions of the *Fruchtbringende Gesellschaft* and because of his facility with languages (besides Latin, he knew several modern languages), he translated a number of works into German (he is particularly known for his Sallust translation). These were highly valued because of their sensitivity and purity in expression and vocabulary. After the Swedes entered the war, he joined their military service and fought in early 1633 under Duke Bernhard of Saxe-Weimar in Franconia. Conermann, *Die Mitglieder der Fruchtbringenden Gesellschaft*, 173–75; Elsmann, "Humanismus," 229–30.

107 Sigl, *Veit Hösers Kriegstagebuch*, 94 (18 November 1633).
108 Sigl, *Veit Hösers Kriegstagebuch*, 148 (24 December 1633). Höser goes on: "My quill, you refuse [to describe the experience] …" The Lutheran pastor, Bartholomæus Dietwar, is another example of someone who did not afford the enemy a single positive characteristic. When he describes the Catholics' "friendlier" treatment of the evangelical ministers

Höser's narrative is more deliberate in its construction than most discussed here. The perspectives, according to which the abbot arranges his material, are his ire and pain over having to leave his cloister, and his separation from his "mother, the abbey," and from his brothers. In Höser's recollections, one cannot find a single episode that throws a mitigating light on the enemy and his destructive rampage – a perspective that coincides with the well-known general narrative of the war. Leaving no room for ambiguities, his gripping tale shows several stylistic characteristics. The editor posits reasonably that the abbot wrote down his *Peregrinatio* when he came to Landshut in early 1634, but he certainly must have taken notes along the way since some of his observations are very detailed, giving not only the date but also the hour of an occurrence. The abbot knew how to make a point: his depictions of various matters, such as torture, first provide a general description and then a concrete example – often from his own experience. The result is a combination of elements both carefully constructed and less so: concise imparting of information, which he sometimes renders in half-sentences as if he merely copied his earlier notes; elaborate, detailed – almost scientific – observations; highly dramatized and stylized studies, in which he gives free rein to his considerable rhetorical skills; and a continual commentary on political and military leaders and their actions as well as on his own brethren that could be scathing and ironic.

While all accounts predominantly report experiences of brutality at the hands of troops (enemy and friendly), many authors include at least some aspects about the enemy that did not fit this straightforward storyline, and a fair number of them relate encounters with the opponents that can only be described as positive. These vignettes run counter to the common assumption of wholesale hostility between the confessional parties. Intriguingly, Höser himself provides an example by a fellow brother that falls into the more moderate rubric of puzzlement about the enemy. Pater Ambrosius Wicht was one of the first to return to the destroyed abbey in April 1634 and in a letter told Höser about its condition. Wicht describes the extensive damage done to both profane and sacred spaces and objects, but he also includes a tale about a commander – "presumably a Catholic" – who took pains to save the church. Still, the relics of the saints were thrown away; yet, other soldiers picked them up and brought them back: "The tomb of our Blessed Albert was broken open and his bones scattered and – this was really astonishing – taken up again by

---

in Kitzingen after the second occupation by the Catholics, he does not trust them and, in the end, sees himself vindicated in his skepticism because the Catholics turned out to be "wolves in sheepskin." LAELKB, MD Uffenheim, Akt. 95.

a good soldier."¹⁰⁹ Wicht is clearly perplexed by these behaviors, which do not fit the common image that all enemies are brutal and barbaric, but he does not edit them out of his report. His observations also upend conventional assumptions that juxtapose more disciplined officers with uninhibited common soldiers. Clearly, honest souls and their opposite could be found on every level of the military hierarchy. The pater adds a further facet when he depicts the destruction of the abbey's various properties. He repeatedly states that all wood was gone; even the pulpit, organ, and oratory were used to keep the fire going. Wicht, however, shows some understanding that the enemy, too, had to keep warm during this ice cold winter of 1634, and notes that not all destruction was gratuitous and unrestrained: "Thus the entire barn was not burned down in a single fire either, but, broken down piecemeal, it had to serve to keep the campfires going."¹¹⁰

Other authors note a positive aspect of the enemy but can explain it only through divine intervention. For example, like many contemporaries, Anna Catharina Frölich of the Angerkloster notes the mild behavior of Gustavus Adolphus when he entered Munich, but she rationalizes this perplexing fact with the vow the citizens had made to the Blessed Lady of Altötting, who in turn implored St. Mary to soften the enemy's heart. Frölich contrasts the Swedish king's previous announcement – that he would plunder and burn the city – with his subsequent about-turn, during which he "allowed no harm to be done to anyone."¹¹¹ Attributing an enemy's behavior that was at odds with the general explanatory model to divine intervention allowed Frölich and others to avoid having to question their assumptions about the enemy.

Besides these fairly short passages describing an opponent who may not be wholly evil and barbaric or who may have been moved by God, one finds more pronounced episodes in some accounts that upset easy dichotomies – then and now – between enemy and friend. The Dominican nuns of Heiliggrab in Bamberg offer a prominent example in this regard. Once the Swedish officers occupied the city, Sister Junius described their encounters all in all as pleasant and beneficial for the nuns. Several high officers made their repeated rounds to the convent, including Duke Bernhard of Saxe-Weimar, the new governor of Franconia. Junius notes how well-behaved the duke was and how beautifully (*mechtig schön*) he talked to the sisters. Commissary Johann Scheibelberger von Wielbronn was a particularly benevolent patron, who considered the Domincan sisters his

---

109 Sigl, *Veit Hösers Kriegstagebuch*, 170. Höser included Wicht's letter in his account.
110 Sigl, *Veit Hösers Kriegstagebuch*, 171.
111 Zwingler, *Klarissenkloster*, 1073 (# 21).

"spiritual daughters." He came every day or, if something prevented him from visiting, sent one of his men to inquire whether the nuns had any complaints. Scheibelberger assured them, if they were pressured in any way, he would come to their aid. The Swedish colonel, Wilhelm von Lohausen, too, whom we encountered earlier in the Jesuit College, became a welcome guest at the Domincan nuns' convent. When he had to leave Bamberg, he sent the nuns a cow as his parting gift, and he and his party took their leave from the sisters "under great pains."[112] He was the one responsible for allowing the Catholic churches and cloisters to continue their worship. Junius had only good things to record about the officers, "who had done them and the whole city so much good ... and who had been so decent and devoted to the city and its citizenry."[113]

One is tempted to suspect ulterior motives on the part of the Dominican nuns for painting the Swedes/Protestants in such favorable colors, but the chronicler of Bamberg's Jesuit College corroborates many of Junius' statements and adds some intriguing components to this multi-faceted picture of relations with the enemy. When Colonel Georg Wolf von Wildenstein, a Calvinist in Swedish service, occupied the Jesuit College after Bamberg's takeover in 1632, the Jesuit chronicler pointed out: "By the way, Wildenstein left the buildings of the *Collegium* and the church unharmed; whatever he could use of the college's furnishings, however, he carefully discovered."[114] The colonel did go after victuals and was most appreciative of the college's "fine wine," but the chronicler did not criticize him for these actions. The armies had to be fed, after all. Wildenstein's successor as occupant of the college, however, the military leader Johann Bülow (of the Baudissinische cavalry), proved to be Wildenstein's opposite: "This company did more damage to the church and college within the shortest period of time than Wildenstein during the whole month [of his residency]." After they had demolished and removed the benches, they used all rooms and buildings as stables. The Jesuit chronicler offers a reasoned, balanced account of the occurrences in and around the college. Besides re-emphasizing that the college's destruction was the fault of Bülow, not Wildenstein, he expresses puzzlement over the fact that a number of items, such as the cover of the altar, pictures, windows, panels, and ovens, were left untouched – a circumstance that was increasingly rare as the conflict wore on.[115] When the Jesuits were forced to leave the college in 1634, the chronicler underlines: "This, too, deserves mention that one did not notice

---

112 Hümmer, ed., "Bamberg im Schweden-Kriege," 52: 129–30, 150–51 (1633).
113 Hümmer, ed., "Bamberg im Schweden-Kriege," 52: 131.
114 *Jesuitenchronik* in Weber, *Bamberg im dreißigjährigen Krieg*, 17.
115 *Jesuitenchronik* in Weber, *Bamberg im dreißigjährigen Krieg*, 18, 23.

a single Swede who was glad of the misfortune of the departing [Jesuits] or who would have mocked them. A guard called to us when we passed through the gate: 'Ey, this is not right.'"[116] On their journey, the brothers continued to receive provisions and support from the officers and soldiers they encountered. Many accounts highlight the irony of "friendly" troops, who were in fact no more friendly, or even less so, than the enemy. On this particular journey, the Jesuits were in luck and evidently encountered real "friendly" troops. The author may well have been aware that this was not the norm, since he notes that "their travel seemed to have stood under a very special protection of providence."[117]

The Jesuit chronicler conveys the diversity among the enemy, who, much like their own troops, consisted of both good and bad men. He readily acknowledges when they had the good fortune of encountering a helpful "enemy," such as in 1633, when "enemy soldiers assisted us with horse and cart so that we could cultivate our estate and transport goods." While these Scots proved to be a great asset to the Jesuits, another Scottish cadet sergeant tried to trick the monks.[118] The range of behaviors thus was wide. Safety and violence often stood side by side, and the reasons why the one was more in evidence than the other were multilayered. It is well known that location mattered, but, as the above examples demonstrate, widely divergent behaviors could exist in the same locales, which underlines the important role of personalities, connections, beneficial strategies, and sheer luck or whatever one may call contingent factors. Even in and around Bamberg, a fairly small space, one group may have had more options, slight advantages, or may have been more resourceful in navigating a difficult situation than another. In 1633 under General Georg Christoph von Taupadel (ca. 1600–1647), for example, the Jesuits experienced safety within their college, while the citizens around them suffered under the lack of military discipline in the city.[119] At times the Jesuits and the Dominican nuns residing in and around Bamberg found their religious status advantageous, while at other times it proved a liability. Reading the situation correctly was therefore of the utmost importance. The confusing dividing lines between enemy and friend got even more complicated with the involvement of the Catholic French on the side of the Protestant Swedes. Politics and confession did not always align, but religious ties could help the Jesuits and other Catholics, even though the French ostensibly were their enemies.[120]

---

116   *Jesuitenchronik* in Weber, *Bamberg im dreißigjährigen Krieg*, 70.
117   *Jesuitenchronik* in Weber, *Bamberg im dreißigjährigen Krieg*, 77.
118   *Jesuitenchronik* in Weber, *Bamberg im dreißigjährigen Krieg*, 56.
119   *Jesuitenchronik* in Weber, *Bamberg im dreißigjährigen Krieg*, 56.
120   *Jesuitenchronik* in Weber, *Bamberg im dreißigjährigen Krieg*, 95.

EXPERIENCES OF WAR 63

The Capuchins by Landshut also reflect a more variegated reality and relationship with the enemy.[121] During the occupation of the city, which was, in many ways, bloody, the friars had been imprisoned. Then an odd confrontation with a Calvinist lieutenant resulted in their release, but things became stranger still.[122] The friars had barely left their prison chamber, when a Swedish officer in charge of peace and order approached them and inquired where they were going. The Capuchins answered they hardly knew themselves, since they had just been freed from imprisonment. They were on their way back to the provostry because they had no other refuge.[123] The Swedish officer immediately warned that "we should not return to our former abode because we would not be safe there since we had no *Salva Guardia* there. Moreover, we would have nothing to eat or live on there, and the next person who would find us would detain us again, lead us away, and demand much of us."[124]

One would think that such a fate would be a desirable outcome for an enemy, and certainly many religious orders experienced the same. But, for some reason, the officer wanted to make sure that nothing bad happened to the friars. Certainly, there existed rules of engagement and contracts with occupiers designed to safeguard the lives of the inhabitants once a city had been taken, but the reality often looked quite different, as various reports on Landshut, including that of the Capuchins' chronicler (Melchior von Straubing), confirm. We do not know what motivated this Swedish officer to ensure the safety of the friars (nor do we know where he came from). He may have felt more duty-bound than others to enforce the negotiated contracts between occupiers and the occupied. Or, even though in this war religion and confession played an important role, he may have considered these friars innocent victims of the conflict (although *religiosi* did not necessarily elicit sympathy – often quite the opposite). Be that as it may, the officer ordered the Capuchins to proceed to the Franciscan monastery, where he had placed a *Salva Guardia* and where they would be safe. Then he gave them a soldier as escort.[125] Thus, both the Capuchins and the Reformed or Observant Franciscans enjoyed the officer's protection.

On their way, the friars had an even more perplexing encounter. When they passed a house full of soldiers, one of them called out to the friars and urged them to come in – they had some useful items for them, namely some clerical

---

121 The Capuchins originated from the Reformed Franciscans in 1517. Their goal was to follow St. Francis to the letter (Heimbucher, *Die Orden*, 1:727).
122 For the larger story, see Chapter 4.
123 The Capuchins had moved from their cloister outside the city walls into the provostry inside Landshut, when the enemy approached the city.
124 StBM, Cgm 2943, 9^v–10^v.
125 StBM, Cgm 2943, 10^v.

and liturgical articles, which the Capuchins decided to take to the Reformed Franciscans. The soldiers also offered them wine and bread for refreshment.[126]

Melchior von Straubing (the Capuchins' chronicler), however, yearned to know what had happened to their cloister, and (with Pater Petronio) obtained the guardian's permission to investigate. His observations of his excursion to the cloister and then of the city show a fascinating picture of contrasts and a fair amount of puzzlement on his side. At the entrance to their cloister, the two friars were greeted by a soldier's wife, who offered them cakes fresh out of the pan. The garden of the cloister had been transformed into a camp, but, differently from most other descriptions, Melchior highlights the orderliness of this "tent-city":

> I can hardly describe how beautiful all things were arranged in it because the entire garden looked like a well-ordered camp; the garden was filled with tents so that it was a pleasure to look at; that is, it was very orderly like the alleys in a city so that one could easily walk through them: here, one person butchered and slaughtered, another fried, the third baked, the fourth boiled, another sewed, sorted, washed, etc.[127]

What is more, several soldiers bestowed candles, robes, and other liturgical and practical items upon them. In contrast, when they came to their church, it looked like a stable. All sorts of animals had been tied to chairs and benches.[128]

Melchior notes his indignation about such ruin of their sacred space, and, yet, his general description highlights the soldiers' disciplined use rather than the abuse of their cloister: the soldiers' camp in the cloister's garden was well-organized and highly serviceable. The cloister's kitchen remained unused since all the cooking was done outside in the camp, but Melchior does not record any gratuitous destruction to the kitchen either. The occupiers used the friars' church as stables – a common practice noted in many accounts, but the friar mentions no tearing out of benches or any other damage to the church. When it comes to sacred spaces, however, the lines between use and abuse are drawn differently. Even though the enemy may have made functional rather than brutal use of the church buildings, he likely knew and intended this act to have a more far-reaching meaning. It signaled dominance, power, and religious mockery. Indeed, it usually represented an act of religious violence toward the defeated.

---

126 StBM, Cgm 2943, 10^v–11^r.
127 StBM, Cgm 2943, 13^{r-v}.
128 StBM, Cgm 2943, 13^v–14^r.

This fascinating narrative lays bare how complicated the navigation between different confessions could be. The basic division between occupier and occupied seemed clear from the distance, and from these divisions emanated certain behaviors, such as violence against possessions and civilians (as Melchior observed around him in the city), the pressuring and extraction of ransoms from or for important persons, and the establishment of dominion over the enemy (especially religious dominion).[129] This can be discerned in the Swedish army's occupation of the Capuchins' cloister and their subsequent use of the church as stable. But beyond these markers, the dividing lines are less clear. The Swedish general's care for the friars' safety diverges from the customary plotline of a conqueror's intent to defeat and destroy, as do the colonels' generous gifts to the friars.

The testimonies do not elaborate regarding what went on in people's minds. While these vignettes are most intriguing in their disruption of neat categories, it is not entirely clear how to interpret the behaviors. Are we here confronted with a case of honorable rules of engagement that treat the enemy with respect as long as the victor is acknowledged? In other words, once the realities of dominance are established, those on each side can be civilized to one another (akin to medieval chivalric practices). Or, do the realities of war appear differently at closer engagement with the "enemy," allowing him to come into view as a human rather than as a representative of an enemy target to be destroyed, not as the "other" but as a mirror image of oneself? Another vignette of Melchior's account points in this direction: while Bernhard of Saxe-Weimar's army occupied Landshut for eight days and inflicted much destruction, especially during the last phase, our chronicler and his brother Pater Richardus of Munich fell deathly ill. His fellow brothers promptly went to the apothecary of the Swedish army and received whatever ointments and medicines were still available since the city's two apothecaries had also been destroyed.[130] In the midst of ruin, one helped one another, whether enemy or friend. This is the other side of the experience that friendly troops were no friendlier than enemy troops. Who was a friend, who an enemy? Sometimes the "enemy" turned out to be a friend. The noise of war and the relative quiet of occupation may also have had an impact on whether one was in a position to "listen" to anything but the official propaganda. When the fires and the noise

---

129 One needs to keep in mind though that the army itself, i.e., its soldiers, was rarely confessionally or religiously motivated, which is reflected in its hodge-podge composition from all countries and confessions.

130 StBM, Cgm 2943, 14^v–15^r.

of war died down, there may have been an opening for encounters beyond the friend-enemy constellation.

Maurus Friesenegger of the Benedictine abbey Andechs offers the occasional moderate narrative of the enemy as well – from admiration toward Gustavus Adolphus and the disciplined behavior of some Swedish officers to an incident of sparing women and children during the storming of Weilheim.[131] More striking, however, is his recurring discussion of friendly troops who act like foes. This motive appears in almost all accounts discussed here, but with Friesenegger it becomes a major theme running through his narrative like a red thread.[132] Early on, the Benedictine observes that friendly and enemy troops represent a similar drain on the region, and he expresses his hope that both Swedish and Bavarian contingents disappear.[133] Soon he comments that the dragoons in charge of guarding the Amper Bridge against marauders "acted themselves, if not worse, then certainly no better than the others. They tyrannized the entire vicinity disgustingly."[134] Importantly, the Benedictine reports time and again that "friendly" soldiers respected sacred spaces and objects no more, and sometimes less, than the enemy. They pillaged churches and desecrated holy sites.[135] Thus, unlike Höser, for Friesenegger the enemy had no monopoly on savagery and sacrilege; such traits could readily be found among one's own troops as well.

By late 1633 Friesenegger equates "riders" (i.e., the cavalry) with "robbers": "Up here with us there raged from village to village thirty riders or robbers, consisting of Croats and Poles, and they acted no better [than the Swedes under von Saxe-Weimar, who had taken Straubing]."[136] When Friesenegger and his brothers returned to Andechs after one of their flights to the nearby Kiental, they found their cloister robbed and their sacred spaces destroyed. He exclaimed: "This was done by our friends, our auxiliary troops! And what else could the enemy have done – except perhaps act better!"[137]

---

131 Friesenegger, *Tagebuch*, 24, 27, 56, 148.
132 The Benedictine also narrates how often one's own neighbors used the chaos of war to steal from the locals. Friesenegger, *Tagebuch*, 28, 33.
133 Friesenegger, *Tagebuch*, 34–35.
134 Friesenegger, *Tagebuch*, 48 (1633).
135 Friesenegger, *Tagebuch*, 49, 79.
136 Friesenegger, *Tagebuch*, 53. Friesenegger calls the Polish soldiers the derogatory name "Polaken."
137 Friesenegger, *Tagebuch*, 80 (1634). Their "friendly troops" were also not always on good terms with one another. Bavaria's armies were sometimes at odds with the Spanish or Austrian imperials, and even more frequently with the allied Croats and Poles (Friesenegger, 100).

As the war dragged on, Friesenegger became ever more disillusioned. In 1646, conveying the sentiments of his community, he notes "we had always been comforted by the hope that our army with imperial support would go to meet the enemy ... but what vain hope and weak trust in the imperials, who themselves lusted for Bavaria more than the enemy!"[138] Enemies and friends could no longer be distinguished since the imperials carried on worse than the Swedes. Indeed, the imperial horsemen plundered in the most "enemy-like" way. Ever since the imperials moved into Bavaria between the Isar and the Lech, "everyone longs for the still better Swedes." No one escaped the imperials' "barbarity and willfulness. They robbed, plundered, and tortured without thinking that they [themselves] are humans and they are dealing with humans." And this all happened without consideration of age or gender: "Such beasts does the ongoing war make of humans!"[139] In contrast, when, a month later, 4,000 Swedes/French took Weilheim after its citizens had resisted, women and children remained "unharmed of honor and life" even though the commanders allowed their soldiers to kill anyone in arms and to plunder the city.[140]

How did contemporaries deal with the fact that friendly troops were worse than the enemy's? And were the Swedes really better than "one's own people"? There were certainly instances when this was the case, particularly when the sources describe concrete occurrences. Moreover, Gustavus Adolphus' civilized behavior was legendary and commented on in numerous writings. Many critical passages were more likely expressions of frustration and anger over the fact that one could not trust one's own troops, that they were as bad as the enemy or worse, and that, in the end, there was no deliverance. The experience of destruction from one's associates shattered one's worldview, the sense of right and wrong. The sociologist Peter Sloterdijk calls these experiences of cognitive dissonance *Stör-Erfahrungen*, a term denoting such encounters "that explode hitherto experiences, convictions, or behaviors that have been taken for granted and that contain a dissonance toward such expectations."[141] Such suffered harm could easily be expressed in ways that reflected the felt outrage rather than the precise reality: the damage done by an ally was articulated more dramatically and juxtaposed with instances of an enemy's more benign behavior.

In December 1633 one company after another made their way to Erling and the cloister – all with varying modes of conduct. Friesenegger notes the

---

138 Friesenegger, *Tagebuch*, 139.
139 Friesenegger, *Tagebuch*, 142–45.
140 Friesenegger, *Tagebuch*, 148.
141 Sloterdijk, *Literatur und Organisation von Lebenserfahrung*, 113.

officers' good behavior: "Some greeted Heiligenberg from afar, others visited the abbey, paid for beer and bread, and gave generous alms." In contrast, the common soldiers gave their *Salva Guardia* and the villagers grief. The cloister housed two Spanish colonels, who were modest and content with two rooms and a bit of beer and bread, offering to pay for anything else. Their servants, however, could not be satisfied and responded violently when their outrageous demands could not be fulfilled.[142]

But in the Benedictine's book officers do not generally fare better than the lowly soldier. Instead, Friesenegger criticizes the higher-ups for their exploitation of the soldiers. He understood well the common soldier's difficult plight. In late December 1633 soldiers were ordered to stay in the Andechs region because no winter quarters had yet been prepared for them: "Heaven! One already saw peasants and soldiers walking around in this coldest of weather – only half-dressed, pale from misery, emaciated from hunger, in their bare feet."[143] The soldiers were so hungry that they ate dogs, cats, and stolen meat, while the peasants often had not even a piece of bread. Friesenegger describes how the starving searched the brothers' garden for herbs and roots. The cloister helped in any way it could by slaughtering the salvaged livestock and baking as much bread as possible. Bakers from places nearby (*fremde Bäcker*) brought bread, but it was not enough for the 1,500 soldiers in the village and over 1,000 refugees from several locales who crowded the cloister. In addition, convoys with provisions were frequently plundered. Thus the hunger rose to disastrous levels among soldiers and villagers, and the officers' money was of no use. The starving troops broke into the church and ate the peasants' seeds for the next year, which was stored underneath the roof. Even though Friesenegger notes the serious consequences for the village's future, he does not pass judgment on the soldiers.

Instead, he depicts the pitiful spectacle during the inspection of the Spanish regiment two days later: "Several only half-filled companies with black and yellow faces; emaciated bodies half-covered or draped with rags; or figures masked in stolen women's clothes. This is what hunger and poverty looks like. In comparison, the officers were attractively and richly dressed people."[144] Friesenegger was well aware that the officers became wealthy off the war, while the soldiers were largely left to fend for themselves, without the promised salaries. With compassion he pointed to the soldiers who were just as hungry as the other men and women who knocked on the abbey's door and asked for

---

142 Friesenegger, *Tagebuch*, 56–57.
143 Friesenegger, *Tagebuch*, 58.
144 Friesenegger, *Tagebuch*, 59.

food.[145] He commented incisively that it was the continuing war that turned soldiers into beasts, and, when toward the end of 1647 their own soldiers marched again through the countryside, Friesenegger remarked: "with what benefit, or damage, to all places is easily imaginable to those who know the soldiers, especially when they have become degenerate [*verwildern*] after so many years under arms."[146] The Benedictine both illustrates and overturns age-old dichotomies: while he underlines the antagonism between soldiers and peasants, he also shows their common condition of misery and hunger. Often at odds with and fighting each other, they could also join hands against a perceived common enemy.

Friesenegger's astute observations and his occasional outcries form an image that does not quite coalesce. He was clearly aware that the war presented them with an exceptional situation in which long-held certainties could no longer be trusted. One could not count on the protection of the government. Moreover, Friesenegger's continuous comparison of the various troops suggests not so much that the Swedes were any better than the Bavarian or imperial units, but rather that there were few, if any, differences between all the armies. Friends and foes were no longer clearly distinguishable. Unlike Höser, Friesenegger observed barbarity and tyranny in all troops, not just the enemy's, and, indeed, at times the enemy turned out to be more humane than the "friend."

This chapter has traced a series of experiences during the Thirty Years' War. From a deep, unshakable fear of violence and the accompanying volatility and disruption, to the harsh realities of hunger and deprivation, people were united in a profound sense of vulnerability. This perception of defenselessness was only heightened by the fact that not only could people no longer rely on help from allied troops; the populace had learned that they could expect worse from their own people. Given this profound sense of vulnerability, how did secular and religious authorities try to help their subjects? What could the populace expect from their lords as they encountered violent attacks, material losses, poverty, and epidemic diseases? We next turn to how governments responded to the needs of their subjects, and examine efforts at providing physical protection, relief for the poor, and control of disease.

---

145 Friesenegger, *Tagebuch*, 61.
146 Friesenegger, *Tagebuch*, 156. "Solche Bestien machet der anhaltende Krieg aus den Menschen!" ("Such beasts does the ongoing war make of humans.") Friesenegger, 145 (1646).

CHAPTER 3

Governmental Support: Hopes, Measures, and Realities

The previous section illustrated many experiences of those who lived through the war – such as fear, volatility, violence, dearth, vulnerability, and instability – experiences that were engendered, exacerbated, or prolonged by the war. How did political and religious authorities attempt to counteract these challenges to their subjects' lives? Protection was a fundamental task of government, and the populace expected authorities to come to their aid and provide at least a degree of safety. Looking closely at a broad range of initiatives – from building or upgrading fortifications, increasing military guards, and entering into negotiations, to providing poor relief, disease control, and taking spiritual precautions – the following sections explore the strategies various governments pursued to ensure stability, deflect harm, and support their severely burdened subjects. The first section traces efforts to protect the populace against military attacks and violence; the second considers measures to stem the growing poverty as well as confront the health crisis in the wake of troop movements and dearth; and the third investigates governmental initiatives directed toward their subjects' spiritual protection. Case studies furthermore illuminate the dynamics between subjects and the multiple levels of authorities that, depending on the situation, could contribute to or hinder the success of these initiatives.

1   Protection against Violence

1.1   *Fortifications*
Franconia's and Bavaria's evolving political and military realities during the Thirty Years' War do not have to be described here in detail since they have received thorough treatment in scholarship.[1] During the 1620s, troops regularly passed through Franconia and took up quarters there, but for this region the conflict began in earnest in 1631, when Gustavus Adolphus led the Swedes

---

[1] See especially von Soden, *Gustav Adolph*, 3 vols.; Donaubauer, "Nürnberg"; Kaiser, *Politik und Kriegsführung*; Kaiser, "Maximilian I"; Kraus, *Maximilian I*; Roeck, "Bayern und der Dreißigjährige Krieg"; Wilson, *Thirty Years War*.

south to aid Augsburg's Protestants, who greeted him enthusiastically.[2] After beating the troops of the Catholic League at Breitenfeld, the Swedes marched through Erfurt, Würzburg, and Bamberg to winter in Eichstätt's diocese. The road from Nuremberg through Eichstätt to Munich was a heavily travelled military route, and thus the populace along this path came to be afflicted with most scourges of the war. While the Frankish circle, including, eventually, Nuremberg, welcomed the Swedish king, Bavaria's elector Maximilian sided with Emperor Ferdinand II, which gave Gustavus Adolphus the justification to invade Bavaria. In April 1632, the Swedes conquered Weißenburg, Donauwörth, and Rain am Lech. Unable to subdue Ingolstadt, the Swedish king, instead, took Munich. After the Swedish Intervention, armies continued to pass through or winter in Franconia and Bavaria. Population losses for these two regions are difficult to determine, but they range between 30–50 percent for Bavaria and 30–40 percent for Franconia.[3]

Considering these realities, physical protection counted among the highest priorities for both subjects and governments, but how well this protection was realized varied widely. The most obvious measure consisted of building protective walls between aggressor and populace. Such remedies were more readily available for people living in urban areas than for those in the countryside, but even among larger cities, a great diversity in levels of fortification existed. Those in many smaller towns found it even harder to secure their location. As a consequence, most cities lacked adequate fortifications to withstand an enemy's attack. There were exceptions to this rule, such as Nuremberg and Ingolstadt, as well as heavily fortified castles, such as Forchheim and Kronach. None of these sites was ever conquered.

Multiple interests and factors influenced the extent of fortification at various locales. State of the art defense systems were expensive. With the war's heavy financial toll, ever fewer communities – especially those in areas of troop movement – were in a position to spend their rapidly diminishing resources on fortifications. There is no mystery why Nuremberg had powerful defenses. As an important imperial city of great political and commercial standing, it had already improved its defensive system during the sixteenth century according to the latest innovations in weapons technology. The upgrading of the city walls was largely completed by the early Thirty Years' War, when under

---

2 Reicke, *Geschichte der Reichsstadt Nürnberg*, 959–60; Endres, "Der Dreissigjährige Krieg in Franken," 11–13. See the map of troop movement in Chapter 1.
3 The large range indicates the difficulty in estimating the number of fatalities. Historians have adjusted the overall death toll to about 15–20 percent of the population (Wilson, *Thirty Years War*, 787–89).

the pressure of war Nuremberg's council began to enhance the safety of its suburbs.[4] During the winter of 1632, the city stepped up its fortifications. With Gustavus Adolphus' arrival in Franconia and his decision to make Nuremberg the basis of his operations, the push toward buttressing the site's defenses reached a new level. In the king's plan, a belt of redoubts was to encircle not only the city's suburbs but also the closest small towns. For sixteen days in mid-1632, 6,000 citizens and peasants worked day and night to finish the fortifications.[5] Because of its stellar defense system, Nuremberg was neither besieged nor taken during the war, but its countryside suffered tremendously when the imperial and Swedish armies faced each other at the *Alte Veste* (Old Fortress) three miles southwest of the city in September 1632.

In Bavaria, Maximilian, too, had been able to strengthen Ingolstadt's defenses just in time for the Swedish attacks.[6] Ingolstadt was Bavaria's old stronghold and proud university city. Like Nuremberg, it was never conquered, although its fortifications were thoroughly tested when Gustavus Adolphus tried to take the city in the spring of 1632. After a week-long siege and several unsuccessful assaults, the frustrated king gave up and instead set his eyes on Munich, Maximilian's court city, which because of its weak fortifications fell into the Swedish king's hands without a siege in May 1632.

Bavaria's elector was not primarily to blame for Munich's inadequate defense system. Indeed, the case of Munich and its lack of adequate fortifications well into the 1630s illustrates the problems many governments of mid-sized cities faced. Maximilian fully understood the importance of military readiness, but his efforts during the decade prior to the war to enhance the medieval walls around Munich were largely in vain, since he could not convince the city's magistrate or the territorial estates to finance such an extensive project. While Munich's council was concerned about its defenses, implementing such an expensive undertaking was a different matter.[7] Although Munich's magistrate finally agreed in 1615 to strengthen its fortifications, the planning progressed only slowly. The beginning of the war in 1618 accelerated preparations, and fieldwork began at last in late 1619 with an initial workforce of 200 men and 300 women, augmented by 2,000 from outside the city, including criminals, beggars, and vagrants. By the middle of the 1620s, however, after the Battle of the White Mountain (1620) and the positive results for Bavaria (for his troubles

---

4 Hofmann, *Nürnberger Stadtmauer*, 67–87.
5 Reicke, *Geschichte der Reichsstadt Nürnberg*, 977; Hofmann, *Nürnberger Stadtmauer*, 67–87. For a detailed discussion of the fortification efforts of 1632, see Willax, "Befestigungsanlagen."
6 On Ingolstadt, see Schönauer, *Ingolstadt*.
7 Stahleder, *Chronik*, 2:286 (13 August 1605). In 1605 the city's financial records show an expense for literature on architecture and fortifications.

Maximilian received the Upper-Palatinate and was made elector of Bavaria), work on fortifications was slacking off again. Since Bavaria had been spared immediate military action during the first decade of the war, people did not see a pressing need for such a considerable effort. Thus, when in the spring of 1632 Gustavus Adolphus marched through Bavaria, taking city after city and aiming for Munich, the court city was ripe for the taking. Munich agreed to an enormous ransom – 300,000 reichsthaler – to avoid plundering at the hands of the Swedish king's troops, and gave Gustavus its keys when he entered the city on 17 May 1632. To ensure remuneration, the king took 42 secular and ecclesiastical hostages.[8]

The lack of physical preparedness was a crucial lesson to both Maximilian and Munich. After the Swedes had left, Maximilian ordered his court city to complete its fortifications at its own expense, but Munich's city fathers begged him to spare them from complying with his demand because of their miserable financial situation. Unmoved, the elector directed the council to have 60 people ready to begin building fortifications at the Anger Gate, and the city responded with several calls to the populace to contribute to this effort.[9] Once Maximilian returned to Munich in 1635 after a three-year absence, he accelerated his efforts to fortify the city and ordered a special tax to pay for the measures.[10] He was so upset about the slow progress and the councilors' lackluster supervision of the work that, in 1638, he fined every councilmember ten reichsthaler.[11] Work on fortifications then gathered speed, with about 20,000 people working (per year) and efforts peaking in 1639. Seven years later, the fortifications were largely completed, and when the Swedish-French armies stood before Munich in 1646, they were confronted with a defensive system constructed in accordance with the latest technology. This time, its fortifications contributed to preventing a hostile takeover of the city.

Besides limited financial resources, another factor impeding sufficient physical protection was the unwillingness of inhabitants to build fortifications. Many authorities echoed the complaint of Nuremberg's councilors:

---

8   The procurement of the sum and the freeing of the hostages became a long and painful business stretching until 1635. In the end, the amount was never fully paid, and several hostages died during captivity.
9   Stahleder, *Chronik*, 2:462–63 (1633).
10 Maximilian left Munich before the Swedes arrived (4 April 1632) and returned in mid-May 1635 after the pestilence had subsided. Much of the time he governed from fortified Braunau on the Inn, some 77 miles east of Munich.
11 Stahleder, *Chronik*, 2:503. Two months later, Maximilian revoked the fine because its threat alone had apparently had the desired effect.

> It displeased us to learn that many have grumbled about the mandatory payments for the redoubts [*Schanzgeld*], and since we left it up to them to either lend a hand themselves or send someone from the household, we discovered that they often sent only old, ravaged, and wasted women or weak, immature children to the redoubts. The old were of little use; the young because of their mischief often a hindrance to others, especially since they frequently left their posts early.[12]

Peasants and citizens most likely sent the feeblest members of their households to labor on fortifications, not because they wanted to defy their authorities or did not desire protection, but because they needed every able-bodied person to work the fields, particularly during a time when they also had to pay contributions and feed the armies. Understandably, they tended to make decisions according to the most immediate and pressing necessities – putting food on the table and paying contributions – not according to decisions, however prudent, for the more distant future, which was a luxury they could not afford.

Strong defensive systems were certainly generally desirable, especially during a military attack, but, as the above discussion suggests, the financial commitment was often too great for a community to shoulder. Ahead of a military action, governments could also be split over the necessity of such an expenditure. In the case of Munich, besides the large financial commitment, the strained rapport between territorial lord and civic leadership hampered a proactive fortification strategy. Their respective assessments differed regarding the military danger for Munich as well as the steps and sacrifices the situation demanded; and their fraught relationship made cooperation even more difficult. After Munich succumbed to the Swedish forces in 1632, Maximilian exerted enough pressure on his city to make sure that such a scenario would not repeat itself. Many cities and towns, however, did not have the resources to boost and improve their fortifications, even though they had learned the same lessons that Munich had. Accordingly, they had to employ other strategies to weather a military offensive.

1.2 *Troops*

Troops were a further means to offer the populace protection, although, as addressed earlier, during the course of the war *all* troops, whether one's own or those of the enemy regiments, came to be associated with harm rather than safety. Especially during times of crisis, cities engaged troops to safeguard

---

[12] StA N, Rst Nbg, M 3, 493 (13 June 1632). See Mummenhoff, *Altnürnberg*, 6–7, on the common nature of these complaints.

its citizens. When Nuremberg became the center of military action in 1632, the city temporarily hired 3,000 soldiers (a regiment of ten troops) as well as three companies of cavalrymen. Gustavus Adolphus sent Nuremberg another 2,000 soldiers.[13] Maintaining a contingent of soldiers to protect a city, however, was expensive, and these regiments were typically released as soon as the immediate danger had passed. When a city was besieged, it depended on the likelihood of relief troops (*Entsatztruppen*) whether its inhabitants defended themselves or negotiated an accord with the enemy. The prospect of rescue troops from the outside made cities hang on during a siege or, conversely, give in to the besiegers.

Besides his military leadership in the war, Maximilian had concerned himself with Munich's safety even before he became duke of Bavaria. Learning from the Hundred Years' War (1337–1453), the wars of his Habsburg ancestors against the Swiss, and the Burgundian wars (1474–1477), he created an infantry of lansquenets, foot soldiers trained by the Swiss. This reflected the tendency of the time toward a standing army and a shift of focus from the cavalry to the infantry.[14] Well before the Thirty Years' War, Maximilian increased his stock of weapons and ammunition and tried to raise the levels of the country militia and the numbers of Munich's civic guards. Maximilian's immediate concern during the early years of his reign was not so much a potential military conflict with the Protestants but the threat of the Turks.[15]

While troops could provide protection, they also posed grave problems for the populace. Feeding the armies was hard enough, but military units used the so-called "contributions system" to extract provisions from local communities. During the Thirty Years' War, this originally regular war tax (*Kontribution*) evolved into a coercive levy, a "fire tax" (*Brandschatzung*), imposed upon the populace to avoid having their property burned down.[16] Moreover, it was very

---

13   These were soldiers Count Heinrich Wilhelm von Solms-Laubach (1583–1632) had recruited from Nuremberg's territory.
14   Mandlmayr and Vogelka, "Vom Adelsaufgebot zum Stehenden Heer," 113–14.
15   See Wilson, *Thirty Years War*, 76–115, on the largely overlooked significance of the Turkish menace for the military readiness at the outset of the Thirty Years' War. The "Long Turkish War" (1593–1606) between the Habsburg and the Ottoman Empires amplified the West's general image of the Turk as the bogeyman. In 1601 Maximilian prohibited the recruitment of his subjects by any authority within or without his territory and cited the Turkish threat as reason for his order (Stahleder, *Chronik*, 2:255, 19 January 1601). Presumably the duke wanted to have enough men to draw from should war ensue. See Heydenreuter, *Der Landesherrliche Hofrat*, 177, n. 493.
16   "*Brandschatzung* was a payment in money or kind extorted by an enemy under the threat of force." (Redlich, "Contributions," 247). Redlich also offers a thorough discussion of the contribution system and its practice.

much in question to what extent the military really protected the people. In late 1633 the Benedictine abbot Veit Höser commented angrily on the authorities' failure to shield their subjects:

> May those search their conscience and bear responsibility who have been entrusted with the protective sword and power! What now? *Inclinate Capita Vestra*, bow your heads, you poor abandoned and forsaken ones, you children of the fatherland, who have been robbed of every help and – harsh are my words! – submit to the enemy or flee! Because the archenemy of the Roman faith and of our ancestral holy religion, Bernhard of Weimar, has already marched across the bridge and through the gates of Straubing toward us ... without anyone's opposition – yes, not even a dog barked at him! ... I, for my part, would rather flee and trust the steadfast assurance of the Lord: "When they persecute you in one city, flee to the next"![17]

Höser's ire here is directed at the imperial military leader Wallenstein, who remained passive as the Swedish enemy moved into Bavaria. Wallenstein's failure to come to Elector Maximilian's aid left Straubing vulnerable to the commander of the Swedish army, Bernhard of Saxe-Weimar. Thus, the populace's best option, Höser advised, lay in flight.

The abbot of Oberalteich may have dramatized his experience of the military situation, but the sense of vulnerability and lack of protection pervades many accounts of the war. Andech's Maurus Friesenegger, too, often expressed frustration with Bavaria's troops, who went after their own booty and left Bavaria unprotected. The chronicler of Bamberg's Jesuit College was similarly critical of the military leadership. Early in 1633, when the Swedish army made renewed inroads into Franconia, Bamberg's citizens and the defensive troops stationed there "agreed to sacrifice blood and life for God and fatherland" in defense of the city. Captain Raab promised publicly that, "if he abandoned the city, they could attach his name to the pillory."[18] Despite Raab's assurance, and unbeknownst to most citizens, however, Maximilian's colonel, Friedrich Schletz, withdrew all troops. The chronicler conveyed the effect of these actions:

---

17   Sigl, *Veit Hösers Kriegstagebuch*, 99. The biblical reference is to Matthew 10:23.
18   *Jesuitenchronik* in Weber, *Bamberg im dreißigjährigen Krieg*, 41.

Even though this happened because of a higher directive and for reasons of state, many complained, not without justification, that they had been misled by the soldiers' empty promises and thus missed the chance to move their belongings to safety; they did not even consider the latter as honorable lest it appeared that they distrusted the officers' bravery and lest [their action] frightened their fellow citizens even more. The fatherland had maintained the cavalry at heavy costs; now the same marched out under the pretense to ferret out or stall the enemy, and they have withdrawn to Forchheim and the [Upper] Palatinate. *Whom could one trust in the future, if one were suddenly abandoned by friendly troops in circumstances that demanded urgent help?*[19]

The citizens' sense of abandonment and loss of trust due to their lacking protection could not be articulated more clearly. While greater concerns of state may have justified the withdrawal of troops, on the local level this action had decidedly negative consequences: the populace saw itself exposed and betrayed. In other words, in the people's eyes, larger reasons of state did not release authorities from protecting their subjects in the regions, and the failure to do so led to a critical loss of trust in their authorities.

Besides regular armies, governments also tried to build up civic and country militias. As Eugen von Frauenholz has shown, initially rulers put greater stock in a territorial defense system than in mercenaries.[20] In the sixteenth and early seventeenth centuries, several important treatises discussed the benefits of such a territorial defense system.[21] Many authors shared the opinion that the peasant, who was used to the outdoors and hard labor, made the best soldier. Subjects serving in the militias were supposed to have more at stake because they were defending their own family and possessions, while foreigners or mercenaries, the argument ran, were interested only in money. Practice and

---

19   *Jesuitenchronik* in Weber, *Bamberg im dreißigjährigen Krieg*, 42 (emphasis added).
20   Frauenholz, *Heerwesen*, 2:v and 17. See Parrott, *Business of War*, who argues that the mercenary armies of the Thirty Years' War were, in fact, quite effective.
21   From Lazarus von Schwendi (1522–1583), military commander and general of the imperial army, who echoed Machiavelli's arguments, and Count Hans Albrecht von Sprinzenstein in the 1580s, to a veritable wave of tracts around and after 1600 on the *Landesdefension* by Count Johann von Nassau-Siegen, Count Moritz von Hessen, Georg Fuchs zum Gastein, Count Abraham zu Dohna, Johann Ludwig von Erlach zu Castelen, and, importantly, Johann Jacobi von Wallhausen. See Frauenholz, *Heerwesen*, 2:8–17.

diligence would make up for lack of military aptitude.[22] Maximilian, in particular, pursued a territorial defense system, and with his usual determination.[23]

In reality, however, such efforts encountered headwind from several directions. The countrymen did not share Maximilian's enthusiasm and turned out to be less reliable than anticipated. The middle authorities were not necessarily supportive of his initiative either since they tried to protect their own power and rights in regard to their subjects. There were many incidents of militias fleeing the scene. Maximilian's colonels, Alexander von Haslang and Hannibal von Herrliberg, had been cautious about the effectiveness of the militias early on, and, indeed, Haslang and a Captain Schöttl reported in 1617 that the feudal lords typically sent their feeblest subjects and kept the capable ones at home. The next year Colonel von Herrliberg confirmed that many among the select were unfit because of advanced age or illness.[24]

These problems came particularly to the fore in 1632, when the Swedes advanced on Bavaria. The councilor and *Rentmeister* of the district Amberg, Ägidius Sickenhauser, informed the elector that the defense unit was supposed to be 3,380 strong, but there were hardly 300 men because almost everyone ran away "to the Nurembergers." The district administrator had cited the subjects twice, but they had not appeared and "instead declared that they would rather leave the country than be selected [for the militia]. Similar reports from other districts reached him as well, and they had a hard time preventing a general uprising." Moreover, the contingent was badly equipped with weapons and clothes since the sons of the well-to-do burghers and peasants had stayed home. In Freising, Lieutenant Colonel Hans Jacob von Fendten informed von Herrliberg that the cavalry of countrymen was useless for patrol, and the other country folk had almost all bolted home: "God save the one who has to fight with these [people]."[25]

Complaints about uncooperative, ill-prepared, inept, and disappearing contingents of countrymen and burghers dominate reports from various locales. A lack of good instructors and able commanders was one of the problems, but

---

22   Georg Fuchs zum Gastein, "Landts Deffension-Ortnung," in Frauenholz, *Heerwesen*, 2: App. 5, 85. Frauenholz underlines that the original purpose of the territorial defense system was not a rural or civic militia for local purposes or a unit that would fight alongside a professional regiment, but the replacement of the mercenary with a draft army. Following these visions, political leaders in the beginning dreamed of replacing the mercenary army with a homegrown militia (Frauenholz, 17).
23   Frauenholz, *Heerwesen*, 2:19–25.
24   Frauenholz, *Heerwesen*, 2:133–34 (App. 12 g and i).
25   Frauenholz, *Heerwesen*, 2:135–36 (App. 12 m, n, and p).

Colonel von Herrliberg disputed that better leadership would have improved the situation:

> Even though Your Electoral Highness has had reports that the subjects in many locales have said they would stand as one man and would protect the beloved fatherland against the enemy if only they would obtain people who would lead them, [I] cannot hide from Your Electoral Highness that such a result is nowhere in evidence, because when I sent the desired leaders, the peasants partly rejected them and partly excused themselves that these [leaders] did not understand them. In other words, there is nothing but confusion. As soon as the [peasants] see the slightest evidence of the enemy, they run away. They pay a fire tax (*Brandsteuer*) for the towns and market towns, which may not be so bad, although I fear this will not prevent the burning, so that the money will have been paid in vain.[26]

These realities prompted Maximilian, who had always pushed to expand the territorial defense system, to move away from it. Instead, he instituted a tax for recruiting trained soldiers. In the end, militias served mostly as auxiliary troops and to take over local tasks, such as guard duties.

The fact that the populace was not eager to fight in the militia does not mean that they did not want protection or refused to contribute to it. There are many examples of peasants and townspeople flocking together to fight the enemy and defend their homes and property. A regular assignment in a country or civic militia, however, was a great burden on top of the countrymen's usual responsibilities. Training took place on Sundays, the one day off work. Peasants likely already felt too overburdened with paying contributions to also supply the defense, for which their government was responsible. However, when the enemy stood before their gates or threatened their crops, they could and did devise ways to defend themselves.[27]

Salva Guardias were another means of providing protection. These could take the form of one or two soldiers, guards whom the occupied could obtain from the occupiers. They had to be paid for and provisioned by those who would be guarded, although there were many instances in which these supposedly protective guards were of little use and were sometimes even harmful, but they were, in any case, always a great financial burden. Our various chroniclers highlight the very uneven performance of the *Salva Guardias*. Some, such as

---

26 Frauenholz, *Heerwesen*, 2:138–39 (App. 12 w).
27 For discussion of the peasants' initiatives, see Chapter 4.3.

Maria Anna Junius, speak well of them, but many more complain about them. Hohenwart's recorder had nothing good to say about their guard, who got drunk rather than help the nuns in their distress.[28] Still others, such as Clara Staiger, underlined the great strain on the convent's economy these guards posed. *Salva Guardias* could also take the form of a letter (a written promise of protection) if no soldier was at hand or a community could not afford the outlay for a lifeguard. While these came with fewer costs and nuisances attached, they commonly proved to be even less effective, but the populace craved any kind of protection no matter how feeble it might be.

1.3 Negotiations and Guidance

Besides fortifications and troops, governments applied other stratagems to avoid or minimize harm, and to calm their people, especially when neither protective walls nor troops were available. Authorities employed expert negotiators, took legal measures, and provided guidelines for their subjects to contain the damage, but when these options were exhausted or fruitless, they could do little else than advise patience. Complaints against plunderers and their brutality pervade the war's official and personal records. Just as evident is the authorities' inability to protect their subjects against violent excesses. Villagers and townspeople petitioned overlords and magistrates, who appealed to military leaders and then the commander in chief. Sympathetic to the problem, the military leadership passed edicts that promised harsh justice for plundering soldiers. This cycle of offense, complaint, resolution, and the occasional crackdown against marauders repeated itself endlessly throughout the war, yet official actions were striking for their failure to curb violence.

A look at various scenes illustrates the authorities' struggles and the subjects' reactions to their government's measures. One of the greatest burdens for any area in the line of troop movement was the passage and billeting of soldiers. Even though many regions in the southeast German lands experienced the troops' debilitating effect, the way each area dealt with the challenge was shaped by its specific set of circumstances and personalities, and could reflect different dynamics between all levels of authorities and their subjects.

The war extracted an enormous amount of contributions from the populace, and many governments enlisted professional or designated negotiators to reduce the stipulated sum.[29] Sometimes magistrates could placate officers

---

28   StBM, HSS, Cgm 5727, 60–61.
29   Negotiations were going on at every level of society – including by peasants, citizens, members of religious orders, and the clergy. These activities will be discussed in Chapter 4.3. This section focuses on governmental actions.

GOVERNMENTAL SUPPORT   81

with gifts, and expert mediators were able to obtain better terms, but, over the course of the war, officers and soldiers raised their demands of payments to such heights that no one could hope to satisfy them.[30] Paying the requested contribution, or at least a good part of it, could deter soldiers from seizing supplies by force. Still, soldiers had to be stationed somewhere. While cities had to pay contributions and were often saddled with the lodging of officers, villages in the countryside were in a much more vulnerable position, since they often faced an unending series of troops housed either in their homes or nearby, and the sheer overwhelming task of keeping them fed. Subjects in Nuremberg's territory charged: "... with every day, more soldiers were quartered [here], and when they had provided one company with food and drink to the best of their ability, ... another would come, which they were forced to supply afresh; nor could they work their fields for fear of [their homes] being robbed in their absence."[31]

The "authorized" provisioning, or foraging, was bad enough, but soldiers and cavalrymen often forcefully extracted further service from the people. The villagers of Egersdorf in Franconia complained that they had fed 40 foot soldiers for eight days, but these people did not content themselves with ordinary fare and pressed the poor people to provide them with money by selling their livestock.[32] In Ödenreuth, a lieutenant made himself at home with three soldiers and asked for meat twice a day.[33] Similar complaints about the intolerable presence and the demands of troops saturate reports from Old Bavaria and, indeed, most regions that endured the movement or billeting of troops.[34]

What advice and potential deliverance did authorities extend to their subjects in the face of such sizable and mounting trials? Nuremberg's political leaders offered their peasants a range of aids. They sent out their consultants to negotiate with regiments in the hope of directing them elsewhere and attempted to spread the burden equally among the subjects.[35] Some communities tried to avoid the billeting of troops in their towns by paying the companies large sums of money, but they could not protect themselves from the plundering of individual soldiers.[36] If peasants sought refuge from the rampage of troops and marauding cavalrymen by fleeing to other villages or a nearby

---

30   See, e.g., HStA M, DK, Akt. 323, 56^r–59^v, 81^r–82^r.
31   StA N, Rst Nbg, RK, B-Laden, Akt. 82 (Nr. 3), 5.
32   StA N, Rst Nbg, RK, B-Laden, Akt. 82 (Nr. 3), 9 (March 1632).
33   StA N, Rst Nbg, RK, B-Laden, Akt. 82 (Nr. 3), 10–11.
34   For Old Bavaria, see HStA M, KB – ÄA 2529, 21^v.
35   StA N, Rst Nbg, RK, B-Laden, Akt. 85 (Nr. 1) (1639).
36   StA N, Rst Nbg, RK, B-Laden, Akt. 82 (Nr. 3), 42–43.

forest, the soldiers at times forced them to return by threatening that, if they refused, the soldiers would destroy everything the villagers had left behind.[37]

Frequently Nuremberg's council instructed the district overseers in the event of troops passing through to have "a bit of beer and bread ready" to placate the soldiers, but admonished them to keep other provisions out of sight.[38] Such guidance could impart a sense of ability to manage a potential threat, but communities quickly found out that regiments were rarely satisfied with "a bit of beer and bread." When Nuremberg's councilors learned that Gräfenberg's administrator had supplied General Octavio Piccolomini's regiment with meat, bread, and wine, they severely reprimanded their overseer for setting a ruinous precedent and told him that the town had to take care of these expenses.[39] It is hard to believe that the councilors were unaware of the substantial and often outrageous demands stationed troops made, and that the subjects had almost no means of opposing such commands without endangering their lives. More likely, Nuremberg's response reflects that the city was in no position to remunerate Gräfenberg or any locale in its territory for such expenses and thus could only reaffirm the set guidelines.

Many government responses and directives signaled in subtle or more emphatic ways their inability to aid their subjects, but Nuremberg's councilors were almost despondent about their lack of resources. Much of the council's resignation had to do with Nuremberg's financial situation. The city had entered the war economically weakened. After the disastrous wars with the margraves in the 1550s, its debt had skyrocketed from 453,000 to 3.5 million florin.[40] That Nuremberg was able to lower its debt to 1.8 million by the beginning of the Thirty Years' War attests to its economic ingenuity and agility. But with the advent of war, this vibrant commercial community suffered especially from the plundering and uncertainty of the roads. The war thus had a highly damaging impact on Nuremberg as a powerhouse of commerce and business. The occasional convoy proved inadequate in protecting traveling merchants. With the decline of trade and the cost of war spiraling out of control, Nuremberg's treasury was depleted by the mid-1630s, and its debt had risen to 7.5 million florin (compared to Augsburg's 1.6 million).[41]

---

37 See, e.g., StA N, Rst Nbg, RK, B-Laden, Akt. 82 (Nr. 3), 62–63.
38 StA N, Rst Nbg, RK, B-Laden, Akt. 83 (Nr. 5), Ratsverlaß of 9 June 1636 and 14 June 1636.
39 StA N, Rst Nbg, RK, B-Laden, Akt. 83 (Nr. 5), Ratsverlaß (15 June 1636).
40 Schultheiss, *Kleine Geschichte Nürnbergs*, 52.
41 Reicke, *Geschichte der Reichsstadt Nürnberg*, 994–95.

GOVERNMENTAL SUPPORT   83

Strapped for resources and faced with a war whose atrocities mounted with every year, Nuremberg's council pursued a course of realism that verged on resignation. On 12 July 1632 a butcher sent a complaint to Nuremberg's council: on his way into the city, he had been robbed by eight Swedish cavalrymen of one calf and eight pounds of lard. Since many carrying victuals to the market were robbed on the streets, he requested that the council pass an ordinance against such crimes and see to their elimination. The council's response was noted on the letter: the matter should be put to rest since nothing could be done to remedy the miserable situation during these difficult times. Instead, the butcher should be advised to be patient.[42] This episode provides insight into Nuremberg's political leaders as well as their subjects. In 1632 the butcher had not abandoned hope that his authorities could right the wrongs done to their subjects. Amazingly, he not only called the council to action, but requested a decree against highway robbery as well. The authorities, however, had already resigned themselves to the probability that neither the law nor any action could reverse the detrimental course of the war. Unable to stem the tide of violence, they directed their subjects to be patient. This inability to protect their own people is underlined by the mockery of soldiers in the neighboring margraviate Brandenburg-Ansbach, who were robbing Nuremberg's peasants and then ridiculing them by saying: "Nuremberg's subjects had a very fine government that not only failed to protect them against hardships but even made beggars out of them."[43] Old animosities and power struggles came to the fore, as the margrave's soldiers and cavalrymen maltreated Nuremberg's subjects, scoffed at their burdened-down neighbors, and claimed that they, the Brandenburg-Ansbachers, were now the lords, even over churches.[44]

The council continued to receive complaints about the billeting of troops in the countryside. A dialogue, this time from the end of the 1630s, highlights once again Nuremberg's own perceived helplessness in alleviating its subjects' burdens. Jeremias Pistorius, prior of Burgdorf, requested that the burgomaster and councilors of Nuremberg remedy the untenable situation due to the billeting of General Franz von Mercy's regiment. Herr von Fürstenberg, director of the war council, privately told Pistorius that he agreed with him entirely, but Pistorius should suggest means how this could be accomplished. The councilors did not know of any.

---

42   "Dies Ansag vff Sich ruhen, vnd weil diesem vnheil bey diesen leidigen beschwerlichen leuffen nicht zu remedirn, Jhn zu gedult weisen laßen." StA N, Rst Nbg, RK, B-Laden, Akt. 82 (Nr. 16), 1.
43   StA N, Rst Nbg, RK, B-Laden, Akt 82 (Nr. 3), 77 (2 May 1632).
44   StA N, Rst Nbg, RK, B-Laden, Akt. 82 (Nr. 3), 5 (1631–1632).

> *Pistorius*: It is not up to me to dictate to Your Majesty and the councilors. They will know themselves what they need to do. There are still means that can be found.
> *Von Fürstenberg*: How?
> *Pistorius*: If one would proceed according to the imperial constitution and the customary observance, and would punish severely those who extracted exorbitant sums, as well as treat the people in such a way that everyone could remain where his livelihood is.
> *Von Fürstenberg*: It has already gone too far.
> *Pistorius*: How do the states in Holland do it? They are always engaged in war and nevertheless flourish.
> *Von Fürstenberg*: That is a different matter. The Bavarians are causing all this chaos. We write, request, and remind them, but nothing comes of it; they don't even answer ...[45]

The councilor's sense of powerlessness in improving the subjects' situation is unmistakable. Von Fürstenberg's last statement also makes clear how limited the war council's options were. After complaints to General Mercy about the excesses of his Bavarian troops yielded no results, the council could do little else.

The responses on various levels of government to their subjects' anxieties also highlight the complex dynamics between central and middle authorities. The district overseers were middle authorities and thus representatives and executive organs of the central powers in the countryside, but they also stood as vital mediators between local administrators and central organs. Crucially, they resided in the locales and had a more immediate knowledge of conditions on the ground. In their letters, they informed the further removed government of the ever-worsening conditions in the countryside and requested help in improving the situation. These texts were carefully constructed not only to inform the central government but also to move it toward action. Often the local administrators' correspondence escalated over time with ever more dire predictions if no aid was forthcoming. The envisioned assistance could be in the form of monetary support, military protection, or deliverance from soldiers quartering in their area.

---

45 StA N, Rst Nbg, RK, B-Laden, Akt. 85 (Nr. 2) (15 September 1639).

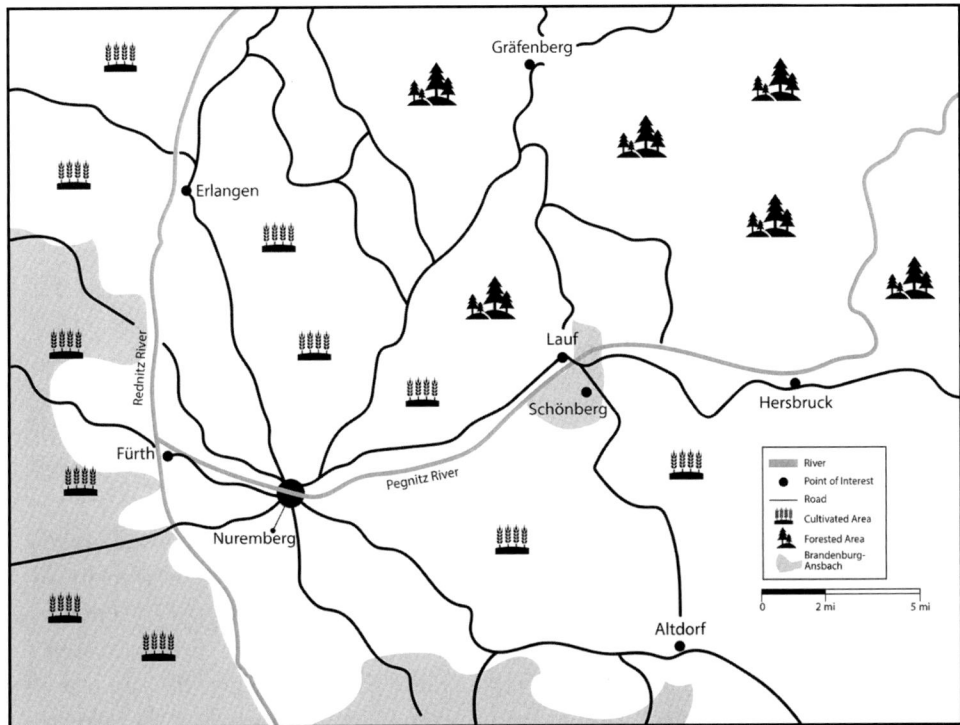

FIGURE 11   Greater Nuremberg

Several intriguing examples of such exchanges come from Nuremberg's territory. The first originates from the district Lauf to the east of the imperial city and illustrates the potential for flights – a common response to troop movements, but it also underlines that the populace's decision about whether they should stay or flee depended largely on their discernment of protection by the authorities, not on a blind sense of panic. Lauf's administrator, Christoff Örtel, notified Nuremberg's council in late 1631 of the situation in his district: When imperial troops entered their territory and started plundering, he called the citizenry together, especially those who had already started packing up, and admonished them to return and await further instructions. But soon people were wondering "whether they had been abandoned entirely and left unprotected. In case they could count on protection, they would exert body and life for their authority." Örtel asked the Nuremberg council what relief it had in store for Lauf and expressed his hope that the councilors would send a contingent of guards the next day. Doubtlessly, he ventured, the lords would make such arrangements, which would give the citizenry a reason for hope.[46]

---

46   StA N, Rst Nbg, RK, D-Laden, Akt. 3031, 17^{r-v} (19 November 1631).

The second example concerns the district Gräfenberg north of Lauf and illuminates the capacity for violence and uprising. Its administrator, Jobst Roggenbach, turned to Nuremberg's council in May 1632, when the countryside around Nuremberg was suffused with friendly and enemy troops ahead of the confrontation between Gustavus Adolphus and Albrecht von Wallenstein. The populace suffered severely under the plundering, and Roggenbach warned Nuremberg's council: "It is to be feared that, if they did not soon find a solution to these hostile proceedings, the subjects will all take up arms to divert such offensive violence as much as possible, from which all kinds of nuisances will arise, which would not serve the common good." Roggenbach suggested that the lords send a contingent of troops, of which one could place a living *Salva Guardia* (not merely a letter) in the most important villages – unless the lords had better solutions to forestall the utter ruin of the subjects. He closed with the reminder to the council: "This [protection] was the Lords' duty and the subjects' desire."[47]

A third example comes from the district Hersbruck east of Lauf and underlines the disillusionment of the populace with Nuremberg's government. In 1635, Hersbruck's overseer, Christoph Enders, began his report with common stories of soldiers' plundering "under the guise of foraging." Enders' distinction between foraging and plundering indicates his familiarity with the laws of war, which condoned "foraging" as occasionally necessary to feed the soldiers, but not "plundering."[48] Even though the peasants had reported such pillaging many times, no help had been offered. Because of these experiences, the subjects were disheartened, particularly with their authorities in Nuremberg, and this disillusionment was expressed in their resolve that "they no longer want to turn to the same [authorities, i.e., Nuremberg] for aid."[49]

Enders continued that the populace's disappointment and loss of faith in their authorities was intensified by another unsettling and widespread experience, namely the fact that one's own troops acted as harmfully or even more so than the enemy's:

> It is shameful that the subjects remain unmolested by the enemy, but are assaulted by our own soldiers worse than by the enemy. Those who should defend them – especially right now so that they can work the fields and sow – rob and devastate them so completely that one has to

---

47 StA N, Rst Nbg, RK, B-Laden, Akt. 86 (Nr. 2), 1^{r-v}.
48 This inserted differentiation may have been designed to preclude a response from Nuremberg rejecting his complaint out of hand.
49 StA N, Rst Nbg, RK, D-Laden, Akt. 239, 1^{r-v} (1 April 1635).

fear, if such insolent and atrocious deeds continue and remain unpunished, the poor populace cannot till the land and will have to leave their empty huts [because this is what they mostly are] – not to mention other punishment we might draw upon us.[50]

Much like Hersbruck's overseer, Enders had concrete suggestions how some of the problems could be remedied, and he reminded the councilors that he had proposed these before. He asked Nuremberg's council to send a commissioner or someone else who would command respect and could keep discipline among the troops. Short of this, he "could no longer remain in office with a good conscience, while he watched how the district's subjects were left helpless as they were entirely ruined by our own troops."[51] In this way, Enders tried not only to compel the central government toward action by warning that their subjects would emigrate should no help and protection be forthcoming – a familiar argument among middle authorities generally; he also threatened his own resignation should the central authorities not do their job.

The council's ability to protect its people from the war's ruinous consequences was often confined to sending out warnings of approaching troops, offering advice on how subjects should behave toward soldiers, and supplying the limited guards that were available during most years of the war. These measures proved entirely insufficient, as the council certainly realized. Besides a portrait of the dismal conditions in the countryside, the above examples convey the populace's growing loss of faith in the ability of their government to shield them from harm. In the early 1630s, one could still find subjects who trusted their government to come to their aid. But by the mid to late 1630s, the peasantry had largely resigned themselves to the fact that their lords could not protect them. The discussed cases also make clear that the district administrators in their powerlessness to help their subjects were similarly fed up with the central authorities' lack of action. Threats that the populace might move elsewhere or take matters into their own hands and answer violence with violence suggest the local administrators' writings were framed with the intention of putting moral and social-political pressure on the central authorities in Nuremberg. These communications also underscore that, in the estimation of the authorities on the ground, Nuremberg's actions – or lack thereof – and its calls for patience fell considerably short of what was required.

In Bavaria, with Maximilian and his various executive officers at Munich's court and in the districts (*Rentämter*), the government was not able to save

---

50   StA N, Rst Nbg, RK, D-Laden, Akt. 239, 1ᵛ.
51   StA N, Rst Nbg, RK, D-Laden, Akt. 239, 1ᵛ–2ʳ.

its subjects from the consequences of violence and deprivation either, but the character and tone of the correspondence with the regional administrators could not be more dissimilar from the exchanges between authorities in Nuremberg's territory. One cannot imagine a mid-level administrator telling the elector what to do or threatening him with resignation if he did not come through with the requested aid. This had much to do with Maximilian's personality and his strong position in Bavaria (and, indeed, the empire), but also with his generally low opinion of the administrators in the districts.

After Gustavus Adolphus' march south toward Augsburg and Munich, Bavaria became not so much a battleground as a territory overrun by troops. The countryside was used as winter quarter, and, over the next few years, many administrators in the districts entreated Maximilian to make the troops pick up and leave. Thus the burgomaster and council of Schärding on the Inn (today part of Upper Austria) wrote Maximilian about the unbelievable burden one platoon after another placed on their subjects. He implored the elector to see to the removal of the troops so that "the poor citizenry would yet be saved from extreme ruin and could remain in their homesteads with their wife and small children."[52] To this petition Schärding's councilors attached Maximilian's earlier order promising the withdrawal of the two companies from their area.[53] The elector responded immediately and declared that the Hauserische company would indeed leave, but the Fuggerische should stay "just a little time." In a complicated move, he committed to some financial relief, which would be reckoned against the contribution payments, and underlined once again that "this would not last much longer but would soon have an end."[54]

In another example, when the town of Neuötting on the Inn refused to let the Schaumburgische soldiers enter their city, Maximilian once again used the stratagem of "a very little time [*ein gar klaine Zeit*]" to soften the hearts and minds of the Neuöttingers, but he also left no doubt that he was giving an order:

> Since the [Schaumburgische] soldiers will have to stay in your town for just a very little time longer, we will instruct that you will receive a bit of support. Because this whole affair will only last a short time and good discipline must be maintained, you have to take in these soldiers and give them decent quarters. And especially in the distribution of the quarters,

---

52   HStA M, KB – ÄA 2529, 21ᵛ (10 April 1634).
53   HStA M, KB – ÄA 2529, 23ʳ (22 March 1634).
54   HStA M, KB – ÄA 2529, 25ʳ⁻ᵛ (11 April 1634).

you have to treat everyone alike so that the poor are not being burdened compared to the rich. We rely on you to make this happen.[55]

These features of middle authorities asking for relief and Maximilian negotiating for endurance pervade the correspondence between the two levels of government. Maximilian was a master at putting off requests and delaying actions by asking administrators to be patient just a little longer and by holding out the hope of the war's impending end. Psychologically, this was an ingenious tactic, because it broke the war's vast millstone into incremental, almost digestible portions – much like one might eat an elephant. He asked them to hold out for just another week, and then another few days, and another. This "gentle touch," however, was buttressed by a stern policy toward his administrators that brooked no opposition.

Maximilian, relying on some of the same strategies as those applied in Franconia, was no more successful than Nuremberg's authorities in protecting his countryside from the brutalities of war. It is also doubtful whether the populace could be placated with Maximilian's delay strategies. The local overseers describe the desperation among their subjects, but we do not hear the administrators inform the elector of people's loss of faith in him as their colleagues in Franconia did. This silence likely has more to do with the dynamics between Maximilian and his administrators than with a more contented populace.

Maximilian, of course, had his hands tied. Despite his sincere wish to help the countryside and his paramount concern for fair treatment, especially toward the poorest of his subjects, the elector could do little else than move the troops around between locales, and this far into the war, his coffers were thoroughly depleted. Witnessing the suffering of his countryside during the 1630s moved Maximilian to seek peace with the other involved parties; however, lasting peace proved elusive until the end of the 1640s. Nevertheless, Bavaria's elector was more effective in portraying a ruler in control of the situation during the war than the authorities in Nuremberg who often looked listless.

In general, then, authorities tried hard to help and protect their subjects, whether it was through physical structures, troops, negotiations with the enemy, or alleviating the burden by providing advice and guidance. No matter how sincere and tireless the governments' efforts, these measures had only very limited success and more often showed up the leaders' inability to shield the populace from harm. But protection against violence and losses was not

---

55   HStA M, KB – ÄA 2529, 27^r.

the only challenge authorities faced. They were also called upon to stem the rising poverty fueled by the repercussions of the war and, in its wake, diseases and pestilence.

2 Stemming Deprivation and Disease

2.1 Poverty and Poor Relief

As the previous section highlighted, poverty suffused most people's lives during the Thirty Years' War. The convergence of colder temperatures, bad harvests, troop movements, contributions, and migration impoverished large parts of the populace, and posed enormous challenges for the government. Efforts at a more effective handling of poor relief go back to the Later Middle Ages, when marked changes in the approaches to the poor occurred.[56] A complicated web of shifts in the economy and in the perception of the poor led to the transformation of poor relief in the Later Middle Ages that involved growing regulation of begging, transfer of supervision from ecclesiastical into communal hands, eviction of foreign beggars, and the establishment of new administrative officers to ensure follow-through. Begging, even for the worthy poor, was ever more circumscribed until, in the early 1500s, it was increasingly banned, particularly in Protestant territories.[57] A by-product of this rationalization process was the institution of firm criteria for deciding who was worthy of aid.[58]

These are the rough outlines of the poor relief system that already began to emerge at the end of the fifteenth century and picked up speed during the

---

56 For the history of poor relief, see Sachße and Tennstedt, *Geschichte der Armenfürsorge*. Scholars of early modern poor relief have focused on the sixteenth century, on the role of the Reformation in shaping policies toward the poor, and on poor relief in cities. See, especially, Jütte, *Obrigkeitliche Armenfürsorge*; Jütte, *Poverty and Deviance*; Lindberg, *Beyond Charity*; Safley, ed., *The Reformation of Charity*; Davis, "Poor Relief"; Grell and Cunningham, eds., *Health Care and Poor Relief in Protestant Europe*; Grell and Cunningham, eds., *Health Care and Poor Relief in Counter-Reformation Europe*; Pullan, "Catholics and the Poor"; Chrisman, "Urban Poor"; Fehler, "The Burden of Benevolence"; Spicer, "Poor Relief and the Exile Communities"; Prak, "The Carrot and the Stick"; and Critchlow and Parker, eds., *With Us Always*.

57 Scholars have pointed out that there was principally no difference between Catholic and Protestant areas in terms of organizing poor relief, although its execution might differ (Sachße and Tennstedt, *Geschichte der Armenfürsorge*, 37, and Jütte, *Poverty and Deviance*, 104).

58 Ideally (in the eyes of governments, if not necessarily of the needy) the more effective system now registered the poor and provided them with visible signs so that they could be recognized and were able to receive aid. Jütte has highlighted the sense of stigmatization associated with these visible signs (*Poverty and Deviance*, 158–65).

Reformation decades. Many of the characteristics present in these earlier initiatives reappeared in the civic and general begging ordinances of Franconia and Bavaria during the early seventeenth century, but one would be mistaken to assume an uninterrupted line of progress from the Later Middle Ages to the Thirty Years' War. The continued hold of old traditions and ways of life led to a very uneven success of these edicts. Moreover, developments toward the end of the sixteenth century – substantial population growth, the "Little Ice Age," stagnating production, inflation, and starvation – brought about a marked deterioration of living conditions and showed the inadequacy of the poor relief system. Rather than moving forward, proponents of poor relief efforts had to retract some of their earlier positions because they were not practicable.[59]

During the war, Franconia and Bavaria struggled to address the escalating poverty and devise measures to alleviate the hardship for their most vulnerable population. In their communications and activities, three concerns are particularly prominent: foreign beggars, effective ordinances, and reliable personnel. Considering the first issue, foreigners had long been regarded with animosity and suspicion, but never more so than during the Thirty Years' War.[60] In Nuremberg, the war's costs and destruction led to a rapid increase in beggars, who congested the streets and strained the city's already depleted resources. Moreover, together with the thousands who fled into the city to escape the brutality of the armies in Nuremberg's territory, these homeless presented a potential health hazard. The city was compelled to act quickly to avoid a major crisis.

In 1624, Nuremberg's council had already published a decree that forbade its subjects in the city and in the countryside, under penalty of fifty gulden, to harbor any foreigner or retired soldier without the authorities' knowledge. An influx of strangers, the councilors argued, would only bring disease and escalate prices.[61] Almost ten years later, with poverty intensifying ever more, Wolff Friedrich Stromer (of the famous Nuremberg family of architects and builders) submitted a proposal to the council that laid out a plan to remedy the problem of foreign beggars.[62] It also bluntly reflected his negative view of them. As officer involved with the fortifications, Stromer's reasoning started from the slow progress of the earthworks. The lack of workers was compounded by the fact that the peasants needed to till the fields for the spring and summer crops, the citizens were already overtaxed with guard and other duties, and

---

59   Sachße and Tennstedt, *Geschichte der Armenfürsorge*, 39–40.
60   Rüger, *Mittelalterliches Almosenwesen*, 49–51.
61   StA N, Rst Nbg, MD3, 444.
62   On Stromer, see Imhoff, *Berühmte Nürnberger*, 158–60.

there were no funds to hire additional people. While pondering solutions to the dilemma, Stromer pointed out how, "besides other disorders, especially the begging in the streets has escalated to such an extent" that no one was free of the beggars' soliciting, even in one's own home. Worse, most of these people were neither from these parts, nor bereft to the point that they could no longer work for themselves; instead, they hailed "from foreign locales and are strong, idle, wicked, and lazy. Out of pure mischief and lethargy, they evade the labor of which they are capable and devise to live on alms." Stromer proposed to solve both problems at once by forcing these "strong, vagabonding rascals" to work on the fortifications. He suggested that the councilors renew their earlier prohibition of begging through a special proclamation for city and countryside, and have any violators arrested and compelled to exert themselves in the redoubts. Thus, the fortifications would not only move forward, but the use of sturdy beggars would also save the city a substantial amount of money, since it would provide them with only a pound of bread rather than the ten to twelve kreuzer per day due a regular worker. Moreover, the streets would be rid of those bothersome beggars, and no end of connected problems would be resolved.[63] Nuremberg's councilors decided to follow Stromer's advice.[64] Two days later the council decreed that the *Bettelordnung* was to be applied not only to foreign beggars and vagabonds, but also to the local poor and homeless.

Bavaria shared Nuremberg's negative view of foreign beggars. Here, efforts at containing poverty were long-standing as well and focused on legitimate begging and limiting the care to one's own poor (the so-called *Heimatprinzip*). Apart from the fact that foreign beggars added to the city's financial burden, Munich's councilors, much like those in Nuremberg and elsewhere, worried about disease and treason. Beggars could be coming from infected places and bringing the epidemic into the city. Or they could be spies of the enemy. Thus, both Maximilian and Munich's councilors followed a hard line against non-native beggars, who were either to be expelled or not admitted, but, as was common practice, unworthy local beggars were not to be permitted either.[65]

The second concern, effective ordinances, is particularly visible in Maximilian's efforts to control the poor relief situation and the growing population of the needy during the later 1620s. Even though there was a war going on and its repercussions were increasingly felt in the south, for Bavaria the late

---

63   StA N, Rst Nbg, RK, B-Laden, Akt. 53 (Nr. 26), 1ʳ–2ʳ (24 May 1633).
64   StA N, Rst Nbg, RK, B-Laden, Akt. 53 (Nr. 26), 1ʳ (13 June 1633). Stromer's recommendation to use sturdy beggars to dig earthworks was not novel, but constituted a fairly common practice during the early modern period, which makes one wonder why the council needed reminding of this strategy.
65   SA M, B&R 60 A 1, BM, Aiiijʳ–ᵛ; Stahleder, *Chronik*, 2:395 (15 December 1623).

1620s were halcyon days, which were just serious enough to prompt legislative action and afford the rulers breathing room to refine them. These years give us a fascinating glimpse into the complicated interactive process between subjects and multiple levels of authorities to address efficiently the issue of poor relief. The backdrop for these activities was the mounting problem of poverty as the 1620s wore on. Even though the war itself with its marauding troops had not yet come to Bavaria, inflation during the early years of the decade (the *Kipper- und Wipperzeit*, i.e., Tipper and See-Saw period) and the financing of war put an increasing strain on its population during the later 1620s.

The process of feedback and legislative adjustment began with Maximilian's demand that Munich's city council evaluate the effectiveness of the reforms aimed at the abolition of begging.[66] Like most other governors and cities during the sixteenth and seventeenth centuries, Maximilian was concerned about 1) channeling help to the appropriate recipients – the poor who could not help themselves and were dependent on public assistance – and 2) eliminating abuses of the meager resources by beggars, who presumably could well take care of themselves. The resulting series of ordinances between 1625 and 1630 is remarkable in several ways. They reflect a process of modifications and reversals in response to problems on the ground and feedback from the populace and local administrators. These pertained to issues such as whether the poor should wear visible signs, carry letters acknowledging their poor status, or neither. Moreover, how should the more vulnerable countryside deal with beggars, especially the unworthy kind who were "not satisfied with any decent offering"?[67]

The outcome of these exchanges was Maximilian's new general begging ordinance of 1630. After five years of trial and error and a confusing earlier edict (1627), the elector settled on several key principles: first, he emphasized knowing the poor in the area so that one could respond to their needs. Accordingly, the native poor were to receive alms in their own town or village, rather than in the larger district where they would not be recognized. Furthermore, each locale needed to keep a register of their poor and give them distinguishable signs, so that authorities could immediately ascertain from which parish or town the beggar hailed and whether he or she was legitimate. The collection and distribution of alms was centralized and tightly regulated – at least in the cities and market towns. Designated officers were to collect alms and victuals, which were to be distributed on a specified day of the week following a sermon. For the countryside, however, Maximilian allowed the poor to go from house

---

66 Stahleder, *Chronik*, 2:401 (24 January 1625).
67 HStA M, KL, fasc. 793/265.

to house on one or two days a week, depending on what the local authorities deemed appropriate.[68]

The 1630 edict merged the intent of the new poor relief organization – an efficient system developed according to the needs of the poor – with the old that paid close attention to the otherworldly rewards of the donors. Not only did the elector stress people's responsibility for Christian charity, he also charged the preachers to remind their parishioners that God would "reimburse the benefactors in a hundred different ways." Spiritual and secular authorities were to shine the way with a strong example.[69]

Besides foreign beggars and effective ordinances, authorities were concerned about a third issue: reliable personnel. The councilors of Nuremberg and Munich were well aware that their orders' success depended to a large degree on their administrators' follow-through, which, however, was rarely to their satisfaction. Maximilian threatened severe monetary penalties and "other exemplary relentless punishment," if his office holders did not see to the execution of his instructions.[70]

In both Franconia and Bavaria, then, governments had made significant efforts at addressing the rising poverty among its populace. Both had a revised poor relief legislation in place, but the next few years brought disasters of such magnitude that it is doubtful even the most sophisticated set of laws could have provided relief. Thus, the implementation of these stipulations during the following years of crises looked quite different from what they had envisioned.

Bavaria is once again a good case in point. Its newly revised begging ordinance did not address the issues that presented themselves during the 1630s and 40s, when the war hit the south in earnest. The flights into cities, the spread of disease, and the escalating number of beggars placed unbearable pressure on the poor relief system. An impoverished populace was largely unable to take care of its regular poor. The ruin of the countryside and the threat of approaching troops led to at least temporary, and, in some cases, permanent, migration to safer and more financially viable places. The increasingly astronomical contributions people had to pay to the armies made beggars out of everyone. The needs were so immense and the people so devastated that an orderly following of begging regulations became unsustainable.

---

68   SA M, B&R 60 B 9, 27, Aij^v–Aiij^r. Nevertheless, the poor in the countryside were not allowed to beg on days other than those specified.
69   SA M, B&R 60 B 9, 27, Aiiij^r.
70   SA M, B&R 60 B 9, 27, Av^v–vj^r.

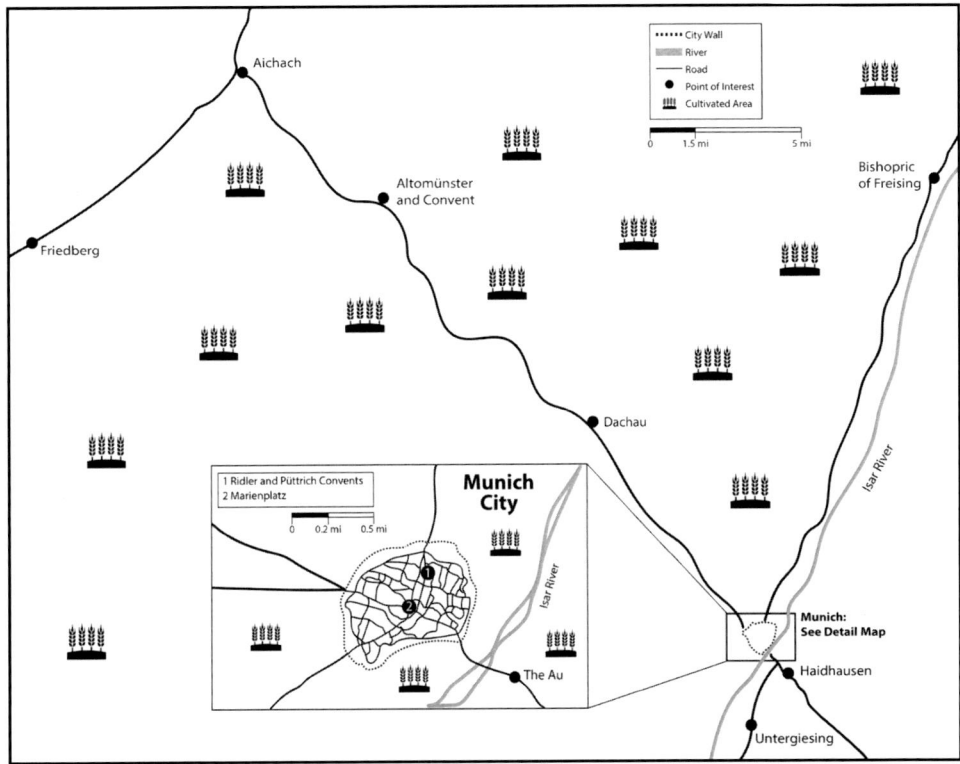

FIGURE 12   Munich and vicinity

The inadequacy of the 1630 ordinance soon became evident. In one of Munich's mandatory reports to Maximilian on the spreading infection in 1634, the councilors' discussion turned to the poor: thousands of people of every social level were flocking into the city to flee the destructive armies, and many poor people, especially the ruined peasants, were dying in the streets because of misery or lack of victuals. Although the city fathers had told foreign beggars to leave the city and had threatened them with expulsion and shaming, the councilors were forced to relent when the Spanish army headed for Munich, since otherwise the poor would have been killed by the troops outside the city walls. Besides, the councilors were irritated by the fact that Maximilian allowed certain outside groups (from Aichach and Friedberg) to reside within Munich – apparently without consulting the city fathers, while demanding that the city follow a strict course against foreigners. Munich's councilors "did not see who would be helped and what good that would do."[71]

---

71   SA M, GW 34, 61ʳ–62ᵛ.

Underlying this exchange is the tug-of-war between the elector and his court city, Munich. The councilors were plainly irritated with Maximilian's interference in city affairs as well as with what they considered unreasonable demands. If the elector wanted the city to get rid of its foreign beggars, then he needed to make a beginning by revoking his order permitting certain outsiders to dwell within the city walls. Munich, therefore, kept its own course of action: while Maximilian renewed his directive to expel beggars and threatened citizens who housed them with punishment, the city gave the 300 refugee peasants in the Au, who were unable to return to their fields, six gulden a week.[72]

Toward the end of the war, between 1646 and 1648, when Swedish and French armies were wreaking havoc on the Bavarian countryside, beggars and the limits of poor relief once again became a central topic, as Munich was flooded with peasants, and the poor sought refuge and relief from the plundering armies. The elector stipulated that the refugees would be allowed into the city only if they were able to provide for themselves for six months. Two weeks later, he reduced the required number of months of provisions from six to four.[73] Even with this reduced number, Maximilian's demand reflected wishful thinking rather than a reasonable response to the dire conditions at hand. Still, his and other rulers' concerns are understandable: overcrowded cities were health hazards and tested the limits of government there. Moreover, when peasants left for the city, their fields lay abandoned, which exacerbated the economic problems. Political leaders were also eager to avoid generating panic. Hordes of fleeing people complete with their belongings sent the signal that things were unravelling, which steered panic among the rest of the populace.

By 1648, the city and its adjacent territories were overwhelmed with poor country folk, and the desperate councilors turned to Maximilian for help. The two often conflicting authorities were united in their concern about the financial fallout and health risks of this latest crisis. The councilors asked the elector to issue a decree that would force the peasants to leave for the surrounding country districts and oblige those districts to take care of the poor.[74] It is evident that the city needed Maximilian's help to deal with the situation – whether it was the force of one of his orders or the manpower at his disposal.

A list of the people who had sought refuge in the Au, Haidhausen, and Untergiesing offers us a glimpse of the spectrum of neediness. The vagueness

---

72   Stahleder, *Chronik*, 2:483 (26 May 1635), 486–87 (30 August 1635).
73   SA M, RSP (SSS) 46 (1646), 123^v–25^r (3 September 1646), 131^v–32^r (18 September 1646).
74   HStA M, DK, Akt. 502, 1^{r-v} (20 May 1648).

of some of the categories make a statistical evaluation impossible, but it is nevertheless highly revealing that approximately:
- 265 households "have nothing."
- 100 (additional) households and 30 persons are explicitly described as "begging."
- 100 households have anywhere from a few loaves of bread to three weeks of provisions.
- 55 households can survive for up to three months.
- 45 households can "live well" for some time. Sometimes half a year is mentioned, sometimes only this vague description.[75]

During this temporary flight, the overwhelming number of refugees were poor with little to no means, while only about 18 percent were able to provide for themselves for any length of time.

The fact that peasants frequently fled to Munich draws attention to what life was like for them in the countryside. The 1636 *Umrittsprotokoll* for the district (*Rentamt*) Munich offers rare insight into the reality of poor relief in the rural areas during what was for Bavaria a catastrophic phase of the war.[76] The *Umrittsprotokoll* of Munich's district describes each visited village and market town (including the number of houses and/or residents) before the Swedish invasion, in 1630, and afterwards, in 1636, during the *Rentmeister*'s visit. Not surprisingly, the records highlight that the handling of poor relief diverged considerably from the theory presented in the electoral begging orders. One important reason for this disjuncture is the widespread ruin of the territory.

---

75   HStA M, DK, Akt. 502, 3^r–46^v (21 May 1648).
76   As a reminder, during the early seventeenth century, Old Bavaria was divided into four, and from 1628 five, *Rentämter* (Munich, Burghausen, Landshut, Straubing, and then Amberg). These districts were each in the hands of a governor, or *Rentmeister*, whose responsibilities included finances as well as law and order and was thus one of the most crucial offices in the government. Roughly every five years, Maximilian ordered his *Rentmeister* to visit each town and village under their jurisdiction and report on the state of their officer; the local administration of justice, accounts, and tax payments; and their *Pollizeywesen* (i.e., the local economy). The result was the so-called *Umrittsprotokolle* (literally "protocols of the circuits on horseback"). I have drawn particularly on the report of Munich's *Rentmeister* written in 1636. Besides examining the local records of the last five or six years, the governor of Munich's *Rentamt* investigated the ministers' performance and the congregations' religious observance. He also noted the degree of destruction in every town and village. The result is a fascinating picture of life in the countryside. On the *Rentmeister* and *Rentamt*, see Heydenreuter, *Der landesherrliche Hofrat*, 50–52. For a map of the districts, see Chapter 1.3.

TABLE 1   Devastation in Munich's *Rentamt*: 1630 vs. 1636

Name	Type	Households			Population		
				Decline			Decline
		1630	1636	%	1630	1636	%
Abendsberg and Altmannstein	District				608	127	79%
Neustadt	District				244	61	75%
Vohburg[a]	District	135	135	0%	808	299	63%
Kösching	District	90	32	64%			
Gerolfing	District				117	67	43%
Pfaffenhofen	District				999	278	72%
Kranzberg	District				1259	324	74%
Mainburg	Market Town	280	81	71%			
Riedenburg	Market Town	104	37	64%			
Altmannstein	Market Town	86	26	70%	86	64	26%
Pförring	Market Town	120	72	40%			
Kösching	Market Town	167	124	26%			
Gaimersheim	Market Town	138	82	41%			
Geisenfeld	Market Town				143	68	52%
Hohenwart	Market Town				159	102	36%
Pfaffenhofen	Market Town	343	160	53%			

a Due to fire insurance contributions, few houses were affected by the Swedish torch although the overall population declined.

SOURCE: STA M, RL, fasc. 33 (1636)

Many locales lost over half of their estates, which were either burned down or deserted. The number of people also shrank markedly.[77]

The *Rentmeister* pursued a differentiated approach tailored to the conditions of each locale. Because of the disruption of the war, many villages did not keep the mandated records on the poor.[78] He admonished the local officers not only to recommence proper record keeping, but also not to permit unworthy

---

[77] StA M, RL, fasc. 33, 124; 40^v–41^r, 52^r, 102^{r-v}, 157^v, 206^v–7^r, 219^r, 233^r, 251^v, 258^v, 275^r, 315^r, 322^{r-v}, 358^v, 393^r, 402^v, 426^v, 435^r.

[78] StA M, RL, fasc. 33, 124; 215^v, 239^r, 245^r, 272^r, 355^r, 397^v, 425^v. In the Pfleggericht Vohburg, the records were inadequate (227^r and following).

GOVERNMENTAL SUPPORT

beggars in their district.⁷⁹ The *Rentmeister* was also concerned that the influx of poor subjects could greatly impede the chances of recovery for places that had been badly hit by the war. Thus, when he came to the market town Geisenfeld, he enjoined the officers to be very careful with regard to whom they admitted, "since there reside mostly poor and ruined burghers in Geisenfeld." Access should be given only to those who could provide sufficient guarantees that he would not resort to begging for the next seven years; otherwise, his sponsors had to take care of him.⁸⁰ Still, it is doubtful whether the local government followed such instructions or whether they were indeed practicable, since the poor refugees had to settle somewhere.

Sometimes the local administrators in charge of begging did not meet the *Rentmeister*'s approval, such as the overseer of begging (*Bettelrichter*) of the market town Pfaffenhofen. This "lazy blighter" (*fauller Tropff*), the *Rentmeister* ordered, should be encouraged initially with imprisonment, and if that did not improve his performance he should be chased out of office and a more reliable one hired.⁸¹ But, more commonly, the *Rentmeister* showed considerable understanding of the difficult situation in the countryside. Often he noted, without rebuke, that there had been no alms boxes for many years and that they had to be newly installed.⁸² Sometimes he remarked that the people were too poor to follow the systematic order of the elector. Thus, only irregular almsgiving was possible – and apparently acceptable.

Most striking is the *Rentmeister*'s attention to the individual. Rather than simply looking at the account books and giving the place a cursory assessment, he paid close attention to the human being behind the record. In the market town Hohenwart, he was particularly troubled about an old poor woman in the hospital, who ought to be treated with more consideration, visited at least once a week, and made more comfortable. He threatened that if the locals did not follow his instructions, he would teach them through penalties how one should take care of the poor.⁸³ In the district (*Pflege*) Gerolfing, the *Rentmeister* noted that, although several beggars resided there, these could not be sustained according to the begging order, since the subjects were ruined and reduced to beggars themselves. Therefore, the poor had to take whatever sporadic donation was available.⁸⁴ Occasionally, he commented on the good order of the

---

79   StA M, RL, fasc. 33, 124; 6ʳ.
80   StA M, RL, fasc. 33, 124; 358ʳ.
81   StA M, RL, fasc. 33, 124; 425ᵛ.
82   StA M, RL, fasc. 33, 124; 77ᵛ, 123ʳ, 178ᵛ, 233ʳ.
83   StA M, RL, fasc. 33, 124; 391ʳ–92ʳ.
84   StA M, RL, fasc. 33, 124; 319ʳ⁻ᵛ.

poor records and that the needy were well taken care of.[85] The *Rentmeister* was also concerned about the closet-poor, especially when the number of poor registered seemed too small in proportion to the size of the town. Thus, he admonished the city of Abensberg: "It has been claimed that right now there are present only three poor persons who are in need of holy alms. However, since this is quite unbelievable, one has to observe the poor burghers more assiduously and inquire more carefully how they keep themselves above water so that those suffering can be helped as much as possible."[86]

In Bavaria, then, we see particularly clearly how the government responded to the crisis of poverty during the war. During the later 1620s, central authorities, administrators at the mid- and local levels, and the populace were involved in the creation of a constructive begging ordinance. In this endeavor, Maximilian was guided by his desire to make the legislation as effective as possible, not by any democratic leanings. The war, however, thwarted these attempts because its repercussions introduced exceptional circumstances, which his edict did not address and might not have been able to meet in any case. The elector's emphasis on effectiveness and fairness was directly tied to a second characteristic of the poor relief law: its local orientation and embeddedness in the reality at hand. Even during the crises of the 1630s, which proved the inadequacy of the system, the focus remained on taking care of the individual and alleviating his or her suffering.

Poor relief, a grave concern in both Franconia and Bavaria, was addressed with vigor, but catastrophic situations during the 1630s and 1640s once again demonstrated the limits of any governing body to contain the crisis. Worse, the war-induced destitution propelled and became caught up with another crisis, epidemic diseases, which presented authorities with even greater challenges, to which we now turn.

2.2 Health and Disease

During the Thirty Years' War, problems of poverty, migration, and disease were intricately linked to one another. Inflation, wet summers, a starved populace, and troops descending on one's region added tremendous potential for sickness and epidemics. Hunger among ever larger parts of the population made them vulnerable to illnesses and infections. The search for protection from marauding armies led to overcrowded cities that threatened to overburden not only the poor relief but also the healthcare system, since the congestion of streets and public places provided a fertile breeding ground for contagious

---

85 StA M, RL, fasc. 33, 124; 256^r.
86 StA M, RL, fasc. 33, 124; 90^{r-v}.

diseases. The situation of soldiers was often dismal as well; with little protection from the elements and few provisions, dysentery, typhus, and other diseases spread easily in their camps. Besides protecting against violence and taking care of the needy, governments thus faced another enormous challenge with the task of safeguarding their subjects' health, or at least minimizing the impact of illnesses.

By the 1600s, Europe had a long history of dealing with epidemic diseases. Since the massive outbreak of the so-called "Black Death" in the mid-fourteenth century, plague epidemics visited Europe about every eleven years until well into the seventeenth century. In the course of their periodic recurrences, European countries adapted to the reality of pestilence. This involuntary familiarity with the plague makes the early modern era different from the medieval period. Common assumptions – that the populace met epidemics with panic, that chaos ruled, and that familial relationships broke down – are much less in evidence for the sixteenth and seventeenth centuries.[87] Over time, authorities developed strategies for dealing with these waves of infectious diseases. Rarely did panic set in; instead, ordinances and mandates about proper procedures were in place, and advisory literature directed the populace toward prophylactic measures or, had one already caught the infection, on how to deal with it. The need to control pestilence propelled governments toward a general organization of healthcare that included epidemics of other diseases as well.[88]

When the plague broke out in the mid-fourteenth century, contemporaries did not know the physical origin of the disease. A persistent explanation located its cause in humanity's sinfulness – an interpretation that endured well into the early modern period.[89] Alongside this religious reasoning, natural concepts developed to account for the disease. One was the *miasma* theory, in which ill-fated planetary constellations caused earthquakes and eruptions of volcanoes, thus setting free poisonous vapors. Natural processes of decay could also produce foul smells, which is why regulations focused on eliminating the sources of putrefaction in cities and towns.[90] During the early modern period,

---

87 See Eckert, *Structure of Plagues*; Ulbricht, ed., *Die leidige Seuche*; and Feuerstein-Herz, ed., *Gotts verhengnis und seine straffe*.
88 Eckert, *Structure of Plagues*, 23. Documents, however, only gradually became more explicit about the kind of "infection" or epidemic with which they were dealing, whether it was a form of pestilence, typhus, dysentery, or smallpox.
89 See, e.g., David Herlicius' *Schreibkalender* of 1636 (HStA M, MSS 522, D^r). According to the Bible, pestilence was one of the four main afflictions (besides war, inflation, and hunger) God sent to chastise humans for their turning away from Him.
90 Porzelt, *Pest in Nürnberg*, 29–30. The *miasma* theory corresponded to the prevalent concept of the four humors in the human body (blood, yellow bile, black bile, and phlegm).

many were swayed by the contagion theory, known since the Great Plague but fully developed only by the Italian physician Girolamo Fracastoro (c. 1476/78–1553).[91] While early modern conceptions and handling of the disease were ever more oriented toward observation and experience with the infection, which confirmed the contagious nature of pestilence, most pronouncements, nevertheless, show an adherence to both theories by addressing the cleansing of the air *and* by separating the infected from the healthy.

During the Thirty Years' War, authorities upheld some of the well-established strategies during outbreaks of pestilence, but the war changed the known parameters in important and dramatic ways. The military conflict, particularly during the 1630s, transformed pestilence into an epidemic of vast proportions. Intriguingly, the period before the Thirty Years' War (1614–21) showed low plague activity.[92] During the next cycle (1622–31), however, the course of the plague became intertwined with events and circumstances of the war, especially the increased mobility of the military and of individuals.[93] When in July 1630 the Swedish army landed in Pomerania and the following year marched southward through the plague zones, it set off "Germany's most devastating mortality crisis," the epidemic cycle from 1632 to 1640.[94]

The following analysis juxtaposes the cases of Bavaria and Franconia. These two territories entered the devastating period from entirely different positions: Bavaria exuded confidence and strength; Franconia, in contrast, was in a severely weakened situation. In some ways, Bavaria is atypical in the history of pestilence. While most regions in Central Europe experienced high mortality during epidemic cycles, Bavaria continuously showed low epidemic activity for much of its territory, except for the last, most severe cycle (1632–1640).[95] This does not mean that there were no cases of pestilence, but rather that death rates did not approach epidemic proportions, i.e., at least four times the

---

The impact of the air on a person depended on the mixture and influence of these humors in one's body.

91 Fracastoro, *Contagione* (1546).
92 Eckert, *Structure of Plagues*, 78–132. Edward Eckert traces the structure of epidemic cycles in Central Europe from 1560, when records were more readily available, until 1640, when the plague began to subside. Each cycle lasted around a decade.
93 Eckert also underlines the influence of seasonal factors on plague activity. The peak usually occurred during the fall months (September until November), whereas February to July showed limited activity. He also stresses the great variations in mortality between individual communities within clusters (*Structure of Plagues*, 143–44).
94 Eckert, *Structure of Plagues*, 134, 136.
95 See Eckert's fascinating epidemiological research on Bavaria (*Structure of Plagues*, 98, 112, 142, 145). Bavarian Swabia, especially Augsburg, however, suffered high mortality in 1627–31.

normal death rate. Despite the recurring nature of this resistance to plague, which suggests certain conditions impeding its spread, there is no clear answer why Bavaria overall suffered only mildly from the epidemic.⁹⁶ Whatever the reason, Bavaria was not immune to pestilence as the catastrophic losses during the 1630s show. Between September 1634 and April 1635, 7,000 people died in Munich alone.⁹⁷

Until this outbreak, Bavaria had handled the control of pestilence similarly to the way other territories had – by staying vigilant and publishing ordinances any time it learned of epidemic activity. The pronouncements underline several characteristics: first, central governments in Bavaria were well aware of the cyclical nature of the epidemic and took care to be informed about its course throughout the neighboring lands. Second, even though Bavaria had been spared major mortality crises during the previous century, authorities prepared diligently to meet the challenge should it actually occur. Third, the ordinances displayed the remarkable assumption that the epidemic would not hit Munich. Thus, they have all the signs of documents aimed at general prevention of misfortune and none of an acute crisis. And finally, authorities exhibited a firm belief in the efficacy of medicine. With God's grace and the physician's skills, the greater part of the sick could be healed as long as they sought medical help at once. Indeed, as the ordinances claimed, for such an illness, the apothecary held many remedies in store.⁹⁸ This confidence is puzzling since, in effect, no medication was available to treat pestilence. The edict's intention was most likely to calm the subjects and prevent panic once cases of infection arose. It perpetuated the perception, shared by many among the populace, that the infection could be managed.

Munich also had a plan in place should the epidemic escalate outside the city. The *General Jnstruction* of 1624 addressed three stages of severity: 1) several locales had contracted pestilence; 2) the pestilence had spread to more than four or five places; and 3) the epidemic became rampant.⁹⁹ These scenarios dictated an increasing vigilance against people from banned places, a closing of ever more gates, and a curtailing of contact with foreigners.¹⁰⁰ In

---

96   Eckert suggests a few possibilities: the type of settlement, which in Bavaria was more dispersed and thus did not reflect the interactive village and town life of many other areas; a different linkage of these settlements; biological factors, such as concentration and types of rodents; and modes of building construction (*Structure of Plagues*, 146).
97   Heimers, *Krieg, Hunger, Pest und Glaubenszwist*, 42. Munich's normal population counted roughly 23,000, but this number does not include the refugees and military.
98   SA M, GW 3.
99   SA M, GW 52.
100 SA M, GW 52, 1ʳ–2ᵛ.

none of these cases did the council articulate the possibility that the epidemic could actually infiltrate Munich. Besides safeguarding against contagion from the outside, the city fathers urged cleansing on the inside so that bad smells were eliminated. Furthermore, the smokehouse was to be opened to fumigate letters and small packages. Larger items of commerce were to be placed under quarantine.[101] In 1628 the city also released an extensive hiring plan, which specified the personnel to be engaged in preparation for a plague epidemic.[102]

At the end of the 1620s, then, Munich still seemed immune to the contagion, but it was well prepared should the worst case indeed occur. While Nuremberg had already experienced periods of epidemics within its walls during the 1620s, Munich's communications sounded as if no harm could come to its citizens as long as they guarded their city carefully against any contagion from the outside and kept the city smelling pleasantly on the inside. The city fathers gave the impression that they had things under control and that the contagion could be mastered. Considering that Bavaria had mostly been spared the experience of pest epidemics, this confidence is understandable, even though the knowledge of plague epidemics elsewhere must have caused some general concern among the government and populace.

In 1634, finally, after the Swedish, Spanish, and other troops had flooded Bavaria, Munich and its countryside faced the kind of plague epidemic that must have surpassed all imagination. The first to act, Maximilian issued a plague ordinance even before the epidemic's escalation.[103] While earlier decrees had only envisioned possible scenarios of the pestilence infiltrating the city, the odds of this happening had become a terrifying reality. The elector showed great concern for the spiritual care of the dying, but the living, too, should turn around their sinful lives and prepare themselves through frequent

---

101   SA M, GW 52. The instruction spelled out precisely how this exchange of items between courier and fumigator was to take place.

102   SA M, GW 52, Ordnung vnd Anstöllungen, 1^r–3^r. Beginning with the spiritual needs of the infected, a special priest was hired for the lazaret, and he was to be paid three times his regular salary. Since the priest had to reside outside the city so as to not bring the infection inside (the lazaret was located outside the city walls), Munich asked the Jesuits and Capuchins who had decided to stay in their houses to care for those infected in the city. Other appointments concerned a nurse, a carrier of the dead, a gravedigger, a midwife, a record keeper, and a barber-surgeon. The order stipulated that those who died were to be replaced with other qualified personnel, which highlights an awareness that these were hazardous jobs.

103   SA M, B&R 60, B 14, Nr. 26, Pestordnung (19 August 1634). Maximilian had left Munich before the Swedes arrived in 1632 and did not return to the city until 1635. Here he responded from Braunau.

confession and communion "so that anytime the Lord might come, He finds them awake and not asleep," that is, ready for death.[104]

On the practical side, besides the common preventive measures of the past, such as cleanliness, fumigation, separation of the sick, and guarding against the pestilence's infiltration from the outside, the city now had to deal with a massive, unprecedented case of epidemic disease. As the plague epidemic increased, both the city and the elector stepped up their efforts. Instructions with guidelines on how to behave during an infection were to be placed on all four main gates.[105] In September, the city opened the pest hospital, but quickly added three more houses to care for the sick and a house with a garden for those who convalesced.

Besides these initiatives, the 1634 plague epidemic also elicited the collection of detailed information on various aspects of the pestilence. In general, the history of disease control in the seventeenth century is accompanied by increased record keeping in an effort to provide more empirical data on the epidemic, which coincided with Maximilian's penchant for meticulous record keeping. To that end, the elector demanded that Munich's city fathers send him comprehensive updates every other day and complained when they were not forthcoming.[106] On 25 September 1634, Munich's burgomaster and council sent the elector one such requested report, and their exasperation over his demands for constant updates is palpable. They pointed out that the physicians had already notified the elector about any epidemic or disease in the city; thus, "we do not see what we should report to you further in this matter."[107]

The exchange between the elector and Munich's councilors reveals some of the underlying reasons for the high degree of irritation between the parties. It is understandable that Maximilian wanted to be fully informed to decide on the best course of action in this health crisis, but it is also evident that he used his system of informants to keep the officers of his court city and the countryside under tight control. Quite plainly, he did not lack information, since he had plenty of sources who furnished him with data, but he criticized Munich's council for its selective delivery of facts and for not providing him with the same particulars he had already received from elsewhere.[108] The overburdened city councilors were annoyed by such time-consuming and what they

---

104   SA M, B&R 60, B 14, Nr. 26.
105   SA M, RSP (URS) 249, 308^v (7 September 1634), 356^v (20 October 1634).
106   These reports were to specify who and how many had died of the contagion, how many and which houses were barred, whether the disease decreased or increased, and whether it had been carried in from other places or where it had originated.
107   SA M, GW 34, Seuchen, Vorbeugemaßnahmen, 59^v.
108   SA M, GW 34, 182^r (19 October 1634).

considered overly exacting or redundant demands, but also by Maximilian's evident desire for control over the council. They may also have been frustrated that the elector did not recognize that they, too, desired and worked toward firm, useful data to get on top of the epidemic. For example, since the city physician treated the pest victims only remotely, they hired a scribe to record vital details, such as whether the illness stemmed from heat or cold, and how long the infected lay sick, so that they could get a better sense of the disease's profile.[109]

The council's report to Maximilian is most illuminating because it offers us a contemporary view of the plague's origins. Divided into four points, the extensive reply suggests that the city had consulted a physician, which was common practice at the time. There was no reference to sin or to God. According to the city authorities, the first reason for the contagion was the lack of food, which resulted in the commoners going hungry: "On the question whether this epidemic had been caused by others or from where it had originated, we judge that this epidemic resulted firstly from the lack of victuals, which the common burgher has to suffer and tolerate in these wretched times, in which he cannot afford them because of the great deprivation and poverty." Next came the fright and grief the people had experienced, beginning with Munich's occupation, then the quartering of troops and the connected abuse. The council pointed out that, according to the judgment of medical men, fear constituted a substantial (*nit geringe*) cause for contagion. A third reason was the lodging of officers and their troops in the city. Some of them fell sick in their houses, but their train and horses also created much refuse that helped spread the contagion. The heavy influx of refugees and their livestock into the city led to overcrowded houses, tremendous stench, and squalor. These refugees died in the streets either because of their great misery and sadness or because of the lack of victuals. The most numerous among them were the ruined and impoverished peasants.[110]

The fourth and foremost reason for the origin of the contagion, so the councilors, was the Spanish army. The officers, who had taken up lodging in the citizens' houses all winter and summer, and the many Spanish soldiers in and outside of the city, produced an extraordinary amount of waste and left behind 150 dead, which was where authorities thought the infection originated. As evidence, they pointed to other places, where the Spanish army left

---

109 See the special instruction for the scribe regarding how to record the information: SA M, GW 52.
110 SA M, GW 34, 60ᵛ–61ᵛ.

behind similar "relics."[111] Given the large garrison and the enormous number of foreign people and their livestock in the city, the councilors' efforts to rid the city of its refuse and restore cleanliness had largely been in vain. Munich's political leaders were evidently well informed about how the contagion spread both within and outside the city. They knew about the route and centers of contagion and were aware of some of the factors that facilitated and enhanced its spread: hunger and crowded living. The councilors also resolutely believed in the importance of cleanliness and good air.

Eventually the tug-of-war between the city government and the elector gave way, at least temporarily, to a joint effort to combat the by now out-of-control contagion. Munich's ordinance of 30 October 1634 laid out principles for countering the health crisis.[112] Although the ordinance built on earlier edicts, it was much more detailed and addressed additional aspects of the issue. Released at the height of the plague epidemic, its severe tone reflected the seriousness of the situation as well as the lack of compliance among the populace, despite the threat of heavy penalties. Accordingly, the council decided to make the ordinance more widely known so that no one could feign ignorance. Second, the city joined forces with Maximilian to put more muscle behind the decree.

The ordinance started out by stating that saving the soul was more important than saving one's life, and thus the most vital measure was to abstain from all sin, since this epidemic was "no doubt" sent by God because of humans' wicked, blasphemous lives. Humility, repentance, and prayer were called for. Gone were the admonitions to attend more fervently the weekly processions. The health crisis was such that gatherings of people had to be avoided. After the foremost directive to correct and improve one's relationship with God, the following 24 articles addressed practical measures – among them the cleansing of air, houses, and the most important civic places; the best diet; the separation of the sick from the healthy; caution toward foreigners; the curtailing of feasts; and the prevention, rather than only the subsequent treatment, of disease. Here, too, the city fathers displayed a belief in the treatability of the contagion. They admonished every housefather to stock up on preventive medicine and pointed to the affordable medical advice literature available at the apothecary.

The epidemic was not confined to overcrowded cities like Munich; it also spread in Bavaria's countryside. The district administrators were particularly vocal about violations of quarantine regulations.[113] Moreover, they complained

---

111   SA M, GW 34, 62ᵛ–63ʳ. Among the locales mentioned were the Tyrol, the districts Rosenheim and Griesbach, Aibling, Weilheim, Tölz, and Swabia.
112   SA M, GW 5, Ratsordnung, die Pestilenz betreffend.
113   StA M, KHHA, A 2608, esp. letter of 6 Sep 1634 to the judge of Wildenwart.

that local authorities did not punish such offenders severely enough.[114] One can only guess at the possible reasons for the authorities' rather moderate approach to quarantine. It is doubtful that the resident administrators lacked an understanding of the principles of quarantine. More likely, they placed other local, especially economic, interests above containing the infection, or regarded the contagion as not overly dangerous – at least not to the same extent as did the central authorities. As soon as the epidemic declined, administrators in the countryside begged the electoral council to relax the quarantine so that their subjects could pursue their business, which suggests that the last two explanations are more to the point.[115] Maximilian, however, had no patience for such light handling of offenders during this health crisis. Breakers of quarantine were a major threat to his territory and subjects, and exemplary sentencing was needed to keep people from following their own – faulty – advice.

The costs of this epidemic, which lasted from September 1634 until April 1635, rose astronomically. In the five houses the council had opened to treat the infected (including a garden house for recuperation), more than 60 lazaret attendants continuously cared for over 300 persons.[116] In order to pay for all these expenses, the administration initiated a collection in the four quarters of the city, which amounted to almost 1,500 florin.[117] Besides what had been collected from the community, the city treasury paid bills in the amount of just under 6,500 florin.[118] The fact that, in 1634, Munich did not collect taxes from its citizenry because of the epidemic added to the city's strapped finances.[119] Additionally, over half of the infected were poor peasants who had fled into the city.[120] Munich, therefore, had to devise ways to raise extra funds. To that end, the councilors requested the elector's permission to add a special tax to beer and meat to pay the enormous costs that had accumulated as a result of the hostages, the infection, and the quartering of the Spanish army. This was to avoid raising taxes in general for the severely impoverished citizenry.[121] During the course of the war, Munich and Bavaria did not again see such a mortality crisis, although, during the renewed convergence of troops in

---

114 StA M, RL, fasc. 33, 124, 159^v, 225^v–26^r; Marckt Altmannstain, (1636).
115 StA M, KHHA A 2608, letter of the judge of Wildenwart to the electoral council (6 February 1635).
116 Additionally, some 250 private houses were placed under quarantine.
117 SA M, Kämmerei 1/241, KR 1634, 158^{r-v}.
118 SA M, SV 251/b, 5^v.
119 The city, however, went after outstanding taxes for 1633. SA M, Kämmerei 1/241, KR 1634, 54^r.
120 SA M, SV 251/b, 2^r.
121 SA M, RSP (URS) 250/2, 123^v (22 September 1635).

1647, the city feared another outbreak of pestilence and stepped up its personnel and its vigilance at the gates and public places.¹²² Fortunately, that time it was spared a similar catastrophe.

Turning from the more unusual case of Munich and Bavaria to Nuremberg and Franconia, one finds both similarities and differences. Franconia experienced the effects of the war on the spread of disease and pestilence much sooner than Old Bavaria because it became a passageway for military troops as early as 1622.¹²³ While Maximilian and his city council hardly contemplated the possibility of pestilence infiltrating the court city, Franconia had to deal with the reality of the plague and other epidemics throughout the 1620s and early 1630s and was much weakened when the great epidemic hit in 1634. Still, the measures and instructions Nuremberg's authorities initiated to prepare for and react to such outbreaks followed the pattern established by authorities in general over the previous century and reflected common attitudes and perceptions of the plague. Two large outbreaks of pestilence in 1562–63 (over 9,000 deaths) and 1574–75 (over 6,500 deaths) propelled Nuremberg to get a handle on disease control. Throughout the next decades, the city was fairly successful in devising measures to contain epidemic diseases to a degree, considering the fact that there was no known medical treatment at the time.¹²⁴ The strain of war, however, challenged everyone's ability to contain diseases and epidemics.

While the plague of 1634 with its massive death count usually commands the most attention, Franconia had already fought smaller outbreaks of diseases throughout the 1620s.¹²⁵ As in Munich, Nuremberg's councilmen complained that hardly anyone bothered with their ordinances. Instead, there were enough "selfish people," both local and foreign, who smuggled heaps of feathers and bedding into the city to sell them, "through which the general citizenry could easily contract a dangerous infection."¹²⁶ The following year (1625) mortality was especially high during the fall months. The deaths did cause fear, but, according to a chronicler, because it disrupted commerce, since passes were blocked and neither people nor goods could get through.¹²⁷ On one hand,

---

122 SA M, SV 251/b, 2^{r-v}.
123 StA N, ASHVMF, HS 219, 190^r. The chronicle speaks of 6,000 Cossacks quartered by Fürth. From then on, there was an almost continuous stream of companies through their territory.
124 Porzelt, *Pest in Nürnberg*, 40–42, 176–77, 291. Like Eckert, Porzelt underlines the lack of pest activity from 1614–1623.
125 StA N, ASHVMF, HS 219; 202^r. As mentioned earlier, the sources are not always reliable on the kind of epidemic. Porzelt speaks of dysentery that came down on the city in October 1624 (*Pest in Nürnberg*, 42).
126 StA N, Rst Nbg, M 3, 448 (3 December 1624).
127 StA N, ASHVMF, HS 219; 206^r.

this is in line with the argument that pestilence did not necessarily spread panic among the populace; on the other, the author makes us understand why people might break the quarantine: anxiety over the plague's impact on business could be more pronounced than over its effect on one's health. For the next couple of years, the number of dead dropped considerably but then started to rise again steeply, which had much to do with the horrendous situation of several large armies settling outside Nuremberg, the subsequent violence against civilians, the flights into the city, the hunger and starvation, and the rise in diseases. While the council already feared an infection in 1632, the city and suburbs were instead plagued by hunger and a kind of typhus, the so-called "head-" or "Hungarian" sickness that, according to the chronicler, led to an astronomical 45,612 dead.[128] Another chronicler, who provides numbers of deaths and baptisms at the end of every year, is more conservative and probably more realistic when he records 4,263 "registered" dead, but suggests that the real number was double that.[129] Considering the death figures for 1631 (2,100) and 1633 (2,678), this is still a shockingly high mortality. Even though the chroniclers' numbers are not always reliable, their notes on the practices around the dead during the epidemic of 1632, prior to the devastating pestilence in 1634, are illuminating. Among the thousands of dead were many young. Every day, six or seven bodies were carried in a procession. Many, however, were simply collected on carts, carried outside the city, and buried there. The lazaret was so overcrowded, mostly from Swedish soldiers, that the dead were stacked like wood in the courtyard until there was time to dig a pit for them.[130]

When the plague struck the imperial city again in 1634, Nuremberg and its countryside were so weakened and decimated that its mortality rate assumed unprecedented proportions. Chroniclers recorded between 11 and 12 thousand deaths for the year 1634, but this figure referred only to those buried in the church yard; the actual number was far higher.[131] For 1635, the number of dead dropped dramatically to 582, which reflects the end of the epidemic but also the shrunken number of inhabitants in the city. Baptisms, however, were twice

---

128   StA N, Rst Nbg, HS 472; 638. He relates that the preacher of Sebald estimated a number of 60,000 including the soldiers in their train.
129   StA N, ASHVMF, HS 219; 230^r. Another chronicle speaks of 5,785 buried bodies, including the Swedes. StA N, ASHVMF, HS 473; 285^r.
130   StBM, Cgm 5642, 389.
131   StA N, ASHVMF, HS 219; 236^v and StA N, ASHVMF, HS 158. Ernst Mummenhoff judged that the real number was twice as high, between 18,000 and 22,000, which would mean a loss of one-half to two-thirds of the city population. Mummenhoff, *Altnürnberg*, 2:72–73.

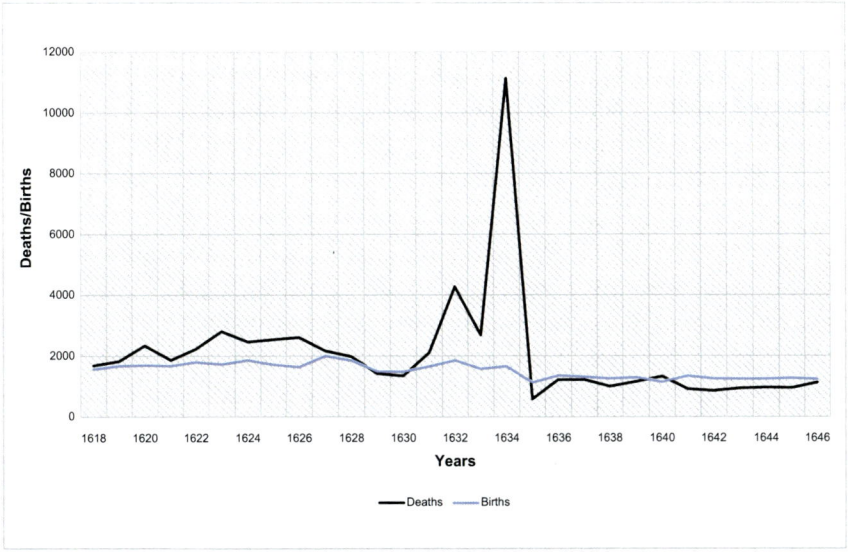

FIGURE 13   Deaths vs. births in Nuremberg, 1618–1646
SOURCE: STA N, ASHVMF, HS 219

as high (1,133).[132] All in all, during the years 1632 to 1634, Nuremberg suffered about 35,000 deaths, including soldiers and refugees. In contrast to developments in the rest of the empire, where demographic numbers reached their pre-war status around 1740, the imperial city did not recover from these losses until the middle of the nineteenth century.[133]

From its experience with regularly occurring waves of pestilence and other epidemics, Nuremberg, along with most cities, developed a system of regulations and offices to deal with the situation, and oriented itself along measures taken during similar incidents in previous years. A broad array of publications was designed to help the subjects face this health crisis in the best possible way.[134] The city hired not only the usual assortment of personnel to deal with the pest – barber-surgeons, ministers, grave diggers, carriers of the dead, midwives, wardens, nurses, cooks, etc. – but also someone to be the connecting

---

132   StA N, ASHVMF, HS 219; 241ᵛ. Two further waves of pestilence during the war were demographically not severe because of the already decimated population (Porzelt, *Pest in Nürnberg*, 43).
133   Porzelt, *Pest in Nürnberg*, 35.
134   Porzelt, *Pest in Nürnberg*, 55–57. These included ordinances regarding dying (*Sterbsordnung*), public edicts, and health pamphlets of civic physicians, as well as the so-called *Pestregiment* with medical advice for the commoner. Curiously, a general edict on contagion for the entire Frankish Circle was not published until 1708.

link between the pest personnel and the council (the *Aufwarter*). His tasks were many, including keeping records of the situation, finances, and discipline. The chief authority lay with the deputies of epidemics, a kind of special commission of four to six men that existed only during an epidemic.[135]

Much less information is available about smaller towns and the countryside during the pestilence.[136] The principle measures involved the quarantining of houses, since no lazaret was available, but such segregation was frequently defied here as well. Some insights about challenges in towns and countryside can be gleaned from the records of the Margraviate Brandenburg-Ansbach west of Nuremberg. Bartholomæus Dietwar, pastor in Kitzingen, gives us a glimpse of the health issues occasioned by the 1632 convergence of armies on their territory. Not only was Kitzingen overcrowded with foreigners and suffering from hunger, but the starved army brought pestilence into town.[137] The spiritual care of the many sick lay in the hands of only one minister and one chaplain, who quickly fell ill and died. Dietwar, asked to assist, recorded the extent of the loss and the progressive deterioration of burial practices. That year 623 persons were buried with the proper procedure, but in 1634, when the plague hit, not all dead could be buried with a procession.[138]

Brandenburg-Ansbach also provides an example of what the spiritual care during an epidemic looked like. The consistory instructed that no one should be denied communion and confession, although these rites could be abbreviated. The minister should take care, however, not to sit too close to the confessing person. In general, pastors were to address the needs of the time in their sermons, especially by encouraging parishioners toward repentance and prayer so that this and other punishments, which they had brought upon themselves because of their many sins, could be averted. The consistory believed that sin was particularly rampant among the common people, who did not even recognize their swearing, drinking, overeating, and promiscuity as sins anymore. Those who died were to be buried "with ringing of the bell and hymns" (*mit Klang und Gesang*).[139] The consistory also warned the ministers

---

135 Porzelt, *Pest in Nürnberg*, 62–63.
136 Porzelt, *Pest in Nürnberg*, 146. Porzelt posits that the health problems in villages and smaller towns were more contained than in the crowded cities with their easy breeding ground for diseases.
137 LAELKB, MD Uffenheim, Akt. 95:67.
138 LAELKB, MD Uffenheim, Akt. 95:70, 77, 80, 84. In 1634, Dietwar buried 477 people.
139 LAELKB, MD Feuchtwangen, Misc. 153a, Kirchliche Verhältnisse während des 30 jähr. Krieges, 1. Verhalten bei Pest (1627), 1^{r-v}; MD Uffenheim, Akt. 95:70. Dietwar notes that, while he helped out in 1632, 2,884 people received communion in church and 345 were served the Eucharist in their houses.

not to abandon their congregations or to raise suspicions that they might leave, since this was the time when the ministers' loyalty and care were needed the most. No one was to be left without physical or spiritual nourishment.[140] Many ministers indeed stayed with their congregations and died performing their office. Their wives and children frequently died as well.[141]

Considering that the consistory expected its personnel to remain in their parishes and districts, it is only understandable that they released instructions on how their ministers could protect themselves as they cared for the sick. For example, "no one would blame them" if they first sent someone to the houses and rooms where the infected lay, so that the rooms could be cleaned and fumigated. The minister himself should be armed with prayer and some preservative, and certainly he should never go out on an empty stomach. In addition, he needed to have utter confidence that God will keep him safe. To be sure, "[God] was more likely to protect him while in office than if he would not do his duty out of fear, in which case he would be in much greater danger with regard to his body, soul, and conscience and would certainly perish, if the plague caught him after having left his post."[142]

Governments, then, were adamant about the practical side of the contagion's prevention and control. Yet, the confluence of epidemic and war burst all known parameters and showed up the inadequacy of well-established mechanisms, especially the blocking off of cities in an attempt to keep the contagion out. Neither refugees nor allied armies could be prevented from entering city gates, and the latter were the most common carriers of epidemic disease. With the massive influx of people and livestock, the rules of cleanliness became a farce. Failing to adhere to quarantine regulations both in the cities and the countryside posed another problem that was exacerbated by the chaos of war. Considering these adverse factors, the government could offer little more than Band-Aids during this unprecedented crisis.

3   Averting Spiritual Harm and Promoting a Decent Life

Political leaders in Franconia and Bavaria saw themselves as responsible not only for the populace's physical care, i.e., protecting the people against bodily harm, poverty, and disease; they also considered themselves accountable for

---

140   LAELKB, MD Feuchtwangen, Misc. 153a, 3^{r-v}.
141   LAELKB, MK Ansbach C, Spez. 14, Alfershausen, vol. 1, 1497–1653 (2 July 1633); Spcz. 883, Uffenheim Dekanat, vol. 1, 1491–1743 (17 March 1635).
142   LAELKB, MD Feuchtwangen, Misc. 153a, 2^{v}–3^{r}.

the spiritual and social well-being of their subjects. In early modern Europe, issues of social and political behavior were closely linked to religion. The traditionally accepted interpretation – as set down by the clergy and the governing authorities – understood war as a manifestation of God's punishment for people's sins. This view led to a flurry of activities on the part of rulers and churchmen to convince God of their heartfelt repentance and their marked improvement toward a more devout and disciplined way of life. Besides prayer hours, sermons, and other explicitly religious observances, governments kept reissuing mandates that addressed a host of religious and social practices, such as drinking, gambling, dancing, and swearing, to evoke in their subjects more pious and orderly behavior.

At the beginning of the war, Brandenburg-Ansbach's consistory directed the deans to call "the young and old [to] attend prayer and worship with greater devotion and zeal than heretofore" and to adjust the usual form of common prayer to the changing situation.[143] Similarly, Nuremberg's council asked its ministers to admonish their parishioners to fervent prayers and a god-pleasing way of life, such as moderation in food, drink, and clothes, as well as restraint from all lavishness and sensual pleasure. Secular music and dancing were prohibited, and weddings and funerals were restricted in size and length. The sharply reduced food supply during the war mandated a more modest frame for festivities, but the magistrates also hoped that a pious and austere lifestyle might appease God and avert further punishment.[144] In the hope of promoting social discipline and religious piety among the populace, Bavaria's elector, too, decreed numerous orders addressing these familiar issues.[145] Like his predecessors and neighbors, Maximilian also assumed ecclesiastical authority whenever he believed the clergy was not doing its job, which, in his estimation, was most of the time. His detailed instructions on religious duties concerned more adamant participation in church visits, catechism classes, special prayers, and almsgiving, as well as abstaining from cursing.[146]

In their attempts to delineate acceptable behavior, however, governments often ran into a wall concerning the execution of their directives. On one hand, the populace had its own ideas about life in these sad times. The authorities' repeated and increasingly forceful admonitions could not move the subjects to curb the little pleasure and comfort they had. Secular and ecclesiastical lords

---

143　LAELKB, MD Uffenheim, Akt. 38, 2 (18 July 1619), 1^{r-v}.
144　Soden, *Gustav Adolph*, 1:33, 320, 359, 421–22; 2:79, 506–7; 3:217–18.
145　SA M, B&R 60 B 1, 171^r, 93^v; B 3, 33^r; B 9, 4^r–6^r; RP (URS) 249, 288^v; 261/1, 196^r.
146　See, for example, StA M, KHHA, A 1725, 24 May 1631, 8 June 1642, 12 June 1645.

GOVERNMENTAL SUPPORT

responded to popular resistance regarding their initiatives with more decrees. Many of these renewed releases follow a pattern much like the 1628 decree of Nuremberg's council against blasphemy and swearing:

> The honorable council of ... Nuremberg ... in Christian consideration of its magisterial office, both in former and in recent years ... has made clear its abhorrence of the terrible, frightening sin of the damnable blasphemy, horrible swearing, and careless cursing through the proclamation and posting of sharp orders as well as the punishment of several found criminals. Consequently, it had justifiably hoped that all citizens, inhabitants, subjects, and associates of the city and in the countryside would pay proper attention to such well-meaning ordinance and would follow the same with due obedience. But with great displeasure the lordships have made the very painful discovery that many of the above-mentioned burghers and subjects have shamefully and wrongfully despised such fatherly admonition ...[147]

Ordinances often began with similar expressions of the governors' hope for a change of behavior among the populace. They then moved to frustration over the lack of the desired changes thereof and next repeated the old decree, sometimes with threats of harsher penalties and always with a reference to God's punishment in case of non-compliance. The repetition of the same and similar orders can have a number of meanings. In a still largely oral society, reiteration of a document was a way to establish its continued validity. Yet, the sense of exasperation conveyed in some of the passages, the increase in punishment, and testimonies from other literature underline that the authorities were largely unsuccessful in persuading the population to alter its ways, particularly in the countryside.[148]

Bavaria's elector did not have any better luck in getting through to his subjects, despite the fact that one could hardly find a more determined governor. Maximilian's often resented attempts to reach into every corner of local life and administration appear like the efforts of a control-obsessed ruler, and his actions could veer in this direction. He was particularly concerned about religious education for children and adults and did not accept the ministers' excuse for cancelling catechism class:

---

[147] StA N, Rst Nbg, M III, Nr. 471 (1 February 1628).
[148] On blasphemy and its ubiquity, see Schwerhoff, *Zungen wie Schwerter*.

> For some time now the clergy has excused itself regarding the neglected catechism class by pointing to the rough winter and to the fact that the children are too cold to walk this far. However, one needs to consider that the children- and catechism class is not only meant for the youth but also for those who are established, for the household, and for those associated with the house, who often need [religious] instruction even more than the children.[149]

Given the fact that most instruction ceased during the summer because every hand was required in the field, canceling the winter classes as well amounted, in essence, to no education at all. Maximilian tried to remove what he considered the major impediment to attending catechism class by prohibiting the popular winter games during instruction time.[150] Realizing, however, that vetoing play did little to persuade children of the value of religious instruction, the elector also decreed that churches should distribute devotional pictures, crosses, and pennies among the youth as positive inducement to come to class.[151]

As in many other areas of disciplining, Maximilian was frequently dissatisfied with the local authorities' failure to execute his orders regarding religious and secular education.[152] Increasingly, therefore, Maximilian relied on other bodies to achieve his goals. The growth of religious foundations under Maximilian is well known, particularly of the Jesuits, but the Capuchins' expansion in Bavaria surpassed even that of the Jesuits. The more disappointed the sovereign became with the inefficiency of his middle and lower officials, the more heavily he leaned on the religious orders, who became crucial agents in the realization of his educational and disciplinary program.[153]

For many local authorities, the conduct that so dismayed the elector simply reflected a traditional way of life and was not intended as a deliberate assault on God and morality. Maximilian, in contrast, could not accept that local authorities followed their own sense of justice rather than the electoral mandates. To him, these officers lacked an understanding of the larger religious, political, and social issues at stake and typically governed with an eye toward local interests and traditional practices. Whether justified or not,

---

149 SA M, B&R 60 B 2, 527^v–28^r (7 July 1631).
150 SA M, B&R 60 B 3, 26^r (16 December 1639).
151 SA M, B&R 60 B 2, 528^{r-v} (16 March 1639). The problem lay not only with children who were more interested in games than in religious instruction, nor with negligent heads of households, but with many ministers who also readily cancelled their classes. SA M, B&R 60 B 3, 18^{r-v} (27 September 1628).
152 SA M, B&R 60 B 9, 37^r; SA M, KHHA, A 1725, 1^r; StA M, RL, fasc. 33, 124, 88^v.
153 Bauerreiss, *Kirchengeschichte Bayerns*, 7:3, 6.

Maximilian believed that this kind of local justice and leadership contributed significantly to the problem of his disorderly territory and God's dissatisfaction with humanity. Indeed, the elector blamed the local administrators more often than the people for failing to establish good discipline. Sometimes, local clerks delayed publicizing the electoral mandates, and their governors ignored such negligence.[154] In 1643 Maximilian exclaimed that he had hoped "in these sad times" his instructions would eliminate the insults against God and the cause of their punishment. But since this had not happened, he commanded his district administrator to try harder:

> Thus we order you graciously and under threat of losing your office and of other punishment that you see to the observation of our earnest general mandate concerning dancing, gambling, drunkenness, swearing, and adultery; similarly that you admonish your subordinate administrators that they, by threat of punishment, do their duty with equal sincerity and apprehend the culprits so that they can be punished adequately.... And that you obediently report to us every quarter [of the year] on these issues.[155]

The elector firmly believed that the common people could not but fail if they were left to themselves or were given bad guidance. Good governors provided signposts and excellent examples for subjects to follow. In turn, Maximilian and the central authorities guided the lower-ranked authorities via mandates and ordinances. However, this chain of command and guidance did not always work.[156]

Maximilian's relentless oversight of his administrators was driven by his concern to uphold justice and fairness.[157] Economic and social standards had declined during the war. When Munich's *Rentmeister* visited the district Mainburg, he found its local economy (*Pollicey wesen*) in a dismal state due to the destruction of the war: "Since the people first have to get settled again at home, the control of weights and measures, of beer, bread, and meat has not been kept up." Maximilian admonished the regional authorities to recommence monitoring the economy's standards "so that the common poor man gets his money's worth."[158] If brewers and bakers overcharged their customers

---

154 StA M, RL, fasc. 33, 124, fol. 44ʳ.
155 StA M, FA Törring-Jettenbach, C 5, 1ʳ⁻ᵛ.
156 StA M, RL, fasc. 33, 124, 155ʳ⁻ᵛ.
157 For further discussion, see Haude, "Social Control and Social Justice."
158 StA M, RL, fasc. 33, 124, 8ʳ⁻ᵛ (1636).

or sold them deficient products, and the local authorities let these abuses go unpunished, then the commoners were the victims. Furthermore, exploitation could also be found among the clergy. During times of plague, some ministers not only overcharged their parishioners but also refused to serve them altogether if they could not pay in advance.[159]

During their visits throughout the district, the *Rentmeister* gathered indisputable evidence that the kind of leadership a village had determined whether a place was able to recuperate from the destruction of war or slide further into desolation. In the market town Geisenfeld, for example, the local economy had made very little progress: "It is evident that the burgomaster and the council are chiefly at fault here because they manage said economy and common weal badly, or because they do not exercise their governmental office. Instead they only concern themselves with their private affairs and neglect everything else."[160] In contrast, the market town Trosburg had "fine and well qualified people who kept a good eye on the local economy. Thus, the bakers, brewers, butchers, and other artisans are under close observation and are held to act responsibly."[161] Exemplary management and guidance could lead to economic prosperity, fairness, and justice as well as to pious and socially commendable living; the opposite could ruin a place.

Maximilian was not interested in promoting social mobility but in enabling a decent life according to one's station. When, due to the dearth of manual workers during the war, the day laborers were demanding higher pay and doing financially better than those of higher social rank, the central authorities intervened. Their concern was the strain on the local economy when day laborers began to demand outrageous pay. But there was also a clear message that everyone had his station, and that it would be unfair to the citizens if laborers began to capitalize on the war and buy up farms and houses to the detriment of those of higher rank who had been hit by the war.[162] Nevertheless, certain situations demanded that the burden be carried by everyone equally, as when contributions became necessary for building fortifications or quartering soldiers.[163] While the parity stipulated here was still always meant as a "proportional equality," disciplined behavior was expected of all.[164] One's birth or rank was no excuse for special exemptions from sumptuary laws, religious observance, and sexual propriety. Bavaria's elector also realized that the war with

---

159   AEM, Realia VN 351, 39^r (7 September 1648); HStA M, NL 84/12, 185 $^{r-v}$ (1 August 1646).
160   StA M, RL, fasc. 33, 124, 323^r.
161   StA M, RA Burghausen, B 13, 7^r (1640).
162   StA M, RA Burghausen, B 13, 65^{r-v}, 273^r.
163   StA M, RL, fasc. 33, 124, 255^v–56^r (1636); SA M, RSP (URS) 248, 244^v (22 July 1633).
164   SA M, RSP (URS) 248, 244^v.

its destructive consequences frequently became a reason for not following the prince's orders.¹⁶⁵ The local conditions were often so dismal that it was impossible to uphold the kind of government he envisioned. Whether by default or by design, the war became an excuse for resisting electoral orders.

Conflicts between authorities and a failure to execute orders also marked Brandenburg-Ansbach.¹⁶⁶ Much like in Bavaria, these issues were long-standing and concerned matters of local autonomy. For example, the government had difficulties enforcing its line of orthodoxy (adherence to the Formula of Concord) not only among the broader populace but also with its own arms of execution, and it chastised the deans for setting aside the princely directive and following their own judgment.¹⁶⁷ The demand of blind obedience could not have sat well with the deans, who understood themselves less as organs of a higher ruler than as authorities in their own right.¹⁶⁸

Discord is also evident between the central authorities and the local clergy. In several locations during the passage of troops and flights from the villages, ministers had reduced or called off the prayer hours. The displeased margrave and consistory charged that this had been done without sufficient cause. These dangerous times, they insisted, called for more rather than less prayer, both in church and at home.¹⁶⁹ Plainly, the consistory and its ministers had different views and approaches to the military situation. For the ministers, times were too dangerous to hold regularly prayer meetings, whereas for the consistory it was too dangerous *not* to hold them. For the parish clergy, practical considerations trumped religious ones.

In their search for consolation and protection, contemporaries – especially Catholics – leaned on sacred treasures.¹⁷⁰ Accounts are full of miraculous acts of holy sites and bodies, but the handling of these objects in the context of war also highlights Catholic authorities' complicated relationship to the protective strength of sacred pieces and images. Political and religious leaders frequently ordered the transfer of holy images to safer places and their subsequent return once the danger had passed. Such actions typically were to be conducted in

---

165 SA M, B&R 60 B 9, 37 (20 September 1636).
166 As a reminder, the margrave's court had put into place a consistory that oversaw deans, who in turn watched over the ministers in the parishes.
167 LAELKB, MD Uffenheim, Akt. 8, Älteste Visitationsakte 1528–1678; Nr. 118, 1ʳ (17 August 1618).
168 The consistory also would have liked to have seen a much more frequent, preferably yearly, visitation of their parishes. Both the resistance to providing specific information and the sluggishness with which the deans organized any visitation point to the fact that the middle authorities tried to avoid interference from the margraves or their executive body.
169 LAELKB, MD Uffenheim, Akt. 38; 38, 1ʳ (1646).
170 For further discussion, see Soergel, *Wondrous in His Saints*.

secret to avoid panic among the populace because such a move could alert the subjects to an approaching threat. The decisions to protect a holy image or relics from damage – rather than let the presumably magic powers of the sacred object protect a community or site – reveals an ambiguity and uncertainty regarding the protective powers of sacred objects. Then again, when no other protection was to be had, authorities tried to calm their subjects by pointing to the potency of such images.[171]

In conclusion, the discussion of governments' responses to the challenges of war showed a complex reality. Despite at times herculean efforts, authorities faced a crisis that by and large surpassed their capabilities. This was not consistently the case and not for all regions at the same time. Nuremberg in the 1620s was in considerably worse shape than Munich, and thus entered the 1630s much more weakened. But even for as engaged and forceful a governor as Maximilian, the confluence of armies, poverty, and pestilence proved too much to handle.

Expectations and responses differed depending on what was at stake. Governments' mandates to improve the populace's spiritual state saw little compliance from the subjects. In this religiously suffused time, averting spiritual harm was a priority for most governments, but central, middle, and local leaders, both secular and religious, as well as the general populace diverged on what was required to achieve it. This disparity in views underlies the poor execution of the many directives toward greater piety and discipline.

How is one to interpret the evidence of non-compliance from large parts of the population? Placing the responsibility wholly with the local and middle authorities, as Maximilian did, leaves the populace not only without fault, but, more importantly, without agency and concerns of their own. Instances of resistance are especially profuse where the orders related to social and religious practices. Even though all three locales were quite distinct in their governing structure and organs, they all faced strikingly similar problems. The rulers' disciplinary agenda was often far removed from the traditions and needs of their subjects. Local and regional administrators frequently assessed the situation on the ground much more accurately than did the central authorities. Consequently, not only peasants and townspeople ignored the mandates, but many local administrators and officers charged with executing the commands did as well.

Regarding the containment of epidemic diseases, the populace did not follow the authorities' directives as fully and as eagerly as required either. The flouting of quarantine regulations was nothing new and can be witnessed from

---

171   HStA M, KL, fasc. 450/12.

the first plague outbreak to our times. Such behavior was prompted by a combination of differing assessments of the situation's seriousness and prioritizing other issues. Especially during the deprivations of the war, economic benefits often outweighed health concerns.

Authorities could expect considerably stronger obedience from their subjects when the regulations pertained to matters of physical safety and protection of life and property. Here the interests of the government and the people converged, but it is also in this area that subjects were most dissatisfied with their rulers. Although troops could protect, they frequently generated poverty and violence. The populace looked toward their government for guidance and deliverance, but rarely received the kind of aid they needed. The directive to keep provisions for armies at a minimum did little to satiate the soldiers, nor was the advice to villages useful that they should be patient when one company after another quartered in one's territory. While unhelpful, these admonitions showed at least the governments' active involvement. Citizens, however, looked particularly unkindly on their leaders' quick retreat to safety during perilous situations. In 1643, after Bamberg had been seized thirteen times, the Jesuit chronicler saw its worst danger yet: "Enemy troops stood there, all eager for booty and full of bitterness." When the city's leadership fled to Forchheim, the helpless and despairing populace "cried that it was entirely abandoned and poured out its bitterness in loud moaning." With its government gone, the citizens felt deserted, rudderless, and unprotected.[172] The subjects' perceived lack of protection led to disillusionment, cynicism, and lack of trust in their government.

This lack of trust not only registered among the broader population; other contemporaries, too, unmistakably articulated their frustration with, and lack of faith in, political and military leaders regarding matters of trust and protection. These issues were extensively discussed in literary circles, such as the *Fruchtbringende Gesellschaft*.[173] Mathematician and astronomer-astrologer David Beineke, of Oranienburg north of Berlin, attests to the fraught

---

[172] Moreover, the broader populace saw their government not only shirking responsibility, namely protecting their subjects, but also claiming for themselves privileges – in this case a safe haven – which many citizens did not have. For a variety of reasons, political and religious leaders were often the first to withdraw. Maximilian, for example, spent the years during the first Swedish advance into Bavaria and during the pest epidemic, from 1632 until 1635, away from Munich and governed from one of his strongholds. He withdrew again when the Swedes returned toward the end of the war. Other governments did the same.

[173] For example, von dem Werder, *Friedens-Rede*. See also Herz, "Aufrichtigkeit, Vertrauen, Frieden."

relationship between rulers and ruled. A year after the German princes and the emperor signed the Peace of Prague (1635), Beineke published an "Astrological Consolation," in which he analyzed the situation in Germany prior to the peace agreement. In Beineke's assessment, the vital trust between rulers and their subjects had disappeared, but after the peace "I have no doubt that, from now on, the war in Germany and in Christendom will subside, and the good German trust (*Vertrawen*) among lords and subjects will blossom anew with happiness and joy."[174]

Beineke's prognosis proved premature, but, more importantly, his analysis of the situation before 1635 echoes the general populace's loss of trust in their authorities. Having been frequently disappointed when looking toward their government for safety, people came to the conclusion that they could expect little help from their leaders. Many contemporaries realized they had to help themselves if they wanted to survive. To these initiatives, we now turn.

---

174   Beineke, *Astrologische Trost Schrifft*, G[r]. The author saw his belief substantiated by astronomical observations. Beineke's writing belonged to the bestselling genre of recording calendars (*Schreibkalender*) and *Astrologica*, publications which people eagerly awaited and devoured.

CHAPTER 4

Coping with the Experiences of War

Political and religious authorities tried hard to manage the crises engendered by the war, but, as has become clear, their generally earnest efforts often fell short of what was needed or what their subjects expected of them. Many instead had to rely on their own resources, if they wanted to live through the war and its detrimental consequences. Their efforts spanned a wide spectrum of practical, physical, spiritual, and mental stratagems. This chapter explores the multifaceted means the weary populace employed to survive and make sense of life's challenges during this military conflict. The various strategies often overlap, but, for the purpose of analysis, they have been separated into distinct sections.

1 To Flee or Not to Flee

Flight counts among the most prevalent actions contemporaries took in the face of violence or rumors of a troop's approach, but this seemingly common response obscures the many variables that came into play with regard to making such a decision. Members of religious orders, the first group under examination, were set apart in various ways from the rest of the population. They lived behind walls and formed a community that could sustain them and in which they could find companionship. Typically, the communities were linked by a wider network of convents and monastic houses to which they could flee or to whom they could appeal for help. Many of them had resources and were the recipients of alms. Moreover, women *religiosi* often were under the "protection" of a male guardian – whatever that might mean. These conceivable advantages were counterbalanced by the more problematic consequences of their status: *religiosi* – in fact, the clergy in general – were frequently the target of violence. In some cases, they were suspected of being more affluent than their lay neighbors; in others, they were taken hostage to extract money from cities and communities. Confessional animosities added to the antagonism toward them. To avoid harassment, monks and nuns on their flights regularly disguised themselves and traveled in secular clothes. Even though monasteries were rarely well fortified, peasants flocked to shelter behind their walls, which turned monasteries into crowded and dangerous places. Subjects also stored their valuables and livestock there, and in doing so transformed monasteries into magnets for marauding soldiers. In short, *religiosi* and their homes were prime targets, and decisions about whether they should stay and face potential violence or flee to a presumably safer haven might determine whether they survived or not. But not everyone had choices. Some had the option to flee, while others did not. For some, the choice lay largely within their power to make; others depended on their superiors who decided which course to take.

The Augustinian nuns outside Eichstätt belonged to those who had a place of refuge. Indeed, they had several options, but they were dependent upon the say-so of their prince-bishop, which was usually communicated through their male guardian of the nearby Augustinian canons in Rebdorf. Every time soldiers were sighted in Eichstätt's vicinity, their guardian ordered Prioress Clara Staiger and her sisters to take their belongings and flee – first to Eichstätt, then to St. Willibald's Castle high above the city, and eventually to Ingolstadt (about 14 miles to the southeast as the crow flies). Still, the degree of protection that could be offered through this guardianship was not only limited but doubtful. Safety could not be guaranteed at any of these places. The enemy conquered both Eichstätt and its castle while the nuns resided there. Nor did Staiger always welcome their guardian's patronage because their flights were not of her own choosing. At times, she would have liked to hold out a little longer in her cloister, but a delay of their departure only earned them their guardian's displeasure.[1]

The Poor Clares of Munich's Angerkloster also had a place to which they could withdraw – in the Tyrol. They, too, were beholden to their male superior, who determined when they would flee, even though their abbess had a hand in choosing and securing a refuge.[2] Fear played a sizable role in the nuns' decision to flee. At first, a few were willing to stay behind to take care of the convent, but once the others were ready to depart, "everyone wanted to leave because they were so frightened." In the end, twelve agreed to remain in the Angerkloster, but seven of them quickly followed the other sisters into exile because of the Swedish menace.[3] Joined by the sisters of Munich's convents Ridler and Püttrich, the travelling community comprised over one hundred

---

1 *Klara Staigers Tagebuch*, 66, 62. For a map of Eichstätt, see p. 29.
2 Zwingler, *Klarissenkloster*, 938. During the Swedes' advance in 1632, the nuns' superior ordered them to be ready for the convoy. The nuns waited – packed and in the same clothes – for four days until he gave the signal.
3 Zwingler, *Klarissenkloster*, 1066.

women and their many escorts. It was difficult to find quarters for such a large group, let alone comfortable ones.⁴

In contrast to these various convents who opted for flight, others decided to remain in their cloister. The Benedictine nuns on the island Frauenchiemsee to the south for the most part did not leave their home. Their situation, however, was quite different in many ways from those of the women religious in Bamberg, Eichstätt, and other places who resided in the middle of military action and troop movement, while the Benedictines lay at its periphery. Their cloister, Frauenwörth, instead became a refuge for the many nuns who had lost their home or were trying to escape the war's violence and destruction. When the Swedes advanced on Bavaria in 1632, Frauenwörth took in the entire Cistercian convent of Niederschönenfeld (Augsburg Diocese), 46 Cistercian sisters of Seligenthal (Landshut; part of the Regensburg Diocese), and 36 Dominican nuns of the Swabian cloister Holzen.⁵ All in all, in 1632 the Benedictine nuns provided for 147 refugee women.⁶

Religious women also stayed in their cloister either because they had no good alternatives, or because, after considering all their options, they decided to remain at home. The Dominican nuns of Heiliggrab by Bamberg had few choices and braved the war mostly without resorting to flight.⁷ As their chronicler Maria Anna Junius tells it, while everyone else fled the scene, she and her sisters trusted in the mercy and assistance of Christ, their bridegroom, and stayed behind:

> The city was in such danger that the prince-bishop, the provost of the cathedral, the canons, the burgomaster, and many other citizens hastened to get to [fortified] Forchheim. They could not tell us enough about [the peril].... But as often as they told us about it, ... we poor, forsaken little orphans, who had no comfort except our beloved bridegroom Jesus, always relied upon his divine mercy and assistance. Although unspeakable fear and horror gripped us numerous times, still we trusted God's

---

4 Seven of the Poor Clares decided halfway to the Tyrol to return to Munich, which underlines the strains of the journey, but remarks from the abbess and the convent recorder also reveal problems because of the forced community with Ridler's and Püttrich's tertiary sisters. These did not abide as strictly to the rules (especially enclosure) as the Poor Clares, who declared they could have done without such sisters (Zwingler, *Klarissenkloster*, 1069).
5 Stalla, *Geschicht Buech*, VI.
6 Brockdorff, "Benediktinerinnenabtei," 378.
7 The Dominican convent fled briefly in 1643 (*Jesuitenchronik* in Weber, *Bamberg im dreißigjährigen Krieg*, 102).

benevolence and, urged by the Holy Spirit, stayed in our dear little cloister Heiligengrab.[8]

The nuns may well have trusted in God's mercy to protect them throughout their embattled years in the convent, but the reasons for remaining in their cloister were more complex than that. This passage depicting a group of nuns seemingly oblivious to the dangers around them and relying solely on their heavenly spouse was preceded by a narrative that suggests another mind-set. Junius' allusion to the sisters as "poor, forsaken little orphans" was not mere rhetoric. Different from the nuns of Mariastein, they had no direct male guardian other than the prince-bishop, Johann Georg Fuchs von Dornheim (r. 1623–1633). When the Dominican nuns of Heiliggrab first heard that the Swedes had taken nearby Königshofen and were likely to move on to Bamberg, they were deeply scared and made ready to flee but did not know where to go. News about violence against brothers and sisters in the vicinity frightened them anew. In their desperation, they turned to Bamberg's prince-bishop, who sat safely behind the walls of the fortress Forchheim, and asked him for advice about where they might go. When the bishop finally answered, counseling them to disperse throughout Bamberg in case of need, it gave them "little comfort." Besides suggesting a break-up of the convent's community and holding out the dubious safety of a city he had just fled, he offered no concrete assistance, no house where they might find refuge. Conferring among themselves what to do, the Catholic nuns decided to turn to the Protestant margravine of Bayreuth, Marie von Brandenburg-Bayreuth (1579–1649), and asked her for a *Salva Guardia* (a military guard). They reminded the margravine that she had been their benefactor in the past and expressed their hope that "she will not leave us poor sisters during this utmost military danger, since we live in great fear, especially as our poor little cloister is situated so far away from the city."[9] The margravine immediately showed the letter to her husband, Margrave Christian of Brandenburg-Bayreuth (1581–1655), whose eyes watered (*ihm gehen die Augen über*) because of his great pity for the Dominican nuns. Christian, one of the founders of the Protestant Union (1608) and an ally to the Swedes, promptly wrote to Gustavus Adolphus to plead their case. The margravine then tried to console the sisters and begged them to stay in their convent, but to make sure that no secular people took refuge there. If they followed her advice, they would have "no reason to be afraid something might happen to

---

8 Hümmer, ed., "Bamberg im Schweden-Kriege," 52:22 (8 December 1631).
9 Hümmer ed., "Bamberg im Schweden-Kriege," 52:15, 17. For a map of Bamberg, see p. 31.

them."[10] Thus, only after the prince-bishop had failed to provide an alternative for the nuns and after their trusted – and, notably, Protestant – patron, Bayreuth's margravine, had strongly advised against leaving their convent, did Junius frame the sisters' stay in Heiliggrab in religious terms.[11]

When the Swedes took Bamberg in February 1632, the sisters were again torn as to whether they should leave their cloister or not. They did not fear death as much as "something else" – presumably rape and the loss of their honor.[12] In the end, however, they decided once again to trust in the mercy of their heavenly spouse, which was a good thing, since the expected military assistance from Bamberg never arrived.

In contrast, the Dominican nuns of St. Katharina in Augsburg represent a convent with options and the power to make its own decisions. This is certainly not unrelated to the fact that many of its members had ties to influential families in the city.[13] The convent's decision-making process, however, turned out to be an exasperating affair, and assessments of the situation changed constantly. The back and forth between the prioress, her convent, and a wide range of secular and religious authorities affords a close-up of the confusion, disbelief, shock, and uncertainty among the Catholic leaders when confronted with the Swedish advance in the early 1630s, and of their reluctant realization that their fortune was about to change. Exchanges range from convictions that all was still well to the slow recognition of potentially very bad outcomes, and the prioress was caught up in the leaders' attempts to find their way in the thicket of war.

When Gustavus Adolphus took Würzburg in 1631, Prioress Maria Kurz was anxious about what would happen next and how best to protect her convent. The nuns had heard that elsewhere many spirituals had fled, and the Swedes had taken hostage any nun they could find: "Therefore [Kurz] suffered the greatest fears, concerns, and doubts whether she should send her convent away or keep [everyone] together in the cloister."[14] As Gustavus Adolphus slowly

---

10 Hümmer, ed., "Bamberg im Schweden-Kriege," 52:20.
11 Hümmer, ed., "Bamberg im Schweden-Kriege," 52:32, 118. Part of the motive behind Junius' repeated references to this issue may have been to justify the nuns' decision to stay in their cloister, since, at various times throughout her chronicle, she mentions others who either had complimented them on staying in Heiliggrab or had recommended that they do so.
12 Hümmer, ed., "Bamberg im Schweden-Kriege," 52:33. For a discussion of rape, see p. 41–43.
13 Bernd Roeck, *Eine Stadt in Krieg und Frieden*, 91. Roeck calls St. Katharina a "premium care facility for the nobility" (*Versorgungsinstitut für den Adel*), which assesses St. Katharina solely from the perspective of the heads of the noble families, not the viewpoint of the women religious residing inside the cloister.
14 DA A, HS 97, 2^r.

closed in on Augsburg, the prioress repeatedly turned to the city's secular and religious leaders for guidance, but their advice for the convent kept changing.[15] First they counseled Kurz to take *all* her nuns to the Tyrol (no one should stay behind!). More than the women's lives, the leaders feared for the nuns' honor.[16] Accordingly, Prioress Kurz made every effort to find a refuge in the Tyrol that was large enough to house the entire convent.[17] In the meantime, however, Augsburg's political leaders advised her to take the sisters to Munich. This suggestion was founded on the conviction that Bavaria was safe, since Elector Maximilian would not let anything happen to it. The religious advisors did not think Bavaria in danger either because no one would let the Swedish king advance this far. But, if it happened after all, "which God may prevent mercifully," Munich and Bavaria were no safer than Augsburg. In this case, the counselors hoped that an accord with the occupiers would ensure their protection. In the end, their father provincial recommended that they stay in Augsburg, since it would place a heavy burden on the prioress to sustain her large convent in exile for a potentially very long time.[18]

The question of flight, however, came up again in early 1632 when rumors circulated that the Swedes were about to take Augsburg. The sisters' religious fathers advised that the women "should absolutely not abandon the cloister entirely but instead leave at least fourteen persons behind for the cloister's protection so that it would not be destroyed entirely by the heretics."[19]

When reliable news (*unfehlbare Zeitung*) arrived in late June 1632 that Gustavus Adolphus had taken Nuremberg and was headed toward Augsburg, the distressed prioress appealed once again to the city's and the convent's administrators and was told that they should all stay.[20] The next communication from Munich described Bavaria as in great danger, but the sisters'

---

15 On Augsburg during the Thirty Years' War, see Roeck, *Eine Stadt in Krieg und Frieden*.
16 DA A, HS 97, 2^{r-v}. As discussed above, rape was rarely mentioned directly.
17 The convent counted 42 women – 31 nuns and 11 lay sisters, plus six Dominican nuns from the convent St. Markus (also called "Marx") in Würzburg, who had sought refuge in Augsburg.
18 DA A, HS 97, 2^v–3^v. In addition, several sisters had relatives in Augsburg and could stay with them. The father provincial told them, however, that their sacred treasure should be sent to Munich.
19 DA A, HS 97, 4^v–5^v. Of the 42 sisters, 29 women agreed to remain. Besides several leaders, 12 older and younger nuns and all 11 lay sisters stayed. The others, who "were quite frightened and of a timid nature and did not want to trust themselves to endure such danger and misery," begged their friends to take them, whether these remained in Augsburg or not.
20 DA A, HS 97, 5^v–6^v. Kurz was shrewd enough to ask for this advice in writing in case things went badly, and no one remembered that they had counseled the prioress to remain in Augsburg.

counselors stuck with their advice that the convent stay because, once the city was taken by accord, the nuns would not have anything to fear. On Easter Day, finally, there was no more escaping the reality: the Swedes had surrounded the city on three sides. The prioress gathered her charges around her, told them the enemy had taken the city, and asked for their decisions regarding staying or leaving. Kurz presented her nuns with several reasons why it was beneficial to remain in the cloister: first, it was advisable to heed the counsel of their administrators, since if those who left the cloister should fall on hard times, they might not expect any help since they had acted against the guidance of "judicious people."[21] More than the authority and wisdom of their political and spiritual leaders, the prioress counted on the persuasiveness of the convent's own history to convince the sisters to stay:

> Although she could not hold back anyone, she nevertheless advised us out of motherly love that we should stay steadfast and think about the example of our most honorable mothers and sisters, who lived in this cloister at the time of the Lutheran heresy [*Lutherey*], and who had preserved the entire cloister with their steadfastness, despite the fact that all spirituals had been expelled from the city so that they did not have any confessors and had been robbed for many years of all their holy sacraments.[22]

Not unlike their own situation, a hundred years earlier most *religiosi* in Augsburg had fled, while St. Katharina's nuns had remained in their cloister. The prioress did not downplay the situation in 1632 and predicted that those who dared to stay could expect not only the deprivations and troubles of their forebears, but also "much hunger, sorrow, fright, and other kinds of misery." Still, she believed that such and more challenges could be borne with God's help.[23]

These are the broad outlines of the entangled consultations on whether the convent ought to flee or not. It shows the tension between a Catholic leadership who, after more than a dozen years of being victorious, had difficulties coming to terms with the altered political and religious landscape, and the prioress' fundamental sense of vulnerability that finds its greatest inspiration in the past courage of their predecessors and their best hope in the protection of God. Augsburg's leadership surrendered with an accord, and next we see Prioress Kurz negotiating with the Swedes to protect her convent – and so the

---

21   DA A, HS 97, 7ʳ–8ᵛ, 9ᵛ. The requested written advice had come on Maundy Thursday.
22   DA A, HS 97, 10ʳ.
23   DA A, HS 97, 10ʳ⁻ᵛ.

sisters (or at least most of them) must have decided to remain. Intriguingly, however – and in contrast to the Augustinian nuns of Mariastein and the Poor Clares of the Angerkloster – despite the eventual pressure on the sisters to stay, in Augsburg the decision lay with the Dominican nuns.

Even though Augsburg's Convent of St. Katharina lay in the line of troop movement, it was at least positioned inside the city. The Capuchins of Landshut, however, were in a more precarious situation, because their monastery was located outside Landshut's city walls. When the Swedes under Bernhard of Saxe-Weimar took Landshut in July 1634, the friars, too, had to decide whether they should stay in their cloister or flee into the city.[24] Their discussion reflects the concerns voiced by many religious: some regarded the retaining of the *community* as the highest priority, while for others the continued viability of the *cloister* was of the utmost importance, which meant that some had to stay behind to maintain its economy. After listening to all suggestions, the Capuchins' guardian, Friar Stanislaus, decided it was best that the entire community move to the city and reside at the vicarage of St. Jobst, from which the priest had already fled. The chronicler, Melchior von Straubing, explained that there were many reasons for their removal, but one in particular: if the city were taken by storm, they – being located outside the city walls – would be the first victims, although in his narrative he is more worried about the loss of their liturgical equipment than of their lives. If they moved into the city, Melchior argued, they could not only save their paraphernalia, but also be of use to the distressed citizenry by administering the sacraments, giving sermons, and reading masses. He added in a critical tone that many clergy had beaten an early retreat (*dann gar viel der Geistlichen sich bey Zeiten aus dem Staube gemacht haben*).[25]

The Benedictine Veit Höser provides another perspective on the decision whether and where to flee. His testimony is a true *Peregrinatio*, in which the abbot rarely found any peace, except at the very end of his wanderings in winter 1634 in Landshut, where he hid for a couple of months. Yet, he admits that the reason for his restless life was his decision to stay close to his abbey, to keep an eye on the events there and in the vicinity, and to be able to quickly return should the opportunity present itself. Had he been willing to flee further – to Passau or Austria, for example, like some of his brethren – his life would have been calmer. Instead he trekked up and down the mountains to various places

---

24   This was the second occupation; the first occurred in 1632 under Gustavus Adolphus. StBM, Cgm 2943, 2^r–3^r.
25   StBM, Cgm 2943, 3^{r-v}. Melchior von Straubing was not in a leadership position but most likely held an administrative position, such as that of a record keeper.

connected with the abbey and returned to Oberalteich or nearby as soon as he got the chance. Thus, he was caught in the Swedish embrace when this otherwise fairly realistic observer of the war's events misread the situation and returned only to be encircled by the Weimarers. His responsibility as the leader of the abbey may have played a role in this decision, as may have his strong relationship with the Benedictine monastery, which he called not only his home but his "mother."[26] Only after he left the proximity of the abbey did he describe himself as exiled and banned. The villagers he observed as he traversed Oberalteich's region, however, who were forced to leave their home for foreign lands, he describes as "exiled."[27]

Veit Höser's testimony furthermore suggests that the choice between flight and staying concerned not only the issue of physical safety but also that of correct moral and spiritual behavior. During his respite in Landshut after six weeks of flight, he sent a letter to his fellow pater, P. Franziskus Höfli, headmaster of the cloister's school:

> Do not believe, my beloved brother, please do not believe that I plunged without reflection, carelessly into this dangerous whirlpool. I have to admit to you I did not want to abscond with the first brethren who were forced to flee, and neither did I want to remain with the very last in the midst of the enemies. As eyewitness I saw both, saw how the first fled and how the last persevered. I endured with the last, but I was not among the very last, who suffered death at the hands of the Swedes and as blood witnesses have proven their persistence until the end. Blushing with shame I have to admit this since it is the duty of the perfect shepherd to sacrifice his soul for his flock. But, alas! I am no perfect shepherd; I would be satisfied if, in the last degree, I were found a little just.[28]

Here the respected reformer and courageous refugee acknowledged the limits of his own strengths and commitment. He regarded it as his Christian responsibility, especially as a religious leader, to hold out to the last, and it pained him that he fell short of this mark.

Decisions among religious leaders over whether to flee or stay home were also informed by the desire not to be taken hostage and in doing so become a financial burden to the cloister. When the chronicler of the Jesuit College describes the flight of the *religiosi* from the monasteries around Bamberg, he

---

26 Sigl, *Veit Hösers Kriegstagebuch*, 103.
27 Sigl, *Veit Hösers Kriegstagebuch*, 93–94.
28 Sigl, *Veit Hösers Kriegstagebuch*, 167 (24 February 1634).

relates that, to the north, the Benedictine abbot of Banz by Bad Staffelstein was "a bit more trusting" and believed he could remain in his cloister. The result was that he not only had to pay a hefty ransom (4,000 reichsthaler in old gold coins) but also sign over the cloister's estates.[29] This concern, among others, also prompted political leaders and other eminent lay people to depart.

The flight of those in leading positions during times of crisis was a thorny issue. Several authors underlined that the leadership was often the first to flee. Authorities tried to set guidelines for who was allowed to withdraw. Nuremberg, for example, was concerned that essential administrators remain in the city to forestall chaos. Certain officers, including the "old lords," were forbidden to leave the city. The reality, nevertheless, often looked quite different, and during an epidemic only a much reduced governing body was available on location. Other, less important offices were simply closed during an outbreak.

During an epidemic, one of the pieces of advice was to flee early, to run far, and to remain away as long as possible. But what of the many people who held posts of some responsibility, such as administrators, the clergy, professors, etc.? When in October 1634 the pestilence reigned in Old Bavaria and in Munich, Elector Maximilian and his princely household, who had already moved to Braunau, ordered the councilors in Munich to relocate to Rosenheim. Ecclesiastical authorities, in contrast, admonished the clergy to remain with their flock. Experts were split about the proper behavior: while physicians counseled in favor of retreat, the clergy advised against it. Since pestilence was a sign of God's judgment, they argued, flight was useless.[30]

Fleeing to elude pestilence was a fairly good option only for the better-off members of the population. Nevertheless, flights were common among the general populace as well, but the graphic descriptions of the Benedictines Höser and Friesenegger underline that this was usually a desperate choice. On his own journey to Weilheim and Polling, Friesenegger observed the misery of the refugees he encountered:

> [I] saw things that were barely endurable. I saw children, of whom each carried weepingly its package; mothers who lugged several children – two on the back and one in their arms; men who laboriously pulled their

---

29   *Jesuitenchronik* in Weber, *Bamberg im dreißigjährigen Krieg*, 36–37 (1632).
30   The question of whether one was allowed to flee in such a situation had famously been discussed by Martin Luther in 1527, and many referred to his treatment of the matter. While Martin Luther's treatise "Ob man vor dem Sterben fliehen möge" ("Whether one may flee death," 1527) did not forbid flight but valued staying behind as morally superior, his colleague Andreas Osiander ("Wie und wohin ein Christ die grausame Plag der pestilenz fliehen soll"; "How and whereto a Christian should flee the gruesome plague of pestilence," 1533) condemned it sharply.

carts loaded with clothes, provisions, the sick, and children, or who drove one or several animals ahead of them.... When I asked where they were headed (and I only asked once; pain suppressed further questions), they gave the answer: where God and our guardian angel will lead us – I don't know yet.[31]

While Friesenegger had both a place of exile and a most comfortable one, peasants had to contend with overcrowded cities or forests at best. Munich's streets were so congested with refugees that "some are driven away from the gates with beatings, and others – which is even more shameful – had to buy their entry with money." Every community on his further flight to Tegernsee was filled with wretched refugees, who hoped for safety in the Alps only to find ice-cold winter.[32]

For the majority of the populace, then, flights implied more profound dangers and hardships. Besides the fact that most of them had few options and resources, they were also disadvantaged regarding another crucial aid: access to reliable news and information.

2   News and Information

Being informed counted foremost among the ways of circumventing the war's damaging impact. Political correspondences and autobiographical accounts continually underscore the importance of obtaining information about the military situation, and that such information might save lives. This crucial precondition for monitoring the war also imparted some sense – however limited – of being in control of the situation.

The Thirty Years' War took place during a veritable "communications revolution" of the early modern era.[33] The arc of its evolution can be traced from the invention of the printing press in the West in the mid-1400s, to the explosion of quickly produced pamphlets and broadsheets during the early Reformation era, the first printed weekly newspapers at the beginning of the 1600s, the daily printed newspapers at mid-century, and the growing role of news reports in media, such as the *Theatrum Europaeum*, *Schreibkalender* (recording calendars or almanacs), and historical novels.[34] These developments toward making

---

31   Friesenegger, *Tagebuch*, 141.
32   Friesenegger, *Tagebuch*, 141–42, 150, 158.
33   See Behringer, *Im Zeichen des Merkur*.
34   On historical novels (*Geschichtsromane*), see particularly Williams, *Mediating Culture*.

more information available were accompanied by more concerted efforts at organizing such knowledge.[35]

Within this ever-expanding media landscape, the Thirty Years' War represented a major news and communications event.[36] Political and religious parties used the media to deride their opponents and promote their own positions. The vivid war scenes and horrid conditions of life provided ample material. Propaganda and dramatic settings, however, were not the only forces driving the surge in news publications. Everyone either involved in or affected by the war, from government official to peasant, was in grave need of information to plan the next move.

To comprehend how people learned about the war in general and the approach of an army in particular, one needs to understand the transmission of news and the complex systems of communication with its manifold forms of communication during this period. In its earliest form, well before the first printed or even handwritten newspaper, *Zeitung(en)* simply referred to "tidings" or "news." This early understanding of *Zeitung* as a passing on of information – regardless of the channel through which news was being transmitted, whether written, printed, or oral – is a reminder that people found multiple ways to convey news and keep informed, and that any analysis needs to address this complex mixture of communication conduits.

The first weekly newspaper had been printed only a few years prior to the war's outbreak.[37] These early printed papers largely refrained from manipulating the news and let the readers form their own opinions.[38] From its beginning, the periodic paper was a great success, mostly because it grew out of and incorporated elements of several existing forms of media, with which people were already familiar. The broad spectrum of news writings included

---

35 See Randolph Head's work, esp. *Making Archives in Early Modern Europe*, and Schock et al., eds., *Dimensions*.

36 Göran Rystad speaks of a "breakthrough in modern propaganda" during the Thirty Years' War (*Kriegsnachrichten*, 3). On the media during the Thirty Years' War, see esp. Barton, *Informationsbedürfnis*; Behringer, "Veränderung der Raum-Zeit-Relation"; Beller, *Propaganda*; Grünbaum, *Über die Publizistik*; Hitzigrath, *Publizistik des Prager Friedens*; and Wolkan, "Politische Karikaturen."

37 The only two extant newspapers are from 1609, but from references in their text it is clear these were not the first issues, and the likely date of the first newspaper is 1605. Bücher, *Gesammelte Aufsätze*, 13, 70; Barton, *Informationsbedürfnis*, 5.

38 Schröder, "Origins," 146. Schröder posits that the early printed newspaper with its "concept of an up-to-date and periodical chronicle, concerned with showing the everyday functions of politics" to "as many people as possible," is the precursor of our "modern communications medium." It was "at once true to reality, empirical, fact-oriented, and non-patronizing." See also his detailed study, *Die ersten Zeitungen*.

pamphlets, broadsheets, *Newe Zeitungen*, monthly communiqués, half-yearly reports at fairs, and handwritten newspapers.[39] Much as they had during the early Reformation, pamphlets and broadsheets (one-page leaflets) played a significant role during the Thirty Years' War, and could come in either a polemical and tendentious form or one that was fairly objective, as in the matter-of-fact style of military intelligence. No other medium reached the general populace as effectively as the broadsheet, whose production peaked around the events of the uprising in Bohemia and the time of Gustavus Adolphus.[40] *Newe Zeitungen*, sporadic publications about a spectacular event, were, like the broadsheets, among the most common and widely read news media. The *Newe Zeitung* addressed the topics that stirred society, from political and religious convictions to personal suffering.[41]

The weekly newspaper, first handwritten and then eventually printed, grew out of several earlier forms of writings. In time, merchants exchanging information on commerce also reported on political and social events, since these had an impact on their business transactions. Scholars, princes, and administrators were also connected through a network of correspondents. This exchange of news, at first sporadic, developed into a regular transmission of information well beyond its original confines. Besides adding a few sentences about world affairs at the end of a personal letter, writers also enclosed separate little notes, "*Zeitungen*," in their communiqués.[42] The scope of these good and bad tidings

---

39   For some of the pertinent literature, see Brednich, *Liedpublizistik*; Bücher, *Gesammelte Aufsätze*; Coupe, *German Illustrated Broadsheet*; Fischer, *Die ältesten Zeitungen*; Groth, *Zeitung*; Harms et al., eds., *Illustrierte Flugblätter*; Paas, ed., *German Political Broadsheet*, vols. 2–3; Wang, "Illustrierte Flugblätter."

40   Schilling, *Bildpublizistik*, 166. For a discussion of broadsheets regarding these events, see Pfeffer, *Flugschriften*.

41   Bücher, *Gesammelte Aufsätze zur Zeitungskunde*, 8–9. Karl Bücher contends *Newe Zeitungen* not only reflected public opinion, they formed it.

42   Princely courts and trading centers maintained and paid correspondents in the big cities that counted as centers of information, and these sent their reports to their commissioner. The intelligence was frequently copied and sent elsewhere. Out of these correspondences grew the *Meßrelationen* (reports ahead of fairs), the *Monatsblätter* (monthly papers), the handwritten weekly newspapers, and, eventually, the printed weekly newspaper. Although *Meßrelationen* were published periodically (two to three times a year just prior to fairs), they lacked the up-to-date quality of later regular newspapers. Still their style of reporting and arranging the news foreshadowed that of the later periodicals. The *Monatsblatt* – the oldest one in existence dates from 1597 – was similarly arranged to the *Meßrelation* and probably took its information from correspondences, much like the *Newe Zeitungen* (Lindemann, *Deutsche Presse*, 1:81–85).

was impressive in its international reach.[43] By the early seventeenth century, all of Western Europe was connected by a system of locales that acted as crossroads for news, and a network for the transmission of news via messengers was in place.

These networks, however, were not enough; other conditions had to be right for a printed weekly paper to be a success. Two technological advancements – the press with movable letters and the invention of a mill (*Mahlwerk*), the so-called *Holländer* – provided a faster and cheaper method of paper production.[44] Additionally, the initial publication and distribution of the printed newspapers were intricately connected with the beginnings of the postal system.[45] And there had to be a desire for a printed periodical among the populace so that the paper could be a profitable business. All these conditions were in place by the beginning of the seventeenth century.[46]

The form of the printed newspaper emulated the handwritten paper exactly. Like the earlier version, it listed the news entries with the places from which they hailed as headings, together with the date when the news was sent. There is no discernible order. The paper might start with an entry from Augsburg, follow with news from other places, and then add another piece of news from Augsburg. Evidently, news was copied as it came in, with few alterations or comments.[47]

---

43 By 1586 these handwritten newspapers provided weekly reports of news from Rome, Venice, Antwerp, Cologne, Paris, Strasbourg, Lyon, and other places. The regular character of the news releases reveals that they came from news agencies. This also explains why news from Antwerp or Rome was not limited to information about the place but provided news from other countries as well (Opel, *Anfänge der deutschen Zeitungspresse*, 10–12, 23–24).

44 Lindemann, *Deutsche Presse*, 1:22, 26.

45 Opel, *Anfänge der deutschen Zeitungspresse*, 1.

46 Newspaper publishers commented on the great desire for news. Publisher Lucas Schultes noted that it is the nature of humankind to find special pleasure in learning about news (Opel, *Anfänge der deutschen Zeitungspresse*, 164).

47 Often the printed papers were simply copied from the written, with some publishers issuing both printed and handwritten papers. Besides the regular printed newspapers, irregular papers or *Extrablätter*, were printed with news that had not made it into the ordinary weekly paper. Frankfurt with its book fair was the main intersection for these handwritten and printed papers. For various reasons, the handwritten paper persisted alongside the printed and other forms of the daily press until well into the eighteenth century. Because handwritten newspapers were less exposed to censorship, they continued to have an advantage over printed newsletters. In general, readers could find more information in written than in printed newspapers. Moreover, during the transition period from scribal to print culture, readers were suspicious of printed newspapers, which in some cases led to the deceptive strategy of printing newspapers in handwritten characters.

The new genre of printed weekly newspapers, written in a compact, concise telegraph style unusual for the period, focused on military and court news, while giving much less space to natural disasters or wondrous occurrences than did the written newspapers. The former explicitly wanted to offer objective and impartial reports – an intention that could be gleaned even from their titles, as in *Unparteiische Zeitung* ("Impartial Newspaper"). Objectivity was also many readers' desire; they demanded unbiased reports so they could draw their own conclusions based on facts rather than on the author's coloring, speculations, comments, and embellishments.[48] Newspaper editors as a rule did not emulate some of the more tendentious daily press, such as the "Laudatory and Triumphal Song about the unexpected, terrible, and magnificent battle, in which the imperial-Bavarian army on the 7th day of September in the year 1631 was chivalrously defeated and driven from the field," a piece dedicated to Gustavus Adolphus.[49] They aimed to offer facts, not conjectures. When newspaper writers were confronted with differing interpretations of an uncertain situation, they presented the range of possibilities: "It is still unknown where this army will turn next. Several say that they are supposed to go and meet with the Danes, others counter that they will make their way through the bishopric Münster. Time will tell."[50] Some news was confirmed twice, particularly when the matter was weighty. If the writers had unconfirmed news, they expressed such ambiguity through their choice of language: "6000 Scotsman *are supposed to* arrive in Holland."[51] The *Novellanten* (newspaper writers) admitted and pointed out uncertainties or lack of information rather than filling in the blanks. One paper declared: "[Mansfeld's] intention cannot be fathomed," or "from Sweden, Courland, or Lower Saxony we know of nothing certain."[52] This common practice of reporting the lack of confirmed information indicates people must have been aware that writers listed news from places according to a geographic sequence. Furthermore, readers expected to see this order maintained in the paper, no matter whether anything newsworthy happened at a location.[53]

Behind all these features is discernible a sense of professional pride that came with this new medium and its claims. Most respectable newspaper

---

48   Opel, *Anfänge der deutschen Zeitungspresse*, 39–40, 139, 143–46.
49   "Leipziger Lobgesang."
50   "Gründlicher vnd Warhafftiger Bericht," (1625).
51   "Andere Wöchentliche Zeitung," (1625) (my emphasis).
52   "Gründlicher vnd Warhafftiger Bericht." Courland (*Churland*) was a duchy in the Baltic region, which from 1569 to 1726 was subject to the king of Poland.
53   If the paper ran out of space, the print size of the entries would become smaller and smaller.

writers found it beneath their honor to print unauthenticated or made-up news in their papers.[54] While interpretative comments were rare, subjective elements, such as a negative comment on the opposing party, nevertheless crept into the periodicals.[55] These "add-ons" likely reflected a shared sentiment among the readership. Newspaper writers also frequently openly sided with a particular confessional party. When the "Mercurij Ordinari Zeitung" of 1632 reported that the Catholic Count Tilly was saved in Bamberg "by the grace of God," the story obviously came from a Catholic supporter. Impartiality was also limited by the fact that Catholic newspapers typically had their sources in Catholic locales (the same was true for the Protestants and their information centers), which likely led to a selective rendition of news because of the partial material.

Newspaper writers strove for accuracy and pertinence in their news, and writers and readers wanted the news hot off the press.[56] Considering that news travelled by postal courier six to ten kilometers (roughly 4–6 miles) per hour depending on the terrain, one is reminded of how much more slowly people received word in the seventeenth century than today.[57] For its time, however, the weekly paper was a considerable achievement, and the *Novellanten* were proud of their timely news delivery. They liked to convey this sense of immediacy in their news coverage. One report from Franconia of 26 October reads: "*Just now someone comes in*, who departed on the 23rd this month at noon from Regensburg." Further below he relates that nothing much happened in Colmar and then interrupts this somewhat dull piece: "*This hour* our people inform us that the enemy is on the march."[58] Most likely the news had indeed just come in, and one can be certain that both writer and reader shared in the excitement about being as much on the edge of the news as one could have been at the time.

---

54 Opel, *Anfänge der deutschen Zeitungspresse*, 170. Newspaper writers resented the *Winkel- und Staudenschreiber* (furtive writers), who just picked up their news from the marketplace without bothering to check their reports.

55 For example, "it would be highly desirable if such vermin would leave, since they ruin the country to both sides of the Rhine entirely" ("Gründlicher vnd Warhafftiger Bericht").

56 Thomas Schröder has pointed to the problem of asynchronicity in newspapers. Current news was always already history, a fact that was even more true during the early phase of the printed paper than it is today. A substantial lag in time existed between the event, the report of the event, and the time the report was made available (*Die ersten Zeitungen*, 226–28).

57 Lindemann, *Deutsche Presse*, 1:30.

58 "Ordentliche Wochentliche Zeitung," 23–28 October (2–7 November) 1633 (my emphasis).

All systems of communication were intricately linked with one another: the printed newspaper depended on handwritten letters and notes and orally transmitted reports. Written and oral cultures further intersected, as peddlers read or sang the news to their largely illiterate audience and as oral networks spread the news further. In short, during the first half of the seventeenth century, the populace and its governments could draw on a broad variety of venues to learn about and spread the news. Oral transmission, writing, and printing were not separate but connected, overlapping spheres. Besides the news media, ideas and opinions about the war were communicated in street literature and erudite discourses. Contemporaries expressed their hope and despair in astrological writings and visions, poems and plays, sermons and treatises.

It is difficult to make precise statements about the readership during the Thirty Years' War. While book production increased during the first two decades of the seventeenth century, it fell off sharply by the late 1630s.[59] The amount of quickly produced daily literature, however, rose with each spectacular event during the war. Particularly the production of printed newspapers expanded during the 1630s but then dropped significantly by the early 1640s. The expansion of the daily press points to a broad readership. In addition to the information channels they already maintained, imperial and royal courts as well as the princely and civic leaders subscribed to several printed newspapers. Furthermore, the clergy, and particularly the members of religious orders, as well as the civic elite, counted among its avid readers. Reading circles (i.e., circles that subscribed to one or more newspapers collectively and passed the papers among their members) and oral communication of news (that had either been passed on by word of mouth or had been heard read) ensured that the news had a much farther reach.[60] Important information was also obtained at markets, where travelers and merchants were urged to share the

---

59 Rolf Engelsing assumes that literacy declined rather than improved during the seventeenth century. He notes that Germany's book production fell from 1,757 new titles in 1618 to 408 titles in 1637 (*Analphabetentum und Lektüre*, 42–44).

60 Bücher, *Gesammelte Aufsätze zur Zeitungskunde*, 76–77. Scholarship has established reading circles for the eighteenth century. While the extent of such reading communities for the early 1600s is still in need of research, it is evident that a similar practice holds for the early phase of the printed newspaper as well. A 1618 case shows the sharing of printed newspapers was practiced from its earliest beginnings. From the signed entries on the front page, one learns that the reading circles counted twelve to seventeen people, their members belonged to the civic elite, the paper circulated among them usually within a day, and the readers were displeased with the contents of the printed paper since they found less information in these than in the handwritten papers.

latest news, and at taverns, churches, pilgrimage sites, and other community centers. The well-known author of recording calendars, Hermann de Werve (1584–1656), judged merchants to be one of the safest sources for reliable news. In his 1640 *Schreibkalender* he advised his readers to get their information about the war from "the impartial and honest merchants, who generally have better and more certain news than the weekly newspapers (which often are studded with great lies)."[61]

Handwritten newspapers clearly had an advantage over the printed version with regard to censorship.[62] During the Thirty Years' War, the restricted views changed with the occupying or winning parties. Censorship also accounts for the odd phenomenon that printed newspapers reported anything from afar but imparted very little local news for fear of running into problems with the resident authorities. Besides this practical consideration, there was genuine interest in news from foreign parts.

The weekly newspaper experienced a great increase in numbers, especially from 1618 until 1635, with news focusing on the "Winterking," Friedrich V of the Palatinate, Tilly, Gustavus Adolphus, and Wallenstein. The 1630s saw a flood of newspaper foundations, especially under the Swedish king, who was keenly interested in up-to-date news and in using the weekly paper as a propaganda vehicle. Along his path through the German lands, he founded post offices or took over existing ones. Where the Swedes went, the Catholic papers disappeared, as in Munich when Gustavus entered the city in 1632. The mounting desolation and destruction of the war brought this period of expansion to an end by 1640. Moreover, while the war fed the hunger for news, it also interrupted its flow. Couriers were hindered, injured, or killed on their travels over dangerous roads, and their newspapers were intercepted. News agents could not obtain information because of the disruptions due to the war.[63]

Of the 34 printed periodic newspapers founded in the seventeenth century, 23 were Protestant and 11 Catholic. Thus, the newspaper continued the trend of the early Reformation period that showed Protestants more involved in new media opportunities than the Catholics.[64] Nuremberg, a center of information

---

61 HStA M, MS, Nr. 345, Diiij^r.
62 Authorities judged the written papers to be more dangerous than the printed because they could not regulate them as easily. One method of keeping control was for the city or governor to issue privileges, i.e., a monopoly for newspaper printing, to certain printers. In imperial cities, censorship lay in the hands of the city council or with a committee designated by the council (Lindemann, *Deutsche Presse*, 1:20, 52–62).
63 Lindemann, *Deutsche Presse*, 1:46.
64 Lindemann points to the tougher legal strictures. Vienna, for example, had a much more elaborate system of control than Hamburg (*Deutsche Presse*, 1:94–98).

during the previous century, had a newspaper office that produced weekly handwritten papers and continued to furnish much of the news, but, intriguingly, it did not generate its own printed newspaper until 1673. Munich, in contrast, printed newspapers from 1628 on.[65]

Contemporaries of the Thirty Years' War, then, had at their disposal a complex and multilayered news and communication system, and many made eager use of these channels. Being well informed became a primary coping strategy for a number of reasons. People needed information to make practical decisions: whether they should stay or flee, and, if the latter, in which direction; if the former, how to prepare for an approaching army, both pragmatically and mentally. This kind of information that kept track of up-to-the minute developments, however, was most readily available through oral communication networks and quickly dispatched letters because they transported news the fastest. Printed and written published reports were much slower in reaching their readership. During especially critical phases of the war, such as the Swedish Intervention, it became difficult to transport written communiqués. The "Mercurij Ordinari Zeitung" of 1632 articulated this problem clearly when it reported the news from Swedish occupied Würzburg (1 March). The city's (Catholic) inhabitants "beg sincerely that one would no longer write to them from foreign places because all letters are being confiscated, and they only came under suspicion because of it." Three days later the newswriter added:

> No one can now get through the country who does not have a passepartout (*Paßzettel*) from the Swedish war officers or Lutheran places. The messengers and travelers passing through, who come from Catholic locales, are considered spies and are taken captive, severely questioned, totally undressed, and examined thoroughly whether they do not, by any chance, carry a secret letter.[66]

The newspaper reported that the messengers risked life and limb. A woman had been caught with a letter in her socks, and as punishment both her ears were cut off.

Women likely played a prominent role in the messenger system. The Dominican nun, Maria Anna Junius, noted that in May 1632 the city of Kronach sent a woman to Bamberg with a letter requesting military assistance. The woman hid the letter on her body and then successfully passed it on to

---

65   Opel, *Anfänge der deutschen Zeitungspresse*, 159–70, 205–7, 212–13, 215, 217; Sporhan-Krempel, *Nürnberg als Nachrichtenzentrum*, 13; Lindemann, *Deutsche Presse*, 1:94.
66   "Mercurij Ordinari Zeitung," 2.

Bamberg's commanding officer.[67] Another female messenger was not so lucky. In January 1633, a woman was beaten with a rod because she carried many letters written by nobles about how they would take back Bamberg.[68] It made sense to employ women in the conveyance of letters and communications because their greater inconspicuousness made them more suitable agents than most men. The fact that neither of the intercepted women lost her life might also indicate that women were treated less harshly than men.[69]

People were largely dependent on oral communication – and whatever letters got through – to learn about any current military developments in their vicinity, and efforts to share intelligence were extensive. We know about Maximilian's constant demand for information, but regional authorities were just as eager for news. Johann Sigmund, Baron of Törring, begged his brother-in-law in 1637 to send him dependable information:

> Dear brother, I want to beseech you most dearly whether you can let me know just the tiniest bit how things stand now with the warfare (*Kriegswesen*), and especially with [Bernard] of [Saxe-] Weimar. Because yesterday our burgomaster Orttner came from Munich and said that *von Weimar* had crossed the Danube again with 13,000 men. Is this indeed so, or what other good news (*gueten Zeittungen*) do you have? Because in Passau there is already again such a clamor that I cannot tell you ...[70]

"Good" news (as in *guete Zeittungen*) could mean "encouraging," but it could also signify "solid," "trustworthy" updates. Indeed, it was crucial to obtain *reliable* news. The private correspondence of Susanne Vitzthum von Eggstätt, mother-in-law of Johann Maximilian, Count of Preysing, affords insight into the thirst for news and the desire to be "part of the conversation" about the military maneuvers, but it also highlights how uncertain and contradictory information often was. In a 1645 letter to her son-in-law, Susanne writes: "the current wartimes are getting more dangerous the longer they last. Moreover, [people] carry on such strange discourses that one does not know how one should conduct one's affairs or whether one should withdraw in the extreme case." She begs her son-in-law, who was Maximilian's privy councilor and treasurer, to advise her:

---

67 Hümmer, ed., "Bamberg im Schweden-Kriege," 52:77.
68 Hümmer, ed., "Bamberg im Schweden-Kriege," 52:102.
69 Some movements under stress, such as the Anabaptists, do show a more pronounced role for women as well as a generally more lenient punishment. See Haude, "Gender Roles."
70 StA M, FA Törring-Jettenbach, C5, 1^v–2^r. The brother-in-law's name is illegible.

[Did he think] I can remain here a while longer or that I should go elsewhere – I myself have no idea. We don't hear anything certain here or even enough so that I could arrange my affairs accordingly. Thus, I hope that the honorable son will not desert me, but will let me know in confidence and in a timely fashion whether there is anything to be feared on account of the French.[71]

In the ever more confusing conflict, dependable news was hard to come by. Some, like Susanne, had personal networks at their disposal to stay as up to date as possible. Cities and towns kept informed by dispatching any news they received via messenger to neighboring communes. In 1636 Nuremberg warned its surrounding towns and merchants about approaching Poles (*Polacken*) without being able to offer any military aid. At the same time, Lichtenau's overseer was advised "to observe the Polish troops closely, and whatever he shall learn he should report to Nuremberg by day or night."[72] The lists of expenditures for such couriers show how extensive this news network was.[73] Authorities also sent out scouts to obtain information, and some prioritized such expenditures over others, like for fortifications.[74]

Much like political leaders, merchants, and the nobility as well as cities and towns were connected through oral communications networks, so were the clergy. Those in religious orders frequently speak of reports that reached their ears, and sometimes they specify their sources. The chronicler of the Benedictine convent Hohenwart noted a nearby parish minister had sent them "news that the enemy was already at Schrobenhausen. Thus they were up all night, but God was merciful and another message arrived."[75] The narratives of the *religiosi* depict the constantly changing and often contradictory news about the military situation in which they found themselves, and they express a healthy distrust of letters and stories that reached them.[76] News came to Maurus Friesenegger of Andechs (1 October 1633) that the Swedes had inflicted much damage upon Stegen and Inning at the Ammersee, but then the message was revised to say that it was actually the imperial troops who were the culprits. During the night the brothers could see ever more firestorms in the area

---

71   StA M, HAA, 2, Akt. 489.
72   StA N, Rst Nbg, RK, B-Laden, Akt. 83, 8 (8–9 July 1636), 1^{r-v}. "Polacken" or "Polaggen" is a derogatory term for Poles.
73   Kroner, *Großhabersdorf*, 43; Kroner, *Ammerndorf*, 86; and Kroner, *Langenzenn*, 53.
74   HStA M, DK, Akt. 337, 40^r (17 Dec 1633).
75   StBM, HSS, Cgm 5727, 66 (1634).
76   Friesenegger, *Tagebuch*, 24: "Because one was often deceived by letters as well as narratives …"

toward Augsburg. They suspected that the Swedes – now that they were done with Bavaria – were intent on destroying everyplace else. The abbey's inhabitants and the people of Erling prepared once more for "the saddest flight," but before they left, they "wanted to seek the truth about the course of this affair" and sent a messenger to Stegen "to look into the matter."[77] In this way, before giving in to panic, they tried to find out the facts of a situation. The Poor Clares of Munich's Angerkloster acted similarly. On their arduous journey into exile in 1632, they were told that the *Köslberg* (Kesselberg) en route was already ruined. Instead of accepting the news, they sent their own envoi during the night "to learn the truth."[78]

Almost all the above accounts of the religious and those of many political administrators show this trait. People such as the Benedictine abbot, Veit Höser, tried to get confirmation of incoming reports so that they could take appropriate rather than blind, panicked action. Clearly, they were in a position to do so, but not everyone had access to either trustworthy information or the means to obtain it. Scouts needed horses and funds, and these were increasingly harder to come by as the war dragged on. Rumors of advancing troops therefore frequently set off large-scale flights of the peasant population to places they believed offered more protection than the open village. In the case of the countryside, this often meant the nearest city. Thus, the council and country judge of Dachau by Munich turned to Elector Maximilian for help when in 1648 the peasants once again fled to Dachau:

> Because of a general rumor in the countryside that there are another 2,000 horsemen heading this way across the Danube, without any knowledge as to where or which place they are going to approach, there has been tonight a great flight from the countryside into Dachau, which is increasing now at night to such an extent that it resembles once again a flight of the entire territory.[79]

While better information may have allowed the religious to prepare for their flight, the broader populace was often caught off-guard. Höser and others describe the chaotic conditions among fleeing villagers. Planning was rarely possible. People had to vacate their homes at once and abandon family, friends, and possessions. In his report to Maximilian, Dachau's country judge

---

77 Friesenegger, *Tagebuch*, 50.
78 Zwingler, *Klarissenkloster*, 1066.
79 HStA M, DK, Akt. 323, 22^r (19 April 1648).

underlines the extent to which the peasants were tossed about on the waves of conflicting rumors, but he himself has no firm news either:

> I just had a report from the district Esting that this night the Friedbergers ... have arrived in Esting with their sheep and animals. They claimed they had been warned from Augsburg that they should flee that same night because the armies have run into each other, and the right wing of the imperials has already been defeated.... Immediately afterwards others came who claimed that it was not so. Therefore, your electoral grace can well imagine what kind of confusion there is in the countryside with such uncertain reports.[80]

Even with better means and access to information, then, everyone was at the mercy of changing and uncertain news. Still, for the Benedictine Maurus Friesenegger, having no information was worse than misinformation.[81]

The longing for news, however, went beyond practical aspects of survival, such as decision making about one's next steps. Being informed was important for one's mind as well. As discussed earlier, the war often led to the separation of a community. In the case of the *religiosi*, many male and female monastics split into groups, one that fled while another kept their economy going at home. A host convent could not always accommodate the entire refugee contingent, and the nuns and monks were frequently separated even further – sometimes for years, as was the case with the Benedictine convent Holzen by Donauwörth in Augsburg's diocese.[82] Yearning to know how each of them was faring, letters and messengers were sent back and forth to apprise the other party of their lives either in exile or at home. When Sister Anna Frölich of the Poor Clares in Munich had to flee with a large contingent of her convent, she could not wait to hear about what was going on at home. In her correspondence with the Poor Clares' housekeeper back in Munich, Frölich begged for information, and not only of the convent but also of the larger community and the city.[83] Even though she lived in an enclosed convent, what happened to Munich and Bavaria affected her on a practical and emotional level: this was her home, her *Heimat*. Other communities – familial, rural, or civic – were disrupted by military aggression as well, and here, too, keeping up with the war's developments was one way of learning something about the others' fortunes.

---

80 HStA M, DK, Akt. 323, 25ʳ (19 April 1648).
81 Friesenegger, *Tagebuch*, 117.
82 See the discussion above Chapter 2.2.
83 Zwingler, *Klarissenkloster*, 1071.

Naturally each group tried to discover via newspapers and other reports how military developments were affecting those from whom they were separated.

People kept up with the news about the war for another vital reason: being informed represented an important way to get a handle on the catastrophe of war – mentally and psychologically. The periodic newspaper contributed to a sense of time as regular, linear, and predictable.[84] Moreover, the regularity of the printed and written newspaper also conveyed to its readers a sense of control and manageability of reality. The weekly, dependable news reports introduced a sense of order, however ephemeral, to the chaotic times of war – something the oral and daily communications that kept overtaking and invalidating one another could not.

Contemporaries were not interested only in receiving news; the *literati* also reproduced such information extensively in their writings. Far from simply copying detailed descriptions about military leaders, strategies, battles, and sieges, male and female authors also commented unreservedly on the war and frequently assessed its causes and outcomes realistically. Both knowing and commenting on the military situation could convey a certain sense of power, since, rather than giving in passively to the whims and commands of others, these men and women engaged with what was happening by applying their knowledge and making a judgment.

The *religiosi* provide a good example in this regard. Contrary to what one might imagine, their seclusion did not make them oblivious or indifferent concerning what was going on in the world. Male and female religious frequently describe the military developments of the war, which means that, whether they were behind walls or not, they had access to news. They gathered this information from a variety of news channels, including letters, messengers, people who passed on information at the speaking window, as well as from newspapers and reports ahead of fairs (*Meßrelationen*).

The Benedictine, Veit Höser, offers us excellent insight into the evolution of his recording. We heard earlier of the abbot's ire because Regensburg and Straubing had been left unprotected, so that the people, including the monks, had to flee.[85] For Höser, the fault for all the misery they experienced lay with the military and political commanders, "who had been entrusted with the protective sword." The Benedictine, however, is not only critical of the leadership; he also offers suggestions for how this situation could have been averted:

---

84   See also Popkin, "New Perspectives."
85   Sigl, *Veit Hösers Kriegstagebuch*, 99 (22 November 1633). See Chapter 3.1.2.

> The Regensburgers and the similarly besieged Straubingers could furnish evidence and produce proof whether [or] not already 2,000 foot soldiers would have been enough to save both cities – albeit under the condition that they would have marched off quickly to stop this very *luderischen* enemy and to protect the cities from their downfall. Would not, I say, 2,000 men have saved Lower Bavaria from this terrible devastation, and so many churches and holy sites, so many people and people's souls from obliteration.[86]

Höser's words may sound like armchair military strategizing, and perhaps some of his thoughts were nothing more than that, but his frustration and pain speak loud and clear, to the point of outrage, in view of the lacking political and military protection.

The Benedictine continues to delve into the various reasons for their disastrous fate and comes to the conclusion that Albrecht von Wallenstein was the prime culprit. His antagonism toward Maximilian, who had advocated the general's dismissal in 1630, had prompted Wallenstein to remain passive as the (Protestant) army of Bernhard of Saxe-Weimar moved into Bavaria and devastated it. Besides conversations with military men, Höser names as his sources the news reports (*Relationen*), which had just been published and were then sold at the spring fairs.[87]

The Augustinian prioress, Clara Staiger, also frequently expressed criticism of the military. From early on she judged the Catholic troops (*Die unsrigen*) to be ineffectual at best and at worst more harmful than the enemy troops.[88] Staiger's assessment of their own troops as neither particularly courageous nor helpful runs like a common thread through her diary. In October 1633 she noted that "our troops were willing to retreat without having achieved anything."[89] The next year, when she received news that the enemy had taken Landshut and had treated its inhabitants very badly, she added "which could well have been prevented by our troops ... if the general [Johann von] Aldringen had not, with faulty strategy (*pratickh*), given the enemy ample scope."[90] Anna Catharina Frölich, the recorder of the Poor Clares in Munich, shared Staiger's frustration with the military leadership as well as the general conviction, "as

---

86 Sigl, *Veit Hösers Kriegstagebuch*, 99 (22 November 1633). "Luder" can mean "hussy," but here it is a play on "Luther." The Latin word in the original is "ludricum."
87 Sigl, *Veit Hösers Kriegstagebuch*, 116, 120, 122.
88 *Klara Staigers Tagebuch*, 61–62, 93.
89 *Klara Staigers Tagebuch*, 104.
90 *Klara Staigers Tagebuch*, 143 (17 July 1634).

voiced by the common soldiers," that "our colonels were the foremost reason why the war did not come to an end."[91]

Maurus Friesenegger, too, frequently commented on the events and actors of the war.[92] Much like Staiger, Friesenegger criticizes the generals and their army for their lack of courage. When in 1648 Bavaria was once again overrun by enemy troops, "our brave, courageous troops everywhere made room for the enemy, indeed [our troops] withdrew to Straubing and relinquished the entire rest of Bavaria to the Swedes."[93] The imperial and electoral troops, the abbot continues, dozed in Lauingen and Passau – their "inhuman looting" being their only vital signs. "[Carl Gustav] Wrangel [1613–1676], the Swedish generalissimo, expected a battle, and everyone else did as well. Only the Bavarians considered themselves too weak – right: [too weak] in courage!"[94]

Far from an odd comment in one or two accounts, appraising the military situation and the usefulness of the leadership were pervasive elements in the narratives of male and female religious. This assessment was certainly fueled by frustration over how the war played out around them, and their writing provided them the opportunity to get their fury and frustration off their chests. Importantly, however, this act also imparted a sense of *doing* something. Their comments and proposals had a participatory dimension. With them they seized the opportunity actively to take a stance rather than just passively observing the ruin around them.

In short, news played an enormously important role in the lives of contemporaries, and the expanding system of communication offered many channels for those in search of information. Updates about battles and details about the enemy's location, size, condition, and direction were essential for military and political leaders, but the rest of the populace was also in grave need of news to plan the next move. Being well informed could make the difference between life and death. Reliable data, however, were not always easy to come by. People with means and connections could more readily obtain trustworthy information than the commoners, who often had to decide on the basis of hearsay whether to flee or not.

The great extent to which authors discussed the news in their writings points to its other vital functions that went beyond practical needs. While people dreaded distressing updates, being informed about what was taking place

---

91 Zwingler, *Klarissenkloster*, 1074 (# 21).
92 Friesenegger, *Tagebuch*, 110–11.
93 Friesenegger, *Tagebuch*, 164.
94 Friesenegger, *Tagebuch*, 165. In contrast to the generals, Maximilian receives the Benedictine's praise because the elector did his best and with determination (Friesenegger, 122–23).

militarily – i.e., getting a handle on the story of the war – was also a means of keeping control to a certain degree. Moreover, the frequent comments and judgments about military leaders and their strategies conveyed a sense that one was not simply a victim of the mayhem but took action. In some form, then, staying *au courant* and commenting on the war's occurrences had important psychological effects that could help those who were living through it combat despondency and desolation.

3   Pragmatism, Resilience, and Initiative

In listening to the narratives of contemporaries, one becomes aware of the many ways in which the populace tried to counteract the negative consequences of the war. People displayed an acute sense of realism and pragmatism – approaches that are underlined by the desire for news and information. This pragmatism manifested itself in multiple forms. The canons of Spalt (in Eichstätt's bishopric) in 1636 sold the silver and bells of their church as well as 44 books so that they could live and cultivate their fields: "Primum est vivere, deinde philosophari," i.e., "living comes first, then philosophizing."[95] Many of those suffering loss and devastation focused on rebuilding their lives and their destroyed property. One might ask what else could they have done, but the case of the Augustinian convent Mariastein outside Eichstätt illustrates just how much determination and dogged perseverance had to be expended in this battle to overcome the war's destructive effects. When Mariastein was destroyed in 1634, Prioress Staiger immediately began to plan the reconstruction of their cloister. Some of the sisters moved back in between the ruins to start the spring crop. Although she and her sisters barely managed to work their own land during the war, the prioress acquired another two fields in February 1634.[96] Over the next decade and a half, her cloister was repeatedly looted and burned down, and each time Staiger immediately went about rebuilding what had been destroyed.

Staiger's resilience and forward-looking perspective are striking, but it is even more amazing when one considers that the nuns had no financial resources. Unlike some of the monasteries discussed above, e.g., Oberaltaich or Andechs, Mariastein was not a rich convent. In the past the sisters had been able to support themselves through dowries, donations, interest (from their property), and the tithe. In addition, begging expeditions (the so-called

---

95   Buchner, "Ruinen," 43.
96   *Klara Staigers Tagebuch*, 121.

terminey) had been part of the nuns' regular duties. During the war, however, sustaining the cloister proved much more difficult, not only because of the widespread violence but also because tithes and interests fell away, and farming was often impossible. Begging had become the sisters' almost exclusive means of securing their livelihood and rebuilding their cloister. It took courage to travel the roads, particularly as a woman. Indeed, after their cloister had been destroyed in 1634, Staiger could only slowly persuade several of her nuns to suffer both pest and soldiers on the women's uncertain begging expeditions. Some of their missions targeted places nearby, but often their trips led them as far afield as Salzburg, Linz, and Vienna.[97]

The sisters showed great ingenuity in their pursuit of alms. During their *terminey* to Ingolstadt in May 1635, for example, they were able to collect over 85 florin because they convinced a discalced friar and a Jesuit to make the convent's case from the pulpit. In another instance, when Staiger learned that the emperor was going to be in Regensburg (1640), she requested permission from the prince-bishop to beg there.[98] The prioress' intrepidness in going to the very top of the political leadership in her search for funds suggests resourcefulness, but it also hints at the increasingly dismal situation for the southeast German lands at this stage in the war. This is highlighted by the fact that Prince-bishop Marquard II (r. 1636–1685) permitted the sisters to beg only in nearby Wemding and the adjacent castles, not in Bavaria or Regensburg. These restrictions point to the general financial strain caused by many years of troops in the region.[99]

Clara Staiger and her sisters felt the economic contraction as their begging expeditions became ever less fruitful. In July 1636 the sisters' pursuit of alms in nearby towns produced 65 florin, but their *terminey* to the Tyrol yielded only 68 florin. The considerably longer journey thus brought a mere three florin more than their search closer to home. Moreover, Staiger narrates that in Innsbruck (Tyrol) the sisters were particularly "unwelcome (*unwerte*) guests, who had to bear much aggravation." It is no wonder, then, that several of her sisters returned to the cloister sick with aches and fever. The next year (1637), two sisters went on a 200-mile journey in search of donations, and, in their letters home, complained about having to endure "much unpleasantness" (*grosse*

---

97   *Klara Staigers Tagebuch*, 180, 182–84, 198–99, 268, 296.
98   *Klara Staigers Tagebuch*, 175–77, 265. The begging expeditions had to be approved by the nuns' prince-bishop, who then issued them a patent for their journey. He also determined how many sisters were allowed to beg and where.
99   *Klara Staigers Tagebuch*, 267. The bishopric of Eichstätt did not lie in Bavaria but in Franconia. Regensburg was part of the Upper Palatinate, which had been given to Maximilian in 1623. Today all these areas belong to Bavaria.

unglegenhait). Often they had to go far for very little money. Months of begging generated only 300 florin and a few useful items.[100]

Beyond sending her sisters on these seemingly interminable travels, the prioress wrote petitions for funds to various people. Staiger was skillful in her pleas for support by applying to people who had been supportive before, prostrating herself before a commander, and appealing to the sisters' religious superiors as well as political leaders for contributions.[101] Indeed, she was not discriminating in whom she approached, begging both friends and foes for any assistance they might be able to give Mariastein. Importantly, her records reveal that an overwhelming number of donations came from women. It may be no surprise that the nuns of Vienna's Augustinian cloister (St. Jakob ob der Hülben) gave generously. They belonged to the same order, and monastic networks played a major supporting role during the war. But other women in Austria and elsewhere were significant benefactors as well. Moreover, during their exile in Ingolstadt in 1634, Staiger and her sisters received many gifts (mostly food and drink), and her meticulous list of donors at the end of their stay demonstrates once again that women outnumbered men by far in their support of the nuns. It is highly likely that the sisters of Mariastein targeted women specifically when they begged locally and farther afield. We see such a practice with the Augustinians' neighbors, the Benedictine nuns of St. Walburg in Eichstätt, who also financed the rebuilding of their destroyed cloister through donations they received while on begging expeditions. Their records show that, in addition to important political figures such as the emperor, they deliberately sought out women.[102]

Besides outright begging, Clara Staiger shrewdly employed the custom of bestowing presents on various parties to augment the pantry and income of her convent. The German term she used – *anbinden* (to bind to) – connotes both the close connection ("bond") that this practice establishes between two people, and the fact that, with this gift, one ties or makes someone indebted to oneself.[103] The reciprocal gesture – *auflösen* (to release from) – continues in the same vein: the other person releases him or herself from this "bond" by reciprocating with a gift. Such habits were long-standing, but they became vitally important survival strategies during the lean years of the war. How successful such tactics were depended on a person's ingenuity in turning precious little into compelling offerings that prompted generous gifts in return. Clara

---

100 *Klara Staigers Tagebuch*, 201, 213–18.
101 *Klara Staigers Tagebuch*, 85–86, 173, 182, 268, 288.
102 *Klara Staigers Tagebuch*, 118–20; "Klosterchronik," 42.
103 See also *Deutsches Wörterbuch*, 1:295–96 ("Anbinden") and 2:31–32 ("Binden"). The sociologist Pierre Bourdieu wrote extensively about gift theory. For an analysis of his theory's evolution throughout his work, see Silber, "Bourdieu's Gift to Gift Theory."

Staiger seems to have been a master at this sort of exchange. In early 1634, for example, the prioress recorded:

> I and Sister Maria Francisca gifted (*anbunden*) her cousin, Mr. Fux, and he released (*auffgelöst*) himself with half a calf.... Monday, 30 January, on St. Adelheid's Day, we presented (*anbunden*) the commander's wife with little gifts of the cloister (*Clostergeblein*). On the evening of *Mariae Lichtmess* [Candlemas; 1 February], we gifted (*anbunden*) the *Junckfrawe* Anna Brigitta, and she responded (*haben sich auffgelest*) with wine, bread, and meat, [some] of which we passed on to the honorable father.[104]

These various exchanges reveal an intricate system of gifting and sharing that sustained the convent and others connected with it. Staiger passed some of the donations on to their religious superior, most likely with the intention of thanking him for past support and incurring his future benevolence toward them. If these transactions appear self-serving, they were, but the sisters were in a difficult financial position, where every loaf of bread counted. The way this system worked underlines that it represented an acknowledged mechanism to assist one another, which was embraced or at least accepted by the involved, often unequal, parties.

The determination and aptitude of Clara Staiger and her nuns in soliciting donations paid off: they managed to keep the convent going, and within a year were able to begin rebuilding their cloister. Ever pragmatic, the sisters helped the workers in erecting the new constructions.[105] That the convent was able to gather such funds reflects not only on their skill and resolve, but also on the strength of religion and the importance of these religious women to many of their contemporaries. It points toward a conviction that alms given to religious houses could improve one's lot – either in this life or the next. Monks and especially nuns had a distinct religious function: they were charged with praying for the wellbeing of a specific person and were often paid for this service they rendered their patrons.

People were willing to help support the sisters and the restoration of their home at a time of great deprivation. Nevertheless, there is no question that these funding strategies became less and less successful as the conflict wore on. At the end of 1637, when Mariastein had not been able to collect interest from its properties for three years and was forced to rebuild and sustain itself

---

104   *Klara Staigers Tagebuch*, 121.
105   *Klara Staigers Tagebuch*, 182.

only through the onerous task of begging (*nur vom pitter sauren ersamelten H.allmueßen baut und gehaußt*), Staiger closes the year with the remarks:

> May our beloved Lord give grace that we will finally get our money from that, which our forefathers have established (*angelegt*) and have left for our benefit, and that our victuals will commence again. We do not know how to sustain ourselves together because the begging around the country is no longer viable, and leaving [the convent for these begging expeditions] is getting increasingly difficult: it is harmful to the spiritual estate and debilitating to worship and work at home.[106]

Staiger was clear-eyed and deeply concerned about the imperiled situation of her convent and her charges. She underlined that Mariastein faced existential challenges not only from the lack of funds, but also with regard to its proper vocation. The sustained crisis induced by the war had led this religious community to a tipping point: its herculean efforts at keeping Mariastein afloat threatened to infringe on its spirituality and the reason for its existence. Despite all the energy, labor, determination, and ingenuity expended on reclaiming their former convent life, then, the positive results were tenuous, could be reversed with any new attack, and were very much in question when one considered the mental and spiritual costs to the sisters.

In all her efforts and times of trials – through the last years of the war, when even the stalwart Staiger's spirits began to falter – her pragmatism nevertheless shines through. When at the end of the war her cloister is destroyed yet again, she concludes: "With everything they took, the damage runs at about 2,000 florin. May God come to our aid in his fatherly way and send us means so that we can begin to put our house back in order, repair our office and farm buildings, and replace the great loss of our mass requisites."[107] Staiger hoped for God's aid, but her answer to the last plunder was a matter-of-fact assessment of what needed to be done next. This pragmatism and purposefulness kept her nuns and herself going throughout the war.

Resourcefulness and expediency were also crucial elements of successful negotiations. A broad spectrum of negotiations occurred on every level of society, not just among political leaders.[108] The gifting discussed above constituted one such effort, which is particularly evident when offerings were employed to

---

106 *Klara Staigers Tagebuch*, 223–24.
107 *Klara Staigers Tagebuch*, 317.
108 For a discussion of negotiations undertaken by government officials, see Chapter 3.2.

propitiate the enemy. Toward the end of the war, in 1648, Maximilian's councilor of war, Herr von Ruepp, urged Abbot Friesenegger to pay the contributions the enemy had assigned to his abbey rather than risk fire; the Benedictine sent his "good and best friend, Herrn Mathias Barbier, merchant [in Munich], who, equipped with courage and eloquence, seemed entirely made for such business," into the enemy camp at Moosburg. Barbier was able to reduce the demanded sum by almost two-thirds and obtain a certificate that none of their properties nor the farms of their subjects would be harmed.[109]

Not all *religiosi*, let alone most contemporaries, had such lofty connections as Abbot Friesenegger, but this did not keep them from using every means at their disposal to obtain a favorable outcome for themselves, their families, and their communities. The Domincan nuns of Heiliggrab, who stayed in their cloister outside Bamberg's city walls during the various military takeovers, are an excellent example. They negotiated their imperiled situation with remarkable pragmatism and ingenuity. Junius and her sisters shielded themselves from harm by establishing good relations with whomever governed their city, whether Protestants or Catholics.[110] When, in February 1632, Bamberg was turned over to the Swedes and no one came to the sisters' aid, the convent rushed to request a *Salva Guardia*. This was a smart move, since, Junius tells us, had they waited until noon, they would have been robbed three times judging from the onslaught at their gate.[111]

The sisters of Heiliggrab not only demonstrated an impressive ability in reading the situation; they also showed themselves as expert negotiators with the Swedish occupying forces. Many of the commanding officers made the wellbeing of the Dominican nuns their personal mission. During the occupation, Heiliggrab had repeatedly been slated for destruction for strategic reasons, and each time the sisters were able to avoid this outcome. One of their staunch defenders was the Swedish general Wilhelm von Lohausen. According to Junius, when in March 1633 the Swedish military considered tearing down the cloister for the second time, von Lohausen stepped in, saying to his superior: "I want you to spare the holy grave [Heiliggrab] since I have 24 daughters there, and I will not allow that they or the cloister will be harmed."[112] Bernhard of Saxe-Weimar had ordered the general to burn down Bamberg,

---

109 Friesenegger, *Tagebuch*, 167–68.
110 These refer to outside forces, whether the Swedes/Protestants or the Catholics, not their own native authorities in Bamberg, with whom the sisters had a tense relationship.
111 Hümmer, ed., "Bamberg im Schweden-Kriege," 52:36–37.
112 Hümmer, ed., "Bamberg im Schweden-Kriege," 52:123. For von Lohausen, see the discussion in Chapter 2.4.

and, when von Lohausen advised against it, at least to raze the suburb where Heiliggrab was located. Yet, as the general related to the sisters during his visit, he firmly held the line against his commander's designs:

> I [General von Lohausen] then said once again that I cannot do such a thing without doing harm to the good maidens of Heiligengrab. Also, I am unable to let something evil happen to my spiritual daughters; I would rather suffer it myself. He also told us: you, my dear daughters, can say in truth that you preserved the suburb [of Bamberg], because if it had not been for you, nothing would be left of the suburb.[113]

Compared to the service and protection the Dominican nuns received from their own authorities, the enemy proved to be much more forthcoming and reliable in his assistance. There was the earlier noted nonchalant and unhelpful response of the prince-bishop to the sisters' request for aid in finding a refuge. Moreover, at times it seemed that the sisters had more to fear from their own government than from the enemy. In early 1634, Heiliggrab underwent what surely must have been one of the most curious and benign enemy inspections of the Thirty Years' War. A Swedish provisions' officer came to their convent to inspect their attic and cellar for supplies. Junius tells the reader that the officer was a "good man, who recorded everything as they told him and did not even go into our cellar. Then he showed us a letter, which one of our pretty councilmen had sent to the colonel..., in which it said that [the Swedes] should just go to Holy Grave [Heiliggrab] on the Münigsberg [Monks mountain] and to St. Clara. There they will find wine and grain aplenty."[114] Even though Junius' description sounds far from objective, it is evident that the city fathers tried to rid themselves of the Swedish pressure by sending the enemy to the supposed bread baskets of the religious orders – and especially to the two

---

113   Hümmer, ed., "Bamberg im Schweden-Kriege," 52:129. Several high officers made their repeated rounds to the convent, including Duke Bernhard of Saxe-Weimar, who was the new governor of Franconia and the prince who had given von Lohausen the above order. Presumably the prince wanted to see for himself why the Dominican nuns attracted such fierce protection from his officers – to the point that his Protestant general called these Catholic nuns his "spiritual daughters"! In August 1633 the Dominican sisters were once again fortunate in their patron, Commissary Johann Scheibelberger of Wielbronn, who also adopted the sisters as his "spiritual daughters." He came every day or, if something prevented him from coming, sent one of his men to inquire whether the nuns had any complaints. If they were pressured in any way, he promised he would come to their aid.
114   Hümmer, ed., "Bamberg im Schweden-Kriege," 52:112.

female convents, Heiliggrab and St. Clara.[115] The Swedes instead sent the sisters money, thanked them for the homemade goods with which the nuns had presented them, and asked whether the sisters "had any complaint on account of our soldiers."[116]

Junius commented disapprovingly on the councilmen's damaging conduct toward them and the citizenry: "This was just the intention of the pretty councilors that, if they could have gotten the Swedes to take much from us, they would have been overjoyed, as they also treated the poor citizens in this way." Rather than protecting its citizens, Junius charged, the councilors set the Swedes upon them and insinuated that the citizenry could pay all right: "Such a comfort was the government to its poor citizens. And the Swedes told us themselves that the councilors … pointed [the Swedes] to us, saying we [the sisters] are rich; they could find with us what they wanted."[117] Junius' remarks, then, suggest that the Dominican nuns were in greater danger from their own city fathers, who may have been motivated by a desire for control over the convent and its women, than from the Swedes who showed abundant concern and consideration for the sisters. The consistently high regard and protection of the Swedes demonstrates that the sisters of Heiliggrab were skilled tacticians, who knew how to turn a dangerous and delicate situation to their advantage.

By protecting the sisters, the generals and colonels may have responded as much to the nuns' appeal to the besiegers' humanity as to their own need to preserve some place of sanity, peace, and gentleness in the midst of mayhem and destruction. Gender played a significant role in these patterns of behavior. The Dominican nuns' relationship with the Swedes was a gendered relationship, just as that of the sisters to Bamberg's councilmen and the Dominican friars, who attempted to control them. Religious women did not necessarily inspire a protective instinct in the enemy (or the friend, for that matter). And, yet, Junius and her fellow nuns were smart enough to exploit the ambiguity about defenseless, religious women by appealing to the besiegers' manliness and to their urge to protect this fragile female community. They also provided something precious during the time of war: a haven of civility and gentleness during this brutal time. Besides the nuns' negotiation skills and their aptitude for bringing out the goodwill in the Swedes, the sisters' unfailingly good relationship with their occupiers suggests that these women filled a need in the

---

115 Junius provides several further examples of the Bamberg's councilors' antagonistic behavior and the Swedes' reassurance that nothing would be taken from them: Hümmer, ed., "Bamberg im Schweden-Kriege," 52:112; 53: 174–75, 182.
116 Hümmer, ed., "Bamberg im Schweden-Kriege," 52:113.
117 Hümmer, ed., "Bamberg im Schweden-Kriege," 53:174–75.

lives of the military men. The convent also offered one of the few spaces where the officers could bring their wives.

The broader populace pursued their own strategies of dealing with the pressures of war. As discussed, peasants regularly opted for flight in response to threats of violence, but the opposite – peasants striking back – was also a widely adopted reaction. At times, authorities tried to harness the defensive potential of their town- and countrymen, for example in the recruitment for country and town militias, but governments also attempted to do so on an ad hoc basis when danger threatened.[118] These measures underline that the political leaders were unable to provide protection through the usual bodies of defense. During the 1632 approach of the Swedes, Maximilian released a general mandate, in which he acknowledged that Bavaria was in need of protection beyond what the already recruited and selected country folk were able to provide: "We have been made aware … that the citizens and peasants in our territory, who are still on hand, show good heart and courage and are eager to defend and save themselves, their wives, children, household, and their dear fatherland with all their might and ability against the enemy, should he advance and enter [our territory] any further."[119] The elector specified that at the first sign of the enemy his subjects should warn the others by a bell stroke or fire signal (*Glockenschlag* or *Fewrzaichen*), and then "gang up (*zusamen rotten*) with their best weapons to attack the marching enemy, and to disperse and follow him."[120] Maximilian must have had some concerns in encouraging untrained commoners to take up arms, since he instructed his local authorities to make sure that those willing to fight were led by "people who had a bit more understanding than others and who could distinguish a friend from an enemy so that our own would not be taken for the enemy's army and attacked."[121]

Nuremberg's political leadership also allowed self-help measures, especially the *Glockenschlag*, by which the local bell was struck to gather the villagers for collective action. Understandably, Nuremberg's magistrates were uneasy about giving executional power to villagers, and they did so only in individual cases. Much like Maximilian, the councilors asked the villagers to use at least a bit more discretion before they killed a soldier and to first determine whether he was a friend or an enemy. When, in June 1632, the suffering peasants organized themselves to answer violence with violence, the council tried to stop them. The magistrates also ordered its local administrators in

---

118   On the disappointing performance of militias, see Chapter 3.1.
119   SA M, B&R 60 A 1: "Landesverteidigung durch Selbsthilfe" (14 April 1632).
120   SA M, B&R 60 A 1.
121   SA M, B&R 60 A 1.

Nuremberg's vicinity not to allow peasants to massacre plundering soldiers. However, this order applied only to Swedish raiders, since the political leaders could not blame their subjects for killing (Catholic) Croats. In addition, the council admonished the peasants not to set the government's authority aside and to report everything.[122] Thus, Nuremberg's leadership tried to walk a fine line between empowering its subjects to ensure a degree of protection and maintaining some control over its enraged people. Their feeble efforts of staying in command, however, reveal that they were not in a position to dictate to their subjects.

In Brandenburg-Ansbach, a 1634 ordinance shows similar concerns regarding peasant resistance and gives insight into the complex situation and reasoning of the court. The government had released regulations to counteract the soldiers' damaging effect to good commerce, agriculture, and the peasantry. The many grievances from the districts, however, had made clear that their efforts had not produced the desired results. Indeed, the *Soldateska* treated their subjects so "barbarically" that the peasants had finally become "desperate," ignored their administrators' orders, and begun to band together with their neighbors for common action. The government feared that this "would soon lead to a general uprising and would most dangerously damage the entire evangelical cause."[123] After underlining that it did not approve of such proceedings, the government entered into a complicated discussion on the rights and limits of both soldier and peasant actions. They condemned the alliance of several peasant communities to attack a cavalry marching through the area because this went beyond the defense of their life and possessions (which was their right). Essentially, the government censured the peasants' *excessive* actions against the army. Similarly, the district administrators were to speak to the armies' commanding officers and to patrol their region to try to forestall unrestrained behavior. But if the officials' entreaties had no effect and the soldiers maltreated the peasants, "then, and in such cases, one cannot blame the subjects if they defend themselves, as much as they are able, through customary striking of the bell and pursuit, in accordance with the imperial *Constitutionen,* and *executions* order, and deter violence with violence."[124] In short, while the court reasonably highlighted the necessity to act within the

---

122 Von Soden, *Gustav Adolph*, 1:173–74, 285, 310, 365–66.
123 StA N, AKTA, Nr. 701, Realindex Tom 71, Nr. 119.
124 StA N, AKTA, Nr. 701, Realindex Tom 71, Nr. 119. The local authorities should try to step in and mitigate, but if the armies would not moderate their excesses, the government could not be held responsible since it had done everything in its power.

legal framework, it signaled that abusive armies had only themselves to blame if peasants fought back.

Although dire situations sometimes forced governments to condone or even encourage commoners toward self-defense, authorities were generally apprehensive of subjects with weapons at their disposal taking matters into their own hands. Whether peasants had been provoked by marauding soldiers or not, hordes of aggressive commoners often triggered fears of a general peasant uprising. These were not only a problem of the past – the Peasants' War of 1524–26 comes to mind – but very much a concern of the present. The rebellions of 1625–26 in Upper Austria (*das Land ob der Enns*, which was part of Bavaria) had already put Bavarian and other political leaders on edge. In 1633–34, Bavaria had to deal with yet another uprising.[125] Importantly, this rebellion broke out in the eastern part between the Isar and Inn rivers, which had been devastated by "friendly" troops, not in the region west of the Isar, where the enemy troops were quartered.[126] It started in December 1633 in Bavaria's southeastern district Kling, where their allied armies had been plundering and devastating the people throughout the year. The situation escalated when Maximilian attempted to place his marauding soldiers in the peasants' and townspeople's homes for the winter. The elector's move graphically illustrates the breakdown of the lord-subject relationship because the subjects could no longer count on protection from their lord in return for service and loyalty.[127] In light of this fact, the subjects refused Maximilian's demand of quarters for his soldiers, and took guarding their houses and homes into their own hands.[128]

The uprising was forcefully put down and its leaders arrested and tried. The subsequent proceedings against them show the dynamic between the central authorities (Maximilian and his privy council), the regional administrators in the *Rentamt* Burghausen where the case was tried, and the accused. As Renate Blickle highlights, the position of the authorities in Burghausen changed after they had interviewed the arrested peasants and citizens. Having first designated the culprits as "rebels," the local administrators eventually came to call them subjects, peasants, or citizens (*Bürger*). The dealings demonstrate two points in particular: Burghausen's government was not simply the executing organ of the elector but had – and defended – its own assessment of the situation. Even more importantly, the subjects had a voice and were heard: they

---

125   For an in-depth discussion of the peasantry and their changing situation over the sixteenth and early seventeenth centuries, see Rebel, *Peasant Classes*, and particularly pp. 230–84 for the rebellion in Upper Austria.
126   Renate Blickle offers a meticulous study of the peasant uprising in Bavaria: "Rebellion," 57.
127   See the discussion above in Chapter 3. Blickle makes this same argument ("Rebellion," 58).
128   Blickle, "Rebellion," 59.

convinced their local authorities that their behavior was not an act of rebellion against their rightful lords, but their way of stepping up where their government had failed, namely in the protection of its subjects.

The insurgence belongs to the more spectacular episodes of commoners' actions, but it does not tell us how the populace in cities and the countryside day-to-day dealt with the violence and deprivation engendered by the war. Only a few autobiographical accounts from these ranks are available, but we hear about some of their activities indirectly through chronicles, official reports, and the *religiosi*'s descriptions. In light of the fact that, during the war, authorities were unable to protect their subjects sufficiently, people saw themselves largely left to take their own actions. Their primary concerns were to protect themselves against violent attacks and plundering, and to ensure their ability to work the fields.

Regarding the first objective, initiatives to guard against violence took many forms. Peasants fought back individually when threatened, as in Windsheim's vicinity in 1640, when a horseman attempted to abuse a peasant working in the field and steal his horse. When the peasant resisted, the rider drew his pistol and tried to shoot the peasant, but the latter, "rather nimble" (*nicht vnbehend*), fired his musket in return and shot the horseman in the head, killing him.[129] More often, however, villagers banded together to take group action either in the pursuit of marauders or to protect themselves as they worked the fields. In March 1632 the peasants of several villages north of Forchheim killed the soldiers stationed there. Even though troops were dispatched to retaliate against the peasants, contrary to the lieutenant's prediction, they did not pay dearly.[130]

Sometimes the promise of imminent military support fortified the populace. When the Swedes besieged Höchstadt (south of Bamberg) in 1633, its burghers refused to surrender, and neither the assurance of being spared if they submitted, nor the threat of death and destruction by fire if they did not, could persuade them to do otherwise. Emboldened by the encouragement they had received from the nearby fortress Forchheim and the assertion that help would come within two hours, they vowed to defend themselves "to the last man." The final defense turned out rather to be that of the women: "When the men could no longer shoot, the women boiled water and poured it [on the soldiers]; they also stirred flour into the boiling water and burned the enemy mightily with it; they threw lots of stones at them as well and caused the enemy

---

129 StA N, *Chronika Windshemiana*. Windsheim was a Franconian imperial city west of Nuremberg.
130 Hümmer, ed., "Bamberg im Schweden-Kriege," 52:52.

COPING WITH WAR   161

great damage." Their "knightly defense" (*riedterliches wehrn*), however, was all in vain since the promised aid never came, and the Swedes followed through on their threats.[131]

Still, neighborhood initiatives were often the most successful strategy of protection. Left to take matters into their own hands, villagers organized themselves to defend their lives and livelihood. Abbot Friesenegger of Andechs provides rich material in describing how burghers and peasants responded to the challenges of war. When in 1632 the Swedes made their way toward Bavaria, the villages Weilheim, Heiligberg, and Seefeld combined forces and occupied the bridge at Stegen with 700 men in an effort to find out about the enemy's progress and to stop any marauder.[132] Over the following months, the Benedictine narrates, the abuse and devastation in the countryside escalated to the point that the peasants fled into the monastery "so that the inside of the cloister is full of men and the outside [still within monastery walls] full of women and children." Soon two companies of riders came to the cloister. While they were able to get rid of the first one with some beer and bread, the second did not leave "until the peasants within the cloister stood together with all manner of weapons and repelled violence with violence." Later that year, when the peasants again sought refuge in the monastery, they defended the cloister once more against small groups of robbers.[133]

Villagers also collaborated to reclaim plundered goods. Fifty armed peasants from Seefeld went after a troop of riders who had robbed them of five horses. The pursuers shot the marauders' leader dead, dispersed the rest, and brought the horses back home. The next day, when another twenty riders pressured Andechs to give them food, drink, and fodder for their horses, and paid no attention to the refusal of the cloister's *Salva Guardia*, the latter called the armed peasants, and the group finally left. At other times, the *Salva Guardia* joined forces with the peasants and pursued the robbers. Plundering by their own (in this case the emperor's) troops was even harder to tolerate than that of the enemy. Indeed, Friesenegger records that, at one time, the peasants joined the Swedes to go after the Croats in Peiting (southwest of the Ammersee), because they were more upset about the latter's plundering than that of the Swedes.[134]

---

131   Hümmer, ed., "Bamberg im Schweden-Kriege," 52:121–22.
132   Friesenegger, *Tagebuch*, 24.
133   Friesenegger, *Tagebuch*, 39 (31 March 1633), 55 (18 December 1633).
134   Friesenegger, *Tagebuch*, 49–50, 55 (1633); 146 (1646). According to the abbot, when soldiers asked politely, the monks gave them provisions.

As the war dragged on and ever more troops with their ordinary and extraordinary demands kept putting pressure on the countryside, peasants went after regular troops as well. This reflected the reality that, after a while, marauders and "legitimate" soldiers were no longer distinguishable. The latters' lawful foraging had evolved into outright plundering, much like that of the raiders. In August 1633, about 150 peasants had taken the Sperreuther (i.e., Swedish) regiment by surprise, shot the guard with a musket through his armpit, and then absconded with their spoils. The regiment's captain (von Eßdorf) requested from the commander in charge of the area (Count of Solms) the return of the robbed items.[135] It is true that retaliation against foraging and plundering soldiers could earn subjects – legally and actually – the death sentence. Some of the official discourses and anecdotal evidence in narrative accounts, however, suggest that governments and their constituents frequently were badly in need of these regulating actions of their subjects. Many examples, like those above, illustrate this point. They also demonstrate that peasants and townspeople were not necessarily punished for their deeds.

At the same time, not everyone was ready and willing (not to mention bold enough) to resist for fear of making things worse. Abbot Johann Dressel of the Cistercian abbey Ebrach (between Würzburg und Bamberg) narrates a fascinating episode that highlights, on one hand, a case of the peasants' readiness to take action against plundering soldiers, and, on the other, the reticence of political leaders and other contemporaries who thought it more expedient not to provoke the enemy by fighting him. Dressel thought that if the abbey's subjects refrained from any aggression, he could save the abbey and village from destruction. To that end, he ordered the peasants in the Steigerwald: "Remain calm, do not rebel either with words or actual deeds against the soldiers, and give [the soldiers] no cause for devastation, scorching, and burning."[136]

The abbot's tactical maneuvering, however, backfired, since the Catholics suspected him of siding with the Swedes and Lutherans. Moreover, the 2,000 thaler, which Colonel Wolf Dietrich Truchseß had exacted from the monastery, had not gone to the army but into the colonel's own coffers. Therefore, the soldiers were about to plunder the cloister, "which would surely have happened, if the peasants, who had entrenched themselves in the forest, had not prevented it." In the end, then, the abbot owed the survival of his abbey to the peasants' refusal to listen to his warning. Dressel does acknowledge that

---

135   StA N, AKA, 53b, Nr. 299. General Tilly also complained to Elector Maximilian that peasants had repeatedly slain his soldiers when they foraged in the countryside (Holzfurtner, "Katastrophe und Neuanfang," 563, fn. 40).
136   Hüttner, "Memoiren," 559 (19 March 1632).

the soldiers were driven to plunder because their colonel only enriched himself rather than take care of his men. After more harassment from the soldiers, the Steigerwald peasants combined forces with the countrymen around Bamberg and Würzburg, attacked the *Salva Guardias* Truchseß had stationed at the villages Bretbach and Sichendorf, arrested them, and took their horses. Suspecting the abbot to be in cahoots with the rebels, the colonel complained to Dressel about the cruel treatment of the *Salva Guardias*, which Truchseß had only posted for the protection of the villagers. He insisted on the return of everything the rebels had taken, telling them that otherwise the abbot and the peasants would be sorry.[137]

The peasants' aggression against the *Salva Guardias* underlines the problematic nature of many of these "protective" guards, whose expenses had to be paid by the locals and who often did little to earn their keep or were destructive. Complaints about these watches are legion, and the fact that the enraged Steigerwald peasants went after them suggests that this contingent had done the communes more harm than good either by extracting unreasonable payment or by using violence against the villagers.

Most commoners may have been fed up with the soldiers' brutality and plunder, but not everyone rebelled or was ready to defend him- or herself. Military training was not an inherent part of a peasant's existence (which is one of the reasons why country militias were generally not successful). Bamberg's subjects in the countryside had been ordered to come into the city; once there, however, they did not know what to do with themselves: "The entire city was full of peasant folk, but not a single one was armed. That is why they were given large clubs and flails, also other weapons, with which they were supposed to fight, but the poor peasants stood there with such fright that they shivered with fear."[138] This vignette, narrated by Junius, not only illustrates that Bamberg saw itself in such need of fighters that it was willing to arm its peasants. It also underlines that fighting, let alone rebellion, was the furthest thing from these peasants' minds. Thus, responses to the violence generated by the war span a broad spectrum. Many peasants and burghers were willing to defend themselves actively and forcefully against aggression and outrageous demands, but not everyone was ready to take up arms. Some were too afraid or did not want to provoke the enemy. The range of responses recorded by the religious also demonstrates that many peasants and burghers embraced a mixture of behaviors: they might flee several times before deciding to fight.

---

137 Hüttner, "Memoiren," 560, 564–65 (12 May 1632). The leader of the uprising had belonged to the cloister's staff.
138 Hümmer, ed., "Bamberg im Schweden-Kriege," 52:74 (8 May 1632).

The choice of action depended on the circumstances, but it also shows that the populace was actively engaged and often chose the moment to take up fight or flight.

Apart from trying to avert violence and plundering, peasants also collaborated to get their work done, which describes their second major concern. Since many felt deserted by their authorities, peasants and others had to come up with ways to put food on the table during great dearth, to sustain themselves, to ensure planting and harvesting, and to protect themselves during their labor.[139] Their solutions exhibit a creative mixture of activities that provides insight into the dynamics in peasant and civic communities. Policies about protecting the countryside did not simply come from above, but peasants and their administrators constantly negotiated what could be done to protect them. Often the initiative came from the peasants, and, as with earlier examples, communal actions proved to be the most effective. The Benedictine Friesenegger notes in April 1633 that, because both the winter and the summer fields had hardly been tended, the inhabitants of Erling "made common cause, harnessed their few horses together, and cultivated almost all the fields. Those who did not work guarded the field against the attack of the marauders and protected the workers with sundry weapons."[140] The peasants to the north in Nuremberg's countryside adopted a similar solution. Since their authorities were unable to provide safety, the roughly 300 peasants of Gräfenberg helped themselves. One hundred kept watch daily and secured the area; the other 200 worked the fields. When Nuremberg's city councilors heard of this procedure, they charged their administrators in the countryside and the war councilors to ponder whether all peasants should imitate this practice so that the harvest could proceed without fail.[141] It appears the subjects were more ingenious than their authorities in responding to the war's challenges.

In another instance, eight villages turned to Nuremberg's councilors and proposed measures to make their field work safer.[142] These took the suggestions to the war officers, who weighed the advantages and disadvantages of several options: The villages had recommended that a strong *Salva Guardia* be stationed at a central location (Poppenreuth), from where the surrounding countryside could be watched and soldiers could be sent out in case of an attack. The war councilors, however, rejected this idea since there were

---

139 Not to mention that they typically had to provide for armies in their vicinity or pay contributions.
140 Friesenegger, *Tagebuch*, 40.
141 StA N, Rst Nbg, RK, B-Laden, Akt. 86, Nr. 6 (6 April 1632).
142 StA N, Rst Nbg, RK, B-Laden, Akt. 86, Nr. 24 (3 March 1638).

still enough woods where plunderers could hide. Another possibility was to hire one or two Croatian soldiers to safeguard the field work, but three or four marauders could easily overcome them, and the guard could not protect every working peasant. A third suggestion was to dispatch a guard to every village, but since Nuremberg regularly had only hundred soldiers who were already employed elsewhere, this was not a viable solution. Instead, the war council suggested a fourth option: As was customary in many locales during wartimes, the peasants should work together and take one field after another, use their horses jointly for the work, and the city would send them those cavalrymen and soldiers who were holding watch that day.[143] Within a day, however, reports about renewed looting arrived, and the peasants feared the worst for their livelihood. Referring to the just released decree, the villages' administrators explained that the council's suggestions did not really work for them since their fields were divided into small parcels that lay dispersed throughout the territory. Moreover, they did not sow just one crop at one particular time, but planted many different seeds.[144] Nuremberg's subjects thus involved themselves actively in the negotiation of how to handle the trials of war and fought hard to come up with solutions that best addressed such omnipresent concerns as protection against marauders and scarcity of draft animals.

Ingenuity and courage played leading roles in survival. Having the ability to read a situation correctly, to size up its possibilities, and to capitalize on windows of opportunities proved to be vitally important. The smart moves and episodes discussed run the gamut from common practical considerations – such as the clergy disguising themselves in secular clothes so as not to draw attention to their identity – to highly audacious ploys. These various responses do not negate the reality of a devastation that often made any kind of creative reaction impossible, but they stress that people did seize and create openings for their own engagement with an eye toward reducing or reversing the war's harmful consequences. In May 1633, for example, when the Benedictine abbey Plankstetten (Berching in Eichstätt's diocese) was destroyed, its monks escaped in disguise. While many conventuals fled to Austria, three brothers remained in Berching camouflaged as schoolmaster, shoemaker, and brewer; several others served neighboring parishes disguised as shepherds and servants. These ruses did not always succeed. One pater, who had posed as a brewer, was betrayed and had to pay dearly to free himself.[145] Camouflage

---

143   StA N, Rst Nbg, RK, B-Laden, Akt. 86, Nr. 24 (6 March 1638). Nuremberg's council concurred and sent a corresponding decree to the villages.
144   StA N, Rst Nbg, RK, B-Laden, Akt. 86, Nr. 24 (8 March 1638).
145   "Chronik von Plankstetten," in Buchner, "Ruinen," 23.

was also the critical tactic with regard to worship. Rather than using the more conspicuous churches, pastors often held services in private homes. Similarly, other ecclesiastical services, such as baptism and weddings, were relocated to the privacy of parishioners' houses.[146]

As observed earlier, the Protestant pastor, Bartholomæus Dietwar, of Hoheim near Kitzingen, belonged to the more courageous and ingenious among his cohort. He had refused to switch his allegiance to the Catholic side after Kitzingen passed from Brandenburg-Ansbach's government to the bishop of Würzburg (1629). When called before the bishop, Dietwar insisted that he was duty bound to the (Protestant) house of Brandenburg-Ansbach and would serve only that government.[147] After the Swedes had retaken Kitzingen in 1632 and the evangelical pastors had returned, they had to deal with the plundering of their own troops. The Hessian and Weimar armies (i.e., those of Bernhard of Saxe-Weimar) – numbering about 25,000 according to Dietwar – had set up camp north of Kitzingen. Dietwar and his parishioners in the nearby village Hoheim drove their livestock into Kitzingen and placed their other valuables into Hoheim's church and vestry, but to no avail: the Weimarers looted these religious sites as well. Dietwar lost a great deal of grain, seeds, bedding, books, and other treasured items. When the soldiers subsequently tried to sell his books at Kitzingen's market, Dietwar confronted them:

> One [soldier] brought in a sack four books in folio and four in quart[o], and when I stood with other foreign ministers at the market, he came to us and told us that he had handsome books and that we should buy them from him. I, however, soon thought that these would be my books, so I charged him to open the sack and showed the other ministers my name in the books. Then I shouted brashly at the soldier and asked who had ordered him to plunder the churches, and I would tell his superior, and he would soon be hanged at the market. This frightened [the soldier], and he relinquished the books to me and went away, but not before he had carried the books to my mother's house.[148]

Dietwar's bold stance was certainly buttressed by his sense of outrage and religious righteousness over the fact that their own troops not only robbed the people they were supposed to protect, but that nothing – not even churches – was sacred to them. The threat of punishment by his commander elicited the

---

146   Großner and von Haller, "Zu kurzem Bericht," 37.
147   LAELKB, MD Uffenheim, Akt. 95.
148   LAELKB, MD Uffenheim, Akt. 95:66–67.

soldier's quick retreat. One can only speculate about the underlying dynamic of this scene. Marauding soldiers, if caught, could expect punishment for their actions, and Gustavus Adolphus, especially, did not look kindly on soldiers despoiling religious sites, but the soldier's hasty reaction also reminds us of the quandary in which the fighting troops found themselves. It is entirely understandable that the populace was critical of soldiers' foraging (an act condoned by the government), which often evolved into plundering. But what were soldiers, who were forced to live off the land because they were not (or only poorly or infrequently) paid, to do when people placed all their valuables in churches and monasteries? Not surprisingly, their need to live trumped any respect for religious sites, although how easily such reverence receded no doubt differed among soldiers and over time. It evidently did not take much for the soldier of Dietwar's story to relent, hand back his spoils, and even lug the books to Dietwar's mother's house!

We heard earlier about the Augustinian nuns of Mariastein by Eichstätt, who braved dangerous roads in search for alms; however, not everyone managed to face the war's frightening reality boldly. For some, the terrifying experience of war with its repercussions proved too much to endure. A particularly graphic example of the literally overwhelming pressures of war comes from the Brigidine cloister Altomünster in the district Dachau near Munich. Most nuns had been able to flee to Munich before the Swedes advanced on their cloister in late April 1632, but two nuns who had been unable to travel starved to death. When the others returned, they found their market ruined and burned down, although the flames had spared their cloister. Shortly after their return in 1634, the plague hit the cloister and killed fifteen sisters. When, in early May 1635, the abbess was unable to find food for her charges, she hanged herself. This is a striking example of the limits of suffering. The overload of one dire crisis after another could well have been too much for anyone, but especially for members of a convent that lacked any support or protection.[149]

As in any community, some were more courageous than others. When danger threatened, Prioress Staiger repeatedly had to leave her cloister earlier than she might have done otherwise, since she had to get the more timid nuns to relative safety. Others were willing to stay behind to look after the cloister and continue working the fields. When the Protestant enemy entered Eichstätt's bishopric in April 1633, Staiger and her nuns were ordered to flee to the castle

---

[149] Liebhart, *Altbayerisches Klosterleben*, 40–41. After the suicide, Bavaria's elector admonished the appropriate institutions to keep better watch over the cloister and render more timely assistance in case of economic dearth, so that in the future such desperate actions could be forestalled.

(St. Willibaldsburg) or the city, but some remained with their laborers. As the enemy drew ever closer, Staiger sent for the remaining sisters to come up to the castle. A few complied, "but several dared [to stay] because they did not like to leave the cloister deserted." Next the antagonists were before the city, and the prioress ordered all sisters moved to the castle, but two still stayed behind. When the Swedes rode toward Mariastein, these two nuns and the household servants tried to escape through the washhouse, onto a boat, across the Hofmühl, and onto the mountain of St. Willibaldsburg. There "they crept back and forth like poor sheep ... because no one was let in or out [of the castle], but when one finally heard that these were people from the cloister Mariastein, the [guard] drew them up over the fortifications and let them enter the castle."[150] This episode illustrates vividly the differing degrees of daring and nerve one might find in a group.

During sieges, men and women worked alongside one another in the defense of a city or a monastery.[151] Some narrators singled out females as particularly courageous or smart. In February 1641, for example, French troops under General Georg Christoph von Taupadel beset Berching in Eichstätt's diocese. While the men had fled the city, the women opened the gates and threw themselves at the feet of the general, who spared the inhabitants but took the church silver.[152]

The Dominican nuns of Heiliggrab by Bamberg proved both smart and gutsy in their dealings with the occupiers. Since the Swedes had taken over the city in 1632, no Catholic mass had been permitted. While their convent was the only one allowed to ring the bell (that tolled the prayer hours), they dearly missed Holy Mass. None of the *Patres* was at hand, so the nuns asked a chaplain, whom they had found disguised as a student in their courtyard, and he willingly obliged. All this had to be done secretly so that the soldiers did not notice him entering and leaving the cloister. One day, however, the soldiers arrived before Holy Mass was over, and the chaplain was trapped inside the cloister with the sisters. The sisters had to hide him all day long – with both parties deeply afraid of being discovered. Worse, during the evening hours, Colonel Grel arrived with his wife and wanted to see the cloister. The sisters were "half dead with fear" because not only did they expect to be plundered; they also did not know what to do with the "good man" they had hidden.

Junius and two other nuns locked the priest in the "new parlor" and reassured him that no one would come to this room. While they told him "not to

---

150   *Klara Staigers Tagebuch*, 81.
151   Friesenegger, *Tagebuch*, 75 (17 April 1634).
152   Buchner, "Ruinen," 23.

be so fainthearted" and that the sisters would defend him, Junius admits: "I did comfort him, but my heart was so full of fear and pain that I cannot express it, because I thought all the time, how will my fellow sisters fare? What do the people want to do here this late [at night]?"[153] In the meantime, their prioress tried to convince the colonel at the speaking window, through which the religious communicated with the world outside the cloister's walls, to come back the next day because of the late hour. But Grel insisted, and so the prioress had to let him, several other military men, and three wives enter. Having all but forced his entry into the convent, Colonel Grel quickly tried to put the sisters at ease: "The worthy mother and sisters should not be afraid or frightened because we came so late ... since we are also bringing our wives, and we do not come as enemies but as your very good friends."[154] Then the colonel asked the prioress to call all her sisters so that he could see them. When Junius and the two nuns who were staying with the chaplain were summoned, they begged to stay behind and suggested they tell the colonel that several of the sisters were sick, "because if we leave, the *gutte herr fridterig* [the man in hiding] would wither away of anguish."[155] Yet when Grel again insisted on seeing all the sisters and was beginning to search the convent, Junius and the two nuns had to join the others. The colonel then demanded dinner for himself and his companions (fourteen people altogether), even though the convent had nothing to offer. The nuns sent to the city for fish, prepared and served it with some of their homemade goods, and asked that the limited provisions be excused. When Grel turned to send one of his servants to his quarters for more food, the latter pointed out that nothing could be unearthed there either.

While in general the relationship between the nuns and the Swedish occupiers was amicable, these exchanges show an important layer to the dynamic. Colonel Grel did not take "no" for an answer, not even from the sisters. When he had his mind set on visiting the nuns, nothing – not the inconvenience to them nor the lateness of the hour – could persuade him to leave. Despite all the expressions of goodwill, the Swedish occupiers, nevertheless, held the power. Still, the colonel seemed intent on making the nuns feel more comfortable and asked his men to put down their swords "so that the good maidens see that we are coming as their good friends and only desire to be merry with them."[156] While the Dominican nuns had to join the visitors in their meal, they could not eat anything out of anxiety over their trapped "pious *herrn fridterig*."

---

153 Hümmer, ed., "Bamberg im Schweden-Kriege," 52:40.
154 Hümmer, ed., "Bamberg im Schweden-Kriege," 52:40–41.
155 Hümmer, ed., "Bamberg im Schweden-Kriege," 52:41.
156 Hümmer, ed., "Bamberg im Schweden-Kriege," 52:42.

"With God's help," one sister was finally able to get him out of the convent without any of the colonels being the wiser.

Junius describes their experience during the meal as "no different than if we had been in purgatory." The colonels, for their part, were at a loss for why the sisters were so miserable and reassured them even more fervently that "[the colonels] were here to protect us; no harm would come to us. We, however, answered that we were not sad, but that this is just our way; and that we were not used to secular people in our cloister." Whenever the nuns had to fetch something, they were so afraid that they did not go alone, which aroused the attention of one of the visitors. Upon his inquiry why no one went by herself, Junius replied: "this is the [Dominican] order's custom that all should be walking in twos or threes, which he believed immediately and said that this was quite proper." Although their visitors were "very chaste and honorable in their conversations," the sisters grew tired of their guests and asked them to leave. The company quickly departed, thanking the nuns "profusely for all the honor and goodness we had shown them, and if we needed something or had any complaint, we should only let them know – [Grel] would protect and help us anytime."[157]

Survival during the Thirty Years' War was not for the fainthearted, and many of the stories recorded show amazing pluck. Nevertheless, as Junius' testimony underlines, such displayed courage was rarely the daredevil kind of fearless bravery, but rather a willingness to act despite being deeply afraid. Women and men facing the war's adversities often exhibit a combination – even a simultaneity – of anxiety and daring, albeit one where either fear or audacity could get the upper hand. If one had the ingenuity and ready wit of some of the Dominican nuns at Heiliggrab who were quick with a smart response, one was in an advantageous position.

Whereas many of the above stories narrate the actions taken by a group or people supported by their community, individuals often could rely only on themselves. Some of their fascinating stories have survived. The visionary Anna Vetter (1630–1703), for example, relates the story of one woman's nerve and resourcefulness: that of her mother. After Anna's father had died of wounds inflicted by marauders, her mother was left in Weißenburg, Franconia, to bring up her four children at a time when no bread was to be had. She swiftly sold her late husband's forging tools, went to Eichstätt to buy bread, and returned to sell it in Weißenburg at a good profit. During the following years she endured much misery: she was robbed on one of her trips to Eichstätt, had to vacate her home, and lost one of her children. Faced with increasing inflation and the

---

157   Hümmer, ed., "Bamberg im Schweden-Kriege," 52:42–43.

plague, and without means to support her remaining children, she bought the beds, on which people had just died, cheaply, carried them for miles, and sold them again. She finally remarried, but she and her husband lost everything when the Swedes raided their village.[158]

The story of Anna's mother shows that one had to be able to adjust quickly to the war's changing conditions and not be beaten by either the gloomiest circumstances nor by the fact that, continually, one had to start all over again. Her methods to ensure survival may have been shady at times, but, like those of the nuns and many others, they demonstrate courage and resilience. Bravery, however, was not always rewarded. When the minister of Oberweiling (in Eichstätt's diocese) boldly fired at the Swedes from the church's tower and then escaped down the bell rope, the enemy responded by burning down the church and village. Oberweiling's authorities were not pleased and wanted to burden the minister with the costs of rebuilding the vicarage since he was responsible for the fire in the first place.[159] Nevertheless, pluck, determination, and ingenuity surface time and again as decisive qualities that might make the difference between life and death.

It is doubtful that the above vignette of Oberweiling's clergyman describes the common reaction of most ministers under the pressure of war, but it does point to the circumstance that many pastors, no matter whether Catholic or Protestant, had to fend for themselves – at least in the countryside. Different from monastics, peasants, and burghers who could take action as a collective, solitary pastors had no such natural communities, unless they resided in a larger town or city where they might be surrounded by other colleagues. Even though they formed an occupational group and belonged to a community, because of their special position, ministers were not necessarily an integrated part of the parish. Typically, they came from different locales, and their education set them apart from their parishioners – again, more so in the countryside than in the city.[160] These circumstances made it more difficult for them, although not impossible, to be incorporated into communal initiatives.

---

158 Beyer-Fröhlich, ed., *Selbstzeugnisse*, 72–73. On Anna Vetter, see Kormann, *Ich, Welt und Gott*, 158–73. Anna Vetter's mother most likely moved these beds elsewhere because they were considered contaminated, and she would have run into trouble with the local authorities.
159 Buchner, *Bistum Eichstätt*, 2:295.
160 This was at first more the case among the Protestant clergy, but after the Council of Trent (1545–1563) the Roman Catholic Church also placed a premium on their priests' education. On the Protestant clergy, see Dixon and Schorn-Schütte, eds., *The Protestant Clergy*, and Schorn-Schütte, *Evangelische Geistlichkeit*.

The minister's position in a congregation during wartime also depended on the kind of stress the parish experienced: whether it faced "only" economic hardships or religious pressures as well (i.e., forced conversion to the confession of the occupiers). In the latter case, if communities decided to resist, their minister often became their spiritual leader, with collective action welding the congregation together in their resistance and sometimes in exile. Many villages, however, struggled with the economic consequences of troops in their area, and, in this case, rural ministers had to confront the grim consequences largely by themselves.

The consistorial records of Brandenburg-Ansbach to the west of Nuremberg show in heart-wrenching ways the extreme destitution of its ministers (*Capitulares*). We know about their wretched circumstances because they took one of the few steps that were left to them to improve their lot: supplications to the consistory.[161] Petitions represented an important initiative of other distressed and enraged contemporaries as well: peasants and local administrators appealed to the next level for relief of numerous kinds, but the ministers' correspondence with the consistory is particularly revealing about the plight of these often solitary figures, who were expected to hold out on their posts during threats and to tend spiritually to the frightened and the sick. One may ask to what degree such reports can be trusted to reflect the true conditions, but, even though the precise measure of neediness may have been exaggerated at times, the repeated and ever more desperate appeals and eventually the departure of at least some ministers speak vividly to the often untenable position in which they found themselves.

At times, one reads about parishioners stepping in when a minister did not receive any pay. Our familiar chronicler Bartholomæus Dietwar relates one such instance when "several good-hearted burghers of Kitzingen voluntarily put together a bit of money" to help out the ministers.[162] More often, however, the pastors complained about lacking salary and having little or no support from their parishioners, who were supposed to contribute to the minister's livelihood. In his supplication of December 1634 to Brandenburg-Ansbach's consistory, Franciscus Artzt, pastor in Altentrüdingen, dolefully narrates his dismal situation.[163] Between plundering troops and firestorms, he had lost all his fortune and had not received the tithe for four years. Then, the previous summer, the entire land, including Altentrüdingen, had been completely

---

161 On petitions, see Gerstenberger, *Der bittende Mensch*.
162 LAELKB, MD Uffenheim, Akt. 95:94–95 (1635).
163 For the following, see Figure 4 on p. 17 (map of Franconia with an insert of the discussed locales).

ruined. Destitute, he had been driven from his parish, and even though he had returned and wanted to continue serving his congregation, he had neither a penny nor a piece of bread to his name. Unless he received assistance, he would be reduced to begging. Reminding the consistory of his twenty-two years of service as a minister and four more as a teacher, Artzt petitioned the lords for a new position, with which he hoped to sustain himself.[164]

Instead of transferring him, the consistory gave him two more parishes, but the following year Artzt reported that, even though he was supposed to receive a little weekly supplement from the three parishes, he kept being put off with empty promises. Then he voiced his deep dismay about his parishioners: "If it were up to them, a minister surely would have to starve to death, because they are more willing to remunerate a shepherd of swine (*Sauhirten*) than a shepherd of souls (*Seelenhirten*)." The consistory tried to mollify its *Capitulares* by suggesting that the lack of support from parishioners had more to do with the hard times than ill will toward their ministers. Artzt eventually caught on that petitions were not enough. The next year he wrote the consistory again, but this time he presented his superiors with a suggestion for a parish.[165]

The lesson that being proactive was the most effective means to improve one's lot also slowly dawned on Tobias Krug, minister of Ammerndorf, whose supplications give us further insight into the plight of the rural clergy. Krug had been taken hostage by enemy soldiers and imprisoned for ten weeks in Pappenheim. Because of the heavy ransom he had to pay and his physical weakness due to the imprisonment, he found himself destitute and heavily indebted. As Krug describes it, his parish in Ammerndorf was a wasteland, his parishioners were in no position to pay him the tithe, and he himself had been plundered many times. Thus, in March 1633, he fervently implored Brandenburg-Ansbach's consistory to provide him with another vacancy, reminding them of his considerable age (58 years) and his 27 years of service. Half a year later, Krug again turned to the consistory, whose lords had responded to his earlier request by adding two more parishes to the one he already had in Ammerndorf, all of which he had served for 14 weeks "not without danger because of the to and fro of the soldiers." With winter just ahead and in view of his advanced age and physical weakness, however, he was concerned that he would be unable to manage the long treks to the various parishes. Moreover, the new congregations – Großhabersdorf and especially Vinzensbronn – were themselves so entirely ruined that they could not sustain a minister. At this point, Krug still showed understanding for the lack of support from the parishioners,

---

164 LAELKB, MK Ansbach, C, Spez. 27, Altentrüdingen, vol. 1.
165 LAELKB, MK Ansbach, C, Spez. 27, Altentrüdingen, vol. 1 (19 August 1635 and 27 May 1636).

who could barely keep themselves from starving and certainly did not have anything left for the minister – "however much they otherwise wanted to give." Therefore, he entreated the consistory once again to transfer him to another post, "where I can spend my life in peace (*Ruhe*)."[166]

His subsequent supplications speak of his mounting debt and lack of victuals. In January 1634, at home in Ammerndorf, he suffered another enemy attack of soldiers from Forchheim, who pushed him around, struck him on the head, and took what little he had left. He was supposed to come with them as prisoner, but when their leader saw him "wounded and stripped entirely" of his clothes, the colonel told him to go home. Evidently, even the enemy took pity on his miserable state. Krug continued to detail his destitute situation, for the first time mentioning his "weak" wife and child. His travels to the two other parishes for Sunday sermons and other duties garnered him little more than a bowl of soup, whereas during the week he had to go hungry. People no longer lent him money, since he could not pay them back, and so he turned to the consistory once again in the hope that it "would, on account of God's mercy, ponder my extreme misery and hardship ... and graciously consider me for a more comfortable (*bequemblichern*) *Translation* (parish transfer)."[167] As before, Krug underlined that he wished to serve God and his church "in quiet" circumstances. Gone were any remarks that expressed understanding for the struggling parishioners, which points to his increasingly desperate situation.

Krug was indeed in a grim position. He soon found out that the minister, who had fled the two parishes in which Krug was serving in addition to Ammerndorf, had returned and was given back his duties. Even though Krug had earlier complained about the inadequacy of these places to support him, it is understandable why he was so incensed about these actions. While he had endured much pain and danger to care for the added congregations during the last nine months and had been able to eke out a meager living, the original minister, who had absconded to a safer place, could just waltz back in and take this however tenuous lifeline away from Krug. Nor was the promised "promotion, for which he had willingly taken [these efforts] upon himself," forthcoming. Krug thus entreated the lords of the consistory once more ardently to nominate him at the first opportunity for a "more comfortable" ("and safer," added in the margins) position. After a long list of all the misfortunes he had borne because of his ministry, he stated his willingness to go any place that was devoted to the Augsburg Confession.[168]

---

166   LAELKB, MK Ansbach, C, Spez. 31 Ammerndorf, vol. 1, Nr. 32.
167   LAELKB, MK Ansbach, C, Spez. 31 Ammerndorf, vol. 1, Nr. 33.
168   LAELKB, MK Ansbach, C, Spez. 31 Ammerndorf, vol. 1, Nr. 34 (20 March 1634).

Finally, in May 1634, things began to take a turn for the better. Krug wrote the consistory again, but this time for a testimony of his qualifications. A position had opened up at the court of Erbach in the Odenwald. Krug told the lords that despite his hope for improvement and assistance his situation had become so unbearable that he was forced to consider "other places for my welfare and needs." The accompanying note from the minister and court preacher, Johann Klein, discloses that Krug had called on the counts of Erbach and had offered his services as *"Exul Christi"* (Exile of Christ).[169] In the end, it was not the consistory but Krug's own initiative in locating an opportunity that improved his situation.

Supplications, then, constituted an important avenue for ministers to pour out their woes and to direct their complaints to the central authorities in the hope of assistance. Krug's and Artzt's examples, however, show that, during critical times of warfare and destruction, the consistory's ability to help their ministers was exceedingly limited. At one point, in 1634, only one secretary was left in the consistory to staff the office and respond to the mounting crises.[170] The lords of the consistory were quite aware of, and certainly not unsympathetic to, the dismal situation of its *Capitulares* in the parishes. In their response to Krug's request to release him, the lords readily confirmed not only his character, but also the truth of his destitute situation, which was brought about especially by the fact that his parishioners were entirely ruined by warfare and had either starved to death or had left, begging staff in hand, for foreign lands (*bittern elend*).[171] Many clergymen likewise approached the consistory because they were facing starvation. The lords tried to find solutions, but they could do little to lessen the burden. As we saw in Krug's and Artzt's cases, one preferred solution was to combine several parishes under one pastor. This procedure mitigated two problems: one, the total number of parishioners from two or three shrunken parishes might generate enough income to sustain a minister; and, two, the policy provided for the parishioners as well, whom the war with its decimation of pastors had left without spiritual guidance. Yet, the minister had to put his life on the line as he traveled on uncertain roads from parish to parish. Moreover, three or more impoverished parishes did not necessarily add up to a sufficient salary. Supplications, then, were a valuable start, but the most promising strategy for ameliorating one's situation consisted in the minister

---

169 LAELKB, MK Ansbach, C, Spez. 31 Ammerndorf, vol. 1, Nr. 35 and 36. The self-identification as exiles of Christ developed especially among educated Lutherans from 1550 on. See von der Osten-Sacken, "Lutheran Exiles of Christ."
170 Wittmann, *Sophia Markgräfin*, 19.
171 LAELKB, MK Ansbach, C, Spez. 31, Ammerndorf, vol. 1, Nr. 37.

conducting his own inquiries regarding vacant parishes and then submitting his request for that parish to the consistory.

Another set of petitions by the minister Elias Otto brings out further nuances concerning the ways in which rural ministers tried to cope with their deteriorating circumstances. Intriguingly, less than two years after Krug had left Ammerndorf for better prospects, Otto requested that parish for himself. He had been a minister in Neuses auf dem Berg, but he had had to go into exile when the enemy occupied his village and installed a Catholic priest. He eventually moved to Nuremberg "to beg Christian compassionate hearts for alms."[172] Apparently Otto saw his only hope in a city like Nuremberg, where he could count on a certain measure of poor relief.

Otto, however, did not remain an "idle beggar" for long, but took pains to find a new position. His letter to the consistory makes clear that, in addition to conducting his own inquiries, he talked to each of the involved parties at the envisioned new locale to ensure they were all on board before he petitioned for the post. From Nuremberg he travelled to Ammerndorf and spoke with the district administrator and the burgomaster. He learned from the community that they would like to have their own minister and caretaker of their souls. For a while, ever since Krug had left, the parson of Roßtal had assumed some of these duties, but he came only about every three weeks, preached his sermon, ate a meal, and hurried back to Roßtal without teaching the youths the catechism. Conversely, in these dangerous times, the villagers did not want to go to church in Roßtal, since they did not dare to leave their homes unattended for fear of the plundering troops.[173] Even though long-winded, the letter makes a compelling – and, as it turned out, successful – case why Ammendorf needed a minister and why this person ought to be Elias Otto.

The stories of Krug and Otto, with the former trying to escape Ammerndorf and the latter seeking to serve its parish, raise some questions. Had Ammerndorf recovered somewhat during the two years since Krug's departure in 1634 to make the locale more attractive to Otto? Or had the parish simply looked more promising to Otto than to Krug because the former considered it at a different juncture in his life than Krug did? Otto had no position and no income whatever, whereas Krug had been toiling desperately in this parish for some time without making any headway, even with the addition of two further parishes. Ten years later, Otto would be in a similar position as Krug in 1633–34: Ammerndorf was so desolate and ruined that Otto was unable to make a living. Once again, he took matters into his own hands and petitioned

---

172 LAELKB, MK Ansbach, C, Spez. 31, Ammerndorf, vol. 1, Nr. 40 (22 June 1636).
173 LAELKB, MK Ansbach, C, Spez. 31, Ammerndorf, vol. 1, Nr. 40.

the consistory to give him an additional parish: Habersdorf. As before, he had done his research and had contacted the commune, which lay about an hour away from Ammerndorf. Because Habersdorf was also ruined, the parish could not maintain its own minister, but it would like to have Otto tend to its spiritual needs.[174] This time the initiative toward multiple parishes in one hand came from the minister himself, not the consistory.

These narrative accounts draw attention to the complexities of people's situations and struggles to maintain life during the war, although the petitions provide only limited insight into the psyche of these two ministers. While it took Krug several rounds of supplications to realize that the consistory could not help him, Otto seemed to have comprehended early on that it was he who needed to make things happen. The reasons for these differences in behaviors may be rooted in different personalities, or they may lie in distinct experiences and conditions. Krug repeatedly mentioned his advanced age as a great burden in his ministry, which made bearing the war's challenges and deprivations more difficult. In addition to the usual war-induced poverty, Krug was also worn down by his large debt. But he might also have been a less "take-charge" kind of person. Conversely, the fact that Otto decided to go to Nuremberg may have been a move of desperation or creative thinking, or both. He may have counted not only on a better poor relief system there, but also on the imperial city as a crossroads of people, where he could more easily obtain information about available positions. His meticulous preparation in obtaining a new post certainly points to someone who was as proactive as one could be in these times.

The stories show that the ministers' neediness was real, but also relative – that is, relative to their strength, position, age, personality, and overall experiences during the war. Krug's letters highlight the exhaustion that came with his attempts to fulfill his duties as a minister during wartimes. Not surprisingly, he repeatedly asked for a parish that would afford him a life in a quieter vein. The testimony of Martin Bötzinger, minister in the Thuringian-Franconian borderland, echoes Krug's sentiments. In his autobiographical account, Bötzinger narrates that he had suffered much during the war and had asked for a transfer into a calmer region. His second move finally placed him in a parish, where the peasants had not been touched by the war and where he was treated with much sympathy. At his new post, he said, he felt as if he had been born again, that he had escaped death, and he finally dared to believe in a better future.[175]

---

174   LAELKB, MK Ansbach, C, Spez. 31, Ammerndorf, vol. 1, Nr. 40 (11 March 1645).
175   Bötzinger, *Leben und Leiden*, 36–37.

As in so many cases during this war, in the end it came down to oneself and how much initiative one was willing and able to take to improve one's situation. Curiously, the consistory's role amounted to little more than signing off on the solutions proposed by the ministers. Instead, the two important partners in the various negotiations were the distressed ministers and the parishioners of underserved parishes, who desired to ensure their spiritual guidance.

4 Connections, Communities, and Space

In many of the above stories, networks and connections enhanced peoples' chances of survival. They played an important role in the stories of the ministers above. Even though they had a difficult time finding a new parish and typically had to fend for themselves, they could at least draw on an ecclesiastical system to ferret out more auspicious locales. Members of religious orders belonged to both a community and an extensive monastic network of their order. Beyond these helpful realities, their status as *religiosi* tied them to the world of the orders at large. Members of different orders helped one another as they could and saw fit. This frequently entailed housing individuals or groups of religious for long periods of time, travelling together into exile, and supporting one another with provisions during lean periods. The coordinate grid of the religious orders also facilitated its members' search for places of refuge. The example of the Augustinian nuns of Mariastein by Eichstätt illustrates that, through their Augustinian network, the sisters relied on contacts to which they could appeal for donations. Likewise, the country and civic elites commonly had networks that afforded them places, to which they could withdraw, and resources they could use.

These avenues did not make it easy to counteract the destructive consequences of the war, but they provided at least passageways, a platform from which to start, or an initial lift for people to regroup and begin again. Moreover, such connections came in different forms and had distinct values. The Dominican sisters of St. Katharina in Augsburg, for example, who hailed from distinguished families in the city, had powerful political protectors, whereas the Dominican nuns of Heiliggrab by Bamberg had more to fear from Bamberg's political leadership than from the Swedes. Still, institutional networks and family assets afforded these groups advantages that were not available to the broader populace, for whom personal and local connections alone provided vital assistance.

The potential of obtaining aid through relationships point to the importance of community. Many of the religious discussed above highlight the vital role community played in their struggles to survive the war. Melchior of Straubing, of Landshut's Capuchins, for example, underlines the essential role of fellowship. When, after their imprisonment, the Swedish colonel sent them to stay with the Reformed Franciscans, the latter welcomed them warmly.[176] In each other's company, they "told one another what they had experienced."[177] Community could offer two of the most essential elements for persevering, namely companionship and being able to talk through and thereby process one's experiences. These fundamental aspects are also underscored by the Benedictine abbot Veit Höser of Oberaltaich. Before Höser and his brethren had to flee in late 1633, their abbey served briefly as refuge for everyone on the run – religious from other monasteries, weighty secular men, and many commoners. While this motley crew exchanged news and tried to verify information about the approaching army, the tables were set, and over thirty strangers shared a meal, "enjoying the food, talking with one another, and discussing everything they had experienced themselves as eyewitnesses."[178] This companionship became even more important during flights. Many people crossed paths on their run and were eager for company. The prelate of Windberg (Michael Fuchs) implored Höser and others: "Let's stay together all day and share our meals, and after supper please stay overnight!" During the night they climbed the mountain to take in the surrounding burning villages: "After we watched the night's spectacle for a while, we returned to the parsonage and ruminated on what we had witnessed but had not digested (*wir kauten das Geschaute, aber nicht Verdaute, in unserer Unterhaltung wieder*)."[179] Only then did they sleep. The company and camaraderie were important, not only because they dispelled loneliness and provided comfort, but also because they enabled them to work through and absorb what they had witnessed: "Everyone told one another extensively about their own misery and mourned and lamented the common disaster."[180] Sharing one's misfortune and talking things through at length provided vital relief and the opportunity to integrate one's own experiences into the larger happenings of the time.

Höser juxtaposes the critical significance of conversation and companionship with the distress over separation from the community. He describes the "fateful night" in November 1634, when "our most beloved community was torn

---

176   As a reminder, the Capuchins were an offshoot of the Reformed Franciscans.
177   StBM, Cgm 2943, 11ʳ.
178   Sigl, *Veit Hösers Kriegstagebuch*, 85.
179   Sigl, *Veit Hösers Kriegstagebuch*, 100–101.
180   Sigl, *Veit Hösers Kriegstagebuch*, 137.

apart, our brotherly unity blown up, and the individual *religiosi* scattered."[181] At first the Benedictine brethren had anticipated that they could soon return to the "monastic family," but presently they lost all hope and trekked separately to various provinces. While fleeing might increase one's chances of survival, it tore apart the community, the crucial framework through which life could be sustained and catastrophic experiences digested. But, as Höser's lines indicate, flights could also lead to chance encounters and foster momentary associations of fate among similarly beleaguered souls, who took the place of one's original circle in absorbing and dealing with what happened. When Clara Staiger and her sisters had to flee to Ingolstadt, they received many alms, "but more from the Neuburgers and foreigners than from the Ingolstädters, who did not greatly respect strangers. The [natives] had neither experienced our grief nor did they understand it."[182] Other refugees understood what they had gone through and shared with them the little they had. Such fellowship during the war's grim periods lifted people's spirits and helped them through their hardship.

Exile, whether temporary or permanent, not only disrupted the community that shaped one's life; it also separated one from home. Space encompasses a complex set of aspects vital to one's life. Most people felt intensely about their home and *Heimat*. The strong affinity with this place and the pain over leaving one's home were expressed countless times in autobiographical accounts. *Heim* (home) and *Heimat* connoted a place one could relate to, of which one had intimate knowledge, and to which one's identity was tied. Typically, this space was where one's community resided – be it one's family, kin, neighbors, or religious family. While these spaces were not free of tensions and problems, they generated a sense of familiarity and connection, a place that offered strength and support during times of upheaval. In contrast, expressions for leaving one's home – going "into misery" or "into strange lands" (*ins Elend* or *in die Fremde gehen*) – carried notions of desolation, despair, grief, and alienation.

At the end of the war, Clara Staiger and her nuns wanted to stay home despite the danger of nearby troops.[183] The Benedictine abbot, Veit Höser, too, postponed going into exile and for the longest time kept evading the enemy by withdrawing from the abbey to places close by but still on the abbey's land, until he finally saw no other option but to leave "his mother," the abbey. When, in February 1633, Bamberg's burgomaster Keim warned Heiliggrab's nuns of approaching enemy troops and asked them to find shelter in the city, they refused saying "we want to remain together in our cloister and live and die

---

181   Sigl, *Veit Hösers Kriegstagebuch*, 105.
182   *Klara Staigers Tagebuch*, 142. Catholic Ingolstadt was never taken by the Swedes.
183   *Klara Staigers Tagebuch*, 315 (1648).

here." Even though all other women and children were called to come inside the city, the nuns "remained steadfast in our little holy grave [i.e., Heiliggrab]."[184]

The members of the Dominican convent St. Katharina in Augsburg also preferred staying in their home, where they could remain together as a community. We heard earlier about the involved decision-making process regarding their course of action. Prioress Kurz reminded them of the convent's special history, namely the staunch defense of their forebears during the Reformation, which must have added to their sense of identity with this space. In the end, the Dominican nuns decided to stay – a decision that was thoroughly tested during the ensuing years. In her distress, Prioress Kurz decided to utilize their space – the cloister – as their bulwark. Her ammunition consisted of shrewd maneuvering and negotiations, which revolved around their enclosure. For the Dominican prioress, enclosure became her most important bargaining chip to keep the occupiers out and her convent safe. By insisting on honoring their enclosure, Kurz was able to protect her community.

The Dominican nuns attracted a considerable amount of attention from the Swedish occupiers. The callers were partly motivated by curiosity, as when several soldiers and evangelical preachers came to St. Katharina's door and desired to see the nuns. The men eventually left, but the following months brought a stream of such demands for entry into their enclosed space. Kurz held against these pressures with all her might. More often, the visitors' intention was of a military nature. Three royal commissioners came by to search their cloister for grain and ammunition that the nuns might be hiding. The men also demanded 20,000 pounds of bread and 50 buckets of beer, as well as access to the cloister. Kurz entreated the men to honor their enclosure, since the sisters had been keeping it for a very long time. She was also determined to protect their granary from the enemy's seizure, and she succeeded in both. When the commissioners confronted the prioress, instead of giving them the keys to the granary, Kurz and the steward "detained and distracted them by talking about other matters so that they forgot [the granary] entirely and no longer thought about it, which was very beneficial to the cloister because the grain was very plentiful at that time."[185] The two senior religious deftly sidestepped the issue and smartly turned the commissioners' minds to other matters, which saved their grain.

With regard to the men's enormous demands for provisioning, Kurz asked them to spare the convent, since it was unable to fulfill such huge requests, but her entreaties and excuses earned her only threats, so that, in the end, the

---

184   Hümmer, ed., "Bamberg im Schweden-Kriege," 52:104–5.
185   DA A, HS 97, 12ᵛ–13ʳ.

convent had to send the requested bread and beer. The chronicler describes the prioress' realistic assessment and clearheaded maneuvering of the situation: "But since the very reverend mother prioress saw that it cannot be otherwise and so that nothing worse might happen to the cloister, she expended every possible effort that [the provisions] were prepared according to their desire." And thus the enclosure was preserved.[186] In other words, Kurz was astute enough to realize that she had to give the occupiers something to protect the assets that were more valuable – her enclosed convent and the granary – since the latter ensured their future provisions.

The pressure on the convent, however, continued. Eventually Kurz hired two soldiers as *Salva Guardia*, which helped some, but maintaining them was very expensive. Over the following months, military men – real and alleged, the chronicler remarked – tried to enter the cloister, but the prioress managed to keep their enclosure intact. In this endeavor, she went so far as to refuse refuge to the abbess of the Benedictine convent Holzen, who was looking for quarters for herself and a few of her charges. Prioress Kurz argued that she had "highly important reasons" for rejecting the abbess' request, "especially regarding enclosure, which would have been broken had they admitted them, and we would have undoubtedly given cause to the Swedes as well as to the local Evangelicals to enter the cloister."[187]

One may wonder about the underlying motives behind Kurz's rigorous stance against the Benedictine abbess of Holzen. After all, as discussed above, supporting one another in times of need proved to be essential in surviving the war. Earlier, prioress Kurz had taken in six nuns of Würzburg for a year, who belonged to the Dominican convent of St. Markus (members of one's own order were allowed into the enclosed space). Moreover, Kurz did attempt to find other solutions for the Benedictine abbess and her charges. She first suggested a room for them in their outer court, but this time their sacristan objected. Then their steward's house was offered, but it was considered too small. In the end, the Benedictine abbess moved into the Dominican cloister of St. Ursula, and the prioress was glad to be rid of this particular problem. While Maria Kurz incurred a lot of criticism for maintaining this stern but painful position, even from relatives of her nuns, she received backing from one of her trusted male advisors (Buechler): "She should by all means turn down [the request] in consideration that at this time the barrier (*Spörr*, i.e., enclosure) is our greatest treasure (*Klainot*), which has protected them this long from

---

186 DA A, HS 97, 12^v–13^r.
187 DA A, HS 97, 61^v.

all danger."[188] Both Buechler and Kurz believed that keeping the nuns' space inviolate – even in the face of those in need – was the best way to safeguard the convent and its community. The Dominican prioress thus capitalized on a male construct supposed to control female religious and employed it to keep the aggressor out and her convent safe.

The Dominican nuns by Bamberg offer us another fascinating example of the use of enclosure, but their strategy could not have been more different from their fellow sisters in Augsburg. At first Heiliggrab was prepared to move along a similar trajectory. When the Swedes threatened Bamberg, Heiliggrab's convent turned for help to the margravine, Marie von Brandenburg-Bayreuth, who advised them to remain in their cloister and let no "secular people" enter their enclosure. "We all kept this [advice] in mind and followed it."[189] As in the case of Augsburg's Dominican convent, enclosure was supposed to afford the sisters the kind of protection governments were unable to provide at this point. Intriguingly this argument in favor of the benefits of enclosure came from the Protestant margravine.

In the end, however, the nuns of Heiliggrab did not keep the margravine's counsel, but instead, under the menace of war, let the occupiers enter their space. Junius explained that the nuns initially resisted the visits and that it was the Swedes who "forced" their way into the cloister so that the nuns had to give in to them. Very quickly, however, any mention of coercion fell away. Earlier, we heard how Heiliggrab became a congenial place, which the officers regularly visited. Junius recorded the comment of a colonel that the sisters were right to allow the officers into their cloister, since they could thus see for themselves how poor the sisters were and that they lived very simply.[190] In short, giving the Protestant commanders access to their convent and insight into their lifestyle was part of ensuring their own protection from plundering and extortion.

It is important to note that Heiliggrab's sisters did not open their enclosure indiscriminately. In September 1634, common soldiers on the Swedish side came to their gate in search of bread and drink as well as fodder for their horses, and the sisters intended to hand them provisions across the cloister's wall:

---

188   DA A, HS 97, 61ᵛ, 64ʳ.
189   Hümmer, ed., "Bamberg im Schweden-Kriege," 52:20.
190   Hümmer, ed., "Bamberg im Schweden-Kriege," 52:118–19. Junius took pains to justify their behavior most likely because the sisters' positive relationship with the Swedes and their frequent visits at the convent, as well as the sisters' breaking of enclosure, aroused criticism.

> The moment our servant climbs the ladder, one [soldier] jumps with unsheathed sword over the wall into [the court] and opens the gate. Immediately four of them ride into [the court]. Among them is a fine man (*Mensch*), whom we implored to shut the gate, which he did right away. Otherwise our entire court would have been full of riders. The rude fellow, however, who had trespassed, proceeds to our door and wants to enter our cloister. Thus, one sister kicked him that he tumbles back, and she tells him: "You are not allowed to enter. No man is allowed to enter. This is enclosure." Thus, all of us were hard pressed to stop this rude fellow so that he would not run inside.[191]

In this particular case, the nuns' insistence on enclosure enhanced the nuns' protection. Their nuanced strategy, which tailored their use of enclosure to the rank and character of the attacker and assessed which tactic might provide the greatest safety, underlines the astuteness of these Dominican nuns in negotiating their survival. This is also underlined by the way they discerned the "fine man" among the soldiers and convinced him to aid their cause. As in many other instances, here, too, Heiliggrab's sisters quickly grasped what the situation demanded and pursued shrewd solutions. As the nun's shoving of the soldier shows, the sisters were not above man-handling a soldier if pushed too far, but more typically they resorted to enlisting men who championed their cause.

Home was an important space, and, as we saw, could be used in ingenious ways, but, especially during war, it was also a threatened space. Not even sacred places, such as churches and monasteries, were exempt from destruction; indeed, often religious animosity erupted into violence against such holy, but oppositional sites. Cities were sometimes able to defend their space, or they negotiated an accord with the occupiers to preserve the community and its place in exchange for a large payment and other conditions. *Salva Guardias* were hired to protect one's space, but more often than not they proved useless and too expansive to maintain. Despite instances of resistance, many people saw no other choice but flight. For them, the preservation of one's home was ultimately less important than protecting one's life and livelihood.

Going into exile, then, often remained the only option for survival. Previous chapters discussed what this experience meant: the destabilizing effects it had on oneself and one's community; the burden of having to make one's home in the wild forest, the crowded city, the monastery, or any place that provided a modicum of safety. Frequently, leaving home proved temporary, although

---

191 Hümmer, ed., "Bamberg im Schweden-Kriege," 53:218.

no one knew for certain how this flight would end. Notably, in the movement of men and women to new living quarters, one can discern that people and places were not created equal. Nuns moved into the spaces their male superiors had left, and commoners crammed into the cities the elites had vacated. The Benedictine, Maurus Friesenegger, alludes to this pattern in 1646:

> Since the elector [Maximilian] has left the city [Munich], the greater part of the inhabitants, especially the nobles and the more affluent, followed him and left house and city to the peasants and the rabble (*Pöbel*), who fled into [the city] from the countryside and who have filled the city with their carts and their rescued stuff (*Plunder*) to such an extent that one can hardly pass through anymore.[192]

Two years later, the abbot commented on the same procedure, but in a more acerbic tone: "the rich dragged their riches on loaded wagons out [of Munich], and the poor hauled their poverty on bleeding backs into [the city]."[193] On their repeated flights, the Augustinian prioress, Clara Staiger, describes a variation on this pattern – in this instance with regard to the nuns and their guardians: when in 1646 Eichstätt's prince-bishop fled St. Willibald's Castle, the sisters moved into the vacated space.[194] In December the peasantry made for the city and the citizens for the castle. Shortly thereafter, the nuns were told to move from the castle down to the city because the bishop had decided to return to St. Willibald's.[195] This curious reshuffling of living quarters evidently proceeded according to a specific hierarchy of power, position, gender, and connections. Plainly, safety could be obtained only consistent with one's station and gender.

Besides temporary exile, people also elected or were forced to leave their *Heimat* permanently, which engendered all the destabilizing experiences discussed earlier. If contemporaries were unable to preserve their home or if staying proved too traumatic, the prospect of finding a new, more tranquil home could at least provide hope. This was unmistakable with some of the ministers, who were so bogged down by the dismal conditions of their parish that envisioning themselves in a new space gave them the energy to go on and create a more promising future in a new space. Still, the situation of the ministers is

---

192 Friesenegger, *Tagebuch*, 140.
193 Friesenegger, *Tagebuch*, 163.
194 *Klara Staigers Tagebuch*, 274 (1641), 309 (1646).
195 *Klara Staigers Tagebuch*, 312. Similarly, as noted earlier, after Bamberg's prince-bishop had left the city for fortified Forchheim, he offered Heiliggrab's nuns refuge in the city he had just fled.

different from that of their parishioners, who typically lived in their village all their lives, whereas their pastors had moved to the village to take up their ministry. Thus, the local ties were more likely stronger with the native population. Moreover, while ministers could take advantage of an ecclesiastical grid to find new parishes, peasants largely had to fend for themselves if their homes and *Heimat* proved beyond recovery.

Networks, connections, community, and spaces thus were of vital importance in surviving the war and its consequences, but it is also evident that their benefits were available to varying degrees. Besides these largely external factors, other forces, to which we now turn, played crucial parts in how men and women sustained themselves during this conflict.

5   Religion and Other Formative Forces

Alongside various practical measures, people relied on mental resources that might help them through the war. Apart from the fact that "religion" and "confession" constituted sizable components in stimulating and sustaining this conflict, in an intensely religious age, many looked toward religion to make sense of the disaster and to find consolation. The topic deserves a book-length study, in which the wealth of religious materials at people's disposal, and how they employed these sources, would be discussed at greater length. This chapter can offer only a first foray into this vast subject.

The following will consider spiritual aids for clergy and laity, and the recourse members of both groups took to religion.[196] In the process, we will address theological interpretations of the war and to what extent these were shared by the general populace. Inevitably we will encounter quite diverse understandings of and approaches to religion, which prompts the question of how to define the term. Here I will use "religion" in the widest sense possible to include versions of orthodox and magic practices, and any mixture thereof. In other words, "religion" is whatever spiritual belief and practice people consider it to be.

5.1   *Official Religious Resources*

Contemporaries had a range of resources to draw from when it came to religious aids and explanations. Prayers, sermons, songs, and instructional texts offered rationales and words of comfort to the suffering. These show both

---

196   Because of the geographic concentration, the religious material is mostly of the Catholic and Lutheran variety.

commonality and divergence, which can in part be explained by differences in Catholic and evangelical positions, stages in the war, and audiences, but the variety also points more generally to a greater diversity in both Protestant and Catholic religious interpretations. Earlier we discussed how secular and ecclesiastical governments released prayers during times of crisis to counteract the war's harmful consequences or to celebrate a victory.[197] While adjusting their specific contents to the changing situation, all prayers interpreted the war as God's just punishment for people's sins and called the populace toward repentance and a return to God.

In their adapted form, prayers reveal contemporary concerns but also familiar religious argumentation. A 1619 supplication speaks to the concerns of Nuremberg's Protestants now that the emperor (who had tolerated the Protestants) was dead, and rumors about war, bloodshed, and "great tyranny" were reaching their ears. This plainly political prayer begins in the usual vein by readily admitting that the fault for the upheaval was entirely on humanity's side, and by entreating God to deal with them according to His mercy rather than His wrath over their wrongdoing. The prayer employs "the costly merit of our mediator and savior Jesus Christ" to counter humans' grievous faults, but then quickly moves into a political mode:

> Work and accomplish, O merciful and benevolent God, that, through lawful and unanimous election, in lieu of the deceased Imperial Majesty, another Christian and capable head will be placed before the common fatherland, under whose government justice will be administered, evil punished, peace and unity preserved for the praise and glory of Your most holy name and the continuous wellbeing of Your Christendom.[198]

The prayer expresses strong concerns about a potentially adverse new emperor and turns to God with pleas to ensure that the imperial crown will be transferred into the right hands. The appeal to God is couched in confessional terms and conveys an "us" versus "them" reasoning. The supplicant begs God to "enlighten the persecutors of Your saving Gospel." Moreover, in his entreaty to preserve them against assaults and destruction, he points out that it was God who planted the vineyard among them. In the words of the Psalmist, the supplicant cries, "Why do you let the heathens say, Where is your God?" and

---

197 See Chapter 3.3.
198 LAELKB, LAA Nbg, 465, Aj^r.

implores God to fight on their side against the enemy "to bestow victory and blessings upon those who love Your holy word ..."[199]

During the course of the conflict, one's religious identity or confession often served as a rallying point for gathering strength and courage. In this time of trial, it became essential to boost one's own religious confession and righteousness by denigrating the opponent's. This is also evident in a particular kind of sermon – the jubilee sermon. Preached on certain anniversaries, such as the centennial of the Augsburg Confession in 1630, the jubilee sermon provided an opportunity to celebrate, mark, and reinforce one's religious identity.[200] These festivities offered comfort to followers by claiming religious if not military victory, and by denying the enemy any justification for his religious claims.

Jubilee sermons were an important implement to strengthen the beleaguered Evangelicals at a critical juncture in the war when all seemed lost. Accordingly, their formulations were decidedly confessional and drew on the entire religious arsenal at their disposal to generate confidence and hope in the evangelical cause. Frequently they employed the simile of the mustard seed (Matthew 13:31), since it was an apt description of the embattled evangelical church, which, like the mustard seed, suffered ridicule because it seemed so small and ineffectual. One homily of 1630 focused on providing comfort by describing the history of the Evangelicals from Martin Luther (1483–1546) and Emperor Charles V (r. 1519–1556) on, and by drawing on the simile of the mustard seed. It included a song that urged trust in God despite all appearances to the contrary: "Even if it looks like He does not want to [come to our aid], don't be alarmed. Because where He is the most present, He wants it to remain a mystery." The preacher ended by encouraging his audience to join him in speaking "very joyfully and confidently" the words of Psalm 46: "God is our refuge and strength, a help in great need."[201]

Another jubilee sermon, also featuring the mustard seed, deplored that they experienced such contempt against their little church both "from those who want to be good Christians and our fellow believers, but also from our opponents, the Papists, who do not believe it is a sin when they disdain, slander, defile, and condemn our teachings to the utmost, as well as persecute those who follow [the evangelical teachings] and drive them with wife and child

---

199   LAELKB, LAA Nbg, 465, Aij^r, Ajv^v (Psalms 79:10 and 115:2).
200   On the jubilee celebrations and their significance for the Thirty Years' War, see Burkhardt, *Der Dreißigjährige Krieg*, 128–43.
201   LAELKB, MD Schwabach, Akt. 34, 4 (23 July/2 August 1630). The preacher was Leonard Teucher.

into bitter exile (*Elend*)."[202] In this precarious situation of being afflicted from all sides, the homily draws on the history of the Lutherans, especially that of Martin Luther himself, who also had to suffer much pain and difficulties: "When, through the initiative of God's Holy Spirit, [Luther] began to attack the erroneous doctrine of the papacy and to teach the Divine doctrine from the Holy Bible, he was banished and condemned to the utmost. And this, alas, is also happening to all righteous believers and steadfast Christians in these highly distressing times of persecution."[203] In other words, their own fate was not much different from Luther's.

These historical references to Luther in his anguish aimed at providing perspective and comfort to the listeners by placing them within a community of sufferers. Anyone who adhered to Christ and His Holy Gospel, whether Luther or a contemporary listener, experienced hostility. The homily fans outrage over such treatment among its audience by enumerating variations of its harassment in pairs of rhyming words: "*Sie werden bedrangt vnd bezwangt, vernicht vnd gericht, verlacht vnd veracht, geneidet vnd gemeidet, verlogen vnd betrogen, verbannt vnd verdambt* (they are being harassed and oppressed, destroyed and executed, ridiculed and despised, envied and avoided, lied to and cheated, expelled and damned)."[204] The fact – indeed, as the homilist pronounced, the miracle – that the enemies had not been able to eradicate the Lutheran Church during the previous one hundred years provided a sound reason to rejoice. Nothing, neither life nor death, could separate them from the love of Jesus Christ.[205]

After fortifying his audience with further references to scriptural texts (Romans 8:35–36 and 1 Samuel 2:30), the homilist exclaimed: "Don't let yourself be bewildered by this hostile and bloodthirsty time of persecution and the terrible ranting and raving of our enemies! The Lord Himself will set out and fight against them (Isaiah 42:13). He will rip their ropes and topple their false teachings."[206] In a final appeal, the homilist called upon his audience to be steadfast and patient in its faith, and he concluded with the prayer: "Ah, stay with us, Lord JESUS CHRIST/ since night and the end are here/ Please do not

---

202 LAELKB, MD Schwabach, Akt. 34, 23:7 (12/22 March 1631) (my pagination). The first group – those who want to be fellow Christians – most likely referred to the Reformed, who, during the second part of the sixteenth century, had labored to be considered a form of Lutheranism under the Peace of Augsburg (1555).
203 LAELKB, MD Schwabach, Akt. 34, 23:7.
204 LKA Nbg., MD Schwabach, Akt. 34, 23:7.
205 LKA Nbg., MD Schwabach, Akt. 34, 23:9–10.
206 LAELKB, MD Schwabach, Akt. 3423:11.

let expire among us/ Your dear word, the bright light/ In this last, bleak time."[207] The sermon does not deny the listeners' wretched conditions, but by juxtaposing the darkness of their situation with the brilliance of Jesus' light, it attempts to give the parishioners hope and strength: Christ's light shines in the darkness.

The strategy of confessional identity politics, as seen in prayers and jubilee sermons, may have worked during the early years of the conflict, but with every passing decade the continued violence and a seemingly unending conflict eventually led to a retreat from such thinking and toward a greater emphasis on ending this war. A 1644 prayer, published by Nuremberg's council for the city and its countryside, began with the customary admission that sinful humanity had caused the long-lasting war and that all of God's punishments (*Zornruthen*) were well deserved, then continued:

> We hoped it would be peace, but nothing good has come; we hoped we would heal, but, behold, more damage occurred. Therefore, we recognize our wrongdoing, and we are heartily sorry that we thus willfully provoked You, our dear God and Father, to anger, and that, so far, we have not acknowledged Your salutary disciplining with penitent gratitude. We beg, therefore, because of the precious merit of Your dear Son, our Lord and Savior, Jesus Christ, that You will forgive out of grace all our sins, and avert from us and alleviate the well-deserved punishments in a fatherly way.[208]

The prayer refers to a late stage during the war, when peace negotiations had begun in Westphalia but resolutions were still far away, and the southeast German lands continued to suffer under troop movements. It speaks of the dashed hopes for peace and recovery. After acknowledging that people's sinful behavior and lack of repentance were still causing God's fury, the prayer employs another common element of "negotiation with God," Jesus Christ's sacrifice for humankind: Why would God want to destroy humanity, if He sacrificed His only Son for its salvation? The supplicant then addresses other factors that prolonged the war:

> Stop anyone who lusts after war and hates peace. Control the brutal bloodshed, murder, burning, robbing, plundering, and all damaging adversity. Guide the hearts and minds of the Imperial Majesty and all electors and estates of the Roman Empire, as well as other potentates toward peace,

---

207   LAELKB, MD Schwabach, Akt. 34, 23:12.
208   LAELKB, LAA Nbg, 455/1 M, Aj^r.

that they pursue the same in earnest, and settle in a Christian way all arisen unrest through wholesome means.²⁰⁹

The long duration of the war, the supplicant suggests, was due not only to humanity's sins, but more specifically to people, especially in leading positions, who love war more than peace. Importantly, there are no references to confessional divides and enemies. Instead, the prayer calls for a "Christian" resolution.

A *Christlich Bußgebet* (Christian Penitential Prayer) of 1646 also concerned itself with the seemingly elusive prospect of tranquility this late in the war. Contrary to the prayer of 1619, when one could only envision the turmoil of war, by 1646 contemporaries had experienced more than their share. The *Bußgebet* was directed toward God as both a prayer of repentance and a "yearning for the dear peace (*Seuffzer vmb den lieben Frieden*)." Cognizant that God knew of all their misfortunes past and present during this war, it nevertheless emphasized:

> We have lost almost everything of ours, everything beautiful we owned has been destroyed; except for the pure Word of God and the correct worship, we have little left ... O faithful GOD, what gruesome destruction and desolation has gone on in the Roman Empire and in our beloved fatherland of the German Nation. How many thousand people miserably and wretchedly have been robbed of goods and chattels, body and life, some even of their souls and salvation. Simply no crisis and death, no sin and evil, no misery and tribulation can be invented that has not been experienced and heard of during this long-lasting German war.²¹⁰

After admitting that they deserved all and more because of their sins, the prayer concentrates on the fact that, despite His great wrath, God had not entirely destroyed them because His mercy was "too intense (*brünstig*)." The supplicant adds that people at all levels in the entire country had sinned and enraged God, and he entreats God to be merciful because who else could save them: "Who will go and obtain peace for us if You do not do it.... You are the LORD, who injures and bandages, who tears apart and heals again, who destroys and rebuilds, who crushes and raises up, who saddens and delights again ..." Much like the previous supplication, this one emphasizes that God is Lord over wars everywhere, and that He can control them – biblical history has proven so. The petitioner thus begs Him: "Speak You Yourself to the hearts of all potentates

---

209 LAELKB, LAA Nbg, 455/1 M, Aij^v.
210 LAELKB, DK Wassertrüdingen, 13, Nr. 5, Aij^r-v.

and to those who lead the war: Peace be with you. Bend and move their minds toward peace and unity."[211]

The tone of lament and yearning is most pronounced in this prayer. People were looking back on decades of warfare and destruction, and even though negotiations for peace had been ongoing for several years, no end seemed in sight. Although carefully constructed, it is a highly emotional prayer, in which the supplicant is close to despair over the unending conflict and damage. With this emotional charge, the penitent steps before the omnipotent God, who has the power finally to propel politicians and military leaders toward peace and bring an end to the war. While prayers of the early years are awash in confessional phrases, these examples of the war's late stage have no such agenda. Instead, they contemplate the damage to the entire German nation, point to the faults of all estates, and pray for God's spirit on every potentate on the battlefield and at the negotiating table.

Much like prayers and sermons, religious songs also tried to offer both meaning behind the misery and ways to go on. A "Fight and Consolation Song" of 1629 set out to buoy all Lutherans who had been persecuted because of the "evangelical truth."[212] This lengthy piece, which is studded with scriptural references, situates the war in the last days, when one can expect things only to get worse, and humans prove the case by behaving ever more shamefully. Admitting that he deserves all punishments, the penitent turns to Jesus Christ and asks Him to put mercy before justice because otherwise everyone would be lost (Psalm 143:2; inserted in the margin). Earlier examples called upon Christ as humanity's savior because of His own suffering and redemption, but here the Son of God is treated as both judge and redeemer, who afflicts and delights. The song tries to bolster trust and faith among the persecuted that Christ has not abandoned His church. Echoing Martin Luther, it exclaims: "Doubt is a devil's trick; woe onto those who despair" (Sirach 2: 14–15 in the margin). Instead, they should not be deterred despite all appearances and taunts of their enemies: "What God promises/ happens for certain."[213] Moreover, God has set limits for the enemies, which they cannot exceed.

This song of 1629, the year of the Edict of Restitution, is cast in an apocalyptic mode, which underlines that the last days are at hand. The turmoil of war is God's *Prognosticon*, His warning to turn one's life around. Intriguingly, the author dismisses any theologizing in favor of Christian practice: "Whatever one now keeps debating/ With regard to the sequence of pure doctrine/ We

---

211 LAELKB, DK Wassertrüdingen, 13, Nr. 5, Aij^v–Aiij^r, Aiv^r–Av^r.
212 StBM, HSS, Cgm 7866, 282^r–306^r.
213 StBM, HSS, Cgm 7866, 283^v, § 5, 284^v, § 12 and 15.

give a pass." After discussing the last days and the Antichrist (who has already been toppled spiritually and will be crushed entirely by Jesus Christ), the author again addresses the importance of a Christian life over correct theology: "Whoever desires more and does not let up/ And always wants to ruminate (*spintisiren*) [and] counterpose (*opponiren*)/ Finally has our answer/ A Christian must practice/ Faith and patience, in love and sorrow/ With enemies, and with friends ..." In short, the author not only rejects theologizing in favor of pious Christian behavior, but also advises practicing love with friends *and* foes. This will be the test of a true follower of Christ in these last days. The song ends with a clear statement of its purpose, namely to comfort and fortify the afflicted: "This song was created for your consolation/ You small flock of God/ And all who are despondent/ ... Fight mightily, brothers, and continue/ Be steadfast without wavering ..."[214]

Some songs provide historical narratives of what happened to a place and its inhabitants at a crucial time during the war, but these accounts are highly stylized to impart a forceful message. "On the Great Heartbreak of the City Rothenburg ob der Tauber" (1631) is one such song that recounts graphically the former glory and then defeat of this Franconian imperial city. The negotiated accord was not honored, and the song renders vividly the plundering, violence, fear, and heartbreak among the citizens. Much like prayers and sermons, the song ends by encouraging Rothenburg's populace to trust in God's protection: "O blessed Rothenburg: Do surrender yourself to God/ Even though the grim enemy takes your body and life/ He cannot damage your soul but quietly nourishes it ... / Remain steadfast in your hope; no hopeful person will be abandoned/ However great the misery, God can rein it in ... / You are destined for eternal life, they for the fires of hell."[215] Similarly, the *Meistersinger* of Nuremberg offered comments and advice in their songs. Ambrosius Metzger (1573–1632), composer and teacher in Nuremberg, wrote several pieces about the critical times and drew on the Psalms, the Easter Lamb, and Jesus' birth and crucifixion to comfort his audience.[216]

These songs were written at a time of great disaster for the Protestants following the Edict of Restitution (1629), and, in different ways, reflect the very limited options the Evangelicals had left. Even though the song of the Protestant city Rothenburg falls into the period after Gustavus' landing, it reflects how

---

214 StBM, HSS, Cgm 7866, 286ʳ, § 19; 287ᵛ, § 28–29.
215 StBM, HSS, Cgm 5289, fasc. 2, 105ᵛ.
216 See especially Metzger's 1630 song, which followed Psalm 130 closely ("Out of the depths have I cried unto thee, O Lord"). StBM, HSS, Cgm 6250, Nürnberger Meisterlieder, Heft 20. Metzger, who never attended a music school, left a collection of 1,400 *Meisterlieder* and 311 of his own melodies (von Imhoff, *Berühmte Nürnberger*, 185–86).

cities could suffer when armies moved through or congregated in their region. Both urge a steadfast trust in God who will come to their aid and proclaim that He is still the One in control over life and war. In Rothenburg's lament, however, the composer shifts the emphasis to the soul, which cannot be taken and will live on into eternity if people remain faithful to God. Furthermore, while people should continue to implore God for mercy, the author now counsels them to set their eyes on the afterlife. In other words, the perspective has swung from this life, which was all but lost, to the next.

Not only parishioners, but their embattled shepherds, too, needed spiritual and mental aids during this time of trial, and the clergy's superiors tried to provide their ministers with guidelines to weather the war. The consistory and deans of Brandenburg-Ansbach, for example, offered practical and spiritual advice in their directives to their *Capitulares* – often in response to specific pleas for help. When several ministers of the church district (*Dekanat*) Uffenheim were plundered, Dean Cöler communicated the consistory's instructions to the maltreated. An intriguing mixture of comforting words, rebuke, and "tough love," the mandate presented the victims a mostly religious rationale for dealing with such negative experiences. Cöler pointed out that, long ago, God had warned humans through the prophet Jeremiah about the consequences of their sins: "Since the true God has now, according to His just judgment, carried out His threat against us in the recent march through, we should therefore not wail about God and the suffered damage, but rather about our severe sin and great wrongdoing." After thus readjusting the ministers' perspective, Cöler underscored the exceptional role and place of the ministers, since they were the essential means through which God's work continued, and then reassured the ministers that God would be fighting on their side against their enemies.[217]

In an effort to shift the pastors' attention from the wrathful God, who was sending one calamity after another, to the merciful One, the consistory and dean employed a fairly common religious argumentation, namely to show proof of God's mercy by pointing toward His consistency: "Since the just God unfortunately made good on His threat to punish us for our manifold sins, there is no doubt – but rather certain and Amen – He will also amply fulfil His comforting promise toward us, according to His bottomless mercy, as long as we stand by Him in true faith and admonish our entrusted congregations toward true penance and a pious life." Therefore, the ministers should not get upset about their material loss. Rather, what they had taught *in theoria* during better days, they should now teach *in praxi*, since "examples teach more than words." Specifically, if the ministers remained with their parishioners, God

---

217   LAELKB, MD Uffenheim, Akt. 38, 1ʳ (21 Nov. 1631).

"would ever more bless and preserve them in everything else." Until God came through with His aid, the brothers should make do with whatever garment they had and with any kind of chalice, for all these were of minor importance (*Hæc enim omnia adiaphora sunt*).[218] In short, the ministers were not only told to focus on their sins rather than their suffered damage, but also to be an example to their parishioners. As consolation, their superiors asked them to trust the fail-proof logic: God has promised both punishment and mercy, and God keeps His promises. The first part He has fulfilled; therefore, He will also keep the second part of His promise toward His people, namely their deliverance.

With Catholics we find similar attempts among the clergy and the laity to provide explanations and spiritual comfort. While they share several characteristics with the Evangelicals, Catholics had a wider array of advocates on which they could draw. In addition to Jesus Christ, they invoked Mary and the saints. From the Middle Ages on, Mary was increasingly perceived as a mother figure, a "reconciler of the world" in Anselm of Canterbury's words, an intercessor par excellence, to whom men turned in their need.[219] A "War Song" of 1637, written from the perspective of a soldier, calls on Mary for help in battle, but it also offers an intriguing example of a soldier's impatient and almost irreverent haggling with the Holy Mother to turn the tide:

> Do you not see the misery,
> Since you see without glasses,
> The way our Lutheran enemy
> Persecutes and chases us.
> O mother, do not abandon us,
> Why does your aid take this long? ...
> Where is your miracle work ...
> How have you abandoned me ...
> How did I incur this
> O great St. Mary,
> Your wrath deals my honor
> A very hard blow
> Previously, you had the highest honor
> And you should be honored!
> I also give [honor] to you daily ...
> But where is mine?[220]

---

218   LAELKB, MD Uffenheim, Akt. 38, 1ᵛ–2ʳ.
219   On the changing images of Mary in the medieval and late medieval periods, see Kreitzer, *Reforming Mary*, 11–19.
220   StBM, HSS, Cgm 5496, 75ʳ–ᵛ.

The soldier treats Mary, the Mother of God, with decidedly less respect than seen in earlier supplications to God. The composer expresses impatience when Mary does not react immediately to reverse the harmful military course, even though, as he points out, she can see clearly enough how much the Lutheran enemy was gaining on the Catholics. Exasperated, the soldier confronts Mary and demands to know why she was not using her great powers for their advantage. These charges underline that Mary was typically seen in the role of advocate for those who entreated her.

Most noticeable in this song is the lack of any acknowledgment of guilt. Whereas other supplications invariably include the common refrain that all misery was a punishment for their transgressions, the soldier asks: how is this my fault? In *quid pro quo* fashion, he readily grants Mary her honor, but demands his own in return. The song's bold tenor mirrors the more brazen mentality of a soldier, but it also points to a different relationship that could exist with Mary, whose maternal qualities conjured up a nurturing mother, as opposed to an omnipotent Father God, who tended to evoke associations of judgment and punishment.

More representative than the soldier's song are prayer books of the time, such as the one from the Augustinian cloister Mariastein by Eichstätt, even though these texts are directed toward members of the religious orders. This book from the seventeenth century provides suggestions for prayers before penance and draws on several similar elements present in Protestant prayers.[221] Others, however, also show marked differences. For example, in one prayer the supplicant pleads that "human weakness" (*menschliche plödigkeit*) made her "forget" herself and she begs God to exercise compassion toward her. She then asks God to consider her present goodwill and to help her "with Your divine grace to accomplish all good things."[222] These passages reveal general theological differences between Catholic and Protestant teachings – not in admitting human weakness, but in the suggestion that such feebleness only obscured the goodwill that was in humans. Luther had famously rejected this position, and, in the footsteps of St. Augustine, had insisted on humans' fundamental sinfulness. Moreover, Protestants would have bristled at the idea that one needed only the "assistance" of God's grace to do good, a stance that smacked of semi-Pelagianism. Rather, any credit for good intentions lay entirely with God.

The prayers in this collection also frequently turn to Mary in the hope that she might assuage the misery. As in medieval times, the penitent invoked the divine mother as a mediatrix between Jesus Christ and herself:

---

221 See, for example, StBM, HSS, Cgm 7252, 29^v–30^v (my pagination).
222 StBM, HSS, Cgm 7252, 33^v–34^r, 44^r.

Therefore, I beg you ardently that you will stand by me and accompany me before the stern judge, your dearest Son, whom I have infuriated with countless heavy sins. Make Him benevolent and mild with your faithful supplication. Sacrifice all your virtue and your holy life for my evil life and wickedness (*vntugent*) and reconcile myself today with **Christo**, as you are eternally reconciled with Him. Amen.[223]

Whereas Protestant texts typically proffered Jesus' sacrifice for the sinners as the reason why God the Father ought to have mercy on them, in this Catholic prayer Jesus steps into the role of the forbidding judge (which in Protestant pieces was usually reserved for the Father), while Mary becomes the intercessor, whose part it is to propitiate Him. This, however, was not the only Catholic perspective on Jesus Christ, who could also hold the position of a mediator between God and humans, and, as we saw above, one can occasionally find elements of Christ the judge in Protestant texts as well. Despite some theological differences, then, the religious movements employed a broad range of religious elements that elude easy categorization and show substantial overlap.[224]

Mariastein's members and the clergy in general also drew on mystical resources as they tried to come to terms with the war. Their religious instructions addressed surrendering one's own will to God's so that they became one.[225] No matter what tragedy befell her – "yes, if the entire world were filled with war and pestilence ... and the heaven would collapse and the ground would open up, and all human and hellish power at once would stand against me and would raise a violent hand against my possessions and blood" – she was to direct her mind and actions entirely toward contemplating God's will and to arrange her remaining short life accordingly. "With the joining of both wills," the nun was to submit to her death "when, where, and how it will please ... God."[226] Since the nuns were wedded to Jesus Christ during their profession and were wearing a ring to mark their marriage, this union also was to give them strength, especially during times of great distress: "With this precious (*cöstlichen*) little ring, you may marry your spouse again spiritually at various

---

223 StBM, HSS, Cgm 7252, 36^r.
224 The Catholic supplicant also relied on other biblical figures to find comfort and ways to appease a wrathful God. In one of the prayerbooks for nuns, the penitent reminded Jesus Christ of his mercy toward "the great sinner, Mary Magdalene," whose faith and tears of repentance saved her. The nuns were encouraged to entreat all the saints (although it mentions only females) to plead their case. StBM, HSS, Cgm 7252, 19^v–20^r, 139^r–41^v.
225 StBM, HSS, Cgm 7254, 142^r (1647) (my pagination). The book dealt with the sisters' profession to their order and the renewal of their vows.
226 StBM, HSS, Cgm 7254, 143^v–44^r.

times, especially when you experience affliction, sadness, and sorrow, and you think that you are abandoned by God and all and every human."²²⁷ *Cöstlich* connotes both "dear" and "valuable" as well as "delicious." The nun's marriage to Christ is thus expressed in the language of bridal mysticism, and the *cöstliche Ringlein* is the physical pledge of that union. As spouse, Christ serves again in the role of the protector and lover of his betrothed rather than in that of the judge.

After several psalms of lamentation, the text returns to Christ. In the framework of the marriage between Him and the nun, His sacrifice is focused on her personally rather than on humanity in general, and is expressed in the more graphic, mystical language:

> O Lord Jesus Christ, I remind (*Erman*) You of the bloody, fearful sweat, which You shed for me, and beg You: come to my aid in all fear and misery, which I will have to suffer during my final days. I remind You also of the precious sweat, which You have shed often and plentifully and out of fear during Your entire life, and beg You that you sacrifice that [sweat] and all physical labor you ever had on earth for me for Your heavenly Father.²²⁸

All Jesus Christ had ever done and suffered became a benefit for His spouse, the nun, and could lift not only her standing with God, the Father, but also her spirits. The parallel nature of their suffering also affords comfort to the distressed sister.

Dated 1647, the collection includes prayers and instructions for desperate times, which reflects the situation in the nuns' lives. Constructed similarly to the Psalms of Lamentation, one supplication advises the nuns to speak these lines when fear and a sense of desertion overwhelmed the sisters:

> O Lord, do not abandon me,
> Do not abandon me everywhere,
> Do not abandon me entirely.
> And even if You have abandoned me,
> Do not let this abandonment be forever,
> But only for a time,
> So that afterwards You will welcome and delight me
> The more affectionately, friendly, tenderly, and compassionately.²²⁹

---

227   StBM, HSS, Cgm 7254, 144ᵛ. These instructions were written in red ink.
228   StBM, HSS, Cgm 7254, 151ᵛ–52ʳ.
229   StBM, HSS, Cgm 7254, 161ʳ.

Abandonment was, of course, the nuns' ever more vividly experienced reality. Between 1646 and 1648, Bavaria was once again the target of Swedish and French troops. With the continued and seemingly endless war, the penitent redirected her entreaties toward the future, since the past and present had been miserable and desolate. Her hope and plea to God were now that He would not desert her forever. Her vision is thus focused on the future, the time of the spouses' happy reunion, and the familiar mystical language vividly evokes the bridal bliss.

This collection of writings is only a small selection of the spiritual resources available, but it nevertheless provides a sense of the theological and religious aids at people's disposal, at least those compiled by the upper and upper-middle classes. Some were specifically geared toward the clergy in their often difficult positions; others were directed at the broader laity, including soldiers; and many were meant for all as comfort. The question, however, remains of how effective these mostly prescriptive or advisory texts were in helping people cope with the war. Can we assume that they indeed offered contemporaries "satisfying" explanations and consolation? This issue is much harder to address, but our autobiographical accounts yield some insights both on the clergy and the communities they observed. Similar to the variety of justifications and theological rationales discussed above, one has to be cognizant of the breadth in religious responses among the populace. This is not surprising, since people are individuals, who are defined not only by their religious, social, political, and cultural associations, but also by more elusive personal characteristics.

Religion played a prominent role in dealing with the war. Contemporaries sought explanations and consolation by looking at God. The conviction that God had sent this affliction as punishment for humanity's sins challenged people to come to terms with a – however justifiably – wrathful God. It also offered a reason for the war's occurrence as well as strategies to redirect humanity's course from misery and destruction to preservation and prosperity. As we heard, people were urged specifically to acknowledge their sins, to repent, to improve their lives, and to entreat God for His mercy. Behind this general statement, however, lie complex ideas about different ways of relying on religion by both laity and clergy.

Among the narrators we encountered before, some contemporaries were quite vocal about their religious outlook, while others rarely mentioned it. The chronicler of the Capuchins just outside Landshut, for example, demonstrates an immersion in their religious world throughout their hardships that one can see in few other testimonies. When Bernhard of Saxe-Weimar's armies attacked Landshut in 1634 and the friars fled to the vicarage of St. Jobst within the city walls, they displayed a remarkable devotion:

> In the meantime all of us offered ourselves to the omnipotent God in humble confession and taking of the sacraments, believing that we were ready and willing to hand in our lives, which we, as true brothers and children of St. Francis and real blood witnesses of Christ according to our blessed rule, had received for a while from our Patriarch, and we gladly stretched out our lives and our bare necks toward this hothead and tyrannical bloodhound [Bernhard of Saxe-Weimar].[230]

According to the chronicler, Melchior von Straubing, the friars understood their lives as on loan from God and were grateful for His plentiful gift. Now, during the enemy's attack, Melchior depicted the brothers as not only ready to give back this granted life, but almost giddy at such a prospect. Certainly, as men of God, they were attuned to and had most likely internalized such thinking, but, as other testimonies show, being among the religious did not necessarily take away fear or transfigure these men and women when they faced the prospect of suffering.

Melchior describes the brothers' insight as the result of a gradual realization: when they "*saw*" – that is, when they came to recognize – that "we were not *supposed to* be afraid of the tyrants, who only kill the body, we directed all of our love toward God."[231] This ostensibly hopeful position was the result of a learning process, a stance that revealed itself to them during this time of crisis. The Capuchins' insight may have been the product of meditation on the dangerous situation and on their religious foundations, or on some of the religious resources discussed above – Melchior does not specify how this spiritual stance came about. His words certainly echo the lines of some of the prayer material at the Augustinian convent Mariastein.

The friars' joyful behavior led to some baffling encounters with the enemy, who was wholly unprepared for the fact that these friars apparently could not be terrorized. It seemed that the Capuchins could think of nothing better than to die as witnesses to their Lord. They quickly opened the doors of the parsonage to their pillaging adversaries, kneeled down in front of them, extended their necks, lifted their hearts and hands toward heaven, and waited eagerly to see "who would be the first among them to carry away triumphantly the bloody cross of victory." Such triumph and heavenly feasts, however, were not to be. Maybe the Lord did not consider them worthy, maybe He wanted to test them a little longer – "God only knows why," Melchior wails. Maybe, the friar muses, they had to suffer some more before the Lord called them to Him. Declaring

---

230 StBM, Cgm 2943, 4ʳ.
231 StBM, Cgm 2943, 5ʳ.

that Heaven certainly was worth any persecutions they had to bear on earth, he wonders whether perhaps their demonstrated "good behavior" made God save them for a more severe battle![232] Melchior here affords us a view at an evolving understanding in this religious community as it confronts the threats of its world at war. Compared to other contemporary testimonies, however, the Capuchins' admirable devotion and their sense of safety in their relationship with God, as expressed in this chronicle, are rather unusual.

Bartolomæus Dietwar, too, evinced a seemingly unshakable trust in God and his guidance. A Lutheran minister, he represents someone who, according to his own account, was wholly convinced that the war and its other plagues were God's just punishment for humans' sins. His *Chronik* offers astute observations on Kitzingen – a territory that underwent several changes, from Lutheran to Catholic, and various stages of coexistence under provisions of an accord. Although written from a decidedly Lutheran point of view, his comments throw light on the multi-faceted world of religion during this conflict and illuminate the religious and confessional landscape in this contested area. His overlord was the consistory of Brandenburg-Ansbach, until Kitzingen fell to the bishop of Würzburg. As we heard earlier, however, Dietwar never acknowledged the bishop and went into exile rather than serve any lord but the one in Brandenburg-Ansbach.

Dietwar provides continuous updates on the state of the military situation both in and around Kitzingen, as well as in places as far afield as Prague, which highlights once again how well informed many contemporaries, especially the clergy, were. Concurrently, Dietwar describes God's hand in all of his life's experiences. God is responsible for the good that happens to Dietwar as well as for the bitter pills he has to swallow. While this is most likely the case with many of his contemporaries – at least in theory – rarely does an author express this conviction so consistently and forcefully as Dietwar. His account of his life and afflictions imparts the sense that he feels secure in God's hands. Time and again, trial after trial, the minister returns to the fact that God acts according to His plan, that Dietwar has a place in His design, and that God has the well-being of His people at heart. This view informs the way the Lutheran minister approaches life, and it enables him to cope constructively with his negative experiences. For example, Dietwar had harvested the grapes of his vineyard in Hoheim and had brought them directly to Mainbernheim, which proved to be a smart move, because the Catholic district magistrate of Kitzingen demanded of Hoheim's mayor

---

[232] StBM, Cgm 2943, 5^{r-v}.

that he confiscate my must (Most), since [the magistrate] assumed that I had [the Most] in Hoheim. Now, if God had not given me the idea that I should have it taken immediately to Mainbernheim, these people would have defrauded me of it without any cause: Thanks be to God, who rescues the miserable from the one who is too strong for him, and the miserable and poor from the robbers.[233]

Dietwar credits God with saving him from a worse fate and overall regards God as the source of all good offerings during this war.[234]

God, however, also continued to discipline his people. In 1634 Dietwar notes that "because of the previous ingratitude, God heaped anew his plagues over the land, especially the city of Kitzingen."[235] His firm faith in God shines through even when he loses one child after another. While infant mortality was high in the early modern period in general, the pressures of war – hunger, flights, violence, and pestilence – greatly increased the odds that a child might not survive. In the case of Dietwar and his second wife, Regina, who bore him eight children, only one daughter survived.[236] Dietwar describes each of the births and deaths with great sensitivity and draws death masks of several of his children in his *Chronik*'s margins. While his words echo the typical phrases used in other autobiographical accounts upon the death of a loved one, they nevertheless show some nuances. When his first son, Johannes (17 November 1638–26 March 1639), dies, Dietwar speaks about the "faithful God," who "struck a deep wound into my heart," and ends with the entreaty that "God help us come together in eternal life."[237] His next child, Barbara, died on 20 April 1641 after almost 33 weeks, and his anguish is palpable: "God feeds me once more with bread of tears (*threnen brott*) and drenches me with a great tankard full of tears," when He took his daughter "from this vale of tears to Himself in His heavenly hall of joy."[238] A year later, his second daughter, also named Barbara, was born. His second son (Johannes-Vitus) died after a week (14 January 1644): "At the beginning of this year, I soon have to drink a very bitter draught of myrrh from the heavy cup (*Creützbächer*) of God, the heavenly housefather ... may God at some point give him back with good joy to his poor

---

233 LAELKB, MD Uffenheim, Akt. 95:43–44.
234 LAELKB, MD Uffenheim, Akt. 95:85, 97, 99–100, 113.
235 LAELKB, MD Uffenheim, Akt. 95:77.
236 Dietwar's first wife died at the age of 50 on 20 July 1634 after sixteen years of childless marriage. On 15 March 1635, Dietwar married his second wife, Regina, a minister's daughter.
237 LAELKB, MD Uffenheim, Akt. 95:103.
238 LAELKB, MD Uffenheim, Akt. 95:106.

parents and, in the meantime, let go of His wrath and displeasure of us."[239] For the first time, Dietwar speaks of the parents' anguish, rather than solely his own, and his pain becomes more expressive. He also entreats God to cease His punishing ire, while never disputing that God has every right to be vengeful.

His third daughter, Martha, "had to leave us according to God's will also much too soon," in 1646, after "twenty-six weeks and two days."[240] The following year, Regina bore him twins:

> but we had simultaneously joy and heartbreak because God had blessed her with two sons. The first came out incorrectly with his small feet first, but was born alive under great danger and pain through God's mercy.... The other came over three hours afterwards also incorrectly and came, alas (*Gott sey es geklagt*), dead into the world.... May God have mercy on him for Christ's sake, and may He in the future preserve me and all pious house fathers from such miserable state.[241]

This time in his pain, Dietwar sees himself in the community of fellow "housefathers," who suffer similarly as he does upon the death of a child. His son remained sickly and died eight weeks and three days later. The year after the war officially ended, Regina bore him his last son, who was also too weak to survive and died after eight and a half weeks. Having witnessed his son's struggle, Dietwar begged God to "award (his son) with a gentle peace (*sanffte ruhe*) and a joyous resurrection to everlasting life, and don't punish me quite so much in His ire, but remember me according to His great mercy."[242]

Although Dietwar experienced each child's death as ever more intolerable, he never questioned God's actions but pleaded with Him to show kindness rather than severity, reminding God that he could bear only so much. Barbara, Dietwar's one surviving daughter, became the focus of his energies and the model of a Christian child, almost a wunderkind and a testimony of his devotion to God.[243] On Christmas 1643, he recorded with pride: "she can recite the Our Father entirely from memory, before she is even two years old. May God continue to bestow His mercy on her." Barbara went to school just after her fourth birthday.[244] We do not hear how Dietwar's wife, Regina, who had borne

---

239   LAELKB, MD Uffenheim, Akt. 95:111.
240   LAELKB, MD Uffenheim, Akt. 95:118–19.
241   LAELKB, MD Uffenheim, Akt. 95:121.
242   LAELKB, MD Uffenheim, Akt. 95:132.
243   This reminds one of the Catholics' dedication of a child to God by placing him or her into an order.
244   LAELKB, MD Uffenheim, Akt. 95:110, 118.

him eight children in eleven years (1638–1649), bore her losses. One must assume that the rigors of childbirth in close succession and constant moves during pregnancies only added to her burden and heartbreak. Regina died in 1658 at age 45 after 23 years of marriage; her husband in 1670 at age 78.

In Dietwar, we see a man who was not easily shaken, who stood firm in his faith, who tolerated exile and deprivation rather than conform to a different faith and political power, and, as we saw earlier, who exhibited ready courage in confronting soldiers. He strikes one as being among the more intrepid of his generation, but it is also evident that he found great comfort and strength in his faith. His reliance on God's power emboldened him. Even though many shared the belief in God's omnipotence and in His right to use punishment or mercy toward His people depending on their behavior, Dietwar's testimony stands out in his unshakable trust in God's wisdom and guidance. Perceiving one's life so wholly and consciously as safeguarded by God, no matter what happened to oneself, provided powerful comfort and a way to make sense of the war.

Other ministers of the margraviate Brandenburg-Ansbach displayed similar views about God's actions, but with many the suffering was more pronounced than the gratitude toward God. A minister of Poppenreuth (Fürth), for example, described the convergence of Ligistic and Swedish troops in 1632 in the area around Fürth: "Even though all the villages situated around the city were devastated, the churches broken open, ... nor the crops of the field spared by the Swedes, the Ligistic [troops] did the same to the margraviate, and enacted God's will on us because of our grave sins, through which great poverty, hunger, inflation, and death were caused in the entire land." The pastor was plainly upset about both enemy and friendly troops' plundering of his (Lutheran) church. In the meantime, he and his family had to reside in exile (*das trawrige Exilium bawen*) and "bottle up much sorrow (*viel leids in mich fressen müßen*), for which God be praise and thanks."[245]

It is difficult to interpret these almost formulaic add-ons. Their stereotypical character does not necessarily make them hollow statements. The way they are inserted into the narrative suggests that the author knows and acknowledges these things to be true. They are part of the mental and religious world in which the minister moves. They might also be a reminder not only to the future reader, but to himself, a "calling to order," i.e., the divine order, in which this war was customarily explained through God's punishment of his subjects' trespasses.

---

245 LAELKB, Fuerth Poppenreuth, PP 12:30. It is not clear, however, whether his use of the passive voice for the Swedish army and the active for troops of the Catholic League was intentional. For a map of the villages around Kitzingen, see Figure 10 in Chapter 2, Sec. 2.

How deeply and unfailingly both clergy and laity embraced this understanding is not easy to answer. As the consistorial records of Brandenburg-Ansbach reveal, clergymen were human, too. Few ministers appeared as sanguine and undeterred as Dietwar in their acceptance of their misery. This became evident in the above discussion of the ministers' ever more desperate letters to the consistory for a new position.

Regarding the broader laity, it is even more challenging to gauge the role of religion in how they coped with the war. Dietwar's chronicle provides some insight into how people responded to the pressure to convert when Kitzingen first went to the Catholics. As might be expected, this action evoked a range of reactions. There were those who were unwilling to convert to Catholicism. Dietwar lists forty-one "souls" in his parish Hoheim, who "remained steadfast in Christ and went into exile (*ins elend*)." Over the years, some risked their lives and possessions to continue attending Sunday services in their home communities, although they tried to minimize the danger by travelling in larger groups.[246]

Even among those who remained in Kitzingen and, under pressure, ostensibly switched their religious allegiance, things appeared anything but straightforward. The Catholics tried to ensure that people stayed in church during the entire service by positioning a soldier in front of the church doors. Those not attending the Catholic Mass (the "idolatry," according to the Evangelicals), were "driven with whips to the church."[247] None of these measures suggests an eager attendance of the Catholic worship. In 1631 the Catholics confiscated the Evangelicals' books for the second time, which indicates that during the first seizure the year before enough books were hidden to warrant a second round of appropriation. Subjects who refused to convert to Catholicism were imprisoned. On fast days, the Catholics forced their way into the Kitzingers' homes and searched the drawers by the fire, and, if they found meat, they punished transgressors severely. The Catholic minister of Hoheim, Zipfel, threatened to throw stones into the gardens of the women if they did not convert to Catholicism.[248] Underneath the outward conversion, then, Lutheranism was evidently much alive. House and garden were the domains of women, and the fact that the Catholics targeted their spheres implies that they identified women as particularly determined in holding on to their faith.

Dietwar's narrative also attests to another much utilized stratagem during the Catholic takeover: *Auslauf*. The term literally means "leaving" or "departure,"

---

246 LAELKB, MD Uffenheim, Akt. 95:49–50, 109.
247 LAELKB, MD Uffenheim, Akt. 95:49.
248 LAELKB, MD Uffenheim, Akt. 95:48–50, 56.

but, importantly, this was only a temporary movement and usually took place on Sundays for the purpose of attending a service of one's own religion in a nearby village. Such *Ausläufe* were also undertaken for baptism and other ecclesiastical acts. The *Auslauf* phenomenon had existed since the time of the Reformation and could be found among both Catholics and Lutherans. David Luebke has emphasized the integrative qualities of this practice that allowed Catholics and Lutherans to coexist during the sixteenth century.[249] At the latest by the early 1600s, however, under the pressure of increased confessional antagonism, the *Auslauf's* integrative powers were much diminished. When, after the Catholic takeover in 1630, several parishioners of Hoheim went to a Lutheran service in Fröhstockheim, they were captured and imprisoned. The next year, the Count of Iphofen and his musketeers chased Protestants, who traditionally went to Speckfeld to worship, like wild animals and imprisoned anyone he could catch. Over the next few years, Kitzingen went back and forth between Lutherans and Catholics, and when it was once more in the latter's hands, its inhabitants were "forbidden to attend the evangelical sermons outside [of Kitzingen]." According to Dietwar, this order did not have the desired effect either: "In Kitzingen, the Evangelicals were severely oppressed, and, as often as someone went to church in Sickershausen, he had to pay a Reichstaler."[250] His words, nevertheless, highlight that something important had shifted in this phase of the war. Dietwar reports fines rather than imprisonment, which might underscore the authorities' dire financial situation by the second half of the 1630s. This change could also point to a new stage in the relationship of the confessions, where a penalizing payment was acknowledgment enough of confessional and political superiority over the opponent.

Dietwar's *Chronik* also highlights the tenuousness of accords with the occupying party. The negotiated terms of coexistence could fall considerably short of the agreement. Not surprisingly, the execution depended on where power was predominantly located at the time and whether violations of the accord had any chance of being addressed, i.e., whether an authority was on hand to defend the agreed upon rights. Otherwise, as in the case of Kitzingen, the bishop of Würzburg could pursue his own interests with impunity.[251] Dietwar's record furthermore exposes that reactions to religious coercion were not uniform. Some switched their religious allegiance, some found ways of continuing their confessional existence, and others emigrated – at least for a while. Various contemporaries echoed Dietwar's observations. In 1641, Neuburg's

---

249   Luebke, *Hometown Religion*, 107.
250   LAELKB, MD Uffenheim, Akt. 95:50, 56, 97, 100 (1637).
251   LAELKB, MD Uffenheim, Akt. 95:90–91 (1635).

government in Eichstätt's diocese ordered an inquisition of those subjects in Lohen and Dixenhausen who refused to accept the Catholic faith. These reprobates trekked instead to the Lutheran village Offenbau that had been rebuilt out of its ruins.[252]

The election of exile, *Auslauf*, and acts of subterfuge underline the importance of one's religion to people's lives, especially at a time of crisis such as the Thirty Years' War. Parishioners were willing to leave their homes, risk lives and livelihood, or pay a substantial amount of money during great scarcity for the opportunity to worship in their own religion. The comfort one's beliefs and religious community could bestow was surely part of what motivated them to make these sacrifices.

5.2 Responses to Official Religious Offerings

While the above testimonies manifest reliance on the religious offers of governments and churches, whether Protestant or Catholic, there is also ample evidence of people pursuing different avenues or at least adding other elements to the official offerings and directives. This more complex reality comes into view when one looks at visitation records, which reflect responses of a broader populace. Moreover, accounts capturing the follow-through rather than the prescription of behaviors also speak to the question of whether and to what extent people embraced the ideas discussed above. An analysis of these sources suggests that 1) considerable segments of the population were not necessarily falling in line with the official interpretations of the war as punishment for their sins; and 2) many looked toward additional means of mental and religious support, such as magic practices. We will address these aspects in turn.

Given the paucity of written records for the broader populace, one has to consult indirect testimonies regarding their mindsets. A first indication comes from people's responses to their lords' mandates and orders. In many locales, governments observed indifference not only toward their pronouncements regarding social discipline, but also toward the offers of the church, such as additional weekday sermons and prayer hours. In Bavaria, Maximilian bemoaned that his subjects continued in their promiscuity, adultery, and blasphemy.[253] While these grievances could be just the voice of an overzealous, hard-to-please elector, other records confirm the very uneven compliance with the electoral orders throughout Bavaria.[254] The situation looks

---

252   Buchner, *Das Bistum Eichstätt*, 2:652.
253   SA M, B&R 60 B 1.
254   I am referring to the so-called *Umrittsprotokolle*. StA M, RL, fasc. 33, 124.

similar in the Protestant territories of Nuremberg and Brandenburg-Ansbach. Nuremberg's city council complained that the longer the church services, the fewer people attended, while Brandenburg-Ansbach's consistory ordered its deacons to inquire among the ministers why people were coming neither to the prayer hours nor to sermons that were scheduled during the week.[255] The war – referred to in so many mandates as divine punishment for their sins – had a grave impact on their subjects, but evidently not in the way authorities desired. It did not necessarily move people toward greater social and religious discipline.

A second indication of people's attitudes toward life and religion comes from the visitation records of Nuremberg's countryside for the year 1637.[256] Most ministers in Nuremberg's countryside saw great "*barbarias*" going on: "all vices, and particularly cursing, had grown rampant because of the war."[257] Similar evidence can be found in other territories. Braunschweig's pastor David Wagentroz complained that people did not listen to the preachers' calls for repentance. It was a myth, Wagentroz contended, that war improved the state of religion and turned people toward God. On the contrary, instead of making them more pious, the war made people nine times worse.[258] One might consider these pessimistic commentators scaremongers, but they had experienced the war's impact on their parishioners firsthand and might well be realists.

It is evident that not only calls for greater social discipline went all but unheeded; large parts of the population were also unimpressed by the church's religious offers, and threats of God's punishment could not change their minds. Visitation and consistorial records can provide some compelling reasons for this attitude. A few ministers of Nuremberg's countryside reported that their parishioners preferred drinking and dancing to attending Sunday sermons and catechism class. Far more prevalent, however, were explanations related to the peasants' work. Especially during harvest time, the ministers noted, parishioners could be found in their fields rather than in church.[259] Complaints about peasants working on the Sabbath, and not only during the morning worship,

---

255 LAELKB, MD Feuchtwangen 16, 881–83.
256 StA N, Rst Nbg, KuO Nbg, LG, 456. The ministers in the countryside were asked questions regarding how long each one has been in the parish; whether he resides there and if not, why not; problems in the parish; whether he faithfully teaches catechism class; how many belong to his parish; the methods of preaching the gospel; how often a week he preaches; the condition of marriage and baptismal registers; the quality of his assistant; the school; and how often he conducts hours of prayer. They also frequently provide information on the condition of the parish.
257 StA N, Rst Nbg, KuO Nbg, LG 456, 20^v, 22^r, 29^v.
258 Wagentroz, "Sanfftes Schlaffkämmerlein," Civ^v (1640).
259 StA N, Rst Nbg, KuO Nbg, LG 456, 4^v, 5^v, 8^r, 17^r, 22^r.

were frequent. Still, people attended the Sunday worship in much larger numbers than they did sermons and prayer hours scheduled during the week.[260] Many ministers justified their parishioners' absence by stressing that peasants had to attend to their work according to the seasons – be it harvesting or wood-cutting. Religious observation took second place after toiling to ensure their livelihood.

Evidence from neighboring Brandenburg-Ansbach points to another reason: a fundamental lack of understanding between church authorities and parishioners. In 1631 the consistory ordered additional prayer hours for one o'clock in the afternoon on Tuesdays and Thursdays because of the dangerous times. When the peasants requested to have the prayer hours moved from one to twelve o'clock so that these might fit better into their work schedule, the consistory refused to negotiate since they desired uniform practices within the margraviate. After all, the prayers were set for only twice a week and took not much more than half an hour, which could easily be made up in the afternoon: "True and diligent Christians will value the general suffering ... as well as their own misery more highly than a slight decrease in their field work."[261] The heightened crisis of the war reveals that the governing elites had scant understanding of their subjects' situation. The consistory assumed that the parishioners felt merely inconvenienced, which carried no weight when it came to matters as severe as divine punishment. Then again, it is hard to believe that the church's argument of uniformity in religious practices persuaded the overburdened peasants. The authorities' unwillingness to meet the peasants' concerns helps explain the tepid response to their orders, even when work did not demand their attention.

Secular and ecclesiastical governments responded to the popular resistance to their initiatives with more decrees, but garnered poor compliance from their subjects, especially in the countryside. To understand why they did not follow their government's precepts and could not be moved even by the reality of war to do so, one might look toward the life and work situation of the peasants, which left little room for religious activities if they wanted to put food on the table. Moreover, their labor largely paid for the contributions extracted by armies crisscrossing the country. At the same time that the authorities demanded much greater religious activity from the populace, the war exacted an enormous sacrifice from the peasants, who had to satisfy the ferocious appetite of the soldiers. One also has to consider that peasant life

---

260   StA N, Rst Nbg, KuO Nbg, LG 456, 15^v, 21^r, 23^{r-v}, 25^r, 28^v. To the disapproval of their superiors, many ministers discontinued these weekday activities because no one came.
261   LAELKB, MD Uffenheim, Akt. 38:11, 1^r–2^r.

was steeped in material culture and religion. Its horizon was defined by the world of the peasant: earth, weather, livestock, food, family, community, and seasonal feasts. Presumably the farmer, his wife, and his household thought about their animals, this year's harvest, their illnesses, or a regiment quartered in the village. In short, their world view was one of much greater immediacy. With the occasional exception – the Italian miller Menocchio comes to mind – most peasants probably did not ponder the potential transcendental consequences of their actions.[262] They did think about the future, but largely in more immediate physical terms, such as whether the ravaging army had just destroyed the seeds for the next crop and therefore ruined their hopes for the future.

Many among the literate populace shared the orthodox view of the war as punishment for man's sins and believed in the need for repentance. Among the commoners, the field was much more diverse. Some showed great loyalty to their church: by going with their pastors into exile when a new leadership forced them to renounce their faith, by continuing their worship despite marauders lying in ambush, or by complaining when their pastors did not regularly hold sermons. But there is also compelling evidence of criticism and non-compliance with the dictates of official religion. The above examples highlighted potential conflicts between central authorities and their subjects, although they do not confirm a fundamental opposition to it. Peasants were critical of some of the orders because they kept them from their work, but they were not completely opposed to them. The peasants were willing to negotiate with the consistory about better times that fit into their work schedule, but they met only intransigence from the authorities. People did not want to be rid of the church or their ministers. Indeed, it was the ministers to whom they often looked for comfort and whom they followed into the woods or into a nearby city if worship in their own villages had become impossible or too dangerous. The ministers had a much better understanding of their parishioners' situation and often tried to mediate between the demands of the central authorities and the needs of their congregants. Because of the war, however, the death rate among ministers was extremely high, and many parishes had to go for years without a pastor or had to share one with several other parishes. People also had a sense about their confessional identity. Congregations repeatedly opted for exile over changing their confessional beliefs. In several cases, major contingents followed their minister into a neighboring town of their religious confession, where he continued to serve his former parishioners. The evidence from visitation records, however, also suggests that people

---

262 For the story of Menocchio, see Ginzburg, *The Cheese and the Worms*.

often augmented these offers with other religious components, which brings us to the second consideration, the role of magic practices.

5.3 Augmenting Official Religious Resources: Magic Practices

Magic practices, of course, predated the Thirty Years' War and had long been part and parcel of religious exercises, despite all efforts of the official churches to eradicate such customs among their congregants. Over the last few decades, scholarship on this subject has undergone enormous developments from a largely patronizing treatment of presumably superstitious, irrational beliefs of ignorant and misguided commoners to a greater awareness of magic's multifaceted dimensions and intricate relationship to the Christian confessions. Protestants considered many Catholic rituals as "superstition" or *Aberglauben*, and, after the Reformation, Catholics, too, tried to cleanse their habits of "superstitious" elements. Even though these labels are nowadays distasteful to historians, early modern German ecclesiastical and official sources, both Protestant and Catholic, regularly and disapprovingly used these designations.

Scholars have emphasized how threatened the world of early modern contemporaries was, and that actual aids to counter dangers and afflictions were quite limited. Thus, people sought protection concerning illnesses, death, sick farm animals, adverse weather, poor harvests, and many other challenges from a host of magic rituals that were supposed to guard against such perils. This broad spectrum of practices – which evolved over time, embodied a creative mixture of magic and ecclesiastical elements, and displayed many regional differences – offered a range of benefits: from relief and support, such as blessings; to protective magic, which could block negative influences; to black magic, which were attempts to reverse or eliminate the damaging effects of dark forces, but also to deploy them to one's own advantage. Particularly in this last area of black magic or *maleficia*, popular ideas about harmful bewitchment touched official teachings of witchcraft. Importantly, authorities *and* subjects agreed that witches caused grave harm and represented a major threat. From the perspective of the commoners' religious horizon, such menaces could be countered with black magic, although this was a dangerous undertaking because it invoked forces not entirely under one's control. In other words, people at times used black magic to defeat witches. For authorities, however, such *maleficia* were another form of witchcraft.[263]

The meanings of and relationship between "magic" and "witchcraft" depend on the time period and on who defines these terms. One person's "magic" could be another one's witchcraft or orthodox practice. That a crisis like the Thirty

---

263   For a detailed discussion of magic folk beliefs, see Labouvie, *Verbotene Künste*.

Years' War with its many ruinous consequences for the populace provided chief occasions for magic practices is not so surprising; the knottier issue is whether the war led to a rise in witchcraft. One might expect that the experience of the war's disasters inevitably led to the search for a scapegoat. A quick look at the timeline – with major episodes of witch persecutions occurring during the Thirty Years' War – seems to justify this intuitive deduction. Even though the war does not feature prominently in most witchcraft studies, several scholars have discussed a possible link between the two. Long ago, Erik Midelfort problematized any easy causal connection between witch hunts and the war.[264] Wolfgang Behringer's work on witchcraft in Bavaria also makes a case against the war as an inducement for witch hunts by pointing to the fact that the first large, trans-regional wave of persecutions around 1590 took place during the long stretch of peace between the Schmalkaldic and the Thirty Years' Wars.[265] In general, Behringer contends that war and witchcraft persecutions did not go well together. Agrarian crises were far more important than war in triggering witch hunts, as were harsher weather conditions due to the "Little Ice Age." Erik Midelfort moreover discredits the thesis that the Swedish advance in the early 1630s ended persecutions in the Catholic territories since witch hunts stopped before Gustavus Adolphus made his way to Bavaria.[266]

In her study of Bamberg, Britta Gehm goes a step further by asserting that, because of its financial stress, the war was detrimental rather than conducive to the persecution of witches. Court proceedings were costly and could not be sustained while also paying the heavy war levies following the Battle of the White Mountain (1620). With an eye toward the witch hunts in Bamberg and Würzburg around 1630, she explains that they occurred "in the slipstream of larger political developments": the political success of the Catholic party and the subsequent military calm stimulated champions of witch hunts "to fight the inner enemy in their territories" as well.[267]

Other historians, however, declare the relationship between witchcraft and the war was more complex, confounding such neat conclusions. Jürgen Schmidt, for example, is not persuaded by Bernd Thieser's claim that military repercussions preempted witch persecutions in the Upper Palatinate during the Thirty Years' War. Schmidt points out that Electoral Palatinate also experienced heavy losses due to the war, but the persecution of witches continued

---

264 Midelfort, *Witch Hunting in Southwestern Germany*, 68, 75–76, 122–23.
265 Behringer, *Hexenverfolgung*, 6. See also Behringer, *Mit dem Feuer vom Leben zum Tod*.
266 Midelfort, *Witch Hunting in Southwestern Germany*, 75, 131, 134, 138. See also Behringer, *Hexenverfolgung*, 105, 107, 312, 321.
267 Gehm, *Hexenverfolgung im Hochstift Bamberg*, 113.

in this region.²⁶⁸ Even studies on the same region disagree with one another. Reinhard Heydenreuter, eminent authority on Munich's archival holdings, challenges Behringer's contention that there were no witchcraft persecutions in electoral Bavaria during the 1630s and 1640s. Heydenreuter's research on Elector Maximilian's Privy Council reveals that, shortly after the Swedish invasion of 1632, Bavaria once again condemned witches to death: "Thus, one cannot talk about an end of witch-persecutions after 1632. New, however, is the fact that now offenses of superstition are punished with particular frequency."²⁶⁹

It is apparent that diverse regional settings and times stimulated different dynamics between war and witchcraft, and one answer regarding any link of the two is unlikely to fit all locales. The conflicting conclusions underline the need for regional and comparative studies to explain more accurately the relationship between war and witchcraft.

Heydenreuter's findings bring us back to the issue of magic practices. The increase in prosecution of superstition in the 1630s and 40s points to a greater reliance on magic aids among the populace during what was for Bavaria an intense phase of the war. In 1611/12, Maximilian had passed an edict on superstition, which underwent a process of revisions and reflects the heated debates among various intellectual, political, and religious elites in Bavaria, debates that pitted proponents against opponents of witchcraft persecutions. Supporters of persecutions understood magic practices and witchcraft as connected and considered superstition as the first step toward witchcraft. Therefore, they advocated holding a rigorous line against any incident of superstition. In contrast, the intellectual critics of prosecutions, who could be found in Munich and at the University of Ingolstadt, saw a qualitative difference between witchcraft and everyday magic, and thus championed a milder punishment for what they considered largely harmless practices.²⁷⁰

Maximilian and his Privy Council attempted to mitigate the original, harsher tone of the edict, but the outcome was a sprawling law and a cumbersome guideline. With such convoluted directives, one might wonder what the reality in the villages looked like. How should one envision the dynamic between subjects and their authorities? With central governments and intellectual elites in conflict, how did local and regional authorities approach the situation on the ground, and how did the populace respond to Protestant and Catholic efforts at ridding the community of so-called "superstitious elements"? A comparison of visitation records of Nuremberg's countryside from 1560–61 with

---

268   Schmidt, *Glaube und Skepsis*, 438–39; Thieser, *Oberpfalz*, 198.
269   Heydenreuter, "Der Landesherrliche Hofrat," 149.
270   Behringer, *Hexenverfolgung*, 296.

those of 1637 during the Thirty Years' War and visitation records of the adjoining Margraviate from the 1570s until the early 1600s suggests some answers.[271] Discrepancies in the catalogue of questions and in the places visited make a statistical evaluation difficult, yet the strong overall impression is one of continuity. The commoners were usually slow in taking advantage of the Christian education that was offered in sermons and catechism classes. And, war or no war, they adhered to a host of "ungodly" practices, from swearing and adultery to playing games and dancing on Sundays as church services were held.

A marked difference, however, is evident in the prevalence of blessings. While blessings were a recurring phenomenon in all visitation records, it is only in the series of the Thirty Years' War that we find statements about the pervasiveness of this practice in several places. Many clergymen reported instances of superstition, the foremost being the ritual of "blessing" (*Segensprechen*), which means that villagers called on healers or other people with allegedly special powers to retrieve lost items or to bless their animals, the crop, or a sick person. Sometimes the ministers spoke only of individual cases in a village; at other times, they claimed blessings were a common occurrence.[272] Kalckreut's pastor believed that "one would find few men and women who were not devoted to blessings and similar practices." In Velden, blessings were not only widespread, but "there were even people who defended such actions." When death spread among the livestock, chances were that people sent for an expert in blessings as far away as Bohemia. This kind of magic was also used to guard one's livestock against wolves and to improve the milk production of cows. Betzenstain's minister concluded that superstition was a strong force among his parishioners, "especially when they were sick."[273]

Evidence from Bavaria underlines some of the same features. When war and destruction finally came to Bavaria in the 1630s and 40s, superstitious practices spread rapidly – among them were fortune telling with mirrors, glasses, and crystals; the so-called "reading of planets"; treasure hunts; magic attempts at healing; and the supposed summon and dismissal of spirits.[274] Particularly disconcerting was the news from the Bavarian Forest, where in the early 1640s belief in werewolves abounded. Incidentally, the rise in werewolves and forms of counter magic coincided with a sharp increase in the population of wolves

---

271 Most of the visitation records of 1560 and 1561 have been published by Gerhard Hirschmann in *Kirchenvisitation*. The visitation records of 1637 for Nuremberg's countryside encompass about 40 parishes and can be found in StA N, Rst Nbg, KuO Nbg, LG, Akt. 456; those for the margraviate in LAELKB, MD Uffenheim, Akt. 8.
272 StA N, Rst Nbg, KuO Nbg, LG, Akt. 456, 5^v, 13^v, 15^{r-v}, 18^v, 20^r, 22^r, 27^r.
273 StA N, Rst Nbg, KuO Nbg, LG, Akt. 456, 5^v, 7^r, 12^r, 13^r, 27^v.
274 Heydenreuter, "Der Landesherrliche Hofrat," 140.

because the war's destruction had led to a lack of cultivation and to wild growth in the Bavarian Forest. Suspicion fell on the shepherds, who supposedly had used sorcery on regular wolves to turn them into werewolves.

This case illuminates many aspects of magic beliefs and people's underlying fears and expectations. Whereas blessings was a common and fairly harmless practice, werewolves occupied the other end of the spectrum of magic beliefs. Those who turned themselves or their animals into werewolves and "bit" (*paizen*) people were employing a dark and dangerous art, and the peasants secretly complained to their authorities about the suspected shepherds – an occupational group long distrusted. The local judge could not make any headway with his investigation because the peasants were intimidated by the shepherds' threats and their presumably sinister powers.[275]

When these reports reached Maximilian in Munich, he was most alarmed, fearing that this blasphemy would infuriate God even more. He sent his own two judges to Regen on the outskirts of the Bavarian Forest so that they could investigate and resolve the matter. The elector was also concerned about another report that at Holy Easter or Pentecost "people carry loads of baptismal water away, and, it is to be suspected, use it for improper and especially for superstitious magic things." Maximilian ordered such habits to be terminated and inquiries to be made for what purpose the holy water was used (as it turned out, the water was used to combat werewolves!). He also wanted to know who taught the commoners such "arts."[276]

The elector pointed to the war as the context for the increase in superstitious practices, but he was also convinced that people fell for such beliefs because they were not properly instructed.[277] Whether in visitation records or official correspondence, observers identified a lack of education as the major impediment in eradicating the irritating magic practices. While complaints about people knowing little about the essentials of their Christian faith predate the war, the situation worsened during the military conflict when uncertain roads made it even more unlikely that the household and children would attend catechism classes. The problem, however, lay not only with the populace, but with their presumed spiritual "guides" as well. Even before the war, visitation records note disconcerting cases of pastors using their "arts" to help their parishioners with supposed protective magic devices and blessings.[278] In

---

275   HStA M, KB HR 270, HRP 1641, 1:135ᵛ–36ʳ.
276   HStA M, KB HR 270, HRP 1641, 1:135ᵛ.
277   HStA M, Jesuiten 584 (1642).
278   AEM, FS 41, VP 1603–1646, 66.

other words, some ministers not only tolerated, but reinforced magic practices among their parishioners.[279]

The war drastically increased the difficulties around education in all directions. As we learned, the conflict took a particularly heavy toll on the ministers. While historians of the Protestant clergy have underlined that after the early decades of the Reformation Protestant ministers were increasingly university-trained and came from the same families, resulting in dynasties of pastors, a glimpse at the visitation records of Nuremberg's territory shows a different picture during this lean staffing period. Many ministers noted that their fathers had been artisans. Similarly, their training was more diverse or "creative" than that of those who had received a strict university education. In short, during long stretches of the war, the diminished clergy at the parishes' spiritual helm exhibited a much greater range of religious formation and were less embedded in an official religious canon taught at a university. One pastor of Fürth-Lonnerstadt opens our eyes to yet another reality in this context: this Catholic priest first served the Catholics in Lonnerstadt. When the Protestants took over, he taught the Evangelicals and pointed out that many priests (*Pfaffen*) were forced to do the same. Some pastors certainly left for places of their own confession during an enemy takeover, but not everyone was able or willing to do so. This continuously shifting confessional situation adds another complicating dimension to the religious profile of parishes.

In the case of the werewolves in the Bavarian Forest, Maximilian, as always, took quick action to address the presumed educational deficiency. Not trusting the bishops of Passau and Regensburg to do the job, he asked the Jesuit provincial for four *Patres* to teach the populace the proper kind of religion. In the end, two Jesuits and three Capuchins were dispatched.[280] According to Bernhard Duhr, an early, eminent historian of the Jesuits, the mission was a great success and proved the elector right – that all that was needed was better instruction. A report on the mission alleged that the people were ignorant but willing to learn. They knew only the Our Father, the Ave Maria, and the Apostolic Creed, which the minister read from the pulpit instead of a catechism. But when the

---

279 In her studies of the Saarland, Eva Labouvie has argued that the "cleansing" process with regard to "superstition" failed in Protestant and Catholic parishes, but it did so for different reasons. From a theological point of view, Protestant ministers could roundly condemn magic practices, whereas Catholic priests had a much harder time explaining to a confused populace the difference between illicit popular and official Catholic magic customs (*Verbotene Künste*, 241–43). Whether the persuasion of the populace miscarried because of a disconnect between ministers and parishioners or because of confounding ambiguity, magic practices continued in all confessional territories.

280 Duhr, *Geschichte der Jesuiten*, 2:35–36.

Patres began to explicate the theological truths, people listened for hours without complaint. They claimed that they had never heard the word of God so clearly, had not known about many issues, and had sinned only because of ignorance and lack of proper teaching. People had not believed their priests since they, while warning against superstition, often adhered to the same practices.[281]

It is doubtful that the populace indeed gave up their magic beliefs as easily and as completely as the report alleged and Duhr surmised, and that it only needed instruction to turn the populace into full-fledged, officially acceptable Christians. As the correspondence between the elector, the provincial of the Jesuits, and the bishop of Regensburg, as well as the report on the mission make clear: spiritual personnel and priests, yes, even a prelate, adhered to these superstitious practices, which suggests that education and catechism class were not all that was needed to convince people of their faulty religious customs. Moreover, the assurance of acting out of ignorance and the easy renouncing of their beliefs echo strategies of other religious groups when they were caught.

Magic practices and beliefs, then, could be found at every level of the social and educational spectrum. Evidence from Franconia corroborates that not only the broader populace, but also members of the upper and upper-middle classes utilized such resources. Velden's councilor fell back on such "means on account of the considerable money he had lost." And the local administrator told Velden's chaplain with regard to the blessings that he should mind his own business.[282] Peter Burke has argued that elites participated in popular culture such as festivals and carnival, even though the same was not true the other way around (i.e., commoners did not and could not participate in the rituals of the elites).[283] Clearly, those upper levels of society also took part in the more superstitious forms of religion.

Unmistakably, diverse social groups and individuals within these groups had varied attitudes toward the war and pursued different venues to make sense of it, to provide consolation, and to find cures for the ravages caused by war.[284] It is reasonable to assume that people affected by the war – whether they were of high or low social status or somewhere in between – shared certain sensitivities (such as horror and fright) about its atrocities. By and large, however,

---

281 Duhr, *Geschichte der Jesuiten*, 2:36–37.
282 StA N, Rst Nbg, KuO Nbg, LG 456, 5ᵛ.
283 Burke, *Popular Culture*, 24.
284 See also Hermann Hörger, who emphasizes that "each stratum experiences and forms ... piety differently" ("Organisational Forms of Popular Piety," 212).

there existed a much greater diversity among the population's views and reactions to the conflict than has generally been acknowledged. This expansive, yet far from complete, discussion of religion and its uses indicates the varied and complex roles religion could play for people coping with the war. Its differentiated applications come down to one issue: whether a religious interpretation or practice could provide comfort and protection in the face of fear and destruction. The question, then, is not so much whether people turned away from "official religion," but rather what it could do for them.

Despite complaints of ecclesiastical and secular authorities about the widespread lack of compliance, people sought comfort in the church. Yet it is also evident that the reality of the war led to a far greater reach for unorthodox practices. The need for protection from harm was so much more urgent during this violent conflict with marauding armies and unbearable demands than during normal times with their habitual uncertainties. Overall, the more extensive reliance on magic suggests that many judged the religious remedies provided by the church – such as an increase in sermons, prayers, and instruction – as insufficient in addressing their pressing concerns. Given this reality, many people sought the best protection and the most comfort by drawing on both orthodox and magic practices.

Furthermore, people were selective in their use of the church's offers. In the end, it was the villagers who determined the form of his or her religion, not the church. Parishioners defended their religious practices against those ordained from above by pointing to their traditions, and they employed this argument both to forego the church's remedies and to embrace unorthodox practices. In Nuremberg's countryside, Vischbach's minister noted his flock came "for the most part only once a year to communion and reasoned that this was their custom." In a couple of villages, the ministers did not conduct any prayer hours on Sundays because their parishioners would not "tolerate novelties." And Endenberg's minister complained his congregation "had retained all kinds of superstitious practices from their forefathers."[285] Consequently, they followed their own blend of religious and social practices to get them through life's crises.

It is noteworthy that these magic remedies transcended confessional boundaries. The customs and traditions, on which the populace insisted, predated the Reformation and thus went back to pre-confessional times. Certainly, the populace incorporated elements of their confessional religion into folk beliefs and practices, but in the end both Protestants and Catholics found consolation and relief in these semi-orthodox mixtures. Not surprisingly, then, recourse to

---

285   StA N, Rst Nbg, KuO Nbg, LG 456, 8^r, 25^v, 26^r, 29^r.

magic aids increased with the crisis of the war irrespective of a region's confessional affinities. Nor were people particular concerning the religious persuasion of a blesser, and one might find Protestant villagers calling on a Jew or a Catholic.[286]

There were many other ways of finding meaning, consolation, and protection in religion, which deserve a fuller discussion than is possible here. Several surfaced in earlier chapters, such as the – albeit ambiguous – reliance on sacred objects for protection.[287] Furthermore, days of prayers and repentance and other ceremonies and rites prompted by the war point to the fact that religion provided not only spiritual nourishment and consolation, but also rituals – in other words, actions and behaviors – to counteract the devastating effects of the war. These rituals could reside squarely within the confines of orthodox religion, or they could be of the more unorthodox, "superstitious" variety.

In their search for protection and preparedness, contemporaries were also attuned to signs, comets, prodigies, and miracles. Several of the autobiographical accounts discussed above recount miracle stories typically in support of one's confession. Some related how people who renounced their faith met with a dire fate.[288] The heavens, too, were explored for signs of what to expect next. Many contemporaries saw the comet of 1618 as the beginning of the war.[289] As always, *Schreibkalender* (recording calendars) and *Prognostica* were in high demand. These writings not only offered sections with astronomical constellations and interpretations; they also included a chapter on war and other calamities, in which the author made predictions for the coming year.[290]

All these diverse religious efforts and understandings are connected by a fundamental desire to find consolation as well as meaning behind the suffering and protection against harm. One might expect that, as a consequence of the great misery, people focused on the presumably happier afterlife in their desire to flee this vale of tears.[291] For some, this was likely the case. In his *Mourning Song for Anna Wolff*, Meistersinger Heinrich Wolff of Nuremberg

---

286 StA N, Rst Nbg, KuO Nbg, LG 456, 18ᵛ, 20ʳ.
287 See the discussion in Chapter 3.3. Sacred objects could be ambiguous in their powers to protect because, while they were supposed to shield the community from harm, they were also moved to safer places so that they would not be destroyed.
288 LAELKB, MD Uffenheim, Akt. 95:58.
289 See Bähr, *Der Grausame Komet*, for a discussion of the 1618 comet and its meanings throughout the war.
290 These publications are a fascinating source, which deserve a more in-depth treatment regarding the war, but this goes beyond what can be offered here.
291 Thus Meumann and Niefanger, "Interdisziplinäre Betrachtung," 10.

(1595–1669) described the miserable lot all humans face here on earth, but because of Christ's deed, they had paradise to look forward to: "Who wants to be afraid of death/ Since it ends all suffering/ And through (death) we come to God/ Into everlasting life."[292] Some of the advice given in the devotional literature also points to the life ahead as a consolation. Yet in the majority of contemporary testimonies, both of the clergy and the laity, such suggestions are quite rare. Clara Staiger's notes, for example, show no preoccupation with the "next world." Rather than yearning to retreat to a safe, more rewarding haven in the beyond, her mind and hands worked continually and resolutely on the present and future here on earth, as did those of her determined fellow sisters at St. Walburg.[293] For Staiger, religion was a consolation, not an escape. Her faith anchored her as the war's mayhem broke out around her, and during an attack she found it more trying not to able to hear the word of God than to lack food and drink. The prayers and invocation of the saints, which only increased as the war dragged on, were her and her sisters' contribution toward an end of the affliction and did not express an eagerness for the next life.

Contemporaries found comfort not only in religion and its practices, but also in a broad range of other routines, which provided stability, comfort, and reassurance as the world around them disintegrated. The days of Mariastein's nuns were marked by a soothing habit of religious acts and words, but the prioress also recorded meticulously the daily chores, to which she and her sisters adhered, even when they were in exile. Washing and cooking, spinning and soap making kept them busy and brought order to days and weeks of disorder. Besides the habitual activities to sustain oneself each single day, there were life's celebrations, such as weddings, baptisms, and funerals, which were just as indispensable. Despite the misery and deprivation, weddings and other feasts abounded in Nuremberg and elsewhere, and neither the magistrates' orders nor the threat of fines could move its inhabitants to celebrate more modestly.[294] The citizens had their own ideas about life in these sad times, and the authorities' repeated and increasingly forceful admonitions could not move their subjects to curb what few pleasures and comfort they had. When the pestilence raged in Nuremberg in 1634, citizens became disheartened because the many victims of the plague had been buried without so much as a hymn or even the ringing of the bell. The council recognized the needs of the population, and,

---

292   StBM, Cgm 6250, Nürnberger Meisterlieder, Heft 21, 3.
293   *Klara Staigers Tagebuch*, 317. This result is concordant with Krusenstjern's findings ("Seliges Sterben," 494).
294   Von Soden, *Gustav Adolph*, 1:369–70; Hambrecht, "'Das Papier ist mein Acker,'" 358, 360–61, 363.

without changing the letter of the law, was willing upon request to make an exception to the rule. In some cases, they even allowed a funeral procession.[295]

Beyond religion and rituals, other formative forces and influences played a role in shaping contemporaries' responses to the war. Once again, such a discussion goes beyond the limits of this study and may indeed not be feasible, but we need at least to be cognizant of this broader spectrum. Whatever education was available to the populace contributed to their outlook. Besides the mystical and devotional literature open to the clergy and other elites, philosophical and further intellectual literature (such as political and legal treatises) influenced their point of view and behavior in working through this crisis. Then, as now, "education," did not exclusively occur in a convent, school, or university, but also in one's family, kin group, and village. Earlier we noted the importance of tradition to the way people behaved. One's upbringing, then, consisted of many variables, only some of which are still visible to us today.

6   Lifting Up the Spirit

We finally turn to several aspects that provided positive energy to overcome the sense of desolation during the war. The previous chapters explored practical strategies and mental resources that helped people survive. Still, one wonders what gave men and women the strength to go on, to be courageous despite fear, and to look optimistically at future options rather than wearily at past and present losses. One's circumstances, formation, and personality are certainly part of the answer, yet there existed other important reserves and occurrences that we usually do not associate with the Thirty Years' War. Contemporaries displayed humor and hope, and engaged in music and other positive encounters to lift and bolster their spirits. The strength of these features can hardly be overestimated.

Some of the above narrators employed humor in dealing with the adversity of war. The two Benedictines, Höser and Friesenegger, show themselves as masters at it with their self-deprecating and funny remarks in some of the most uncomfortable situations. The witty Friesenegger, for example, relates an especially humorous incident that occurred in 1634 when, during a time of great dearth, the allied soldiers went after Andechs' pigs. The monks asked the soldiers' officers for help, and Friesenegger describes the ensuing scene: "If in these times we still had laughter in us, then this was a truly ridiculous spectacle as the common [soldiers] went after the pigs, and the officers after

---

295   Von Soden, *Gustav Adolph*, 2:573–74.

the commoners in the field so that the rags of the one and the hair of the others flew skyward."[296] Clearly, even in these grim times, Friesenegger had not lost his ability to spot the humor in this bizarre tableau. Looking at reality with wit and finding absurdity in the brutishness of war provided new perspectives on an otherwise dismal situation. These devices worked toward cutting the enemy down to size by showing him to be laughable and thus lightening their threatening experience.

The easing power of laughter comes through time and again. While the larger contingent of the Poor Clares of Munich's Angerkloster had fled to the Tyrol, the previous prioress, Walburgia Hengsberger, who had remained in the cloister, came out of retirement and lifted the spirits of those who kept the cloister going. Sister Constantia Grindl praised the old prioress, who was patient and "laughs often so sweetly that it strengthens my heart." Hengsberger herself added a postscript to Grindl's letter to those in the Tyrol, in which she assured the exiled sisters that "we are all very cheerful as if there were no war in the whole world."[297]

By employing laughter and cheerfulness, people resolutely tried not to give in to the destructive maelstrom created by the war. These episodes highlight once again the determination to retain control of their lives and not be browbeaten by the forces of war. Exhibiting joyfulness amid adversity constituted a particularly subversive move. Humor and laughter, then, were powerful means for surviving the war. By turning a menacing situation into a humorous or cheerful one, contemporaries denied the enemy the ability to dictate the terms of the war and, instead, claimed that power for themselves. What is more, humor and joyousness represented ways of upholding and affirming life in the face of misery and afflictions.[298]

Many of the testimonies discussed above display an appreciation for the good things that did come people's way. As much as women and men suffered during hard times, they also rejoiced in a plentiful harvest and a good wine. Not letting fear and misery engulf one entirely – having the capacity to see light within darkness – was a powerful antidote to the destructive nature of war.[299] Importantly, our authors testify to the strength of hope during bleak times. Hope for peace and a brighter future sustained many individuals and communities. Such hope fueled projects to rebuild communities, homes, and lives. The

---

296 Friesenegger, *Tagebuch*, 66.
297 Zwingler, *Klarissenkloster*, 1060–61, letter # 14 (1632).
298 On humor see Fischer, "Ethnicity," 224; and Hutcheon, *Irony's Edge*, 25–27.
299 Good and bad experiences stand side by side in their testimonies and do not invalidate each other. In this respect, early modern autobiographical accounts are much less "shaped" than modern ones.

Benedictine abbess, Agnes von Neuegg of Holzen, conveys this hope following the Catholics' regaining of Augsburg and the Peace of Prague (1635). After their exile in Salzburg (1633–1635), she returned to Holzen with a core group of her convent to restore their monastic community. She had sent the other twenty-nine sisters to various monastic houses, but she took "the remainder ... with me in the incessant, confident hope that the loving God will bestow upon us the earnestly longed-for peace and enough grace so that I could retrieve one by one the dispersed children and take them to me again, which was both my and their deepest wish."[300] Whether well-founded or not, hope carried people forward. The hope for imminent peace, especially, propelled people not to give up on the future.[301]

While a military conflict as horrendous as the Thirty Years' War invariably draws our attention to its violence and destruction, it is also true that the war engendered great physical movement, during which people from other countries, faiths, and cultures met. Besides the devastation, the movement of people and ideas brought about more positive encounters. Sometimes testimonies reflect mystery, impatience, and confusion during such interactions; at other times, the writers manifest curiosity as well as greater knowledge and appreciation of the other. While vilifying an enemy as a barbarian or Antichrist could strengthen people's resolve and heighten the distance between opponents, an awareness of commonality could begin to bridge the gap between them.

Earlier we discussed some of the remarkable experiences of concern and care for the other.[302] Taking up this strand, we turn once again to Melchior von Straubing, chronicler of the Capuchins by Landshut. We recall that, during the Swedish threat to the city in 1634, the friars decided to move into the city's parsonage, from which the minister had fled. The general outline of what happened next conforms to the well-known narrative of destruction during the Thirty Years' War: the occupiers ransacked Landshut, burned parts of it down, and killed or harassed its inhabitants. Melchior von Straubing, too, underlines the harmful character of the occupation. In fact, one of their brothers who had become separated from their group was killed in a public square. In other respects, however, Melchior's narrative runs counter to the familiar storyline. Neither the friars nor the soldiers conformed to their respective expectations of one another. Melchior and his brothers anticipated death and martyrdom, but the occupiers did not oblige. The friars, in turn, did not behave according to the officer's ideas either. A convoluted and almost comical back and forth ensued

---

300 HStA M, KL, fasc. 739/59, 1ᵛ.
301 E.g., Hümmer, ed., "Bamberg im Schweden-Kriege," 52:26.
302 See Chapter 2.3.

between the lieutenant, who seemed stupefied because the friars' behavior confounded his clear directive from above, and the friars who time and again hoped that now their chance had come for blessed martyrdom. Instead of killing the Capuchins, the English Calvinist officer took the friars prisoner and escorted them through the city to an inn. While there was mayhem all around them, no one harmed the friars because of the lieutenant. Melchior credited God with the protection of the entire *familia*.[303]

The lieutenant pursued different venues with the friars. He demanded 100 Gulden ransom from them, and when they pointed out that they had no possessions, he threatened to kill two or three of them if they did not cooperate. While he let them "stew" in their cell for an hour, their guard took pity upon them and gave them a piece of his bread.

The negotiations regarding the ransom are intriguing. When the officer returned with several soldiers to press his demand, the friars explained their rule (*regula*) to him and why it was of no use to ask for money. They simply had none! As a Calvinist from England, where religious orders had been dissolved a century earlier, the officer may indeed have required some tutoring about the Capuchins and their principles. At last he exclaimed they should turn to their bishop or governor to obtain the sum, but the friars quickly disabused him of this idea as well, informing him that they had no bishop. It was also fruitless to ask their secular lord for money since he hardly could liberate all the religious who had been taken hostage.[304]

The situation in Landshut became ever more volatile. The soldiers had already started setting fire to several houses before Bernhard of Saxe-Weimar could prevent it. When a house close to where the Capuchins were held captive caught fire, the lieutenant tried to pressure them again. Whether he – literally – wanted to "smoke out" any deceit among the friars, was unwilling to accept defeat with regard to his ransom, or had fundamental difficulties understanding the friars and their sanguine attitude toward him and the menacing situation, in the end he must have realized the futility of his attempts, and he let them go.[305]

There is the puzzlement of the Calvinist English lieutenant when he encountered the Capuchins and their pious and fearless comportment discussed earlier. Not only did these friars thwart his orders, but their example did not align with the typically confessionally distorted image of a Catholic and a friar to

---

303   StBM, Cgm 2943, 6ᵛ–7ʳ. At this point the group consisted of six *Patres*, three clerical brothers, and three lay brothers.
304   StBM, Cgm 2943, 7ᵛ–8ᵛ.
305   StBM, Cgm 2943, 8ᵛ–9ʳ.

boot. We do not know what went on in the lieutenant's mind. The realities of war may have appeared differently at closer engagement with the "enemy," who comes into view as a human rather than a target to be destroyed. The "other" may seem not so different from oneself, or, as in the case of the Capuchins, unusual and perplexing enough to give one pause. When one examines the war at the personal, immediate level, chances are one encounters the other as a human being, as an individual, rather than as representative of an enemy force. Whatever the lieutenant's thoughts, it is evident that the new encounter engendered at least confusion and potentially a shaking of his views.

The movement and continuous motion generated by the war, then, not only left people unmoored, but also led to unexpected and at times eye-opening encounters. According to our testimonies, many of these meetings took place in monastic settings, which brings up the question why Protestants in this confessionally divided conflict sought out conversations and companionship with members of religious orders who epitomized so much of what was considered wrong with the Roman Catholic Church. The narratives of the *religiosi* point us in some fruitful directions regarding what stimulated such exchanges.

One of the driving forces was curiosity about the other. Testimonies note the desire to discuss matters, to learn of the other's views, and to exchange knowledge and information. The Capuchins of Landshut again provide a case in point. After the friars had joined the Reformed Franciscans in their residence and after the bloodshed in the city had somewhat subsided, several colonels of the occupying party came to visit and inquire how the friars were faring. Melchior von Straubing notes that the Swedish officers were particularly interested in discussing politics with the Capuchins and Franciscans. The colonels wanted to know what the friars thought about the emperor, Bavaria's elector Maximilian, and several military leaders of the Catholic party. In the end, the officers asked whether they had enough food. When the friars told them that, between nine Franciscans and eleven Capuchins, they had two loaves of bread for lunch, the colonels sent them meat, flour, and bread.[306]

Another example of such friendly discourse comes from the unknown chronicler of Bamberg's Jesuit College. The Protestant General Wilhelm von Lohausen, whom Junius had praised so highly, held a special place among the Jesuits as well. The chronicler described von Lohausen as a man of sincerity and decency. He paid the Jesuit College several "friendly visits" and sometimes invited the monks to dinner, "which he spiced up with almost learned disputations with our father about matters of faith."[307] According to the author,

---
306 StBM, Cgm 2943, 12ʳ–13ʳ.
307 *Jesuitenchronik* in Weber, *Bamberg im dreißigjährigen Krieg*, 43.

one action weighed heavily on von Lohausen's conscience: his fierce dealings with the town Staffelstein north of Bamberg at the order of Bernhard of Saxe-Weimar. Recognizing among the Jesuits a fellow countryman from the Bergische Land (Pater Adolph Clever), the general was eager to learn what the pater thought of the carnage.[308] When von Lohausen departed Bamberg, Pater Clever gave him the devotional writings of Jeremias Drexel (1581–1638), a Jesuit teacher and court preacher. The general reciprocated by donating to the college the works of a Lutheran theologian and presenting Pater Clever with the cosmography of the sixteenth-century mathematician and astronomer, Peter Apianus (1495–1552).[309]

These exchanges are telling in their particulars. To begin with, good terms between occupier and occupied could be facilitated by points of connection. In this case, the common geographic origin of von Lohausen and Pater Clever provided an opening for talks, and the Jesuit chronicler emphasizes that the college benefitted from this connection. In von Lohausen's case, his concern did not depend on such a contact, as his care for the Dominican nuns in Bamberg illustrates, but generally links of locality, kin, or religion surely helped along friendly exchanges among contemporaries who otherwise hailed from different universes – religiously, politically, and culturally. Once Catholic France openly entered the war on the side of the Protestants in 1635, we see more of these "understandings" between ostensibly hostile parties taking place.

The kind of gifts von Lohausen and Pater Clever exchanged is also noteworthy: The Jesuit gave the Protestant general the works of Jeremias Drexel, who had been born a Lutheran but had converted to Catholicism during his youth. Drexel's many non-polemical and largely practical books found broad appeal among Protestants as well.[310] And although von Lohausen does not identify the Lutheran author of the book he bestowed upon the college, his choice of a scientific work for the pater underlines the desire to focus on areas less fraught with controversy.

The male orders, however, were not the only ones that attracted the Protestant officers' curiosity. Junius' narrative reveals that they were also intensely interested in getting to know religious women. When Colonel Grel approached the Dominican convent's mother superior regarding stationing animals in

---

308   *Jesuitenchronik* in Weber, *Bamberg im dreißigjährigen Krieg*, 40. Bernhard of Saxe-Weimar believed Staffelstein's inhabitants had betrayed him. The Bergische Land is a region in the southeast corner of modern North Rhine-Westphalia.
309   *Jesuitenchronik* in Weber, *Bamberg im dreißigjährigen Krieg*, 43. Apianus was a professor of mathematics in Ingolstadt from 1527 until his death in 1552 and was also a printer. The chronicler does not identify the Lutheran theologian.
310   Kratz, SJ: "Drexel, Jeremias."

their courtyard, one sister overheard the exchange and misunderstood him to mean that he would place soldiers in their courtyard. The sister begged him not to do so, whereupon Grel laughed and said: "How is it possible that you nuns are so hostile toward men?"[311] Contrary to the sisters' expectations, the colonel showed himself helpful. When the nuns asked him for wood, he said that they would get however much they needed. He also told them to send to his quarters for wine.

It took time to get to know and appreciate one another, especially when one started out on opposite sides. The attitude of Bamberg's Dominican women toward the occupying Swedes evolved over a longer period. Early on, Junius recalls the sisters seeing and listening to a Lutheran camp service. The preacher stood right by the convent walls to preach to the military in the redoubts, and thus the nuns could see and hear what was going on:

> First the preacher began to sing, and the officers chimed in. Then he prayed for his little bunch of *Helbutzen* (hellish spirits) that God would preserve them. When the sermon was over, he began to sing once again, but no one sang with him. However, when everything was over and the preacher had barely said the last word, there was such laughter and yelling and clamor all at the same time that it was worse than in a Jewish school. This was their devotion and betterment that followed from their sermon.[312]

Junius here echoes a common criticism toward Lutherans that their faith made no difference in their lives. Rather than responding piously to the sermon, they displayed lewdness and gaiety.

At the beginning of their acquaintance with the Swedish occupiers, then, the sisters' confessional biases were firmly in place, as was their distrust of the enemy, but the officers paid the sisters frequent visits. The nuns, for their part, sat together and continued spinning, sewing, or whatever they were doing: "Then [the officers] greeted us in a very friendly way and went from one to the other and gave us their hand. Then they talked to us for a while, but they behaved toward us in such a friendly, polite, chaste, and maiden-like (*Jungfreülich*) way that we could not marvel enough about it."[313] The officers' behavior mystified the Dominican nuns, who still felt threatened by the men's presence. Such negative expectations were reasonable, since the sisters had

---

311 Hümmer, ed., "Bamberg im Schweden-Kriege," 52:43.
312 Hümmer, ed., "Bamberg im Schweden-Kriege," 52:49–50 (7 March 1632).
313 Hümmer, ed., "Bamberg im Schweden-Kriege," 52:44.

heard reports of violence against the religious in nearby locations. Instead, their experience proved quite different. Some of the officers were tongue-tied when they saw the congregated sisters, and the men did not know what to do or say. It was up to the nuns to start talking and make them feel comfortable in the religious women's presence. The officers apologized for any inconveniences they may have caused them and said that, "if they could be of service to us in some way and we would be in need of their help, they would always be prepared to do so for us." The men also promised that nothing would happen to the convent. Junius and her sisters thanked them kindly but remained suspicious: "Our hearts were always heavy with fright and fear because we continuously thought: O God, who knows whether your heart conforms to what your mouth speaks."[314]

Over the next few months, the Protestant high officers regularly visited Heiliggrab. They often ate with the sisters after having sent provisions for the evening meal and engaged in discourses over religion and politics. Among the visitors was Colonel Georg Wolf von Wildenstein, the Calvinist in Swedish service whom we encountered earlier in the Jesuit chronicle, who had treated the Jesuit College with such notable forbearance. In her testimony, Junius relates a conversation in which Wildenstein accuses the nuns (and by extension the Catholics) of praying only for themselves and for their own benefit and fortune, while they wished misfortune upon the enemy, the Protestants. The nuns responded: on the contrary, "we pray for peace and unity/ also for the cause of the entire Christendom." Another "Swede" countered that "[the Swedes/ Protestants] pray for friend and foe."[315]

This purported discourse between occupier and occupied touches upon fundamental questions about how to act in a religiously divided country. How Christian was it to pray only for one's own people and wish death upon the enemy? And even if the nuns contended that they had the welfare of the "entire Christendom" at heart, the Protestants had no part in this Christendom since the Catholics considered them to be heretics. Whether consciously or not, these queries tug at the confessional divisions and rationale behind the war. A curious conversation with Duke Bernhard of Saxe-Weimar, who also visited the convent, points in the same direction. Junius conveys that he spoke to them "beautifully" (*mechtig schön*) and inquired about the founder of their

---

314 Hümmer, ed., "Bamberg im Schweden-Kriege," 52:45. As mentioned earlier, there is also an element of justification in Junius' account for staying behind and for their good relations with the Swedes. She continues: "Thus, we had to pretend to be friendly toward them against our will, although we much rather wanted to cry."
315 Hümmer, ed., "Bamberg im Schweden-Kriege," 52:47 (March 1632).

order, Catherine of Siena, the fourteenth-century theologian and mystic, who, he mused, brought about so much goodness, peace, and unity in Christendom. Then the prince sighed: "If only God would once again raise such a woman among you who would bring peace. Then he desired that we sing the *complet* (evening office), since he wanted to hear us sing."[316] According to Junius, Bernhard of Saxe-Weimar not only expressed a desire for peace; intriguingly, he formulated a vision in which God empowered a pious woman, not a military leader, to bring about concord. Moreover, the prince did not frame the peace initiative in confessional terms. His point of reference lay in the pre-Reformation era and concerned a person every confession could look upon with admiration.

These are remarkable words attributed to a military leader known in other testimonies as "bloodhound" and "tyrant," and one might wonder, like Melchior von Straubing, whether one is dealing with a wolf or a sheep. The context of a dinner group at the Dominican convent is certainly important here. Different settings induce different behaviors and comments, but these ascribed lines also remind us to give the war's protagonists credit for a more complex spectrum of impulses and behaviors than we often do. It is not unreasonable to assume that even an aggressive military leader grew tired of the war.

Over time, the nuns learned and allowed themselves to appreciate the Swedes; and the officers, in turn, came to respect the sisters. When von Lohausen visited Heiliggrab in early March 1633 and the sisters pointed out to him that they were poor and did not own anything of value, he responded: "Everything about you pleases me because Christ the Lord was also poor on earth." Another colonel chimed in that, indeed, "everything was modest (*schlecht*, i.e., *schlicht*) and clean (*sauber*). That is why we are all heartily pleased with your life and cloister, because it is simple and right (*gerecht*)."[317]

Time and, once again, space are important elements in these encounters. If such meetings were to have more fruitful results than blows and abuse, they required time and space to unfold, which some of these monastic locales provided. The Dominican convent of Heiliggrab outside of Bamberg represented such a space, where one could learn about the other. The officers were able to get to know these religious women over conversations and by looking at their space. Conversely, the sisters learned about the military men through their words and actions.

The impulse to look for common ground rather than animosity and to learn about the other is also evident in the areas of religious music and liturgy.

---

316   Hümmer, ed., "Bamberg im Schweden-Kriege," 52:125 (March 1633).
317   Hümmer, ed., "Bamberg im Schweden-Kriege," 52: 118–19.

As Rebecca Wagner Oettinger has pointed out, in the early decades of the Reformation, evangelical reformers used songs and music as effective tools of propaganda, but their polemical function declined by the 1560s.[318] Musicologist Alexander Fisher, whose work focuses on Counter-Reformation Bavaria, even argues that there is no such thing as confessional music.[319] Junius' testimony highlights these findings. We heard of Bernhard of Saxe-Weimar's rapt attention to the nuns' singing. Several other Protestant high officers visited the Dominican convent to experience, and in some cases participate, in its religious rituals, which reminds us of Gustavus Adolphus and his respect for the Catholic service in Munich. Junius tells of another episode when the cloister's new military guard was installed and brought its own Protestant preacher. As the nuns sang the *salve regina* (a Marian hymn), the Protestants "also began to sing. Their preacher stood right among them, and the soldiers had all gathered around him, and thus they sang their Lutheran songs very beautifully (*mechtig schön*)." The next day, "the soldiers started again to sing very nicely. Afterwards their preacher preached to them. When the sermon was over, they sang again. These [Protestants] were certainly very devout ..."[320] Junius' words convey a very different assessment of Protestant worship than those she made the previous year, when she criticized the Lutherans for their lacking pious comportment. Here she highlights the Swedes' religious seriousness. Undeniably, much like the simple lifestyle of the nuns, their music became a common denominator for the Protestant officers and the Dominican nuns.

The story of the Dominican nuns of Heiliggrab is fascinating. Their convent became a meeting ground, where people learned about each other and shared ideas about religion, politics, piety, and music. Outside the convent, the Swedes continued to be the enemy, but within its walls, harmony and caring and civility reigned. Indeed, the nuns' cloister not only remained a home for the sisters living there; it also became a refuge of sorts for the besiegers. Officers, sometimes with their wives, trekked to the cloister to be with the sisters, to eat with them, to hear them sing, and to watch them go through their religious routine of vesper and complet. No doubt, these hardened men regarded the convent as a safe haven from the turmoil of war, a civilized place where one could recover briefly from the brutishness and messiness around them.

---

318   Oettinger, *Music as Propaganda*, 9.
319   Fisher made the comment during his presentation at the 2015 conference *Frühe Neuzeit Interdisziplinär* in Nashville. See also Fisher, *Music, Piety, and Propaganda*.
320   Hümmer, ed., "Bamberg im Schweden-Kriege," 52: 142–43 (July 1633).

Despite the fact, then, that the war posed daunting challenges, inflicted unspeakable violence, and caused horrendous losses, contemporaries seized opportunities to counter this reality in creative and often effective ways. People employed humor and laughter to offset negative situations; held on to hope and positive thinking regarding a better future; and, when the place and time were right, engaged with the "other" over music and conversation. These constructive and brighter moments were not the norm, but where they existed, they changed the dynamic of the war. Through them, contemporaries affirmed the strength of life despite all evidence to the contrary.

CHAPTER 5

Conclusion: Life Beyond Devastation

This study has taken us from people's wartime experiences to their actions in response to the hardships they faced, and one thing has become undeniably clear: the vital actors of the Thirty Years' War were the people. Pounded by violence, homelessness, loss, and poverty, the populace in their profound sense of vulnerability had first looked toward their governments for protection. The rulers tried to help their subjects as best they could, but this war showed up their exceedingly limited resources. In many ways the war thus gave the initiative to the populace. *They* needed to make it happen, and they did so in countless small ways. Whereas the scholarly focus has traditionally been on military and political leaders and their actions, the real heroes of survival were to be found among the populace. This reality becomes evident when one explores an aspect largely left out of historical treatments on the Thirty Years' War: how those who lived through it tried to survive this dramatic and prolonged struggle.

Moving from the panoramic view of the conflict, where the extent of human and material loss was overwhelming, to the more specific occurrences on the ground, the inquiry offered a series of micro studies situated in their broader social and political contexts. Testimonies of members of religious orders and the clergy – besides communicating their own experiences and coping strategies – offered invaluable windows onto the communities, in which they lived. Not only their monastic groups but also the peasant society around them came to life in the narratives of the religious and in scores of other contemporaneous accounts.

In this scaled down perspective, the rich vignettes of contemporaries afforded us glimpses into the devastation and trauma the war brought to so many people and a look at how they met these challenges. People encountered fear, displacement, dearth, violence, instability, and volatility. Notwithstanding their great variety, all of these experiences were rooted in a deep sense of vulnerability toward the ordeals of war.

In their often traumatic experiences, many looked to their authorities for help. The analysis uncovered that a disaster such as the Thirty Years' War showed most of the procedures in place were entirely insufficient. Fortifications and troops were too few to provide any widespread protection from violence, plundering, and extortion. Both poor relief and disease control had developed administrative systems that had continually adapted to the needs of the times, but these, too, proved unable to handle the disaster, when several calamities – troop movement, a starved populace, and an epidemic cycle – converged in 1634. Notably, not all governmental efforts at protection, especially those regarding quarantine, gained the desired cooperation of the subjects or even of the local authorities, but this was largely due to divergent assessments of dangers and priorities.

Bavaria and Franconia, both areas hit hard by the war, showed some differences between (mostly) Protestant Franconia and Catholic Bavaria, but more striking were the similarities between these regions and their inhabitants in the way they handled the crisis. Factors such as whether one lived in the city or countryside, the local situation, or the availability of networks held far greater sway in shaping responses than did people's religious persuasions. Some variances can be traced to disparities in governing bodies, long-standing power dynamics, and personalities, such as the forceful Maximilian of Bavaria. But here, too, one frequently finds the application of very similar strategies – for example, governors' standard temporizing when faced with an exhausted and exasperated populace's call for help. In the end, then, as the analysis laid bare, authorities were largely unable to provide assistance to their subjects, which, in turn, led to people's loss of trust and confidence in their lords and to the realization that they were essentially thrown back on their own wits and relationships, if they wanted to outlive the war.

Unwilling to take the war lying down, women and men, commoners and nobles, monastic communities and the clergy attempted to elude, thwart, or mitigate the war's destructive consequences and responded to its formidable challenges with creative acts of survival. Many of the stratagems and resources are well known. From the practical choices of flights and negotiations to the mental comforts of community, hope, and religion, the behaviors constitute frequently applied measures during such crises, then and now. The importance of these actions lies not so much in their occurrence than in the many shapes they took and the complex ways in which people applied and executed them. Significantly, people's experiences and their responses to them were deeply embedded in their personal and local circumstances. The responses tell us something about who these people were and show them in their everyday lives and struggles.

As we bring into focus how people coped with the hostilities' many repercussions and its enormous challenges, a much more complex image of the war comes into view. Against our largely uniform understanding of the time as wholly devastating, I have argued that, even in areas where the war raged exceedingly, we find not only resignation and despair. Rather, people regularly countered the disaster with pragmatism and ingenuity. Although the conflict with its profoundly harmful consequences claimed numerous lives and not everyone had the opportunity to act, the stories underline that many refused to be simply victims and instead worked hard to find solutions to the trials of war. Their resilience and their willingness to respond imaginatively in the face of often overwhelming odds turns our perception of the Thirty Years' War as an event that steamrolled the populace to one where people grasped the nettle and acted, even under the most trying circumstances.

And, finally, this study highlighted that, during the war, experiences proved to be much more diverse and often more perplexing than a straightforward story line of violence and destruction can capture. The inquiry aimed to expand our view of the war to include other, at times brighter, realities. This is not to deny the tremendously ruinous impact of the war, but to acknowledge that the range of experiences included positive ones as well. If the modern reader is surprised by this facet, so were the war's contemporaries. As much as the aggression of friendly troops confused, disoriented, and angered people, so did positive encounters with their enemies perplex them.

In some areas of life, constructive meetings were to be expected. For example, old political alliances facilitated diplomatic negotiations, and talks among these parties continued throughout the war. Merchants with their international networks also paid more attention to their bottom line than to political and religious differences. Humanists, too, valued stimulating discourses with people from all confessional and political quarters, and the much discussed Wilhelm von Lohausen was only one of many with similar interests. Powered by a common desire to promote the German language, humanism, and peace, literary societies such as the *Fruchtbringende Gesellschaft* counted among their members predominantly men of Protestant faith but several Catholics as well. Proponents of science and law also transcended confessional antagonism, as they trained their minds on the growth of knowledge.

Productive exchanges in these circles were not only aided by common interests; they also depended on the personalities involved and – likely to an even larger extent – on connections and established conduits of regular dialogues. The often international and trans-confessional networks fostered encounters among a diverse range of people who traded in goods and ideas. Yet, among the broader populace, such opportunities were rare. The war, however, changed the physical and mental boundaries within which women and men tended to operate in important ways. The movement of soldiers and noncombatants brought new contacts to a much wider circle of individuals and communities, many of whom had not previously been exposed to this variety of persons, impressions, faiths, and cultures. The result was violent clashes on one hand; but, on the other, the exposure led at times to enlightening meetings.

Enemy occupations could be harrowing experiences; however, in some cases – especially when given time and space to evolve – they also offered opportunities to learn about and even begin to appreciate the other. Curiosity was a driving force in these exchanges.

We thus need to expand our view of the war to include not only its – albeit predominantly – destructive power, but also its occasional positive encounters. Relationships between the opposing parties were not exclusively of the violent kind. Some of these more fruitful interactions were no doubt driven by practical considerations, but the movement of people from other countries, faiths, and cultures also led to curiosity about and regard for the other. In the overall assessment of the war's impact, these brighter experiences cannot offset the conflict's devastating realities. Acknowledging these more complex dimensions, however, opens new perspectives on the war. By coloring in critical areas of an otherwise black and white picture, it imparts a fuller understanding of this key event in European history.

The long-lasting peace negotiations finally came to an end in October 1648, and so-called heralds of peace (*Friedensreiter*) traversed the country to proclaim the Peace of Westphalia. Cities organized celebrations with fireworks and fountains spouting wine to regale the citizenry. Beyond these heady moments, however, the reality was more complicated, and relief was hard to come by. Many German lands and their infrastructures had been devastated to such an extent that it took them decades to recover. Some places, like Nuremberg, never regained their former status. Soldiers lingered until they were paid, which could take years and continued the drain on the populace.

Religion, too, took a beating. With the buildup of unspeakable atrocities on both sides over three decades, religion's content, function, and justification came under review. In the succeeding era, the very real experiences of extraordinary and seemingly unending human suffering led to an overwhelming distaste for warfare in the name of religion. This does not mean that, with the end of the Thirty Years' War, Europe became de-Christianized and entered the age of secularization, but rather governments no longer went to war to enforce one particular religion over another.[1] Instead, religious skepticism and more inward-looking forms of religion (such as pietism) that steered clear of confessionalism grew as the century wore on. At the same time, the experience

---

1   As legal historian Michael Stolleis has noted: "The public life and the governmental system during the seventeenth and eighteenth centuries were thoroughly Christian ... no one considered a modern separation of state and church. The goal was not de-Christianization of public life, but prevention of violent enforcement of religious disputes" (Stolleis, ed., *Staatsdenker*, 17).

of the war intensified the search for reliable foundations and incontrovertible truths, and helped move the pursuit of natural law and the sciences to center stage.

The psychological impact of the war is much more difficult to gauge – no matter how resilient substantial sections of the population showed themselves in their responses to its challenges. Questions arise regarding the war's long-term mental and emotional consequences. Did people trust the Peace? Were they willing to believe in the sustainability of their future? Over the centuries, *literati* from Hans J. C. von Grimmelshausen (1621–1676) and Johann Schiller (1759–1805) to Bertolt Brecht (1898–1956) and Günter Grass (1927–2015) have wrestled with the meaning and lessons of the war. In the popular imagination of the German people, too, the Thirty Years' War fills a prominent place, which points to the trauma this conflict triggered for generations to come. Importantly, the calamities this war precipitated and the larger questions this study engaged – coping with disaster, violence, exile, poverty, and disease – are still very much with us.

Glossary

Brandschatzung or *Brandsteuer*.   Literally: "fire tax." This was a sum of money (or goods) the army imposed upon the populace to avoid having their property burned down. See also "Contributions."

Catholic League.   Formed in 1609 in response to the creation of the Protestant Union (1608), the Catholic League was a political coalition of Catholic Estates with the goal of safeguarding the Catholic religion in the Holy Roman Empire. It played a major role in the first half of the Thirty Years' War until 1635.

Confession/Confessional.   In the seventeenth century, "confession" or "confessional" denotes one's belonging to a religious community that is bound by, or "confesses to," a doctrinal statement (e.g., the Augsburg Confession of the Lutherans). Therefore, Lutheranism, Calvinism/Reformed Religion, and Roman Catholicism are referred to as "confessions," not denominations.

Contributions.   During the Thirty Years' War, this originally regular war tax (*Kontribution*) evolved into a coercive levy, a "fire tax" (*Brandschatzung*). This tax was imposed upon the populace so that they could avoid the burning down of their property.

Edict of Restitution (1629).   Emperor Ferdinand II (r. 1619–1637) released the Edict of Restitution after a decade of victories over the Protestants. The edict demanded that all Catholic Church property taken by the Protestants since 1552 be returned (i.e., the Peace of Passau was taken as the normative year or *Normaljahr*).

Elector (also: **prince-elector**).   A member of the electoral college of princes in the Holy Roman Empire who elected the emperor. They consisted of three archbishops (Mainz, Cologne, and Trier) and four secular princes (the Palatinate, Brandenburg, Saxony, and the king of Bohemia). In 1623 the Palatinate lost its electorate to Bavaria following the Battle of the White Mountain (1620), but the Palatine electorate was reinstated at the end of the war, which brought the number of electoral titles up to eight.

Habsburgs.   Originally from Switzerland, the Habsburgs became the premier dynasty of the Holy Roman Empire that supplied its emperors from 1452 until 1740.

Imperial Immediacy.   A privileged constitutional status, according to which any imperial entity in the Holy Roman Empire (whether a region or a city) or an individual (such as an imperial knight), was exempt from the authority of the local lord and placed under the direct (i.e., immediate) authority of the emperor and the imperial diet.

Kipper- und Wipperzeit.   Literally: "Tipper and See-saw Time." This term refers to the financial crisis from 1621 to 1623, when German governments debased coins with cheaper metals to finance the war.

Ligistic Troops. Troops belonging to the Catholic League (see entry above).

Peace of Augsburg (1555). Peace treaty between the Lutherans and Roman Catholics that recognized Lutheranism as a religion alongside Roman Catholicism. The treaty stipulated that the ruler of the empire determined the religion of his territory, hence the formula: whose region, his religion (*cuius regio eius religio*). Calvinism/the Reformed religion was not included in this treaty.

Peace of Prague (1635). A peace treaty between the Habsburg Emperor Ferdinand II (r. 1619–1637) and Elector John George I of Saxony (r. 1611–1656), it was signed by several, but not all, German princes. It suspended the Edict of Restitution, revised the normative year to 1627, and spelled the end for the Catholic League. The edict included neither Sweden nor France, who continued the war. The treaty nevertheless represents an important steppingstone toward the Peace of Westphalia.

Peace of Westphalia (1648). Peace treaty that ended the Thirty Years' War. Consisting of two treaties (one signed by the Catholics in Münster, the other by the Protestants in Osnabrück), the Peace confirmed the Peace of Augsburg (1555), added Calvinism/the Reformed religion as a third recognized religion, and placed the relationships between European states on a new footing.

Pollizeywesen. In the seventeenth century, this term referred to issues pertaining to the local economy, such as weights and measures as well as the quality and price of meat, bread, and beer.

Protestant Union. A military alliance (1608–1621) among the Protestant estates of the Holy Roman Empire for mutual protection against the growing power of the Roman Catholic estates.

Religiosi. Members of religious orders. Also referred to as "religious."

Rentamt (pl. *Rentämter*). These connote administrative districts in (Old) Bavaria, which was divided into four, and from 1628 five, *Rentämter* (Munich, Burghausen, Landshut, Straubing, and then Amberg).

Rentmeister. A *Rentmeister* was the central administrator of a *Rentamt*, or district, in Bavaria. By the time of Maximilian, the *Rentmeister*'s responsibilities included finances as well as law and order. He thus held one of the most crucial offices in the princely government.

Salva Guardia. These could consist of one or more soldiers hired from the enemy for the protection of a locale and its inhabitants. SG could also come in the form of a letter to protect a group at home or on its travels. These letters were less expensive than soldiers.

Schmalkaldic League. A Protestant defensive league created in 1531 to protect the interests of the Protestants against potential Catholic aggression.

Schmalkaldic War (1546–1547). Fighting between Emperor Charles V (r. 1519–1556) and the Catholic estates of the Holy Roman Empire, on one side, and the

Protestant Schmalkaldic League, on the other. The emperor, intending to put down Protestantism, won this war. However, a series of setbacks eventually led to the Peace of Augsburg (see above) that acknowledged the Lutheran religion.

Umrittsprotokoll. Literally: "protocol of the circuit on horseback." These are visitation-style records of the *Rentmeister*, who recorded his observations concerning all the locales he visited on his circuit through his *Rentamt*. Maximilian of Bavaria ordered his *Rentmeister* to undertake his rounds ideally every five years. Besides examining the local records of the previous five years, he investigated the ministers' performance and the congregations' religious observance. He also noted the condition of every town and village.

Bibliography

Manuscript Sources

Archiv des Erzbiztums München und Freising [AEM]
FS 41 (Old Signature: B 598), Visitationsprotokolle [VP] 1603–1646.
Realia VN 351, Ordinariat: Generalvikar, Verschiedene Verfügungen gegen ansteckende Krankheiten betr. Bistum Freising, 1625ff.

Diozesanarchiv Augsburg [DA A]
HS 97: "Kurtze Beschreibung Wie eß mit, vnd Jn vnsserm loblichen Closster, vnd Conuent Jn dem Schwedischen Krieg gestanden, und ergangen Ist."
HS 108: Friesenegger, Maurus. "Ephemerides Andecenses sive res gestae memoriae dignae de Monte sancto et Pago Erlingano congestae (1627–1649)."

Hauptstaatsarchiv München [HStA M]
Dreißigjähriger Krieg [DK], Akt. 323, 337, 502.
Jesuiten 584, Die Mißiven in den bayer Wald durch die P.P.S.J. betr. 1642.
Klosterliteralien [KL], fasc. 13/1a, Dominikanerkonvent Altenhohenau.
Klosterliteralien [KL], fasc. 393/1831, Klarissenkloster München.
Klosterliteralien [KL], fasc. 423/1, Püttrichkloster München.
Klosterliteralien [KL], fasc. 450/12, Karmelitenkloster in München und geistliche Raths-Acta die Verhältnisse des Karmeliten-Klosters zu München in Kriegszeiten betr., 1632–1802.
Klosterliteralien [KL], fasc. 739/59, Benediktinerkonvent Holzen by Donauwörth.
Klosterliteralien [KL], fasc. 793/265, Kurfürstliches Bettelmandat (28 August 1626).
Kurbayern [KB], Äußeres Archiv [ÄA] 2529.
Kurbayern [KB], Hofrat [HR] 270, Hofratsprotokolle [HRP] 1641, vol. 1 (Jan–March).
Manuskriptensammlung [MS], Nr. 345, Schreibkalender (1640).
Manuskriptensammlung [MS], Nr. 522, Schreibkalender (1636).

Landeskirchliches Archiv der Evangelisch-Lutherischen Kirche in Bayern [in Nuremberg] [LAELKB]
Fuerth Poppenreuth, PP 12.
Landalmosenamt Nürnberg [LAA Nbg], 455/1 Mandate [M].
Landalmosenamt Nürnberg [LAA Nbg], 465.
Markgräfliches Dekanat [MD] Feuchtwangen, Akt. 16.
Markgräfliches Dekanat [MD] Feuchtwangen, Miscellanea [Misc.] 153a, Kirchliche Verhältnisse während des 30 jähr. Krieges, 1. Verhalten bei Pest (1627).

Markgräfliches Dekanat [MD] Schwabach, Akt. 34, Jubelpredigten.
Markgräfliches Dekanat [MD] Uffenheim, Akt. 8, Älteste Visitationsakte 1528–1678; Nr. 118 (1618).
Markgräfliches Dekanat [MD] Uffenheim, Akt. 38.
Markgräfliches Dekanat [MD] Uffenheim, Akt. 95, Chronik Bartholomæus Dietwar.
Markgräfliches Dekanat [MD] Wassertrüdingen, Akt. 13: Acta die Anordnung der Kirchengebete, dann Buß- v. Bet- auch Dank- u. Jubelfeste betr. 1630–1766, Nr. 5.
Markgräfliches Konsistorium [MK] Ansbach C, Spez. 14, Alfershausen, vol. 1, 1497–1653.
Markgräfliches Konsistorium [MK] Ansbach C, Spez. 27, Altentrüdingen, vol. 1, 1491–1747.
Markgräfliches Konsistorium [MK] Ansbach C, Spez. 31, Ammerndorf, vol. 1, Nr. 31–37, 40.
Markgräfliches Konsistorium [MK] Ansbach C, Spez. 883, Uffenheim Dekanat [Dk], vol. I, 1491–1743.

Staatsarchiv München [StA M]

Familienarchiv [FA] Törring-Jettenbach, C 5.
Hohenaschauer Archiv [HAA] vol. 2: Akten [Akt.], 489.
Kirchen in der Herrschaft Hohenaschau [KHHA], A 1725.
Kirchen in der Herrschaft Hohenaschau [KHHA], A 2608.
Rentmeister – Literalien [RL], fasc. 33, 124, Umrittsprotokoll des Rentamts München (1636).
Rentmeisteramt [RA] Burghausen, B 13, Protokoll über das Rentmeisterische Umreiten im Rentamt Burghausen (1640).

Staatsarchiv Nürnberg [StA N]

Ansbacher Kreistagsakten [AKTA] 701, Realindex Tom 71, Nr. 119: Fürstl. Brandenb. Onolzbach. Verordnung der unbefugten Zusammenrottung der Unterthanen und welcher Gestalt sich künfftig bey fernern Durchmärschen zu verhalten (24 January 1634).
Ansbacher Kriegsakten [AKA], 53b, Nr. 299.
Archivaliensammlung des Historischen Vereins für Mittelfranken [ASHVMF], Handschriften [HS] 219, Nürnberger Chronik bis 1687.
Archivaliensammlung des Historischen Vereins für Mittelfranken [ASHVMF], Handschriften [HS] 473, Nürnberger Chronik bis 1678, *von anderer Hand fortgesetzt bis 1689*.
Reichsstadt Nürnberg [Rst Nbg], Handschriften [HS] 472: Ein Schöne und kurtz: Doch wohl gegründete Cronica der weltberühmten Stadt: Nurnberg. Von ihren anfang Ursprung u: erweiterung. Auch mancherley Krieg: und = Thatten: fleißig und ordentlich gefertiget und zusamen getragen, bis 1673.

Reichsstadt Nürnberg [Rst Nbg], Kirchen u. Ortschaften [KuO] Nbg Landgebiet [LG], 456.
Reichsstadt Nürnberg [Rst Nbg], Mandate [M], lose, 3, Nr. 444, 448, 471, 493.
Reichsstadt Nürnberg [Rst Nbg], Ratskanzlei [RK], B-Laden, Akt. 53, Nr. 26.
Reichsstadt Nürnberg [Rst Nbg], Ratskanzlei [RK], B-Laden, Akt. 82, Nr. 3 and 16.
Reichsstadt Nürnberg [Rst Nbg], Ratskanzlei [RK], B-Laden, Akt. 83, Nr. 5 and 8.
Reichsstadt Nürnberg [Rst Nbg], Ratskanzlei [RK], B-Laden, Akt. 85, Nr. 1 and 2.
Reichsstadt Nürnberg [Rst Nbg], Ratskanzlei [RK], B-Laden, Akt. 86, Nr. 2 and 6.
Reichsstadt Nürnberg [Rst Nbg], Ratskanzlei [RK], B-Laden, Akt. 86, Nr. 24, Chronika Windshemiana, von Manasse Flentsch. Windsheim, 1650.
Reichsstadt Nürnberg [Rst Nbg], Ratskanzlei [RK], D-Laden, Akt. 239 and 3031.

Staatsbibliothek München – Handschriftensammlung [StBM HSS]

Cgm 2943, Melchior von Straubing, "Relatio Was sich in dem Schweden Krieg zu Lanndshut mit dennen Capucineren zu getragen" (1634).
Cgm 5289, fasc. 2. Historische Volkslieder Ms 1620–1714: "Der Stadt Rothenburg an der Tauber grosses Hertzenleyd." G. D. Hoff (1631).
Cgm 5496, Politische Gedichte, Schwänke, 1614–1638. Kriegslied mit Anrufung der Hl. Maria (1637).
Cgm 5642, Cronica von Nürnberg bis 1679.
Cgm 5727: Hohenwarter Chronik.
Cgm 6250, Nürnberger Meisterlieder (Nürnberger Gedichte aus dem 17. Jahrhundert), Heft 20, Ambrosius Metzger, Psalm 130 (March 1630).
Cgm 6250, Nürnberger Meisterlieder, Heft 21, Heinrich Wolff, Trauerlied auf Anna Wolff.
Cgm 7252, Gebetbücher aus dem Kloster Mariastein bei Eichstätt (17. Jahrhundert); Beichtgebete.
Cgm 7254, "Volkomne auff opfferung des menschlichen willen in den willen gottes" (1647).
Cgm 7866, "Pasquilli sive Collectanea satyrico-politico-historica ad illustrationem historicae, 16. und 17. Jh.: Evangelico-Luteranam Christlicher Exulanten Bogen, das ist Kampf vnd Trostlied …" (1629).
Clm 1326, ("Viti Hoeseri Abbatis Hist. Miscella PEREGRINATIONIS Durante per inferiorem Bauariam …"), vol. 3 of his "Monomonastikon."

Stadtarchiv München [SA M]

Bürgermeister und Rat [B&R], 60 A 1.
Bürgermeister und Rat [B&R], 60 B 1, 2, 3, 9, 14.
Gesundheitswesen [GW] 3, Sterbeläufe.
Gesundheitswesen [GW] 5, Ratsordnung, die Pestilenz betreffend.

Gesundheitswesen [GW] 34, Seuchen – Vorbeugemaßnahmen. Polizeiverfassung. Gesundheitspolizei. Sterbeläufe, Pest vnd Contagien vnd die dagegen getroffenen Anstalten betreffend (1634–1635).

Gesundheitswesen [GW] 52, Polizeiverfassung. Gesundheitspolizei. Sterbeläufe Pest vnd Contagien vnd die dagegen getroffenen Anstalten betreffend (1592–1632).

Historischer Verein [HV], Manuskripte 151/1–2, Chronik des Dorfes Unterammergau, von Johann Baptist Prechtl, 1854, vol. 1.

Kämmerei 1/241, Kammerrechnungen [KR] 1634.

Ratssitzungsprotokolle [RSP] (Stadtschreiberserie [SSS]) 46.

Ratssitzungsprotokolle [RSP] (Unterrichterserie [URS]) 248, 249, 250/2, 261/1.

Stadtverteidigung 251/b.

Printed Primary Sources and Aids

"Andere Wöchentliche Zeitung vnd Advisen. Vom groben Soldaten/ Welcher zu Newstadt in Besatzung ligt/ vnd isst lebendige Hund vnd Katzen/ Hüner/ vnd allerley Thier hinweg/ ja die Hennen vnd andere Thier mit Federn/ Haut/ Haar/ Bein/ vnd Jngeweid/ lest nicht vbrig. 1625. Jtem/ Was sich mehr mit dem Kriegswesen begeben/ wird hierinnen vermeldt/ Gedruckt zu Franckfurt am Mayn/ Bey Sigmund Latomo/ Jm Monat September." HAB, T 553 Helmst 40 (5).

Beineke, David. *Astrologische Trost Schrifft/ Am gestirnten Firmament deß Himmels/ durch die wunderthätige starcke Hand GOttes/ in der Himmlischen Jnfluentz auffgezeichnet: Darauß der gute Grund vnd feste Bestand deß nunmehr im H. Römischen Reich publicirten. Hochgewünschten Friedens/ Sonderlich Anno 1635. 36. vnd 38. auß etlichen nachdencklichen Vmbständen: Jedermänniglich zum Besten vnd Nachrichtung: Wolgemeinet abgemahlet/ vnd mit Frewden zu betrachten fürgestellet wird*: Durch David Beineken, Misn. D. Mathematicum Uranoburgicum. 1636. HAB, 127.4 Quod. (9).

Beyer-Fröhlich, Marianne, ed. *Selbstzeugnisse aus dem Dreissigjährigen Krieg und dem Barock*. Darmstadt: Wissenschaftliche Buchgesellschaft, 1970.

Bierther, Kathrin, ed. *Die Politik Maximilians I. von Bayern und seiner Verbündeten 1618–1651*. Briefe und Akten zur Geschichte des Dreissigjährigen Krieges, NF, Part 2, vol. 8 (Januar 1633–Mai 1634). Munich: Oldenbourg, 1982.

Bötzinger, Martin. *Leben und Leiden während des Dreißigjährigen Krieges in Thüringen & Franken 1618–1648. Ein Augenzeugenbericht*. Bad Langensalza: Rockstuhl, 1994.

Buchner, Franz X. "Ruinen, Not und Notverordnungen infolge des 30 jährigen Krieges im Bistum Eichstätt." *Sammelblatt des Historischen Vereins Eichstätt* 38 (1933): 9–52.

Dietwar, Bartholomäus. *Leben eines evangelischen Pfarrers im früheren markgräflichen Amte Kitzingen von 1592–1670, von ihm selbst erzählt. Zugleich ein Beitrag zur*

Geschichte des 30 jährigen Krieges in Franken. Edited by Volkmar Wirth. Kitzingen: Staßel'sche Buch- & Kunsthandlung, 1887.

Fracastoro, Girolamo. *De contagione et contagiosis morbis et eorum curatione*, vol. 3. Venice, 1546.

Friesenegger, Maurus. *Tagebuch aus dem 30jährigen Krieg.* Edited by Willibald Mathäser. Munich: Süddeutscher Verlag, 1974.

Fritz, Gerhard, and Mathias Klink. "Außergewöhnliche Sulzbacher Kirchenbucheinträge aus der Zeit des Dreißigjährigen Krieges." *Württembergisch Franken Jahrbuch* 76 (1992): 177–234.

Grimm, Jakob, and Wilhelm Grimm. *Deutsches Wörterbuch von Jacob und Wilhelm Grimm.* Munich: Deutscher Taschenbuch Verlag, [1860] 1984.

Großner, Rudolf, and Bertold Frhr. v. Haller. "Zu kurzem Bericht umb der Nachkommen willen: Zeitgenössische Aufzeichnungen aus dem Dreißigjährigen Krieg in Kirchenbüchern des Erlanger Raumes." *Erlanger Bausteine zur fränkischen Heimatforschung* 40 (1992): 9–107.

"Gründlicher vnd Warhafftiger Bericht/ Vom jetzigen Kriegswesen/ so sich im Anfang des Monats September zu Wasser vnd zu Lande/ Auff beyderseits begeben verlauffen vnd zugetragen. Jtem/ wie der Herr General Hertzog zu Friedlandt sey vmb Eger vffgebrochen/ vnd mit der gantzen Armada vff Schmalkalten vnd Hessen/ dem General Tyllen zuzuziehen." Auß den Franckfurdischen Zeitungen vnd Wöchenlichen Avisen gedruckt/ Erstlich zu Franckfurdt am Mayn/ Bey Sigmund Latomo/ Jm Mont. Sept. 1625. HAB, T 553 Helmst 40 (26).

Güntzer, Augustin. *Kleines Biechlin von meinem gantzen Leben. Die Autobiographie eines Elsässer Kannengießers aus dem 17. Jahrhundert.* Edited by Fabian Brändle and Dominik Sieber. Cologne: Böhlau, 2002.

Hagen, Karl. "Politische Flugschriften aus dem 16. Jahrhundert und dem dreißigjährigen Krieg. Dritte Abteilung: Flugschriften aus dem dreißigjährigen Kriege." In *Zur Politischen Geschichte Deutschlands*, edited by Karl Hagen, 304–39. Stuttgart: Buchhandlung Franck, 1842.

Haidenbucher, Maria M. *Geschicht Buech de Anno 1609 biß 1650: Das Tagebuch der Maria Magdalena Haidenbucher (1576–1659), Äbtissin von Frauenwörth.* Edited by Gerhard Stalla. Amsterdam & Maarssen: APA-Holland University Press, 1988.

Hambrecht, Rainer. "'Das Papier ist mein Acker....': Ein Notizbuch des 17. Jahrhunderts von Handwerker-Bauern aus dem nordwestlichen Oberfranken." *Jahrbuch der Coburger Landesstiftung* 29 (1984): 317–450.

Handwörterbuch des deutschen Aberglaubens, vol. 3. Edited by Hanns Bächtold-Stäubli. 3rd ed. Berlin: de Gruyter, 2000.

Härter, Karl, and Michael Stolleis, eds. *Repertorium der Policeyordnungen der Frühen Neuzeit*, vol. 3.1: *Wittelsbachische Territorien (Kurpfalz, Bayern, Pfalz-Neuburg, Pfalz-Sulzbach, Jülich-Berg, Pfalz-Zweibrücken).* Edited by Lothar Schilling and Gerhard Schuck. Frankfurt am Main: Klostermann, 1999.

Heberle, Hans. *Zeytregister.* See under Zillhardt, Gerd.
Heymach, F. "Aufzeichnungen des Pfarrers Plebanus von Miehlen aus den Jahren 1636/37. Im Auszug mitgeteilt." *Annalen des Vereins für Nassauische Altertumskunde* 38 (1908): 255–85.
Hirschmann, Gerhard. *Die Kirchenvisitation im Landgebiet der Reichsstadt Nürnberg 1560 und 1561. Quellenedition.* Neustadt an der Aisch: Degener & Co., 1994.
Hümmer, Friedrich K., ed. "Bamberg im Schweden-Kriege. Nach einem Manuscripte (Mittheilungen über die Jahre 1622–1634)." *Bericht über Bestand und Wirken des historischen Vereins zu Bamberg* 52 (1890): 1–168 (part 1); and 53 (1891): 169–230 (part 2).
Hüttner, Franz. "Memoiren des Zisterzienserabts Johann Dressel von Ebrach aus den Jahren 1631–1635." *Studien und Mitteilungen aus dem Benediktiner- und dem Cistercienser-Orden* 26 (1905): 76–85, 294–305, 551–73.
Hüttner, Franz, ed. "Selbstbiographie des Stadtpfarrers Wolfgang Ammon von Marktbreit (d. 1634)." *Archiv für Kulturgeschichte* 1 (1903): 284–325.
Jesuitenchronik "Historia Collegii S. J. Bambergensis, Litterae Annue." Translated in excerpts by Heinrich Weber, *Bamberg im dreißigjährigen Krieg. Nach einer gleichzeitigen Chronik bearbeitet.* In *Bericht des Historischen Vereins Bamberg* 48 (1886): 1–132.
"Klosterchronik." In *Die Abtei St. Walburg, 1035–1935. 900 Jahre in Wort und Bild.* Edited by the Abtei St. Walburg, Eichstätt. Augsburg: Literarisches Institut von Haas & Grabherr, 1934.
Krusenstjern, Benigna von. *Selbstzeugnisse der Zeit des Dreißigjährigen Krieges. Beschreibendes Verzeichnis.* Berlin: Akademie Verlag, 1997.
"Leipziger Lobgesang, Vnd TRiumph Liedt/ Vber die vnvermuthlich/ erschreckliche vnd herrliche grosse Feldschlacht/ darinn die Kayserliche/ Bayerische Armee am 7. Tag Septemb Anno 1631 Ritterlich erlegt/ vnd aus dem Feld geschlagen worden." Leipzig 1631. HAB, T 553 Helmst 40 (6).
Leuchtmann, Horst. "Zeitgenössische Aufzeichnungen des Bayerischen Hofkapellaltisten Johannes Hellgemayr aus den Jahren 1595–1633." *Oberbayerisches Archiv* 100 (1975): 142–229.
Lorenz, Gottfried, ed. *Quellen zur Vorgeschichte und zu den Anfängen des Dreißigjährigen Krieges.* Darmstadt: Wissenschaftliche Buchgesellschaft, 1991.
Luther, Martin. "Ob man vor dem Sterben fliehen möge. 1527." [WA 23; 338–79]. In *Erneuerung von Frömmigkeit. Martin Luther Ausgewählte Schriften,* 2. Edited by Karin Bornkamm and Gerhard Ebeling. Frankfurt am Main: Insel, 1982.
Mayer, M. Stephan. "Kurze Aufzeichnungen aus den Zeiten des Schwedenkrieges, 1625–45." *Deutsche Gaue* 11 (1910): 26–31.
Medick, Hans, ed. *Der Dreissigjährige Krieg: Zeugnisse vom Leben mit Gewalt.* Göttingen: Wallstein, 2018.
Medick, Hans, and Benjamin Marschke, eds. *Experiencing the Thirty Years War: A Brief History with Documents.* Boston: Bedford/St. Martin's, 2013.
"Mercurij Ordinari Zeitung Auff das 1632. Jahr." HAB, 202. 63 Quod. (61).

Meyers Großes Konversations-Lexikon: Ein Nachschlagewerk des allgemeinen Wissens, vol. 5. 6th ed. Leipzig: Bibliographisches Institut, 1906.

Mußinan, Joseph von. *Über das Schicksal Straubings und des baierischen Waldes während des dreyßig jährigen Krieges vom Oktober 1633 bis April 1634*. Straubing: Lerno, 1813.

New York Times. "Population Control, Marauder Style." 6 November 2011. Section SR, 7.

Opel, Julius O., and Adolf Cohn, eds. *Der Dreißigjährige Krieg: Eine Sammlung von historischen Gedichten und Prosadarstellungen*. Halle: Waisenhaus, 1862.

"Ordentliche Wochentliche Zeitung." 23–28 October (2–7 November) 1633. HAB, 202. 63 Quod. (zu 59).

Osiander, Andreas. *Wie und wohin ein Christ die grausame Plag der pestilentz fliehen soll: Ein Predig, aus dem 91. Psalm*. Nuremberg: Petreius, 1533.

Peters, Jan, ed. *Ein Söldnerleben im Dreißigjährigen Krieg: Eine Quelle zur Sozialgeschichte*. Berlin: Akademie Verlag, 1993.

Pitschmann, Benedikt. "Aus dem Tagebuch eines Flüchtlings des Dreißigjährigen Krieges: Abt Karl Stengel von Anhausen in Kremsmünster." *Studien und Mitteilungen zur Geschichte des Benediktiner-Ordens* 88 (1977): 53–145.

Radspieler, Hans. "'Wer dieses lesen wirt ...': Die Notizen des Rebdorfer Subpriors P. Wunibald Hueber über den Dreißigjährigen Krieg." *Historische Blätter für Stadt und Landkreis Eichstätt* 20 (1971): 18–20.

Reischl, Georg A., ed. *Hohenwarter Klosterchronik 1500–1700. Veröffentlichungen des Historischen Vereins für Schrobenhausen und Umgebung* 8 (1931).

Rullmann, Jakob, ed. "Die Einwirkungen des 30jährigen Krieges auf die Stadt Schlüchtern und ihre Umgegend, aus Kirchenbüchern zusammengestellt." *Zeitschrift des Vereins für hessische Geschichte und Landeskunde* N.F. 6 (1875): 201–50.

Scheible, Johann, ed. *Die Fliegenden Blätter des 16. und 17. Jahrhunderts*. Hildesheim: Olms, [1850] 1972.

Schnorr von Carolsfeld, Franz L. "Zwei neue Meistersängerhandschriften." *Archiv für Litteraturgeschichte* 3 (1874): 49–62.

Sigl, Rupert. "Wallensteins Rache an Bayern: Der Schwedenschreck." *Veit Hösers Kriegstagebuch*. Grafenau: Morsak, 1984.

Stahleder, Helmuth, ed. *Chronik der Stadt München. Belastungen und Bedrückungen*, vol. 2: *Die Jahre 1506–1705*. Ebenhausen and Hamburg: Dölling and Galitz, 2005.

Staiger, Klara. *Klara Staigers Tagebuch: Aufzeichnungen während des Dreißigjährigen Krieges im Kloster Mariastein bei Eichstätt*. Edited by Ortrun Fina. Regensburg: Pustet, 1981.

Stemmler, Otto. "Die Ortenau in Abt Gaissers Tagebüchern (1621–1655)." *Die Ortenau* 29 (1949) [= N.F. 1]: 43–68.

Thomas, Johann. *Friedensgedancken*. New Imprint of 1st ed. 1650. Edited by Detlef Ignasiak. Jena: Drucks- und Verlagshaus Jena, 1994.

Veit Hösers Kriegstagebuch. See under Sigl, Rupert.

Wagentroz, M. David. "Sanfftes Schlaffkämmerlein vnd Ruhebettlein frommer Christen/ darein sie sich verbergen/ biss auff den bald hereinbrechenden lieben Jüngsten Tag/ vnd süsse in Gott schlaffen nur eine Augenblickszeit ... Das ist: Eine Gast- vnd Trostpredigt/ genommen aus den Worten des geistreichen Propheten Esaiae am 26. Capitel v. 20. vnd den 19. Novembris im Thumb zu Braunschweig Anno 1640 gehalten." Braunschweig, 1640. HAB, J 93 40 Helmst. (17).

Werder, Paris von dem. *Friedens-Rede/ In Gegenwart vieler Fürsten/ Fürstinnnen vnd Fräwlein/ auch grosser Anzahl Hochadelicher gelehrter vnd anderer vornehmen Manns-Frawen- vnd Jungfräwlichen Personen*. Hamburg, 1639. HAB, 171. 42 Quod. (9).

Wurster, Herbert W. "Johann Heinrich Ursinus: Mein Lebens-Lauff. Die Autobiographie eines Regensburger Superintendenten aus dem 17. Jahrhundert." *Zeitschrift für bayerische Kirchengeschichte* 51 (1982): 73–105.

Ziegler, Walter, ed. *Altbayern von 1550–1651: Dokumente zur Geschichte von Staat und Gesellschaft in Bayern, Abt. I: Altbayern vom Frühmittelalter bis 1800*, vol. 3/1 and 3/2. Munich: Beck, 1992.

Zillhardt, Gerd, ed. *Der Dreißigjährige Krieg in zeitgenössischer Darstellung: Hans Heberles 'Zeytregister' (1618–1672). Aufzeichnungen aus dem Ulmer Territorium*. Ulm: Kohlhammer, 1975.

Zwingler, Irmgard E. *Das Klarissenkloster bei St. Jakob am Anger zu München: Das Angerkloster unter der Reform des Franziskanerordens im Zeitalter des Dreißigjährigen Krieges*. Munich: Verein für Diözesangeschichte von München und Freising, 2009.

Secondary Sources

Abel, Wilhelm. *Massenarmut und Hungerkrisen im vorindustriellen Europa: Versuch einer Synopsis*. Hamburg: Parey, 1974.

Adam, Wolfgang. "Das Flugblatt als kultur- und literaturgeschichtliche Quelle." *Euphorion* 84 (1990): 187–206.

Adam, Wolfgang, ed. *Geselligkeit und Gesellschaft im Barockzeitalter*, vol. 1. Wiesbaden: Harrassowitz, 1997.

Adrians, Frauke. *Journalismus im 30jährigen Krieg. Kommentierung und "Parteylichkeit" in Zeitungen des 17. Jahrhunderts*. Konstanz: UVK Medien, 1999.

Albrecht, Dieter. *Maximilian I. von Bayern 1573–1651*. Munich: Oldenbourg, 1998.

Amelang, James S. *The Flight of Icarus: Artisan Autobiography in Early Modern Europe*. Stanford: Stanford University Press, 1998.

Amelang, James S. "Vox Populi: Popular Autobiographies as Sources for Early Modern Urban History." *Urban History* 20 (1993): 30–42.

Aretin, Johann C. Freyherr von. "Geschichte des Aufstands der baierischen Bauern in den Jahren 1633 und 1634." In *Beyträge zur Geschichte und Literatur*, edited by Johann C. Freyherr von Aretin, vol. 2.3: 60–76. Munich: Scherersche Kunst- und Buchhandlung, 1804.

Arnold, Klaus, et al., eds. *Das dargestellte Ich. Studien zu Selbstzeugnissen des späteren Mittelalters und der frühen Neuzeit.* Bochum: Winkler, 1999.

Asbach, Olaf, and Peter Schröder, eds. *War, the State and International Law in Seventeenth-Century Europe.* Farnham, UK: Ashgate, 2010.

Asche, Matthias, et al., eds. *Krieg, Militär und Migration in der Frühen Neuzeit.* Berlin: LIT Verlag, 2008.

Asche, Matthias, and Anton Schindling, eds. *Das Strafgericht Gottes. Kriegserfahrungen und Religion im Heiligen Römischen Reich Deutscher Nation im Zeitalter des Dreißigjährigen Krieges.* Münster: Aschendorff, 2001.

Aston, Trevor, ed. *Crisis in Europe 1560–1660. Essay from Past and Present.* London: Routledge & Kegan Paul, 1975.

Ay, Karl-Ludwig. *Land und Fürst im alten Bayern 16–18. Jahrhundert.* Regensburg: Pustet, 1988.

Bachmann-Medick, Doris. *Cultural Turns: New Orientations in the Study of Culture.* Berlin: de Gruyter, 2016.

Bahlcke, Joachim, ed. *Glaubensflüchtlinge. Ursachen, Formen und Auswirkungen frühneuzeitlicher Konfessionsmigration in Europa.* Berlin: Lit Verlag, 2008.

Bahlcke, Joachim, et al., eds. *Konfessionelle Pluralität als Herausforderung: Koexistenz und Konflikt in Spätmittelalter und Früher Neuzeit. Winfried Eberhard zum 65. Geburtstag.* Leipzig: Leipziger Universitätsverlag, 2006.

Bähr, Andreas. *Furcht und Furchtlosigkeit: Göttliche Gewalt und Selbstkonstitution im 17. Jahrhundert.* Göttingen: V&H Unipress, 2013.

Bähr, Andreas. "Gottes Wort, Gottes Macht und Gottes Furcht: Gewaltdrohung und Sprache im 17. Jahrhundert." In *Blutige Worte: Internationales und interdisziplinäres Kolloquium zum Verhältnis von Sprache und Gewalt in Mittelalter und Früher Neuzeit*, edited by Jutta Eming and Claudia Jarzebowski, 213–32. Göttingen: V&R Unipress, 2008.

Bähr, Andreas. *Der Grausame Komet: Himmelszeichen und Weltgeschehen im Dreißigjährigen Krieg.* Reinbek bei Hamburg: Rowohlt, 2017.

Bähr, Andreas. "Remembering Fear: The Fear of Violence and the Violence of Fear in Seventeenth-Century War Memories." In *Memory before Modernity. Practices of Memory in Early Modern Europe*, edited by Erika Kuijpers et al., 269–82. Boston: Brill, 2013.

Barton, Walter. *Informationsbedürfnis und persönliche Betroffenheit. Zeitungskritik und Zeitungskunde im 17. Jahrhundert, überprüft an Presseberichten zum Krieg um Ostfriesland 1622/24*. Oldenburg: BIS-Verlag, 1994.

Bauer, Richard. *Geschichte Münchens: Vom Mittelalter bis zur Gegenwart*. Munich: Beck, 2003.

Bauerreiss, Romuald. *Kirchengeschichte Bayerns*, vol. 7. St. Ottilien: Eos, 1977.

Behringer, Wolfgang. *Hexenverfolgung in Bayern. Volksmagie, Glaubenseifer und Staatsräson in der Frühen Neuzeit*. Munich: Oldenbourg, 1987.

Behringer, Wolfgang. *Im Zeichen des Merkur: Reichspost und Kommunikationsrevolution in der Frühen Neuzeit*. Göttingen: Vandenhoeck & Ruprecht, 2003.

Behringer, Wolfgang. *Mit dem Feuer vom Leben zum Tod. Hexengesetzgebung in Bayern*. Munich: Hugendubel, 1988.

Behringer, Wolfgang. "Veränderung der Raum-Zeit-Relation. Zur Bedeutung des Zeitungs- und Nachrichtenwesens während der Zeit des Dreißigjährigen Krieges." In *Zwischen Alltag und Katastrophe. Der Dreißigjährige Krieg aus der Nähe*, edited by Benigna von Krusenstjern and Hans Medick, 39–81. Göttingen: Vandenhoeck & Ruprecht, 1999.

Behringer, Wolfgang. "Von Krieg zu Krieg: Neue Perspektiven auf das Buch von Günther Franz 'Der Dreißigjährige Krieg und das deutsche Volk' (1940)." In *Zwischen Alltag und Katastrophe. Der Dreißigjährige Krieg aus der Nähe*, edited by Benigna von Krusenstjern and Hans Medick, 543–91. Göttingen: Vandenhoeck & Ruprecht, 1999.

Behringer, Wolfgang, ed. *Kulturelle Konsequenzen der "Kleinen Eiszeit"* [*Cultural Consequences of the "Little Ice Age"*]. Göttingen: Vandenhoeck & Ruprecht, 2005.

Beller, Elmer A. *Propaganda in Germany during the Thirty Years War*. Princeton: Princeton University Press, 1940.

Benedict, Philip, and Myron P. Gutmann, eds. *Early Modern Europe: From Crisis to Stability*. Newark: University of Delaware Press, 2005.

Bircher, Martin, ed. *Deutsche Schriftsteller im Porträt: Das Zeitalter des Barock*. Munich: Beck, 1979.

Bircher, Martin, and Ferdinand van Ingen, eds. *Sprachgesellschaften, Sozietäten, Dichtergruppen: Arbeitsgespräch in der Herzog August Bibliothek Wolfenbüttel 28. bis 30. Juni 1977*. Hamburg: Hauswedell & Co., 1978.

Bireley, Robert. *The Jesuits and the Thirty Years War*. Cambridge: Cambridge University Press, 2003.

Bireley, Robert. *Maximilian von Bayern, Adam Contzen S. J. und die Gegenreformation in Deutschland 1624–1635*. Göttingen: Vandenhoeck & Rupprecht, 1975.

Bireley, Robert. *Religion and Politics in the Age of the Counterreformation: Emperor Ferdinand II, William Lamormaini, S. J., and the Formation of Imperial Policy*. Chapel Hill: University of North Carolina Press, 1981.

Bischoff, Doerte, and Susanne Komfort-Hein, eds. *Literatur und Exil. Neue Perspektiven*. Berlin: de Gruyter, 2013.

Blickle, Renate. "Das Land und das Elend. Die Vier-Wälder-Formel und die Verweisung aus dem Land Bayern. Zur historischen Wahrnehmung von Raum und Grenze." In *Menschen und Grenzen in der frühen Neuzeit*, edited by Wolfgang Schmale und Reinhard Stauber, 131–54. Berlin: Spitz, 1998.

Blickle, Renate. "Laufen gen Hof – Die Beschwerden der Untertanen und die Entstehung des Hofrats in Bayern. Ein Beitrag zu den Varianten rechtlicher Verfahren im späten Mittelalter und in der frühen Neuzeit." In *Gemeinde und Staat im alten Europa*, edited by Peter Blickle, 241–66. Munich: Oldenburg, 1997.

Blickle, Renate. "Rebellion oder natürliche Defension. Der Aufstand der Bauern in Bayern 1633/34." In *Verbrechen, Strafen, und soziale Kontrolle. Studien zur historischen Kulturforschung III*, edited by Richard van Dülmen, 56–84. Frankfurht am Main: Fischer Taschenbuch, 1990.

Blome, Astrid, ed. *Zeitung, Zeitschrift, Intelligenzblatt und Kalender: Beiträge zur historischen Presseforschung*. Bremen: Edition Lumière, 2000.

Blühm, Elger. "Deutsches Zeitungswesen im 17. Jahrhundert." In *Bücher und Bibliotheken im 17. Jahrhundert in Deutschland*, edited by Paul Raabe, 126–34. Hamburg: Ernst Hauswedell & Co., 1980.

Bog, Ingomar. *Die bäuerliche Wirtschaft im Zeitalter des Dreißigjährigen Krieges: Die Bewegungsvorgänge in der Kriegswirtschaft nach den Quellen des Klosterverwalteramtes Heilsbronn*. Coburg: Veste, 1952.

Bogel, Else, and Helga Blühm, eds. *Die Deutschen Zeitungen des 17. Jahrhunderts: Ein Bestandsverzeichnis mit historischen und bibliographischen Angaben*. Bremen: Schünemann, 1971.

Bohatcová, Mirjam. *Irrgarten der Schicksale: Einblattdrucke vom Anfang des Dreissigjährigen Krieges*. Prague: Artia, 1966.

Böttcher, Diethelm. "Propaganda und öffentliche Meinung im protestantischen Deutschland 1628–1636." In *Der Dreissigjährige Krieg. Perspektiven und Strukturen*, edited by Hans U. Rudolf, 325–67. Darmstadt: Wissenschaftliche Buchgesellschaft, 1977.

Bouwsma, William J. "Anxiety and the Formation of Early Modern Culture." In *After the Reformation: Essays in Honor of J. H. Hexter*, edited by Barbara C. Malament, 215–46. Philadelphia: University of Pennsylvania Press, 1980.

Brady, Thomas A., Jr. *German Histories in the Age of Reformations, 1400–1650*. Cambridge: Cambridge University Press, 2009.

Brady, Thomas A., Jr., ed., *Die deutsche Reformation zwischen Spätmittelalter und Früher Neuzeit*. Munich: Oldenbourg, 2001.

Brändle, Fabian et al., eds. "Texte zwischen Erfahrung und Diskurs: Probleme der Selbstzeugnisforschung." In *Von der dargestellten Person zum erinnerten Ich. Europäische*

Selbstzeugnisse als historische Quelle (1500–1850), edited by Kaspar von Greyerz et al., 3–31. Cologne: Böhlau, 2001.

Brecht, Martin et al., eds. *Pietismus und Neuzeit. Ein Jahrbuch zur Geschichte des neueren Protestantismus*. Göttingen: Vandenhoeck & Ruprecht, 2006.

Brednich, Rolf W. *Die Liedpublizistik im Flugblatt des 15. bis 17. Jahrhunderts*, vol. 1. Baden-Baden: Koerner, 1974.

Breuer, Dieter, ed. *Religion und Religiosität im Zeitalter des Barock*, 2 vols. Wiesbaden: Harrassowitz, 1995.

Briegel, Manfred, and Wolfgang Frühwald, eds. *Die Erfahrung der Fremde: Kolloquium des Schwerpunktprogramms "Exilforschung" der Deutschen Forschungsgemeinschaft*. Weinheim: VCH Verlagsgesellschaft, 1988.

Brink, Claudia. "'Mars als Widersacher der Künste.' Ein Thema der Malerei in eigener Sache." *Morgen-Glantz* 9 (1999): 93–128.

Brockdorff, Silvia Gräfin von. "Die Benediktinerinnenabtei Frauenchiemsee im 17. Jahrhundert." *Studien und Mitteilungen zur Geschichte des Benediktiner-Ordens* 54 (1936): 366–96 and 55 (1937): 63–99.

Brod, Walter M. "Die sogenannten 'Schweden-Blätter.'" *Mainfränkisches Jahrbuch für Geschichte und Kunst* 30 (1978): 25–35.

Brownmiller, Susan. *Against Our Will: Men, Women and Rape*. New York: Simon and Schuster, 1975.

Brückner, Wolfgang. "Christlicher Amulett-Gebrauch der frühen Neuzeit – Grundsätzliches und Spezifisches zur Popularisierung der Agnus Dei." In *Frömmigkeit. Formen, Geschichte, Verhalten, Zeugnisse. Lenz Kriss-Rettenbeck zum 70. Geburtstag*, edited by Ingolf Bauer, 89–134. Munich: Deutscher Kunstverlag, 1993.

Brückner, Wolfgang et al., eds. *Literatur und Volk im 17. Jahrhundert. Probleme populärer Kultur in Deutschland*, vol. 2. Wiesbaden: Harrassowitz, 1985.

Brutscher, Ludwig. *Rieser Schicksale im Dreißigjährigen Krieg*. Nördlingen: Steinmeier, 1984.

Bücher, Karl. *Gesammelte Aufsätze zur Zeitungskunde*. Tübingen: Laupp, 1926.

Buchner, Eberhard. *Religion und Kirche. Kulturhistorisch interessante Dokumente aus alten deutschen Zeitungen (16. bis 18. Jahrhundert)*. Munich: Langen, 1925.

Buchner, Franz X. *Das Bistum Eichstätt: historisch-statistische Beschreibung, auf Grund der Literatur, der Registratur des Bischöflichen Ordinariats Eichstätt sowie der pfarramtlichen Berichte*, vol. 2. Eichstätt: Brönner & Däntler, 1938.

Buchstab, Günter. *Reichsstädte, Städtekurie und Westfälischer Friedenskongreß. Zusammenhänge von Sozialstruktur, Rechtsstatus und Wirtschaftskraft*. Münster: Aschendorff, 1976.

Bühl, Walter L. *Krisentheorien: Politik, Wirtschaft und Gesellschaft im Übergang*. Darmstadt: Wissenschaftliche Buchgesellschaft, 1984.

Bulst, Neithard, and Robert Delort, eds. *Maladies et Société (XIIe–XVIIIe siècles): Actes du colloque de Bielefeld*. Paris: Imprimerie Louis-Jean, 1989.
Burke, Peter. *Popular Culture in Early Modern Europe*. New York: Harper & Row, 1978.
Burkhardt, Johannes. *Der Dreißigjährige Krieg*. Frankfurt am Main: Suhrkamp, 1992.
Burkhardt, Johannes. "Der Dreißigjährige Krieg als frühmoderner Staatsbildungskrieg." *Geschichte in Wissenschaft und Unterricht* 45 (1994): 487–99.
Burkhardt, Johannes. "Das größte Friedenswerk der Neuzeit: Der Westfälische Frieden in neuer Perspektive." *Geschichte in Wissenschaft und Unterricht* 10 (1998): 592–612.
Burkhardt, Johannes. *Der Krieg der Kriege: Eine neue Geschichte des Dreißigjährigen Krieges*. Stuttgart: Klett-Cotta, 2018.
Burkhardt, Johannes. "The Summitless Pyramid: War Aims and Peace Compromise among Europe's Universalist Powers." In *1648: War and Peace in Europe*, vol. 1, edited by Klaus Bussmann and Heinz Schilling, 51–60. Munich: Veranstaltungsgesellschaft 350 Jahre Westfälischer Friede, 1998.
Burkhardt, Johannes. "Worum ging es im Dreißigjährigen Krieg? Die frühmodernen Konflikte um Konfessions- und Staatsbildung." In *Wie Kriege entstehen: Zum historischen Hintergrund von Staatskonflikten*, edited by Bernd Wegner, 67–87. Paderborn: Schöningh, 2000.
Burkhardt, Johannes, and Christine Werkstetter, eds. *Kommunikation und Medien in der Frühen Neuzeit*. Munich: Oldenbourg, 2005.
Bussmann, Klaus, and Heinz Schilling, eds. *1648: War and Peace in Europe*, vols. 1–2. Munich: Veranstaltungsgesellschaft 350 Jahre Westfälischer Friede, 1998.
Carlin, Claire L., ed. *Imagining Contagion in Early Modern Europe*. New York: Palgrave Macmillan, 2005.
Certeau, Michel de. *The Practice of Everyday Life*. Translated by Steven Rendall. Berkeley: University of California Press, 1984.
Chrisman, Miriam Usher. "Urban Poor in the Sixteenth Century: The Case of Strasbourg." In *Social Groups and Religious Ideas in the Sixteenth Century*, edited by Miriam Usher Chrisman and Otto Gründler, 59–67. Kalamazoo, Michigan: The Medieval Institute, Western Michigan University, 1978.
Conermann, Klaus, ed. *Die Mitglieder der Fruchtbringenden Gesellschaft 1617–1650*, vol. 3. Weinheim: VCH Edition Leipzig, 1985.
Conrad, Anne. *Zwischen Kloster und Welt: Ursulinen und Jesuitinnen in der Katholischen Reformbewegung des 16./17. Jahrhunderts*. Mainz: von Zabern, 1991.
Coupe, William A. *The German Illustrated Broadsheet in the Seventeenth Century: Historical and Iconographical Studies*, vol. 1. Baden-Baden: Heitz, 1966.
Coy, Jason et al., eds. *The Holy Roman Empire, Reconsidered*. New York: Berghahn, 2010.
Crecelius, W. "Das geschichtliche Lied und die Zeitung im 16. und 17. Jahrhundert." *Zeitschrift des Bergischen Geschichtsvereins* 24 (1888): 1–22.

Creveld, Martin van. *Supplying War: Logistics from Wallenstein to Patton.* Cambridge: Cambridge University Press, 1987.

Critchlow, Donald T., and Charles H. Parker, eds. *With Us Always: A History of Private Charity and Public Welfare.* New York: Rowman & Littlefield, 1998.

Cubero, José-Ramón. *La femme et le soldat: viols et violences de guerre du Moyen Âge à nos jours.* Paris: Imago, 2012.

Czezior, Patricia. *Die Heimatlosigkeit im Werke zweier romantischer Grenzgänger: Joseph von Eichendorff und Heinrich Heine.* Berlin: Wissenschaftlicher Verlag Berlin, 2004.

D'Addario, Christopher. *Exile and Journey in Seventeenth-Century Literature.* Cambridge: Cambridge University Press, 2007.

Dallmeier, Martin. "Die Funktion der Reichspost für den Hof und die Öffentlichkeit." In *Europäische Hofkultur im 16. und 17. Jahrhundert*, vol. 3, edited by August Buck et al., 589–94. Hamburg: Hauswedell, 1981.

Dane, Gesa. *"Zeter und Mordio": Vergewaltigung in Literatur und Recht.* Göttingen: Wallstein, 2005.

Davies, Mererid Puw, et al., eds. *Autobiography by Women in German.* Bern: Lang, 2000.

Davis, Natalie Z. "Poor Relief, Humanism, and Heresy." In *Society and Culture in Early Modern France*, edited by Natalie Z. Davis, 16–64. Stanford: Stanford University Press, 1965.

Deine, Christa. *Die Schwedische Epoche in Franken von 1631–1635.* Würzburg: Gugel, 1966.

Demandt, Dieter, and Hans-Christoph Rublack. *Stadt und Kirche in Kitzingen: Darstellung und Quellen zu Spätmittelalter und Reformation.* Stuttgart: Klett-Cotta, 1978.

Dengler-Schreiber, Karin. "'Ist alles oed vnd wüst ...': Zerstörung und Wiederaufbau in der Stadt Bamberg im Zeitalter des Dreißigjährigen Kriegs." *Jahrbuch für fränkische Landesforschung* 57 (1997): 145–61.

Deventer, Jörg et al., eds. *Zeitenwenden: Herrschaft, Selbstbehauptung und Integration zwischen Reformation und Liberalismus. Festgabe für Arno Herzig zum 65. Geburtstag.* Münster: Lit-Verlag, 2002.

Diefenbacher, Michael, and Wiltrud Fischer-Pache, eds. *Das Nürnberger Buchgewerbe: Buch- und Zeitungsdrucker, Verleger und Druckhändler vom 16. bis zum 18. Jahrhundert.* Nuremberg: Stadtarchiv Nürnberg, 2003.

Dinges, Martin. "Frühneuzeitliche Armenfürsorge als Sozialdisziplinierung? Probleme mit einem Konzept." *Geschichte und Gesellschaft* 17 (1991): 5–29.

Dinges, Martin. "'Historische Anthropologie und Gesellschaftsgeschichte.' Mit dem Lebensstilkonzept zu einer 'Alltagskulturgeschichte' der frühen Neuzeit." *Zeitschrift für Historische Forschung* 24 (1997): 179–214.

Dinges, Martin, and Thomas Schlich, eds. *Neue Wege in der Seuchengeschichte.* Stuttgart: Steiner, 1995.

Dixon, Scott C. "Popular Astrology and Lutheran Propaganda in Reformation Germany." *History* 84 (1999): 403–18.

Dixon, Scott C., and Luise Schorn-Schütte, eds. *The Protestant Clergy of Early Modern Europe*. New York: Palgrave MacMillan, 2003.

Dollinger, Heinz. "Kurfürst Maximilian I. von Bayern und Justus Lipsius: Eine Studie zur Staatstheorie eines frühabsolutistischen Fürsten." *Archiv für Kulturgeschichte* 46 (1965): 227–308.

Donaubauer, Stephan. "Nürnberg in der Mitte des dreißigjährigen Krieges." *Mitteilungen des Vereins für Geschichte der Stadt Nürnberg* 10 (1893): 69–240.

Dooley, Brendan. "News and Doubt in Early Modern Culture: Or, Are We Having a Public Sphere Yet?" In *The Politics of Information in Early Modern Europe*, edited by Brendan Dooley and Sabrina A. Baron, 275–90. London: Routledge, 2001.

Dooley, Brendan, and Sabrina A. Baron, eds. *The Politics of Information in Early Modern Europe*. London: Routledge, 2001.

Duffy, Christopher. *Siege Warfare: The Fortress in the Early Modern World 1494–1660*. London: Routledge & Kegan Paul, 1979.

Duhr, Bernhard. *Geschichte der Jesuiten in den Ländern deutscher Zunge in der ersten Hälfte des XVII. Jahrhunderts*, vol. 2. Freiburg im Breisgau: Herdersche Verlagshandlung, 1913.

Dülmen, Richard van. "Einleitung." In *Kultur der einfachen Leute: bayerisches Volksleben vom 16. bis zum 19. Jahrhundert*, edited by Richard van Dülmen, 7–16. Munich: Beck, 1983.

Dülmen, Richard van, ed. *Entdeckung des Ich: Die Geschichte der Individualisierung vom Mittelalter bis zur Gegenwart*. Cologne: Böhlau, 2001.

Dunant, Sarah, and Roy Porter, eds. *The Age of Anxiety*. London: Virago Press, 1996.

Durchhardt, Heinz. "Interstate War and Peace in Early Modern Europe." In *War, Peace and World Orders in European History*, edited by Anja V. Hartmann and Beatrice Heuser, 185–95. London: Routledge, 2001.

Durchhardt, Heinz. *Studien zur Friedensvermittlung in der Frühen Neuzeit*. Wiesbaden: Steiner, 1979.

Durchhardt, Heinz, and Martin Espenhorst, eds. *Frieden übersetzen in der Vormoderne: Translationsleistungen in Diplomatie, Medien und Wissenschaft*. Göttingen: Vandenhoeck & Ruprecht, 2012.

Durchhardt, Heinz, and Gerhard May, eds. *Union – Konversion – Toleranz: Dimensionen der Annäherung zwischen den christlichen Konfessionen im 17. und 18. Jahrhundert*. Mainz: von Zabern, 2000.

Durchhardt, Heinz, and Patrice Veit, eds. *Krieg und Frieden im Übergang vom Mittelalter zur Neuzeit: Theorie – Praxis – Bilder*. Mainz: von Zabern, 2000.

Eberhardt, Otto. "Exil im Mittelalter. Einige Streiflichter." In *Weltanschauliche Orientierungsversuche im Exil*, edited by Reinhard Andress, 13–36. Amsterdam: Rodopi, 2010.

Ebermeier, Werner. *Landshut im Dreißigjährigen Krieg: Das Schicksal der Stadt und ihrer Bewohner im historischen Zusammenhang*. Landshut: Stadtarchiv Landshut, 2000.

Eckert, Edward A. *The Structure of Plagues and Pestilences in Early Modern Europe: Central Europe, 1560–1640*. Basel: Karger, 1996.

Edel, Andreas. "Auf dem Weg in den Krieg: Zur Vorgeschichte der Intervention Herzog Maximilians I. von Bayern in Österreich und Böhmen 1620." *Zeitschrift für bayerische Landesgeschichte* 65/1 (2002): 157–251.

Ehrenpreis, Stefan, ed. *Der Dreißigjährige Krieg im Herzogtum Berg und in seinen Nachbarregionen*. Neustadt an der Aisch: Schmidt, 2002.

Ehrenpreis, Stefan et al., eds. *Wege der Neuzeit: Festschrift für Heinz Schilling zum 65. Geburtstag*. Berlin: Duncker & Humblot, 2007.

Elmer, Peter, and Ole Peter Grell, eds. *Health, Disease and Society in Europe 1500–1800*. Manchester: Manchester University Press, 2004.

Elsmann, Thomas. "Humanismus, Schule, Buchdruck und Antikenrezeption: Anmerkungen zur Bremer Entwicklung bis 1648." In *Stadt und Literatur im deutschen Sprachraum der Frühen Neuzeit*, vol. I, edited by Klaus Garber, 203–38. Tübingen: Niemeyer, 1998.

Endres, Rudolf. "Der Dreißigjährige Krieg in Franken: Anlaß – Ablauf – Schrecken – Schutzmaßnahmen – Auswirkungen – Wiederaufbau." In *Gustav Adolf, Wallenstein und der Dreissigjährige Krieg in Franken: Ausstellung des Staatsarchivs Nürnberg zum 350. Gedenkjahr (1632–1982)*, edited by Günther Schuhmann, 11–26. Munich: Degener & Co., 1982.

Endres, Rudolf. *Der Fränkische Reichskreis*. Regensburg: Pustet, 2003.

Engelsing, Rolf. *Analphabetentum und Lektüre: Zur Sozialgeschichte des Lesens in Deutschland zwischen feudaler und industrieller Gesellschaft*. Stuttgart: Metzler, 1973.

Engelsing, Rolf. *Der Bürger als Leser: Lesergeschichte in Deutschland 1500–1800*. Stuttgart: Metzler, 1974.

Engelsing, Rolf, and Pavel Hrnčiřík. *Nördlingen 1634: Die Schlacht bei Nördlingen – Wendepunkt des Deißigjährigen Krieges*. Weißenstadt: Späthling, 2009.

Engerisser, Peter. *Von Kronach nach Nördlingen: Der Dreißigjährige Krieg in Franken, Schwaben und der Oberpfalz 1631–1635*. 2nd ed. Weißenstadt: Späthling, [2004] 2007.

Evans, R. J. W. *The Making of the Habsburg Monarchy 1550–1700: An Interpretation*. Oxford: Clarendon Press, 1979.

Evelein, Johannes F., ed. *Exiles Traveling: Exploring Displacement, Crossing Boundaries in German Exile Arts and Writings 1933–1945*. Amsterdam: Rodopi, 2009.

Fahlenbock, Michaela. *Der schwarze Tod in Tirol: Seuchenzüge – Krankheitsbilder – Auswirkungen*. Innsbruck: StudienVerlag, 2009.

Fassl, Peter et al., eds. *Forschungen zur bayerischen und schwäbischen Geschichte: Gesammelte Beiträge von Pankraz Fried. Zu seinem 65. Geburtstag*. Sigmaringen: Thorbecke, 1997.

Fätkenheuer, Frank. *Lebenswelt und Religion: Mikro-historische Untersuchungen an Beispielen aus Franken um 1600*. Göttingen: Vandenhoeck & Ruprecht, 2004.

Fehler, Timothy. "The Burden of Benevolence: Poor Relief and Parish Finance in Early Modern Emden." In *Reformations Old and New: Essays on the Socio-Economic Impact of Religious Change c. 1470–1630*, edited by Beat A. Kümin, 219–36. Aldershot: Scolar Press, 1996.

Feuerstein-Herz, Petra, ed. *Gotts verhengnis und seine straffe – Zur Geschichte der Seuchen in der Frühen Neuzeit*. Ausstellungskatalog der Herzog August Bibliothek. Braunschweig: Schönberg, 2005.

Fischer, Heinz-Dietrich. "Die Zeitung als Forschungsproblem." In *Deutsche Zeitungen des 17. bis 20. Jahrhunderts*, edited by Heinz-Dietrich Fischer, 11–24. Pullach bei Munich: Verlag Dokumentation, 1972.

Fischer, Helmut. *Die ältesten Zeitungen und ihre Verleger*. Augsburg: Schwabenland-Verlag, 1936.

Fischer, Michael M. J. "Ethnicity and the Post-Modern Arts of Memory." In *Writing Culture: The Poetics and Politics of Ethnography*, edited by James Clifford and George E. Marcus, 194–233. Berkeley: University of California Press, 1986.

Fisher, Alexander J. *Music, Piety, and Propaganda: The Soundscapes of Counter-Reformation Bavaria*. Oxford: Oxford University Press, 2014.

Fisher, Alexander J. "Themes of Exile and (Re-)Enclosure in Music for the Franciscan Convents of Counter-Reformation Munich During the Thirty Years' War." In *Enduring Loss in Early Modern Germany: Cross Disciplinary Perspectives*, edited by Lynne Tatlock, 281–306. Leiden: Brill, 2010.

Fisher, Jaimey, and Barbara Mennel. "Introduction." In *Spacial Turns. Space, Place, and Mobility in German Literary and Visual Culture*, edited by Jaimey Fisher and Barbara Mennel, 9–23. Amsterdam: Rodopi, 2010.

Fleischmann, Peter. *Rat und Patriziat in Nürnberg: Die Herrschaft der Ratsgeschlechter vom 13. bis zum 18. Jahrhundert*, 3 vols. Neustadt an der Aisch: Schmidt, 2008.

Forster, Marc R. *Catholic Revival in the Age of the Baroque: Religious Identity in Southwest Germany, 1550–1750*. Cambridge: Cambridge University Press, 2001.

Forster, Marc R. "The Thirty Years' War and the Failure of Catholicization." In *The Counter-Reformation in the Villages: Religion and Reform in the Bishopric of Speyer, 1560–1720*, 144–77. Ithaca: Cornell University Press, 1992. Reprinted in *The Counter-Reformation: Essential Readings*, edited by David M. Luebke, 163–97. Malden, Massachusetts: Blackwell Publishers, 1999.

François, Etienne. *Die unsichtbare Grenze: Protestanten und Katholiken in Augsburg 1648–1806*. Sigmaringen: Thorbecke, 1991.

Franz, Günther. *Der Dreissigjährige Krieg und das deutsche Volk: Untersuchungen zur Bevölkerungs- und Agrargeschichte*. Jena: Fischer, 1940.

Frauenholz, Eugen von. *Das Heerwesen in der Zeit des Dreissigjährigen Krieges*, vol. 1. *Das Söldnertum*. Munich: Beck, 1938.

Frauenholz, Eugen von. *Das Heerwesen in der Zeit des Dreissigjährigen Krieges*, vol. 2. *Die Landesdefension*. Munich: Beck, 1939.

Freund, Cajetan, ed. *Die München-Augsburger Abendzeitung: Ein kurzer Abriß ihrer mehr als 300jährigen Geschichte 1609–1914*. Munich: Bruckmann, 1914.

Frevert, Ute, and Wolfgang Braungart, eds. *Sprachen des Politischen: Medien und Medialität in der Geschichte*. Göttingen: Vandenhoeck & Ruprecht, 2004.

Friedrichs, Christopher R. *Urban Society in an Age of War: Nördlingen, 1580–1720*. Princeton: Princeton University Press, 1979.

Fritz, Gerhard, and Mathias Klink. "Außergewöhnliche Sulzbacher Kirchenbucheinträge aus der Zeit des Dreißigjährigen Krieges." *Württembergisch Franken Jahrbuch* 76 (1992): 177–234.

Fulbrook, Mary, and Ulinka Rublack. "In Relation: The 'Social Self' and Ego-Documents." *German History* 28 no. 3 (2010): 263–72.

Fussel, Paul. *The Great War and Modern Memory*. New York: Oxford University Press, [1975] 1989.

Garber, Klaus, et al., eds. *Erfahrung und Deutung von Krieg und Frieden: Religion – Geschlechter – Natur und Kultur*. Munich: Fink, 2001.

Gebhardt, Hartwig. "Das Interesse an der Pressegeschichte: Zur Wirksamkeit selektiver Wahrnehmung in der Medienhistoriographie." In *Presse und Geschichte: neue Beiträge zur historischen Kommunikationsforschung*, vol. 1:11–19. Munich: Saur, 1987.

Gehm, Britta. *Die Hexenverfolgung im Hochstift Bamberg und das Eingreifen des Reichshofrates zu ihrer Beendigung*. Hildesheim: Olms, 2000.

Geissler, Paul. "Die Älteste Zeitung im Bereiche des heutigen Bayern: Richard Schmidbauer zum 75. Geburtstag am 15. November 1956." *Gutenberg Jahrbuch* (1957): 192–99.

Gerstenberger, Erhard S. *Der bittende Mensch: Bittritual und Klagelied des Einzelnen im Alten Testament*. Neukirchen-Vluyn: Neukirchener Verlag, 1980.

Giesecke, Michael. "Der 'abgang der erkantnusz' und die Renaissance 'wahren Wissens': Frühneuzeitliche Kritik an den mittelalterlichen Formen handschriftlicher Informationsverarbeitung." In *Pragmatische Schriftlichkeit im Mittelalter: Erscheinungsformen und Entwicklungsstufen* (Akten des Internationalen Kolloquiums 17.–19. Mai 1989), edited by Hagen Keller et al., 77–93. Munich: Fink, 1992.

Gindhart, Marion. *Das Kometenjahr 1618: Antikes und zeitgenössisches Wissen in der frühneuzeitlichen Kometenliteratur des deutschsprachigen Raumes*. Wiesbaden: Reichert, 2006.

Ginzburg, Carlo. *The Cheese and the Worms: The Cosmos of a Sixteenth-Century Miller*. Baltimore: Johns Hopkins University Press, 1980.

Ginzburg, Carlo. "Mikro-Historie: Zwei oder drei Dinge, die ich von ihr weiß." *Historische Anthropologie* 1 (1993): 169–92.

Glaser, Hubert, ed. *Um Glauben und Reich: Kurfürst Maximilian I. Beiträge zur Bayerischen Geschichte und Kunst 1573–1657*. Munich: Hirmer und R. Piper & Co., 1980.

Glaser, Rüdiger. *Klimageschichte Mitteleuropas: 1200 Jahre Wetter, Klima, Katastrophen*. 2nd rev. ed. Darmstadt: Wissenschaftliche Buchgesellschaft, [2001] 2008.

Goldmann, Karlheinz, ed. *Gebt uns den Frieden: Aus den Anfängen des Pegnesischen Blumenordens*. Ausstellungskatalog des Instituts für Fränkische Literatur der Stadtbibiothek Nürnberg. Nuremberg: Fränkische Verlagsanstalt und Buchdruckerei, 1968.

Goodale, Jay. "The Clergyman between the Cultures of State and Parish: Contestation and Compromise in Reformation Saxony." In *The Protestant Clergy of Early Modern Europe*, edited by Scott C. Dixon and Luise Schorn-Schütte, 100–119. New York: Palgrave MacMillan, 2003.

Gotthard, Axel. "Maximilian und das Reich." *Zeitschrift für bayerische Landesgeschichte* 65/1 (2002): 35–68.

Gould, Peter, and Rodney White. *Mental Maps*. 2nd ed. Boston: Allen & Unwin, [1974] 1986.

Grell, Ole Peter, and Andrew Cunningham, eds. *Health Care and Poor Relief in Counter-Reformation Europe*. London: Routledge, 1999.

Grell, Ole Peter, and Andrew Cunningham, eds. *Health Care and Poor Relief in Protestant Europe 1500–1700*. London: Routledge, 1997.

Greyerz, Kaspar von. "Deutschschweizerische Selbstzeugnisse (1500–1800) als Quellen der Mentalitätsgeschichte: Bericht über ein Forschungsprojekt." In *Das dargestellte Ich: Studien zu Selbstzeugnissen des späteren Mittelalters und der frühen Neuzeit*, edited by Klaus Arnold et al., 147–59. Bochum: Winkler, 1999.

Greyerz, Kaspar von, "Ego-Documents: The Last Word?" *German History* 28 no. 3 (2010): 273–82.

Greyerz, Kaspar von. "Religion in the Life of German and Swiss Autobiographers (Sixteenth and Early Seventeenth Centuries)." In *Religion and Society in Early Modern Europe: 1500–1800*, edited by Kaspar von Greyerz, 223–41. London: Allen & Unwin, 1984.

Greyerz, Kaspar von. *Vorsehungsglaube und Kosmologie: Studien zu englischen Selbstzeugnissen des 17. Jahrhunderts*. Göttingen: Vandenhoeck & Ruprecht, 1990.

Greyerz, Kaspar von, ed. *Religion and Society in Early Modern Europe: 1500–1800*. London: Allen & Unwin, 1984.

Greyerz, Kaspar von, ed. *Selbstzeugnisse in der Frühen Neuzeit: Individualisierungsweisen in interdisziplinärer Perspektive*. Munich: Oldenbourg, 2007.

Greyerz, Kaspar von, et al., eds. *Interkonfessionalität – Transkonfessionalität – binnenkonfessionelle Pluralität: Neue Forschungen zur Konfessionalisierungsthese*. Gütersloh: Gütersloher Verlagshaus, 2003.

Greyerz, Kaspar von, et al., eds. *Von der dargestellten Person zum erinnerten Ich: Europäische Selbstzeugnisse als historische Quelle (1500–1850)*. Cologne: Böhlau, 2001.

Greyerz, Kaspar von, and Kim Siebenhüner, eds. *Religion und Gewalt: Konflikte, Rituale, Deutungen (1500–1800)*. Göttingen: Vandenhoeck & Ruprecht, 2006.

Grießhammer, Birke, ed. *Drutenjagd in Franken 16.–18. Jahrhundert*. Katalog zur Wanderausstellung: Hexenverfolgung in Franken. 2nd ed. Erlangen: Wagner, [1998]1999.

Grinberg, León, and Rebeca Grinberg. *Psychoanalyse der Migration und des Exils*. Munich: Verlag Internationale Psychoanalyse, 1990.

Groh, Dieter, et al., eds. *Naturkatastrophen: Beiträge zu ihrer Deutung, Wahrnehmung und Darstellung in Text und Bild von der Antike bis ins 20. Jahrhundert*. Tübingen: Narr, 2003.

Groth, Otto. *Die Zeitung. Ein System der Zeitungskunde (Journalistik)*, vol. 4. Mannheim: Bensheimer, 1930.

Grünbaum, Max. *Über die Publicistik des Dreissigjaehrigen Krieges von 1626–1629*. Halle: Niemeyer, 1880.

Günther, Bettina. *Die Behandlung der Sittlichkeitsdelikte in den Policeyordnungen und der Spruchpraxis der Reichsstädte Frankfurt am Main und Nürnberg im 15. bis 17. Jahrhundert*. Frankfurt am Main: Lang, 2004.

Haas, Robert. *Die Musik des Barocks*. Wildpark-Potsdam: Akademische Verlagsgesellschaft Athenaion, 1928.

Hacke, Daniela, ed. *Frauen in der Stadt. Selbstzeugnisse des 16.–18. Jahrhunderts: 39. Arbeitstagung in Heidelberg, 17.–19. November 2000*. Ostfildern: Thorbecke, 2004.

Hanke, Gerhard. "Zur Sozialstruktur der ländlichen Siedlungen Altbayerns im 17. und 18. Jahrhundert." In *Gesellschaft und Herrschaft: Forschungen zu sozial- und landesgeschichtlichen Problemen vornehmlich in Bayern. Eine Festgabe für Karl Bosl zum 60. Geburtstag*, edited by Richard van Dülmen, 219–69. Munich: Beck, 1969.

Hanke, Gerhard, and Wilhelm Liebhart. *Der Landkreis Dachau*. Dachau: Verlagsanstalt Bayerland, 1992.

Harms, Wolfgang. "Feindbilder im illustrierten Flugblatt der Frühen Neuzeit." In *Feindbilder: die Darstellung des Gegners in der politischen Publizistik des Mittelalters und der Neuzeit*, edited by Franz Bosbach, 141–77. Cologne: Böhlau, 1992.

Harms, Wolfgang. "Das illustrierte Flugblatt im Rahmen der Publizistik der frühen Neuzeit." In *Wege zur Kommunikationsgeschichte*, edited by Manfred Bobrowsky and Wolfgang R. Langenbucher, 259–65. Munich: Ölschläger, 1987.

Harms, Wolfgang. "Die kommentierende Erschließung des illustrierten Flugblatts der frühen Neuzeit und dessen Zusammenhang mit der weiteren Publizistik im 17. Jahrhundert." In *Presse und Geschichte: neue Beiträge zur historischen Kommunikationsforschung*, vol. 1: 83–111. Munich: Saur, 1987.

Harms, Wolfgang, et al., eds. *Illustrierte Flugblätter des Barock. Eine Auswahl.* Tübingen: Niemeyer, 1983.

Härter, Karl. "Soziale Disziplinierung durch Strafe? Intentionen frühneuzeitlicher Policeyordnungen und staatliche Sanktionspraxis." *Zeitschrift für historische Forschung* 26 (1990): 365–79.

Hartinger, Walter. "*Aberglaubens*-Mission der Jesuiten und Kapuziner im Bayerischen Wald 1642." In *Regensburg, Bayern und das Reich. Festschrift für Peter Schmid zum 65. Geburtstag*, edited by Tobias Appl and Georg Köglmeier, 479–98. Regensburg: Schnell & Steiner, 2010.

Hartinger, Walter. "Glaube – Aberglaube – Volksglaube? Zauberpraktiken der Frühen Neuzeit in Ostbayern." In *Religiöse Prägung und politische Ordnung in der Neuzeit. Festschrift für Winfried Becker zum 65. Geburtstag*, edited by Bernhard Löffler and Karsten Ruppert, 31–53. Cologne: Böhlau, 2006.

Hartinger, Walter. "Konfessionalisierung des Alltags in Bayern unter Maximilian I." *Zeitschrift für bayerische Landesgeschichte* 65/1 (2002): 123–56.

Hartinger, Walter. "Rechtspflege und Volksleben: Zur Funktion des Rechts im absolutistischen Bayern." In *Das Recht der kleinen Leute: Beiträge zur rechtlichen Volkskunde. Festschrift für Karl-Sigismund Kramer zum 60. Geburtstag*, edited by Karl S. Kramer et al., 50–68. Berlin: Schmidt, 1976.

Hartinger, Walter. "*… wie von alters herkommen …*": *Dorf-, Hofmarks-, Ehehaft- und andere Ordnungen in Ostbayern*, vol. 1, Niederbayern. Passau: Bischöfliches Seelsorgeamt Passau, 1998.

Hartmann, Anja V. "Identities and Mentalities in the Thirty Years' War." In *War, Peace and World Orders in European History*, edited by Anja V. Hartmann and Beatrice Heuser, 174–84. London: Routledge, 2001.

Hartmann, Peter C. *Der Bayerische Reichskreis (1500 bis 1803): Strukturen, Geschichte und Bedeutung im Rahmen der Kreisverfassung und der allgemeinen institutionellen Entwicklung des Heiligen Römischen Reiches.* Berlin: Duncker und Humblot, 1997.

Hartmann, Wilhelm. "Wolfenbüttel als Druckort des »Aviso« von 1609, der ältesten periodisch gedruckten Zeitung." *Niedersächsisches Jahrbuch für Landesgeschichte* 31 (1959): 175–89.

Haude, Sigrun. "The Experience of Disaster during the Thirty Years' War: Autobiographical Writings by Religious in Bavaria." In *Disaster, Death and the Emotions in the Shadow of the Apocalypse, 1400–1700*, edited by Jennifer Spinks and Charles Zika, 135–53. New York: Palgrave Macmillan, 2016.

Haude, Sigrun. "The Experience of War." In *Research Companion to the Thirty Years' War*, edited by Olaf Asbach and Peter Schroeder, 257–68. Franham, UK: Ashgate, 2014.

Haude, Sigrun. "Female Religious Communities During the Thirty Years' War." In *Embodiment, Identity, and Gender in the Early Modern Age*, 97–108. Ed. David Whitford and Amy Leonard. London: Routledge, 2021.

Haude, Sigrun. "Gender Roles and Perspectives among Anabaptist and Spiritualist Groups." In *A Companion to Anabaptism and Spiritualism, 1521–1700*, edited by John D. Roth and James M. Stayer, 425–65. Leiden: Brill, 2007.

Haude, Sigrun. "Life, Death, and Religion during the Thirty Years' War." *Continuity and Change: The Harvest of Late-Medieval and Reformation History. Essays Presented to Heiko A. Oberman on his 70th Birthday*, edited by Robert J. Bast and Andrew C. Gow, 417–30. Leiden: Brill, 2000.

Haude, Sigrun. "Religion während des Dreißigjährigen Krieges (1618–1648)." In *Frömmigkeit – Theologie – Frömmigkeitstheologie: Contributions to European History. Festschrift für Berndt Hamm zum 60. Geburtstag*, edited by Gudrun Litz et al., 537–53. Leiden: Brill, 2005.

Haude, Sigrun. "Social Control and Social Justice under Maximilian I of Bavaria (r. 1598–1651)." In *Politics and Reformations: Communities, Polities, Nations, and Empires. Essays in Honor of Thomas A. Brady Jr.*, edited by Christopher Ocker et al., 423–39. Leiden: Brill, 2007.

Haude, Sigrun. "The Thirty Years' War (1618–1648): Moving Bodies – Transforming Lives – Shifting Knowledge." In *Knowledge in Motion. Constructing Transcultural Experience in the Medieval and Early Modern Periods (1200–1750)*. Ed. Christian Schneider and Gerhild Scholz Williams. Special Issue of *Daphnis: Zeitschrift für Mittlere Deutsche Literatur und Kultur der Frühen Neuzeit (1400–1750)*, 45/ 3–4 (2017): 475–91.

Haude, Sigrun. "War – A Fortuitous Occasion for Social Disciplining and Political Centralization? The Case of Bavaria under Maximilian I." In *Police Forces: A Cultural History of an Institution*, edited by Klaus Mladek, 13–23. New York: Palgrave Macmillan, 2007.

Haude, Sigrun. "Warfare and Artistic Production in the German Lands during the Thirty Years' War." In *Artful Armies, Beautiful Battles: Art and Warfare in Early Modern Europe*, edited by Pia Cuneo, 35–58. Leiden: Brill, 2001.

Haude, Sigrun. "The World of the Siege in New Perspective: The Populace During the Thirty Years' War." In *The World of the Siege*, 21–43. Ed. Anke Fischer-Kattner and Jamel Ostwald. Leiden: Brill, 2019.

Haude, Sigrun. "Zorn und Schrecken, Buße und Gnade. Diskurse in astrologischen Schriften des 17. Jahrhunderts." In *Die Sterne lügen nicht: Astrologie und Astronomie im Mittelalter und in der Frühen Neuzeit*. Ausstellungskatalog der Herzog August

Bibliothek, edited by Christian Heitzmann, 170–200. Memmingen: Memminger MedienCentrum, 2008.

Head, Randolph C. *Making Archives in Early Modern Europe: Proof, Information, and Political Record-Keeping, 1400–1700*. Cambridge: Cambridge University Press, 2019.

Heal, Bridget. "Images of the Virgin Mary and Marian devotion in Protestant Nuremberg." In *Religion and Superstition in Reformation Europe*, edited by Helen Parish and William G. Naphy, 25–46. Manchester: Manchester University Press, 2002.

Hegeler, Hartmut. *Reinhard Wolf: Pfarrerschicksal im Dreißigjährigen Krieg*. Nordhausen: Bantz, 2008.

Heimbucher, Max. *Die Orden und Kongregationen der katholischen Kirche*, 2 vols. Paderborn: Schöningh, 1907.

Heimers, Manfred P. *Krieg, Hunger, Pest und Glaubenszwist: München im Dreißigjährigen Krieg*. Munich: Buchendorf, 1998.

Helm, Winfried. *Obrigkeit und Volk: Herrschaft im frühneuzeitlichen Alltag Niederbayerns, untersucht anhand archivalischer Quellen*. Passau: Neue Presse, 1993.

Helml, Stefan. *Die Oberpfalz im 30jährigen Krieg, der Deutschland und Europa in seinen Bann zog*. Amberg: Scherer, 1990.

Herold, Hans-Jörg. *Markgraf Joachim Ernst von Brandenburg-Ansbach als Reichsfürst*. Göttingen: Vandenhoeck & Ruprecht, 1973.

Heydenreuter, Reinhard. "Die Behördenreform Maximilians I." In *Wittelsbach und Bayern*, 2/1: *Um Glauben und Reich: Kurfürst Maximilian I. Beiträge zur Bayerischen Geschichte und Kunst 1573–1657*, edited by Hubert Glaser, 237–51. Munich: Hirmer, 1980.

Heydenreuter, Reinhard. "Finanz- und Verwaltungsreform unter Herzog und Kurfürst Maximilian I." *Zeitschrift für bayerische Landesgeschichte* 65/1 (2002): 101–121.

Heydenreuter, Reinhard. "Gerichts- und Amtsprotokolle in Altbayern: Zur Entwicklung des gerichts- und grundherrlichen Amtsbuchwesens." *Mitteilungen für die Archivpflege in Bayern* 25/26 (1979/80): 11–46.

Heydenreuter, Reinhard. "Herrschen durch Strafen: Zur Entwicklung des frühneuzeitlichen Staates im Herzogtum und Kurfürstentum Bayern 1550–1650." Habilitation (unpublished). Universität Eichstätt-Ingolstadt, 1996.

Heydenreuter, Reinhard. "Der Landesherrliche Hofrat in München und die Hexenprozesse in den letzten Regierungsjahren des Herzogs und Kurfürsten Maximilian I. (1598–1651)." *Zeitschrift für bayerische Landesgeschichte* 55 (1992): 137–50.

Heydenreuter, Reinhard. *Der landesherrliche Hofrat unter Herzog und Kurfürst Maximilian I. von Bayern (1598–1651)*. Munich: Beck, 1981.

Heydenreuter, Reinhard. "Der Magistrat als Befehlsempfänger: Die Disziplinierung der Stadtobrigkeit 1579 bis 1651." In *Geschichte der Stadt München*, edited by Richard Bauer, 189–210. Munich: Beck, 1992.

Heyl, Gerhard. "Der Geistliche Rat in Bayern unter Kurfürst Maximilian I. 1598–1651 mit einem Ausblick auf die Zeit bis 1745." Dissertation. Ludwig-Maximilian-Universität Munich, 1956.

Herz, Andreas. "Aufrichtigkeit, Vertrauen, Frieden: Eine historische Spurensuche im Umkreis der *Fruchtbringenden Gesellschaft*." *Euphorion* 105 (2011): 317–59.

Herz, Andreas. "'... ma fatale destinèe ...': Krisen- und Leidenserfahrungen Fürst Christians II. von Anhalt-Bernburg (1599–1656) in seinen Tagebüchern und anderen Zeit- und Lebensdokumenten." In *Passion, Affekt und Leidenschaft in der Frühen Neuzeit*, vol. 2, edited by Johann A. Steiger, 981–1035. Wiesbaden: Harrassowitz, 2005.

Hille, Martin. *Ländliche Gesellschaft in Kriegszeiten: Bäuerliche Subsistenz zwischen Fiskus und Feudalherrschaft am Beispiel des oberbayerischen Pfleggerichts Weilheim und des Klostergerichts Benediktbeuern im 17. Jahrhundert*. Munich: Beck, 1997.

Hitzigrath, Heinrich. *Die Publicistik des Prager Friedens*. Halle: Niemeyer, 1880.

Höbelt, Lothar. "The Westphalian Peace: Augsburg Mark II or Celebrated Armistice?" In *The Holy Roman Empire, 1495–1806: A European Perspective*, edited by R. J. W. Evans and Peter H. Wilson, 19–34. Leiden: Brill, 2012.

Hoffmann, Carl A. *Landesherrliche Städte und Märkte im 17. und 18. Jahrhundert: Studien zu ihrer ökonomischen Entwicklung in Oberbayern*. Kallmünz/Opf: Lassleben, 1997.

Hofmann, Hanns H. *Die Nürnberger Stadtmauer*. Nuremberg: Nürnberger Presse, 1967.

Holzfurtner, Ludwig. "Katastrophe und Neuanfang: Kriegsschäden im Dreißigjährigen Krieg im Spiegel der Stiftbücher oberbayerischer Klöster." *Zeitschrift für bayerische Landesgeschichte* 58 (1995): 553–76.

Höpfl, Simon. *Die Belagerungen Regensburgs in den Jahren 1633 und 1634 durch Bernhard von Weimar und durch die Kaiserlichen und Ligisten*. Amberg: Böes, 1913.

Hörger, Hermann. *Kirche, Dorfreligion und bäuerliche Gesellschaft: Strukturanalysen zur gesellschaftsgebundenen Religiosität ländlicher Unterschichten des 17. bis 19. Jahrhunderts, aufgezeigt an bayerischen Beispielen*, vol. 1. Munich: Seitz & Höfling, 1978.

Hörger, Hermann. "Organisational Forms of Popular Piety in Rural Old Bavaria (Sixteenth to Nineteenth Centuries)." In *Religion and Society in Early Modern Europe 1500–1800*, edited by Kaspar von Greyerz, 212–22. London: Allen & Unwin, 1984.

Hortschausky, Klaus. "Everyday Musical Life during the Thirty Years' War." In *1648: War and Peace in Europe*, vol. 2, edited by Klaus Bussmann and Heinz Schilling, 409–16. Munich: Veranstaltungsgesellschaft 350 Jahre Westfälischer Friede, 1998.

Huber, Johann G. B., ed. *Geschichte der Stadt Burghausen in Oberbayern*. Burghausen: Lutzenberger, 1862.

Huf, Hans-Christian, ed. *Mit Gottes Segen in die Hölle: Der Dreissigjährige Krieg*. Munich: Econ, 2003.

Hutcheon, Linda. *Irony's Edge: The Theory and Politics of Irony*. 2nd ed. London: Routledge, [1994] 1995.

Imhof, Arthur E. *Die Verlorenen Welten: Alltagsbewältigung durch unsere Vorfahren – und weshalb wir uns heute so schwer damit tun*. Munich: Beck, 1985.

Imhoff, Christoph von. *Berühmte Nürnberger aus neun Jahrhunderten*. 2nd revised ed. Nuremberg: Hofmann, [1984] 1989.

Immler, Gerhard. *Kurfürst Maximilian I. und der Westfälische Friedenskongress: Die bayerische auswärtige Politik von 1644 bis zum Ulmer Waffenstillstand*. Münster: Aschendorff, 1992.

Immler, Gerhard. "Maximilian I.: Der Große Kurfürst auf der Bühne der europäischen Politik." In *Die Herrscher Bayerns*, edited by Alois Schmid and Katharina Weigand, 202–17. Munich: Beck, 2001.

Immler, Gerhard. "Quellen und Quelleneditionen zur Epoche Maximilians I." *Zeitschrift für bayerische Landesgeschichte* 65/1 (2002): 25–34.

Ingen, Ferdinand van. "Bußstimmung, Krisenbewusstsein und Melancholie – Deutungsmuster der Frühen Neuzeit?" In *Pietismus und Neuzeit: Ein Jahrbuch zur Geschichte des Neueren Protestantismus*, vol. 32, edited by Martin Brecht et al., 57–78. Göttingen: Vandenhoeck & Ruprecht: 2006.

Jäger, Wieland. *Katastrophe und Gesellschaft: Grundlegungen und Kritik von Modellen der Katastrophensoziologie*. Darmstadt, Neuwied: Luchterhand, 1977.

Jakubowski-Tiessen, Manfred, et al., eds. *Jahrhundertwenden: Endzeit- und Zukunftvorstellungen vom 15. bis zum 20. Jahrhundert*. Göttingen: Vandenhoeck & Ruprecht, 1999.

Jakubowski-Tiessen, Manfred, and Hartmut Lehmann, eds. *Um Himmels Willen: Religion in Katastrophenzeiten*. Göttingen: Vandenhoeck & Ruprecht, 2003.

Jancke, Gabriele. *Autobiographie als soziale Praxis: Beziehungskonzepte in Selbstzeugnissen des 15. und 16. Jahrhunderts im deutschsprachigen Raum*. Cologne: Böhlau, 2002.

Jancke, Gabriele, and Claudia Ulbrich, eds. *Vom Individuum zur Person: Neue Konzepte im Spannungsfeld von Autobiographietheorie und Selbstzeugnisforschung*. Göttingen: Wallstein, 2005.

Jarzebowski, Claudia. "Gewalt und Erfahrung: Überlegungen zu den Memoiren der Wilhelmine von Bayreuth (1709–1758)." In *Blutige Worte: Internationales und interdisziplinäres Kolloquium zum Verhältnis von Sprache und Gewalt in Mittelalter und Früher Neuzeit*, edited by Jutta Eming and Claudia Jarzebowski, 187–211. Göttingen: V&R Unipress, 2008.

Jehl, Rainer, and Wolfgang E. J. Weber, eds. *Melancholie: Epochenstimmung – Krankheit – Lebenskunst*. Stuttgart: Kohlhammer, 2000.

Jenny, Marcus, and Edwin Nievergelt, eds. *Paul Gerhardt: Weg und Wirkung*. Zurich: Gotthelf, 1976.

Jürgens, Henning P., and Thomas Weller, eds. *Religion und Mobilität: Zum Verhältnis von raumbezogener Mobilität und religiöser Identitätsbildung im frühneuzeitlichen Europa*. Göttingen: Vandenhoeck & Ruprecht, 2010.

Jürgensmeier, Friedhelm, and Regina E. Schwerdtfeger, eds. *Orden und Klöster im Zeitalter der Reformation und Katholischer Reform 1500–1700*. Münster: Aschendorff, 2005.

Jütte, Robert. *Obrigkeitliche Armenfürsorge in deutschen Reichsstädten der Frühen Neuzeit: Städtisches Armenwesen in Frankfurt am Main und Köln*. Cologne: Böhlau, 1984.

Jütte, Robert. *Poverty and Deviance in Early Modern Europe*. Cambridge: Cambridge University Press, 1994.

Kaffenberger, Philipp, and Wilhelm Kraft. *Roßdorf und Gundernhausen im Dreißigjährigen Krieg*. Roßdorf: Historischer Verein Roßdorf und Gundernhausen, 1987.

Kaiser, Michael. "Inmitten des Kriegstheaters: Die Bevölkerung als militärischer Faktor und Kriegsteilnehmer im Dreißigjährigen Krieg." In *Krieg und Frieden: Militär und Gesellschaft in der Frühen Neuzeit*, edited by Bernhard R. Kroener and Ralf Pröve, 281–303. Munich: Schöningh, 1996.

Kaiser, Michael. "Maximilian I. von Bayern und der Krieg: Zu einem wichtigen Aspekt seines fürstlichen Selbstverständnisses." *Zeitschrift für bayerische Landesgeschichte* 65/1 (2002): 69–99.

Kaiser, Michael. *Politik und Kriegsführung: Maximilian von Bayern, Tilly und die Katholische Liga im Dreissigjährigen Krieg*. Münster: Aschendorff, 1999.

Kaiser, Michael. "Überleben im Krieg – Leben mit dem Krieg: Zur Alltagsgeschichte des Dreißigjährigen Krieges in den niederrheinischen Territorien." In *Der Dreißigjährige Krieg im Herzogtum Berg und in seinen Nachbarregionen*, edited by Stefan Ehrenpreis, 181–233. Neustadt an der Aisch: Schmidt, 2002.

Kaiser, Michael, and Andreas Pečar, eds. *Der zweite Mann im Staat: Oberste Amtsträger and Favoriten im Umkreis der Reichsfürsten in der Frühen Neuzeit*. Berlin: Duncker & Humblot, 2003.

Kampmann, Christoph. *Arbiter und Friedensstiftung: Die Auseinandersetzung um den politischen Schiedsrichter im Europa der Frühen Neuzeit*. Paderborn: Schöningh, 2001.

Kampmann, Christoph. *Europa und das Reich im Dreißigjährigen Krieg: Geschichte eines europäischen Konflikts*. Stuttgart: Kohlhammer, 2008.

Kampmann, Christoph, and Ulrich Niggemann, eds. *Sicherheit in der Frühen Neuzeit: Norm – Praxis – Repräsentation*. Cologne: Böhlau, 2013.

Kaplan, Benjamin J. *Divided by Faith: Religious Conflict and the Practice of Toleration in Early Modern Europe.* Cambridge: Cambridge University Press, 2007.

Karant-Nunn, Susan C. "The Emergence of the Pastoral Family in the German Reformation: The Parsonage as a Site of Socio-religious Change." In *The Protestant Clergy of Early Modern Europe*, edited by Scott C. Dixon and Luise Schorn-Schütte, 79–99. New York: Palgrave MacMillan, 2003.

Kasper, Cordula. *Die bayerische Kriegsorganisation in der zweiten Hälfte des Dreißigjährigen Krieges 1635–1648/49.* Münster: Aschendorff, 1997.

Kästner, Alexander. *Tödliche Geschichte(n): Selbsttötungen in Kursachsen im Spannungsfeld von Normen und Praktiken (1547–1815).* Konstanz: UVK Verlagsgesellschaft, 2012.

Kastner, Ruth. *Geistlicher Raufhandel: Form und Funktion der illustrierten Flugblätter zum Reformationsjubiläum 1617 in ihrem historischen und publizistischen Kontext.* Frankfurt am Main: Lang, 1982.

Kaufmann, Thomas. "The Clergy and the Theological Culture of the Age: The Education of Lutheran Pastors in the Sixteenth and Seventeenth Centuries." In *The Protestant Clergy of Early Modern Europe*, edited by Scott C. Dixon and Luise Schorn-Schütte, 120–36. New York: Palgrave MacMillan, 2003.

Kaufmann, Thomas. *Dreißigjähriger Krieg und Westfälischer Friede: kirchengeschichtliche Studien zur lutherischen Konfessionskultur.* Tübingen: Mohr Siebeck, 1998.

Keller, Hagen et al., eds. *Pragmatische Schriftlichkeit im Mittelalter: Erscheinungsformen und Entwicklungsstufen* (Akten des Internationalen Kolloquiums 17.–19. Mai 1989). Munich: Fink, 1992.

Kist, Johannes. *Fürst- und Erzbistum Bamberg: Leitfaden durch ihre Geschichte von 1007 bis 1960.* 3rd ed. Bamberg: Historischer Verein Bamberg, [1953] 1962.

Knauer, Martin, and Sven Tode, eds. *Der Krieg vor den Toren: Hamburg im Dreißigjährigen Krieg 1618–1648.* Darmstadt: Weihert, 2000.

Knemeyer, Franz-Ludwig. "Polizeibegriffe in Gesetzen des 15. bis 18. Jahrhunderts: Kritische Bemerkungen zur Literatur über die Entwicklung des Polizeibegriffs." *Archiv des öffentlichen Rechts* 92 (1967): 153–80.

Koepke, Wulf. "On Time and Space in Exile – Past, Present and Future in a No-Man's Land." In *Exiles Traveling: Exploring Displacement, Crossing Boundaries in German Exile Arts and Writings 1933–1945*, edited by Johannes F. Evelein, 35–49. Amsterdam: Rodopi, 2009.

Kohler, Alfred. *Das Reich im Kampf um die Hegemonie in Europa 1521–1648.* Munich: Oldenbourg, 1990.

Köhler, Hans-Joachim. "Fragestellungen und Methoden zur Interpretation frühneuzeitlicher Flugschriften." In *Flugschriften als Massenmedium der Reformationszeit: Beiträge zum Tübinger Symposium 1980*, edited by Hans-Joachim Köhler, 1–27. Stuttgart: Klett-Cotta, 1981.

Kollar, Josef, ed. *Markt Dietenhofen: Rund um die Scharwachtürme. Aus dem Leben einer 750jährigen Rangaugemeinde*. Ansbach: Gebhardt, 1985.

Koopmann, Helmut. "Exil als geistige Lebensform." In *Exil: Transhistorische und transnationale Perspektiven*, edited by Helmut Koopmann and Klaus D. Post, 1–19. Paderborn: mentis Verlag, 2001.

Koopmans, Joop W., ed. *News and Politics in Early Modern Europe (1500–1800)*. Leuven: Peeters, 2005.

Kormann, Eva. "Heterologe Subjektivität: Zur historischen Varianz von Autobiographie und Subjektivität." In *Autobiography by Women in German*, edited by Mererid Puw Davies, 87–104. Bern: Lang, 2000.

Kormann, Eva. *Ich, Welt und Gott: Autobiographik im 17. Jahrhundert*. Cologne: Böhlau, 2004.

Koselleck, Reinhart. *Vergangene Zukunft: Zur Semantik geschichtlicher Zeiten*. Frankfuhrt am Main: Suhrkamp, 1989.

Koselleck, Reinhart, and Wolf-Dieter Stempel, eds. *Geschichte – Ereignis und Erzählung*. Munich: Fink, 1973.

Koszyk, Kurt. "Zur Soziologie der Medientechnik." In *Wege zur Kommunikationsgeschichte*, edited by Manfred Bobrowsky and Wolfgang R. Langenbucher, 223–34. Munich: Ölschläger, 1987.

Krabbe, Otto. *Aus dem kirchlichen und wissenschaftlichen Leben Rostocks: Zur Geschichte Wallensteins und des Dreissigjährigen Krieges*. Cologne: Böhlau. 1994.

Kratz, Wilhelm. "Drexel, Jeremias." *Neue Deutsche Biographie* (1959): 119–20 [online edition]; http://www.deutsche-biographie.de/pnd118680749.html.

Kraus, Andreas. *Maximilian I.: Bayerns Großer Kurfürst*. Graz: Pustet, 1990.

Kraus, Eberhard. *Exulanten aus dem westlichen Waldviertel in Franken (ca. 1627–1670): Eine familien- und kirchengeschichtliche Untersuchung*. Nuremberg: Gesellschaft für Familienforschung in Franken, 1997.

Krauss, Marita. "Heimat – Begriff und Erfahrung." In *Heimat, liebe Heimat: Exil und Innere Emigration (1933–1945)*, edited by Herrmann Haarmann, 11–27. Berlin: Bostelmann & Siebenhaar, 2004.

Kreitzer, Beth. *Reforming Mary: Changing Images of the Virgin Mary in Lutheran Sermons of the Sixteenth Century*. Oxford: Oxford University Press, 2004.

Kriss, Rudolf. "Zum Problem der religiösen Magie und ihrer Rolle im volkstümlichen Opferbrauchtum und Sakramentalienwesen." In *Magie und Religion: Beiträge zu einer Theorie der Magie*, edited by Leander Petzoldt, 385–403. Darmstadt: Wissenschaftliche Buchgesellschaft, 1978.

Kriss-Rettenbeck, Lenz. *Bilder und Zeichen religiösen Volksglaubens: Rudolf Kriss zum 60. Geburtstag*. Munich: Callwey, 1965.

Kroener, Bernhard R. "'Kriegsgurgeln, Freireuter und Merodebrüder.' Der Soldat des Dreißigjährigen Krieges: Täter und Opfer." In *Der Krieg des kleinen Mannes: Eine*

Militärgeschichte von unten, edited by Wolfram Wette, 51–67. Munich: Piper, [1992] 1995.

Kroener, Bernhard R. "'... und ist der jammer nit zu beschreiben': Geschlechterbeziehungen und Überlebensstrategien in der Lagergesellschaft des Dreißigjährigen Krieges." In *Landsknechte, Soldatenfrauen und Nationalkrieger: Militär, Krieg und Geschlechterordnung im historischen Wandel*, edited by Karen Hagemann and Ralf Pröve, 279–96. Frankfurt: Campus, 1998.

Kroener, Bernhard R., and Ralf Pröve, eds. *Krieg und Frieden: Militär und Gesellschaft in der Frühen Neuzeit*. Munich: Schöningh, 1996.

Kroner, Michael. *Ammerndorf: Geschichte einer Marktgemeinde an der Bibert*. Führt: Walbinger, 1989.

Kroner, Michael. *Cadolzburg: Im Wandel von der Hohenzollernresidenz und dem Ämtersitz zum gewerblich-industriellen Markt*. Fürth: Walbinger, 1993.

Kroner, Michael. *Großhabersdorf: Eine Gemeinde im Wandel der Geschichte*. Heilsbronn: Schulist, 1986.

Kroner, Michael. *Langenzenn: Vom Königshof zur Gewerbe- und Industriestadt*. Fürth: Walbinger, 1988.

Krüger, Kersten. "Kriegsfinanzen und Reichsrecht im 16. und 17. Jahrhundert." In *Krieg und Frieden: Militär und Gesellschaft in der Frühen Neuzeit*, edited by Bernhard R. Kroener and Ralf Pröve, 47–57. Munich: Schöningh, 1996.

Krüger, Kersten, ed. *Europäische Städte im Zeitalter des Barock: Gestalt – Kultur – Sozialgefüge*. Cologne: Böhlau, 1988.

Krusenstjern, Benigna von. "Buchhalter ihres Lebens: Über Selbstzeugnisse aus dem 17. Jahrhundert." In *Das dargestellte Ich: Studien zu Selbstzeugnissen des späteren Mittelalters und der frühen Neuzeit*, edited by Klaus Arnold et al., 139–46. Bochum: Winkler, 1999.

Krusenstjern, Benigna von. "Das Schiff, der Steuermann und die Kriegsfluten: Staatserfahrung im Dreißigjährigen Krieg." In *Erfahrung als Kategorie der Frühneuzeitgeschichte*, edited by Paul Münch, 425–32. Munich: Oldenbourg, 2001.

Krusenstjern, Benigna von. "Seliges Sterben und böser Tod: Tod und Sterben in der Zeit des Dreißigjährigen Krieges." In *Zwischen Alltag und Katastrophe: Der Dreißigjährige Krieg aus der Nähe*, edited by Benigna von Krusenstjern and Hans Medick, 469–96. Göttingen: Vandenhoeck & Ruprecht, 1999.

Krusenstjern, Benigna von. "Was sind Selbstzeugnisse? Begriffskritische und quellenkundliche Überlegungen anhand von Beispielen aus dem 17. Jahrhundert." *Historische Anthropologie* 2 (1994): 462–71.

Krusenstjern, Benigna von, and Hans Medick, eds. *Zwischen Alltag und Katastrophe: Der Dreißigjährige Krieg aus der Nähe*. Göttingen: Vandenhoeck & Ruprecht, 1999.

Kunstmann, Hartmut H. *Zauberwahn und Hexenprozeß in der Reichsstadt Nürnberg*. Nuremberg: Stadtarchiv Nürnberg, 1970.

Labouvie, Eva. *Verbotene Künste: Volksmagie und ländlicher Aberglaube in den Dorfgemeinden des Saarraumes (16.–19. Jahrhundert)*. St. Ingbert: Röhrig, 1992.

Labouvie, Eva. *Zauberei und Hexenwerk: Ländlicher Hexenglaube in der frühen Neuzeit*. Frankfurt am Main: Fischer Taschenbuch, 1991.

Labuda, Gerard. "Kulturgeschichte als Geschichte der kreativen Innovationen." *Archiv für Kulturgeschichte* 75 (1993): 195–220.

Lademacher, Horst, and Simon Groenveld, eds. *Krieg und Kultur: Die Rezeption von Krieg und Frieden in der Niederländischen Republik und im Deutschen Reich 1568–1648*. Münster: Waxmann, 1998.

Lammert, Gottfried. *Geschichte der Seuchen, Hungers- und Kriegsnoth zur Zeit des Dreissigjährigen Krieges*. Niederwalluf bei Wiesbaden: Sändig, [1890] 1971.

Landwehr, Achim. *Frühe Neue Zeiten: Zeitwissen zwischen Reformation und Revolution*. Bielefeld: transcript Verlag, 2012.

Landwehr, Achim. *Geschichte des Sagbaren: Einführung in die Diskursanalyse*. Tübingen: edition diskord, 2001.

Lang, Helmut W. "Die Neue Zeitung des 15. bis 17. Jahrhunderts: Entwicklungsgeschichte und Typologie." In *Presse und Geschichte: neue Beiträge zur historischen Kommunikationsforschung*, vol. 1: 57–70. Munich: Saur, 1987.

Langer, Herbert. *Kulturgeschichte des 30jährigen Krieges*. Leipzig: Kohlhammer, 1978.

Langer, Herbert. *1648, der Westfälische Frieden: Pax Europaea und Neuordnung des Reiches*. Berlin: Brandenburgisches Verlags-Haus, 1994.

Lauster, Jörg. *Die Verzauberung der Welt: Eine Kulturgeschichte des Christentums*. Munich: Beck, 2014.

Leder, Klaus. *Kirche und Jugend in Nürnberg und seinem Landgebiet 1400 bis 1800*. Neustadt an der Aisch: Degener, 1973.

Lehmann, Hartmut. *Das Zeitalter des Absolutismus: Gottesgnadentum und Kriegsnot*. Stuttgart: Kohlhammer, 1980.

Lehmann, Hartmut. "Frömmigkeitsgeschichtliche Auswirkungen der 'Kleinen Eiszeit.'" In *Volksreligiosität in der modernen Sozialgeschichte*, edited by Wolfgang Schieder, 31–50. Göttingen: Vandenhoeck & Ruprecht, 1986.

Lehmann, Hartmut. "Zur Bedeutung von Religion und Religiosität im Barockzeitalter." In *Religion und Religiosität im Zeitalter des Barock*, vol. 1, edited by Dieter Breuer, 3–22. Wiesbaden: Harrassowitz, 1995.

Lehmann, Hartmut, and Anne-Charlott Trepp, eds. *Im Zeichen der Krise: Religiosität im Europa des 17. Jahrhunderts*. Göttingen: Vandenhoeck & Ruprecht, 1999.

Lehmann-Haupt, Ingeborg. "German Woodcut Broadsides in the Seventeenth Century." In *An Introduction to the Woodcut of the Seventeenth Century*, edited by Helmut Lehmann-Haupt, 229–66. New York: Abaris Books, 1977.

Leistikow, Oskar. *Sperreuter: Ein schwedischer, kaiserlicher und venetianischer Söldnerführer*. Neustadt an der Aisch: Degener, 1968.

Leutenbauer, Siegfried. *Das Delikt der Gotteslästerung in der Bayerischen Gesetzgebung.* Cologne: Böhlau, 1984.

Lieberich, Heinz. "Die Anfänge der Polizeigesetzgebung des Herzogtums Baiern." In *Festschrift für Max Spindler zum 75. Geburtstag,* edited by Dieter Albrecht et al., 307–78. Munich: Beck, 1969.

Liebhart, Wilhelm. *Altbayerisches Klosterleben: Das Birgittenkloster Altomünster 1496–1841.* St. Ottilien: Eos, 1987.

Liebhart, Wilhelm. *Altomünster: Kloster, Markt und Gemeinde.* Altomünster: Plabst, 1999.

Liebhart, Wilhelm. "Krise, Reform und Blüte: Das Brigittenkloster Altomünster im Barock." In *Der Brigittenorden in der Frühen Neuzeit: Beiträge der Internationalen Tagung vom 27. Februar bis 2. März 1997 in Altomünster,* edited by Wilhelm Liebhart, 237–60. Frankfurt am Main: Lang, 1998.

Liebhart, Wilhelm, and Günther Pölsterl. *Die Gemeinden des Landkreises Dachau.* Dachau: Verlagsanstalt Bayerland, 1992.

Lindberg, Carter. *Beyond Charity: Reformation Initiatives for the Poor.* Minneapolis: Fortress Press, 1993.

Lindemann, Margot. *Deutsche Presse bis 1815: Geschichte der deutschen Presse,* 1. Berlin: Colloquium Verlag, 1969.

Locher, Gottfried. "The Theology of Exile: Faith and the Fate of the Refugee." In *Social Groups and Religious Ideas in the Sixteenth Century,* edited by Miriam Usher Chrisman and Otto Gründler, 85–92. Kalamazoo, MI: The Medieval Institute, Western Michigan University, 1978.

Loetz, Francisca. "Sexualisierte Gewalt in Europa 1520–1850: Zur Historisierung von 'Vergewaltigung' und 'Missbrauch.'" *Geschichte und Gesellschaft* 35 (2009): 561–602.

Löffler, Bernhard, and Karsten Ruppert, eds. *Religiöse Prägung und politische Ordnung in der Neuzeit. Festschrift für Winfried Becker zum 65. Geburtstag.* Cologne: Böhlau, 2006.

Looshorn, Johann. *Das Bisthum Bamberg von 1556 bis 1622.* Bamberg: Handelsdruckerei, 1903.

Looshorn, Johann. *Das Bisthum Bamberg von 1623 bis 1729.* Bamberg: Handelsdruckerei, 1906.

Lorey, Elmar M. *Heinrich der Werwolf: Eine Geschichte aus der Zeit der Hexenprozesse mit Dokumenten und Analysen.* Frankfurt am Main: Anabas, 1998.

Loserth, Johann. "Zur Emigration des steiermarkischen Herren- und Ritterstandes." *Beiträge zur Erforschung steirischer Geschichte* 41, NF 9 (1918): 2–64.

Lottes, Günther. "Stadtchronistik und städtische Identität: Zur Erinnerungskultur der frühneuzeitlichen Stadt." *Mitteilungen des Vereins für Geschichte der Stadt Nürnberg* 87 (2000): 47–58.

Lotz-Heumann, Ute, and Matthias Pohlig. "Confessionalization and Literature in the Empire, 1555–1700." *Central European History* 40 (2007): 35–61.

Louthan, Howard, et al., eds. *Diversity and Dissent: Negotiating Religious Difference in Central Europe, 1500–1800*. New York: Berghahn, 2011.

Lucassen, Jan, and Leo Lucassen. "The Mobility Transition Revisited, 1500–1900: What the Case of Europe Can Offer to Global History." *Journal of Global History* 4 (2009): 347–77.

Lüdtke, Alf, ed. *The History of Everyday Life: Reconstructing Historical Experiences and Ways of Life*. Princeton: Princeton University Press, 1995.

Luebke, David M. *Hometown Religion: Regimes of Coexistence in Early Modern Westphalia*. Charlottesville: University of Virginia Press, 2016.

Luebke, David M., et al., eds. *Conversion and the Politics of Religion in Early Modern Germany*. New York: Berghahn, 2012.

Luebke, David M., and Mary Lindemann, eds. *Mixed Matches: Transgressive Unions in Germany from the Reformation to the Enlightenment*. New York: Berghahn, 2014.

Luria, Keith P. *Sacred Boundaries: Religious Coexistence and Conflict in Early Modern France*. Washington, DC: Catholic University of America Press, 2005.

Lutz, Heinrich. *Das Ringen um deutsche Einheit und kirchliche Erneuerung: von Maximilian I. bis zum Westfälischen Frieden, 1490 bis 1648*. Berlin: Propyläen, 1983.

Lynn, John A. "Soldiers on the Rampage." *Military History Quarterly* 3 (1991): 92–101.

Mandlmayr, Martin, and Karl G. Vogelka. "Vom Adelsaufgebot zum stehenden Heer: Bemerkungen zum Funktionswandel des Kriegswesens der frühen Neuzeit." In *Spezialforschung und "Gesamtgeschichte": Beispiele und Methodenfragen zur Geschichte der frühen Neuzeit*, edited by Grete Klingenstein and Heinrich Lutz, 112–25. Munich: Oldenbourg, 1982.

Marigold, W. Gordon. "Lieddichtung als Reformmittel und als Brücke zwischen den Konfessionen: ein katholisches Beispiel." In *Religion und Religiosität im Zeitalter des Barock*, vol. 2., edited by Dieter Breuer, 611–20. Wiesbaden: Harrassowitz, 1995.

Martens, Wolfgang. "Lesen auf dem Lande, in freier Natur, im 17. und 18. Jahrhundert." In *Wege zur Kommunikationsgeschichte*, edited by Manfred Bobrowsky and Wolfgang R. Langenbucher, 296–303. Munich: Ölschläger, 1987.

Marti, Hanspeter. "Der Dialog mit Gott im Gebet: Die *Rhetorica caelestis* des Jesuiten Jeremias Drexel." In *Religion und Religiosität im Zeitalter des Barock*, vol. 2, edited by Dieter Breuer, 509–21. Wiesbaden: Harrassowitz, 1995.

Marti, Hanspeter. "Gesellschaftliches Leben und 'unio mystica' am Beispiel der Mystiktheorie des Jesuiten Maximilian Sandäus (1578–1656)." In *Geselligkeit und Gesellschaft im Barockzeitalter*, vol. 1, edited by Wolfgang Adam, 199–209. Wiesbaden: Harrassowitz, 1997.

Matthäus, Klaus. "Zur Geschichte des Nürnberger Kalenderwesens." *Archiv für Geschichte des Buchwesens* 9 (1969): 965–1396.

Medick, Hans. "Mikro-Historie." In *Sozialgeschichte, Alltagsgeschichte, Mikro-Historie. Eine Diskussion*, edited by Winfried Schulze, 40–53. Göttingen: Vandenhoeck & Ruprecht, 1994.

Medick, Hans. "Orte und Praktiken religiöser Gewalt im Dreißigjährigen Krieg: Konfessionelle Unterschiede und ihre Wahrnehmung im Spiegel von Selbstzeugnissen." In *Religion und Gewalt: Konflikte, Rituale, Deutungen (1500–1800)*, edited by Kaspar von Greyerz and Kim Siebenhüner, 367–82. Göttingen: Vandenhoeck & Ruprecht, 2006.

Medick, Hans, and David Sabean, eds. *Emotionen und materielle Interessen: Sozialanthropologische und historische Beiträge zur Familienforschung*. Göttingen: Vandenhoeck & Ruprecht, 1984.

Meise, Helga. *Das archivierte Ich: Schreibkalender und höfische Repräsentation in Hessen-Darmstadt 1624–1790*. Darmstadt: Hessische Historische Kommission Darmstadt, 2002.

Meise, Helga. "Höfische Tagebücher in der Frühen Neuzeit: Überlegungen zu ihrer Edition und Kommentierung." In *Edition von autobiographischen Schriften und Zeugnissen zur Biographie*, edited by Jochen Golz, 27–37. Tübingen: Niemeyer, 1995.

Mennecke, Ute. "Paul Gerhardts Lieder zu Krieg und Frieden." In *Paul Gerhardt – Dichtung, Theologie, Musik*, edited by Dorothea Wendebourg, 175–205. Tübingen: Mohr Siebeck, 2008.

Merzhäuser, Andreas. "Das 'illiterate' Ich als Historiograph der Katastrophe: Zur Konstruktion von Geschichte in Hans Heberles 'Zeytregister' (1618–1672)." *Zeitenblicke* 1/2 (2002): 1–15.

Meumann, Markus. "Soldatenfamilien und uneheliche Kinder: Ein soziales Problem im Gefolge der stehenden Heere." In *Krieg und Frieden: Militär und Gesellschaft in der Frühen Neuzeit*, edited by Bernhard R. Kroener and Ralf Pröve, 219–36. Munich: Schöningh, 1996.

Meumann, Markus, and Dirk Niefanger. "Für eine interdisziplinäre Betrachtung von Gewaltdarstellungen des 17. Jahrhunderts. Einführende Überlegungen." In *Ein Schauplatz herber Angst: Wahrnehmung und Darstellung von Gewalt im 17. Jahrhundert*, edited by Markus Meumann and Dirk Niefanger, 7–23. Göttingen: Wallstein, 1997.

Meumann, Markus, and Dirk Niefanger, eds. *Ein Schauplatz herber Angst: Wahrnehmung und Darstellung von Gewalt im 17. Jahrhundert*. Göttingen: Wallstein, 1997.

Meyer, Christian. "Geschichte der Burggrafen Nürnberg und der späteren Markgrafenschaften Ansbach und Bayreuth." In *Tübinger Studien für Schwäbische und Deutsche Rechtsgeschichte*, vol. 2, edited by Friedrich Thudichum, 1–184. Tübingen: Laupp, 1911.

Midelfort, H. C. Erik. *Witch Hunting in Southwestern Germany, 1562–1684: The Social and Intellectual Foundations*. Stanford: Stanford University Press, 1972.

Miggelbrink, Ralf. *Der Zorn Gottes: Die Bedeutung einer anstößigen biblischen Tradition.* Darmstadt: Wissenschaftliche Buchgesellschaft, 2002.

Miggelbrink, Ralf. *Der Zorn Gottes: Geschichte und Aktualität einer ungeliebten biblischen Tradition.* Freiburg: Herder, 2000.

Milger, Peter. *Der Dreissigjährige Krieg: Gegen Land und Leute.* Munich: Bertelsmann, 1998.

Moezer, Hans. "Cadolzburg während des Dreißigjährigen Krieges." *Fürther Heimatblätter* 32 (1982): 40–50.

Mohrmann, Ruth-E. "Fest und Alltag in der Frühen Neuzeit – Rituale als Ordnungs- und Handlungsmuster." *Niedersächsisches Jahrbuch für Landesgeschichte* 72 (2000): 1–10.

Mohrmann, Ruth-E. "Zwischen den Zeilen und gegen den Strich: Alltagskultur im Spiegel archivalischer Quellen." *Der Archivar* 44 (1991): 234–46.

Moore, Cornelia Niekus. *The Maiden's Mirror: Reading Material for German Girls in the 16th and 17th Centuries.* Wiesbaden: Harrassowitz, 1987.

Mortimer, Geoff. *Eyewitness Accounts of the Thirty Years War, 1618–1648.* New York: Palgrave, 2002.

Mortimer, Geoff. "Models of Writing in Eyewitness Personal Accounts of the Thirty Years War." *Daphnis* 29 (2000): 609–47.

Mortimer, Geoff. *The Origins of the Thirty Years War and the Revolt in Bohemia, 1618.* Basingstoke: Palgrave Macmillan, 2015.

Mortimer, Geoff. "Style and Fictionalisation in Eyewitness Personal Accounts of the Thirty Years War." *German Life and Letters* 54 (2001): 97–113.

Mortimer, Geoff. *Wallenstein: The Enigma of the Thirty Years War.* Basingstoke: Palgrave Macmillan, 2010.

Müller, Arnd. "Zensurpolitik der Reichsstadt Nürnberg: Von der Einführung der Buchdruckerkunst bis zum Ende der Reichsstadtzeit." *Mitteilungen des Vereins für Geschichte der Stadt Nürnberg* 49 (1959): 66–169.

Mummenhoff, Ernst. *Altnürnberg in Krieg und Kriegsnot.* Nuremberg: Schrag, 1916.

Münch, Paul, ed. *Erfahrung als Kategorie der Frühneuzeitgeschichte.* Munich: Oldenbourg, 2001.

Naphy, William G., and Penny Roberts, eds. *Fear in Early Modern Society.* Manchester: Manchester University Press, 1997.

Naumann, Robert. "Ein Band fliegender Blätter aus den Jahren 1631 und 1632." *Serapeum* 15 (1863): 225–31.

Neuhaus, Helmut. "Maximilian I., Bayerns Grosser Kurfürst." *Zeitschrift für bayerische Landesgeschichte* 65/1 (2002): 5–23.

Newman, William R., and Anthony Grafton, eds. *Secrets of Nature: Astology and Alchemy in Early Modern Europe.* Cambridge, MA: The MIT Press, 2001.

Niefanger, Dirk. *Barock.* Stuttgart: Metzler, 2000.

Niggl, Günter, ed. *Die Autobiographie: Zu Form und Geschichte einer literarischen Gattung*. Darmstadt: Wissenschaftliche Buchgesellschaft, 1989.

Noehles, Karl. "Altartabernakel, Retabel und Kirchenraum des Hochbarock: Anmerkungen zu ihrem formalen und theologischen Bezugssystem." In *Religion und Religiosität im Zeitalter des Barock*, vol. 1, edited by Dieter Breuer, 331–52. Wiesbaden: Harrassowitz, 1995.

Nolting, Uta. *Sprachgebrauch süddeutscher Klosterfrauen des 17. Jahrhunders*. Münster: Waxmann, 2010.

Oestmann, Günther, et al., eds. *Horoscopes and Public Spheres: Essays on the History of Astrology*. Berlin: de Gruyter, 2005.

Oestreich, Gerhard. *Antiker Geist und Moderner Staat bei Justus Lipsius (1547–1606). Der Neustoizismus als Politische Bewegung*, edited by Nicollete Mout. Göttingen: Vandenhoeck & Ruprecht, 1989.

Oestreich, Gerhard. *Geist und Gestalt des frühmodernen Staates. Ausgewählte Aufsätze*. Berlin: Duncker & Humblot, 1969.

Oestreich, Gerhard. "Das politische Anliegen von Justus Lipsius' De Constantia ... in publicis malis (1584)." In *Festschrift für Hermann Heimpel*, edited by Max-Planck-Institut für Geschichte, 618–38. Göttingen: Vandenhoeck & Ruprecht, 1971.

Oettinger, Rebecca Wagner. *Music as Propaganda in the German Reformation*. Aldershot: Ashgate, 2001.

Opel, Julius O. *Die Anfänge der deutschen Zeitungspresse 1609–1650*. Leipzig: Börsenverein der Deutschen Buchhändler, 1879.

Opel, Julius O. "Über einige alte deutsche Zeitungen." *Serapeum* 15 (1863): 302–4.

Oschmann, Antje. *Der Nürnberger Exekutionstag 1649–1650: Das Ende des Dreissigjährigen Krieges in Deutschland*. Münster: Aschendorff. 1991.

Osten-Sacken, Vera von der. "Lutheran Exiles of Christ in the Sixteenth Century. A Survey." *Journal of Early Modern Christianity* 3 (2016): 31–46.

Outram, Quentin. "The Socio-Economic Relations of Warfare and the Military Mortality Crises of the Thirty Years' War." *Medical History* 45 (2001): 151–84.

Paas, John R. "The Changing Image of Gustavus Adolphus on German Broadsheets, 1630–3." *Journal of the Warburg and Courtauld Institutes* 59 (1996): 205–44.

Paas, John R. *The German Political Broadsheet 1600–1700*, vols. 2–3. Wiesbaden: Harrassowitz, 1986/91.

Parish, Helen, and William G. Naphy, eds. *Religion and Superstition in Reformation Europe*. Manchester: Manchester University Press, 2002.

Parker, Geoffrey. *Global Crisis: War, Climate Change and Catastrophe in the Seventeenth Century*. New Haven: Yale University Press, 2013.

Parker, Geoffrey. "The Soldiers of the Thirty Years' War." In *Krieg und Politik 1618–1648: Eurpäische Probleme und Perspektiven*, edited by Konrad Repgen, 303–315. Munich: Oldenbourg, 1988.

Parker, Geoffrey, ed. *The Thirty Years' War*. London: Routledge, 1984.

Parrott, David. *The Business of War: Military Enterprise and Military Revolution in Early Modern Europe*. Cambridge: Cambridge University Press, 2012.

Pastenaci, Stephan. "Probleme der Edition und Kommentierung deutschsprachiger Autobiographien und Tagebücher der Frühen Neuzeit, dargestellt anhand dreier Beispiele." In *Edition von autobiographischen Schriften und Zeugnissen zur Biographie*, edited by Jochen Golz, 303–315. Tübingen: Niemeyer, 1995.

Patrouch, Joseph F. *A Negotiated Settlement: The Counter-Reformation in Upper Austria under the Habsburgs*. Boston: Humanities Press, 2000.

Paul, Markus. *Reichsstadt und Schauspiel: Theatrale Kunst im Nürnberg des 17. Jahrhunderts*. Tübingen: Niemeyer, 2002.

Peter, August. "Zu den Nürnberger Kirchenvisitationen des 17. Jahrhunderts." *Beiträge zur Bayerischen Kirchengeschichte* 25 (1918): 97–107 and 145–61.

Peter, Lambert F. *Der Handel Nürnbergs am Anfang des Dreissigjährigen Krieges: Strukturkomponenten, Unternehmen und Unternehmer – Eine Quantitative Analyse*. Stuttgart: Steiner, 1994.

Peters, Jan. "Wegweiser zum Innenleben? Möglichkeiten und Grenzen der Untersuchung popularer Selbstzeugnisse der Frühen Neuzeit." *Historische Anthropologie* 1 (1993): 235–49.

Petrick, Christine. "Bemerkungen zur Entwicklung von Buchdruck und Buchhandel in den während des Dreißigjährigen Krieges von Schweden eroberten Reichsgebieten." *Wissenschaftliche Zeitschrift der Ernst-Moritz-Arndt-Universität Greifswald. Gesellschafts- und Sprachwissenschaftliche Reihe* 32 (1983): 72–74.

Pfarr, Kristina. "Die Neue Zeitung: Empirische Untersuchung eines Informationsmediums der frühen Neuzeit unter besonderer Berücksichtigung von Gewaltdarstellungen." Dissertation. Johannes Gutenberg Universität Mainz, 1994.

Pfeffer, Maria. *Flugschriften zum Dreissigjährigen Krieg: aus der Häberlin-Sammlung der Thurn- und Taxisschen Bibliothek*. Frankfurt am Main: Lang, 1993.

Pfeiffer, Gerhard, ed. *Nürnberg – Geschichte einer europäischen Stadt*. Munich: Beck, 1971.

Pfister, Christian. *Bevölkerungsgeschichte und Historische Demographie 1500–1800*. Munich: Oldenbourg, 1994.

Pfister, Kurt. *Kurfürst Maximilian von Bayern und sein Jahrhundert*. Munich: Ehrenwirth, 1948.

Pieper, Dietmar, and Johannes Saltzwedel, eds. *Der Dreissigjährige Krieg: Europa im Kampf um Glaube und Macht 1618–1648*. Munich: Deutsche Verlags-Anstalt, 2012.

Pietsch, Andreas, and Barbara Stollberg-Rilinger, eds. *Konfessionelle Ambiguität: Uneindeutigkeit und Verstellung als religiöse Praxis in der Frühen Neuzeit*. Gütersloh: Gütersloher Verlags-Haus, 2013.

Piltz, Eric, and Gerd Schwerhoff, eds. *Gottlosigkeit und Eigensinn: Religiöse Devianz im konfessionellen Zeitalter*. Berlin: Duncker & Humblot, 2015.

Polisenský, Josef. *Der Krieg und die Gesellschaft in Europa 1618–1648*. Prague: Böhlaus, 1971.

Popkin, Jeremy D. "New Perspectives on the Early Modern European Press." In *News and Politics in Early Modern Europe (1500–1800)*, edited by Joop W. Koopmans, 1–27. Leuven: Peeters, 2005.

Popkin, Richard H. *The Third Force in Seventeenth-Century Thought*. Leiden: Brill, 1992.

Pörnbacher, Karl. *Jeremias Drexel: Leben und Werk eines Barockpredigers*. Munich: Seitz, 1965.

Porzelt, Carolin. *Die Pest in Nürnberg: Leben und Herrschen in Pestzeiten in der Reichsstadt Nürnberg (1562–1713)*. St. Ottilien: Eos, 2000.

Prak, Maarten. "The Carrot and the Stick: Social Control and Poor Relief in the Dutch Republic, Sixteenth to Eighteenth Centuries." In *Institutionen, Instrumente und Akteure sozialer Kontrolle und Disziplinierung im frühneuzeitlichen Europa*, edited by Heinz Schilling, 149–66. Frankfurt am Main: Klostermann, 1999.

Pröve, Ralf, ed. *Klio in Uniform? Probleme und Perspektiven einer modernen Militärgeschichte der Frühen Neuzeit*. Cologne: Böhlau, 1997.

Pullan, Brian. "Catholics and the Poor in Early Modern Europe." In *Transactions of the Royal Historical Society*, 5th Series, vol. 26: 15–34. London: Butler & Tanner, 1976.

Pültz, Gernot. "Das kurfürstliche Dekret zum Abschluß der Münchener Stadtvisitation aus dem Jahre 1642." In *Quellen zur Verfassungs-, Sozial- und Wirtschaftsgeschichte Bayerischer Städte in Spätmittelalter und Früher Neuzeit. Festgabe für Wilhelm Strömer zum 65. Geburtstag*, edited by Elisabeth Lukas-Götz et al., 133–67. Munich: Kommission für Bayerische Landesgeschichte, 1993.

Quint, Wolfgang. *Souveränitätsbegriff und Souveränitätspolitik in Bayern: Von der Mitte des 17. bis zur ersten Hälfte des 19. Jahrhunderts*. Berlin: Duncker & Humblot, 1971.

Rädlinger, Christine. *Armenwesen und Armenanstalten in München vom 14. bis zum 18. Jahrhundert*. Munich: Verlag des historischen Vereins von Oberbayern, 1992.

Ranger, Terence, and Paul Slack, eds. *Epidemics and Ideas: Essays on the Historical Perception of Pestilence*. Cambridge: Cambridge University Press, 1992.

Rast, Rudolf. "Heitere Episoden in ernster Zeit (1631–1635)." *Mitteilungen des Vereins für Geschichte der Stadt Nürnberg* 20 (1913): 95–131.

Rebel, Hermann, *Peasant Classes: The Bureaucratization of Property and Family Relations under Early Habsburg Absolutism, 1511–1636*. Princeton: Princeton University Press, 1983.

Rechter, Gerhard. "Der fränkische Reichskreis." In *Tag der Franken: Geschichte – Anspruch – Wirklichkeit*, edited by Andrea M. Kluxen and Julia Hecht, 17–30. Würzburg: Ergon, 2010.

Rechter, Gerhard. *Das Land zwischen Aisch und Rezat: Die Kommende Virnsberg Deutschen Ordens und die Rittergüter im oberen Zenngrund.* Neustadt an der Aisch: Degener & Co, 1981.

Rechter, Gerhard. "Der Obere Zenngrund im Zeitalter des Dreißigjährigen Krieges." *Jahrbuch für Fränkische Landesforschung* 38 (1978): 83–122.

Reddy, William M. *The Navigation of Feeling: A Framework for the History of Emotions.* Cambridge: Cambridge University Press, 2001.

Redlich, Fritz. "Autobiographies as Sources for Social History." *Vierteljahrschrift für Sozial- und Wirtschaftsgeschichte* 62 (1975): 380–90.

Redlich, Fritz. "Contributions in the Thirty Years' War." *The Economic History Review* 12 (1959): 247–54.

Redlich, Fritz. *De Praeda Militari: Looting and Booty 1500–1815.* Wiesbaden: Steiner, 1956.

Reicke, Emil. *Geschichte der Reichsstadt Nürnberg von dem ersten urkundlichen Nachweis ihres Bestehens bis zu ihrem Übergang an das Königreich Bayern (1806).* Nuremberg: Raw'sche Buchhandlung, 1896.

Renczes, Andrea. *Wie löscht man eine Familie aus? Eine Analyse Bamberger Hexenprozesse.* Pfaffenweiler: Centaurus, 1990.

Repgen, Konrad, ed. *Das Herrscherbild im 17. Jahrhundert.* Münster: Aschendorff, 1991.

Repgen, Konrad, ed. *Krieg und Politik 1618–1648: Europäische Probleme und Perspektiven.* Munich: Oldenbourg, 1988.

Ritter, Moritz. *Deutsche Geschichte im Zeitalter der Gegenreformation und des Dreißigjährigen Krieges (1555–1648),* vol. 3: *Geschichte des Dreißigjährigen Krieges.* Darmstadt: Wissenschaftliche Buchgesellschaft, 1962.

Robisheaux, Thomas. *Rural Society and the Search for Order in Early Modern Germany.* Cambridge: Cambridge University Press, 1989.

Rodríguez, Havidán, et al., eds. *Handbook of Disaster Research.* New York: Springer Science+Business Media, 2006.

Roeck, Bernd. *Als wollt die Welt schier brechen. Eine Stadt im Zeitalter des Dreissigjährigen Krieges.* Munich: Beck, 1991.

Roeck, Bernd. "Bayern und der Dreißigjährige Krieg: Demographische, wirtschaftliche und soziale Auswirkungen am Beispiel Münchens." *Geschichte und Gesellschaft* 17 (1991): 434–58.

Roeck, Bernd. "Der Dreißigjährige Krieg und die Menschen im Reich: Überlegungen zu den Formen psychischer Krisenbewältigung in der ersten Hälfte des 17. Jahrhunderts." In *Krieg und Frieden: Militär und Gesellschaft in der Frühen Neuzeit,* edited by Bernhard R. Kroener and Ralf Pröve, 265–79. Munich: Schöningh, 1996.

Roeck, Bernd. *Eine Stadt in Krieg und Frieden: Studien zur Geschichte der Reichsstadt Augsburg zwischen Kalenderstreit und Parität,* 2 vols. Göttingen: Vandenhoeck & Ruprecht, 1989.

Roper, Lyndal. "Jenseits des linguistic turn." *Historische Anthropologie: Kultur – Gesellschaft – Alltag* 7 (1999): 452–66.
Rosa, Mario. "Die Ordensschwester." In *Der Mensch des Barock*, edited by Rosario Villari, 181–231. Essen: Magnus, 1997.
Rublack, Hans-Christoph, ed. *Die lutherische Konfessionalisierung in Deutschland: Wissenschaftliches Symposion des Vereins für Reformationsgeschichte 1988.* Gütersloh: Mohn, 1992.
Rublack, Ulinka, ed. *Gender in Early Modern German History.* Cambridge: Cambridge University Press, 2002.
Rückert, Christoph. *Ipsheim: Die Chronik eines Fränkischen Dorfes.* Ipsheim: Marktgemeinde Ipsheim, 1989.
Rudersdorf, Manfred. "Brandenburg-Ansbach und Brandenburg-Kulmbach/Bayreuth." In *Die Territorien des Reichs im Zeitalter der Reformation und Konfessionalisierung: Land und Konfession 1500–1650*, vol. 1: *Der Südosten*, edited by Anton Schindling and Walter Ziegler, 10–30. Münster: Aschendorff, 1989.
Rudolf, Hans U., ed. *Der Dreissigjährige Krieg: Perspektiven und Strukturen.* Darmstadt: Wissenschaftliche Buchgesellschaft, 1977.
Ruff, Julius R. *Violence in Early Modern Europe 1500-1800.* Cambridge: Cambridge University Press, 2001.
Rüger, Willi. *Mittelalterliches Almosenwesen: Die Almosenordnungen der Reichsstadt Nürnberg.* Nuremberg: Verlag der Hochschulbuchhandlung, 1932.
Rutz, Andreas. *Bildung – Konfession – Geschlecht: Religiöse Frauengemeinschaften und die Katholische Mädchenbildung im Rheinland (16.–18. Jahrhundert).* Mainz: von Zabern, 2006.
Rutz, Andreas. "Ego-*Dokument* oder Ich-*Konstruktion*? Selbstzeugnisse als Quellen zur Erforschung des frühneuzeitlichen Menschen." *Zeitblicke* 1/2 (2002): 1–19.
Rystad, Göran. *Kriegsnachrichten und Propaganda während des Dreissigjährigen Krieges: Die Schlacht bei Nördlingen in den gleichzeitigen, gedruckten Kriegsberichten.* Lund: Gleerup, 1960.
Sabean, David W. *Power in the Blood: Popular Culture and Village Discourse in Early Modern Germany.* Cambridge: Cambridge University Press, 1984.
Sabean, David W. "Production of the Self during the Age of Confessionalism." *Central European History* 29 (1996): 1–18.
Sachße, Christoph, and Florian Tennstedt. *Geschichte der Armenfürsorge in Deutschland: Vom Spätmittelalter bis zum Ersten Weltkrieg.* Stuttgart: Kohlhammer, 1980.
Safley, Thomas M., ed. *A Companion to Multiconfessionalism in the Early Modern World.* Leiden: Brill, 2011.
Safley, Thomas M., ed. *The Reformation of Charity: The Secular and the Religious in Early Modern Poor Relief.* Boston: Brill, 2003.

Scarry, Elaine. *The Body in Pain: The Making and Unmaking of the World.* New York: Oxford University Press, 1985.

Schade, Richard. "The King-for-a-Day Theme and Extra-Literary Realities in the Writings of Hollonius, Gryphius, Harsdörfer and Krüger." *Daphnis* 17 (1988): 37–53.

Schenk, Gerrit J., ed. *Katastrophen: Vom Untergang Pompejis bis zum Klimawandel.* Ostfildern: Thorbecke, 2009.

Schenk, Gerrit J., and Jens I. Engels, eds. *Historical Disaster Research: Concepts, Methods and Case Studies. Historical Social Research* 32 (2007) 3. Special Issue: Disaster.

Schiewek, Ingrid. "Zur Manifestation des Individuellen in der frühen deutschen Selbstdarstellung: Eine Studie zum Autobiographen Bartholomäus Sastrow (1520–1603)." *Weimarer Beiträge* 13 (1967): 885–915.

Schilling, Heinz, ed. *Institutionen, Instrumente und Akteure sozialer Kontrolle und Disziplinierung im frühneuzeitlichen Europa.* Frankfurt am Main: Klostermann, 1999.

Schilling, Heinz, and István György Tóth, eds. *Cultural Exchange in Early Modern Europe,* vol. 1: *Religion and Cultural Exchange in Europe, 1400–1700.* Cambridge: Cambridge University Press, 2006.

Schilling, Michael. *Bildpublizistik der frühen Neuzeit: Aufgaben und Leistungen des illustrierten Flugblatts in Deutschland bis um 1700.* Tübingen: Niemeyer, 1990.

Schilling, Michael. "Medienspezifische Modellierung politischer Ereignisse auf Flugblättern des Dreißigjährigen Krieges." In *Sprachen des Politischen: Medien und Medialität in der Geschichte,* edited by Ute Frevert and Wolfgang Braungart, 123–38. Göttingen: Vandenhoeck & Ruprecht, 2004.

Schindler, Norbert. "Die Prinzipien des Hörensagens: Predigt und Publikum in der Frühen Neuzeit." *Historische Anthropologie* 1 (1993): 359–93.

Schindling, Anton, and Walter Ziegler, eds. *Die Territorien des Reichs im Zeitalter der Reformation und Konfessionalisierung: Land und Konfession 1500–1650,* 7 vols. Münster: Aschendorff, 1989–1997.

Schlögel, Karl. *Im Raume lesen wir die Zeit: Über Zivilisationsgeschichte und Geopolitik.* Frankfurt am Main: Fischer, 2006.

Schlögl, Rudolf. *Bauern, Krieg und Staat: Oberbayerische Bauernwirtschaft und frühmoderner Staat im 17. Jahrhundert.* Göttingen: Vandenhoeck & Ruprecht, 1988.

Schlögl, Rudolf. "Zwischen Krieg und Krise: Situation und Entwicklung der bayerischen Bauernwirtschaft im 17. Jahrhundert." *Zeitschrift für Agrargeschichte und Agrarsoziologie* 40 (1992): 133–67.

Schlosser, Hans. "Gesetzgebung und Rechtswirklichkeit im Territorialstaat der frühen Neuzeit. Am Beispiel des Landesfürstentums Bayern (16./17. Jahrhundert)." In *Diritto e Potere nella Storia Europea: Atti in onore de Bruno Paradisi,* edited by the Società italiana di storia del diritto, 525–42. Florence: Olschki, 1982.

Schmid, Adolf. "Georg Gaisser (1595–1655): Prior von St. Nikolaus und Herr im Klosterbad Rippoldsau." *Die Ortenau* 61 (1981): 87–102.

Schmid, Alois. "Zur Konfessionspolitik Herzog Albrechts V. von Bayern." In *Forschungen zur bayerischen Geschichte. Festschrift für Wilhelm Volkert zum 65. Geburtstag*, edited by Wilhelm Volkert and Dieter Albrecht, 99–114. Frankfurt am Main: Lang, 1993.

Schmid, Alois, and Katharina Weigand, eds. *Die Herrscher Bayerns: 25 historische Portraits von Tassilo III. bis Ludwig III.* Munich: Beck, 2001.

Schmidt, Hans. "Militärverwaltung in Deutschland und Frankreich im 17. und 18. Jahrhundert." In *Krieg und Frieden: Militär und Gesellschaft in der Frühen Neuzeit*, edited by Bernhard R. Kroener and Ralf Pröve, 25–45. Munich: Schöningh, 1996.

Schmidt, Jürgen M. *Glaube und Skepsis. Die Kurpfalz und die abendländische Hexenverfolgung 1446–1685*. Bielefeld: Verlag für Regionalgeschichte, 2000.

Schmidt-Fölkersamb, Ursula. "Der Große Krieg im Nachleben." In *Gustav Adolf, Wallenstein und der Dreissigjährige Krieg in Franken: Ausstellung des Staatsarchivs Nürnberg zum 350. Gedenkjahr (1632–1982)*, edited by Günther Schuhmann, 117–33. Munich: Degener & Co., 1982.

Schnabel, Werner W. *Österreichische Exulanten in oberdeutschen Reichsstädten: Zur Migration von Führungsschichten im 17. Jahrhundert*. Munich: Beck, 1992.

Schneider, Joachim. "Anfänge in der Stadtgeschichte: Über Legenden in der mittelalterlichen Nürnberger Stadtchronistik und ihren historischen Auskunftswert." *Mitteilungen des Vereins für Geschichte der Stadt Nürnberg* 87 (2000): 5–46.

Schock, Flemming, et al., eds. *Dimensions of the Early Modern Theatrum-Metaphor: Order and Representation of Knowledge*. Metaphoric.de. 14/2008 – Tagungsband. Hannover: Wehrhahn, 2008.

Schönauer, Tobias. *Ingolstadt in der Zeit des Dreißigjährigen Krieges: Soziale und wirtschaftliche Aspekte der Stadtgeschichte*. Ingolstadt: Stadtmuseum und Stadtarchiv Ingolstadt, 2007.

Schöne, Walter. *Die deutsche Zeitung des siebzehnten Jahrhunderts in Abbildungen*. Leipzig: Harrassowitz, 1940.

Schorn-Schütte, Luise. *Evangelische Geistlichkeit in der Frühneuzeit: deren Anteil an der Entfaltung frühmoderner Staatlichkeit und Gesellschaft: dargestellt am Beispiel des Fürstentums Braunschweig-Wolfenbüttel, der Landgrafschaft Hessen-Kassel und der Stadt Braunschweig*. Gütersloh: Gütersloher Verlagshaus, 1996.

Schott, Dieter. *Stadt und Katastrophe*. Berlin: Deutsches Institut für Urbanistik, 2003.

Schreiner, Klaus. *Maria: Jungfrau, Mutter, Herrscherin*. Munich: Hauser, 1994.

Schröder, Stephan M. "Hamburg und Schweden im 30jährigen Krieg – vom potentiellen Bündnispartner zum Zentrum der Kriegsfinanzierung." *Vierteljahrsschrift für Sozial- und Wirtschaftsgeschichte* 76 (1989): 305–31.

Schröder, Thomas. *Die ersten Zeitungen: Textgestaltung und Nachrichtenauswahl*. Tübingen: Narr, 1995.

Schröder, Thomas. "The Origins of the German Press." In *The Politics of Information in Early Modern Europe*, edited by Brendan Dooley and Sabrina A. Baron, 123–50. London: Routledge, 2001.

Schuhmann, Günther, ed. *Gustav Adolf, Wallenstein und der Dreissigjährige Krieg in Franken. Ausstellung des Staatsarchivs Nürnberg zum 350. Gedenkjahr (1632–1982)*. Neustadt an der Aisch: Degener & Co., 1982.

Schulte, Regina. *Die verkehrte Welt des Krieges: Studien zu Geschlecht, Religion und Tod.* Frankfurt am Main: Campus, 1998.

Schulte, Rolf. *Hexenmeister. Die Verfolgung von Männern im Rahmen der Hexenverfolgung von 1530–1730 im Alten Reich*. Frankfurt am Main: Lang, 2000.

Schultheiss, Werner. *Kleine Geschichte Nürnbergs*. 3rd ed. Edited by Gerhard Hirschmann. Nuremberg: Spindler, [1966] 1997.

Schulze, Winfried. "Ego-Dokumente: Annäherung an den Menschen in der Geschichte? Vorüberlegungen für die Tagung 'EGO-DOKUMENTE'." In *Ego-Dokumente: Annäherung an den Menschen in der Geschichte*, edited by Winfried Schulze, 11–30. Berlin: Akademie Verlag, 1996.

Schunka, Alexander. "Zeit des Exils – Zur argumentativen Funktion der Zeit bei Zuwanderern im Kursachsen des 17. Jahrhunderts." In *Die Autorität der Zeit in der Frühen Neuzeit*, edited by Arndt Brendecke et al., 149–69. Berlin: LIT Verlag, 2007.

Schwaiger, Georg, ed. *Lebensbilder aus der Geschichte des Bistums Regensburg*, vol. 1. Regensburg: Verlag des Vereins für Regensburger Bistumsgeschichte, 1989.

Schwerhoff, Gerd. "Böse Hexen und fahrlässige Flucher: Frühneuzeitliche Gottlosigkeiten im Vergleich." In *Gottlosigkeit und Eigensinn: Religiöse Devianz im konfessionellen Zeitalter*, edited by Eric Piltz and Gerd Schwerhoff, 187–206. Berlin: Duncker & Humblot, 2015.

Schwerhoff, Gerd. "Zentren und treibende Kräfte der frühneuzeitlichen Hexenverfolgung – Sachsen im regionalen Vergleich." *Neues Archiv für sächsische Geschichte* 79 (2008): 61–100.

Schwerhoff, Gerd. *Zungen wie Schwerter: Blasphemie in alteuropäischen Gesellschaften 1200–1650*. Constance: UVK Verlagsgesellschaft, 2005.

Scott, Joan W. "The Evidence of Experience." *Critical Inquiry* 17 (1991): 773–97.

Seethaler, Josef. "Die Kalenderdrucke – ein frühes 'Massenmedium'? Anmerkungen zu einigen Charakteristika der Wiener Kalenderproduktion des 15. bis 17. Jahrhunderts." In *Zeitung, Zeitschrift, Intelligenzblatt und Kalender: Beiträge zur historischen Presseforschung*, edited by Astrid Blome, 223–36. Bremen: Edition Lumière, 2000.

Siegenthaler, Hansjörg. *Regelvertrauen, Prosperität und Krise: Die Ungleichmäßigkeit wirtschaftlicher und sozialer Entwicklung als Ergebnis individuellen Handelns und sozialen Lernens*. Tübingen: Mohr Siebeck, 1993.

Silber, Ilana F. "Bourdieu's Gift to Gift Theory: An Unacknowledged Trajectory." *Sociological Theory* 27 (2009): 173–90.

Šimeček, Zdeněk. "Geschriebene Zeitungen in den böhmischen Ländern um 1600 und ihr Entstehungs- und Rezeptionszusammenhang mit den gedruckten Zeitungen." In *Presse und Geschichte: neue Beiträge zur historischen Kommunikationsforschung*, vol. 1: 71–82. Munich: Saur, 1987.

Simon, Matthias. *Nürnbergisches Pfarrerbuch: Die evangelisch-lutherische Geistlichkeit der Reichsstadt Nürnberg und ihres Gebietes 1524–1806.* Nürnberg: Verein für Bayerische Kirchengeschichte, 1965.

Simonov, Vladimir I. "Die gesellschaftlichen Funktionen und die Sprache der deutschen Zeitungen des 17. Jahrhunderts." In *Presse und Geschichte: neue Beiträge zur historischen Kommunikationsforschung,* vol. 1: 171–83. Munich: Saur, 1987.

Sloterdijk, Peter. *Literatur und Organisation von Lebenserfahrung: Autobiographien der Zwanziger Jahre.* Munich: Hanser, 1978.

Smith, Pamela H., and Benjamin Schmidt. "Knowledge and Its Making in Early Modern Europe." In *Making Knowledge in Early Modern Europe: Practices, Objects, and Texts, 1400–1800,* edited by Pamela H. Smith and Benjamin Schmidt, 1–16. Chicago: University of Chicago Press, 2007.

Smolinsky, Heribert. *Deutungen der Zeit im Streit der Konfessionen: Kontroverstheologie, Apokalyptik und Astrologie im 16. Jahrhundert.* Heidelberg: Winter, 2000.

Soden, Franz Freiherr von. *Gustav Adolph und sein Heer in Süddeutschland von 1631 bis 1635: Zur Geschichte des dreißigjährigen Krieges,* 3 vols. Erlangen: Bläsing, 1865–1869.

Soergel, Philip M. *Wondrous in His Saints: Counter-Reformation Propaganda in Bavaria.* Berkeley: University of California Press, 1993.

Sörensson, Per. "Das Kriegswesen während der letzten Periode des Dreissigjährigen Krieges." In *Der Dreissigjährige Krieg: Perspektiven und Strukturen,* edited by Hans U. Rudolf, 431–57. Darmstadt: Wissenschaftliche Buchgesellschaft, 1977.

Sperling, Jutta G. *Convents and the Body Politic in Late Renaissance Venice.* Chicago: University of Chicago Press, 1999.

Spicer, Andrew. "Poor Relief and the Exile Communities." In *Reformations Old and New: Essays on the Socio-Economic Impact of Religious Change c. 1470–1630,* edited by Beat A. Kümin, 237–55. Aldershot: Scolar Press, 1996.

Spindler, Max. *Bayerischer Geschichtsatlas.* Munich: Bayerischer Schulbuchverlag, 1969.

Spindler, Max. *Handbuch der Bayerischen Geschichte,* vol. 3: *Franken, Schwaben, Oberpfalz bis zum Ausgang des 18. Jahrhunderts.* Munich: Beck, 1971.

Spohnholz, Jesse. "Multiconfessional Celebration of the Eucharist in Sixteenth-Century Wesel." *Sixteenth Century Journal* 39 (2008): 705–29.

Spohnholz, Jesse. *The Tactics of Toleration: A Refugee Community in the Age of Religious Wars.* Newark: University of Delaware Press, 2011.

Spohnholz, Jesse, and Gary K. Waite, eds. *Exile and Religious Identity, 1500–1800.* London: Pickering & Chatto, 2014.

Sporhan-Krempel, Lore. "Buchdruck und Buchhandel in Nürnberg im 17. Jahrhundert." In *Bücher und Bibliotheken im 17. Jahrhundert in Deutschland,* edited by Paul Raabe, 25–37. Hamburg: Hauswedell & Co., 1980.

Sporhan-Krempel, Lore. *Nürnberg als Nachrichtenzentrum zwischen 1400 und 1700.* Nuremberg: Verein für Geschichte der Stadt Nürnberg, 1968.

Staber, Josef. *Kirchengeschichte des Bistums Regensburg.* Regensburg: Habbel, 1966.

Starn, Randolph. *Contrary Commonwealth: The Theme of Exile in Medieval and Renaissance Italy.* Berkeley: University of California Press, 1982.

Steiger, Heinhard. "Concrete Peace and General Order: The Legal Meaning of the Treaties of 24 October 1648." In *1648: War and Peace in Europe*, vol. 1, edited by Klaus Bussmann and Heinz Schilling, 437–45. Munich: Veranstaltungsgesellschaft 350 Jahre Westfälischer Friede, 1998.

Stieve, Felix. *Das kirchliche Polizeiregiment in Baiern unter Maximilian I. 1595–1651.* Munich: Rieger, 1876.

Stieve, Felix. "Über die ältesten halbjährigen Zeitungen oder Messrelationen und insbesondere über deren Begründer Freiherrn Michael von Aitzing." In *Abhandlungen der Historischen Classe der Königlich Bayerischen Akademie der Wissenschaften*, vol. 16, sec. 1: 177–265. Munich: Verlag der K. Akademie, 1881.

Stolberg, Michael. *Homo patiens: Krankheits- und Körpererfahrung in der Frühen Neuzeit.* Cologne: Böhlau, 2003.

Stolleis, Michael. "Religion und Politik im Zeitalter des Barock: 'Konfessionalisierung' oder 'Säkularisierung' bei der Entstehung des frühmodernen Staates?" In *Religion und Religiosität im Zeitalter des Barock*, vol. 1, edited by Dieter Breuer, 23–42. Wiesbaden: Harrassowitz, 1995.

Stolleis, Michael, ed. *Staatsdenker im 17. und 18. Jahrhundert: Reichspublizistik – Politik – Naturrecht.* 2nd ed. Frankfurt am Main: Metzner, [1977] 1987.

Strange, Carolyn, et al., eds. *Honor, Violence and Emotions in History.* London: Bloomsbury, 2014.

Strasser, Ulrike. "Cloistering Women's Past: Conflicting Accounts of Enclosure in a Seventeenth-Century Munich Nunnery." In *Gender in Early Modern German History*, edited by Ulinka Rublack, 221–46. Cambridge: Cambridge University Press, 2002.

Strasser, Ulrike. *State of Virginity: Gender, Religion, and Politics in an Early Modern Catholic State.* Ann Arbor: University of Michigan Press, 2004.

Strasser, Ulrike. "Vom 'Fall der Ehre' zum 'Fall der Leichtfertigkeit': Geschlechtsspezifische Aspekte der Konfessionalisierung am Beispiel Münchner Eheversprechens- und Alimentationsklagen (1592–1649)." In *Konfessionalisierung und Religion*, edited by Peer Frieß and Rolf Kießling, 227–46. Konstanz: Universitätsverlag Konstanz, 1999.

Straßner, Erich. *Zeitung.* Tübingen: Niemeyer, 1999.

Sträter, Udo. *Meditation und Kirchenreform in der lutherischen Kirche des 17. Jahrhunderts.* Tübingen: Mohr Siebeck, 1995.

Stricker, Käthe. *Deutsche Frauenbildung vom 16. Jahrhundert bis Mitte des 19. Jahrhunderts*. Berlin: Herbig, 1929.

Stübing, Ursula. "Literatur als historische Quelle: Krieg und Soldatenwesen in einer Satire Johann Michael Moscheroschs." *Militärgeschichte* 29 (1990): 241–45.

Sturm, P. Angelus. "Abt Veit Hösers Schwedenflucht." *Benediktinische Monatschrift zur Pflege religiösen und geistigen Lebens* 10 (1928): 457–66.

Sührig, Hartmut. "Niedersächsische Schreibkalender im 17. Jahrhundert: Zur Kulturgeschichte eines populären Lesestoffs." In *Bücher und Bibliotheken im 17. Jahrhundert in Deutschland*, edited by Paul Raabe, 145–70. Hamburg: Hauswedell & Co., 1980.

Tallett, Frank. *War and Society in Early Modern Europe, 1495–1715*. London: Routledge, 1992.

Tanner, Jakob. "Körpererfahrung, Schmerz und die Konstruktion des Kulturellen." *Historische Anthropologie: Kultur – Gesellschaft – Alltag* 2 (1994): 489–502.

Teske, Gunnar. *Bürger, Bauern, Söldner und Gesandte: Der Dreißigjährige Krieg und der Westfälische Frieden in Westfalen*. Münster: Ardey, 1997.

Theibault, John. "The Demography of the Thirty Years' War Revisited." *German History* 15 (1997): 1–21.

Theibault, John. *German Villages in Crisis: Rural Life in Hesse-Kassel and the Thirty Years' War, 1580–1720*. Atlantic Heights, NJ: Humanities Press, 1995.

Theibault, John. "Jeremiah in the Village: Prophecy, Preaching, Pamphlets, and Penance in the Thirty Years' War." *Central European History* 27 (1994): 441–60.

Theibault, John. "The Rhetoric of Death and Destruction in the Thirty Years War." *Journal of Social History* 27 (1993): 271–90.

Thieser, Bernd. *Die Oberpfalz im Zusammenhang des Hexenprozeßgeschehens im Süddeutschen Raum während des 16. und 17. Jahrhunderts*. Bayreuth: Rabenstein, 1992.

Thorndike, Lynn. *A History of Magic and Experimental Science*, vols. 5–8. New York: Columbia University Press (MacMillan), 1923–1958.

Thuillier, Jacques. "The Thirty Years' War and the Arts." In *1648: War and Peace in Europe*, vol. 2, edited by Klaus Bussmann and Heinz Schilling, 15–27. Munich: Veranstaltungsgesellschaft 350 Jahre Westfälischer Friede, 1998.

Tlusty, B. Ann. *The Martial Ethic in Early Modern Germany: Civic Duty and the Right of Arms*. London: Palgrave Macmillan, 2011.

Trim, David J. B. "English Military Émigrés and the Protestant Cause in Europe, 1603–c. 1640." In *British and Irish Emigrants and Exiles in Europe, 1603–1688*, edited by David Worthington, 237–58. Leiden: Brill, 2010.

Trinkner, Diana. "Von Spionen und Ohrenträgern, von Argus' Augen und tönenden Köpfen: Anmerkungen zu Kontrollmechanismen in der Frühen Neuzeit." In *Zeremoniell in der Krise: Störung und Nostalgie*, edited by Bernhard Jahn et al., 61–77. Marburg: Jonas, 1998.

Tschopp, Silvia Serena. *Heilsgeschichtliche Deutungsmuster in der Publizistik des Dreißigjährigen Krieges: Pro- und antischwedische Propaganda in Deutschland 1628 bis 1635*. Frankfurt am Main: Lang, 1991.

Tuan, Yi-fu. *Landscapes of Fear*. New York: Pantheon Books, 1979.

Tucker, George H. *Homo Viator: Itineraries of Exile, Displacement and Writing in Renaissance Europe*. Geneva: Droz, 2003.

Ukema, Peter. "Tagesschrifttum und Öffentlichkeit im 16. und 17. Jahrhundert in Deutschland." In *Presse und Geschichte: Beiträge zur historischen Kommunikationsforschung*, 35–53. Munich: Verlag Dokumentation, 1977.

Ulbrich, Claudia, et al., eds. *Gewalt in der Frühen Neuzeit: Beiträge zur 5. Tagung der Arbeitsgemeinschaft Frühe Neuzeit im VHD*. Berlin: Duncker & Humblot, 2005.

Ulbricht, Otto, ed. *Die leidige Seuche: Pest-Fälle in der Frühen Neuzeit*. Cologne: Böhlau, 2004.

Vasold, Manfred. "Die deutschen Bevölkerungsverluste während des Dreissigjährigen Krieges." *Zeitschrift für bayerische Landesgeschichte* 56 (1993): 147–60.

Vigarello, Georges. *Concepts of Cleanliness: Changing Attitudes in France since the Middle Ages*. Translated by Jean Birrell. Cambridge: Cambridge University Press, 1988.

Vigarello, Georges. *A History of Rape: Sexual Violence in France from the 16th to the 20th Century*. Translated by Jean Birrell. Malden, MA: Polity Press, [1998] 2001.

Walker, Garthine. "Sexual Violence and Rape in Europe, 1500–1750." In *The Routledge History of Sex and the Body 1500 to the Present*, edited by Sarah Toulalan and Kate Fisher, 429–43. New York: Routledge, 2013.

Wallner, Ida. *Clara Staiger: Ein Lebens- und Kulturbild aus dem 30 jährigen Krieg*. Bamberg: Buchner, 1957.

Walter, François. *Katastrophen: Eine Kulturgeschichte vom 16. bis ins 21. Jahrhundert*. Stuttgart: Reclam, 2010.

Wang, Andreas. "Illustrierte Flugblätter im 17. Jahrhundert." *Philobiblon* 21 (1977): 184–210.

Wappmann, Volker. *Durchbruch zur Toleranz: Die Religionspolitik des Pfalzgrafen Christian August von Sulzbach 1622–1708*. Neustadt an der Aisch: Degener & Co., 1995.

Warmbrunn, Paul. *Zwei Konfessionen in einer Stadt: Das Zusammenleben von Katholiken und Protestanten in den paritätischen Reichsstädten Augsburg, Biberach, Ravensburg und Dinkelsbühl von 1548–1648*. Wiesbaden: Steiner, 1983.

Warneken, Bernd Jürgen. *Populare Autobiographik: Empirische Studien zu einer Quellengattung der Alltagsgeschichtsforschung*. Tübingen: Tübinger Vereinskunde für Volkskunde, 1985.

Weber, Johannes. *Avisen, Relationen, Gazetten: Der Beginn des europäischen Zeitungswesens*. Oldenburg: Bibliotheks- und Informationssystem der Universität Oldenburg, 1997.

Weber, Leo. *Veit Adam von Gepeckh Fürstbischof von Freising, 1618 bis 1851*. Munich: Seitz & Höfling, 1972.
Weber, Reinhard. *Würzburg und Bamberg im Dreißigjährigen Krieg: Die Regierungszeit des Bischofs Franz von Hatzfeldt 1631–1642*. Würzburg: Echter, 1979.
Wedgwood, Cecilia V. *The Thirty Years War*. New York: Anchor Book/Doubleday & Company, [1938] 1961.
Wegner, Bernd, ed. *Wie Kriege entstehen: Zum historischen Hintergrund von Staatenkonflikten*. Paderborn: Schöningh, 2000.
Weigelt, Klaus. "Heimat – der Ort personaler Identitätsfindung und sozio-politischer Orientierung." In *Heimat und Nation: Zur Geschichte und Identität der Deutschen*, edited by Klaus Weigelt, 15–25. Mainz: Hase & Koehler, 1984.
Weigl, Andreas, ed. *Wien im Dreißigjährigen Krieg: Bevölkerung – Gesellschaft – Kultur – Konfession*. Vienna: Böhlau, 2001.
Weiss, Hildegard. *Historischer Atlas von Bayern. Teil Franken, 1/21: Stadt- und Landkreis Bamberg*. Munich: Kommission für Bayerische Landesgeschichte, 1974.
Weller, Emil. "Dialoge und Gespräche des siebzehnten Jahrhunderts." *Serapeum* 11 (1863): 161–70 and 12 (1863): 176–88.
Weller, Emil. *Die Lieder des Dreissigjährigen Krieges*. Basel: Georg, 1858.
Welsch, Klaus. "Oberfranken im Dreißigjährigen Krieg: Unter Berücksichtigung des Verhältnisses zwischen dem Bistum Bamberg und der Markgrafschaft Bayreuth." Dissertation. Universität Bayreuth, 1979.
Wette, Wolfram, ed. *Der Krieg des kleinen Mannes: Eine Militärgeschichte von unten*. Munich: Piper, 1995.
der Wieden, Brage bei. "Niederdeutsche Söldner vor dem Dreißigjährigen Krieg: Geistige und mentale Grenzen eines sozialen Raums." In *Krieg und Frieden: Militär und Gesellschaft in der Frühen Neuzeit*, edited by Bernhard R. Kroener and Ralf Pröve, 85–107. Munich: Schöningh, 1996.
Wildgruber, Martin. "Wasserburg im Tagebuch der Äbtissin Haidenbucher von Frauenchiemsee 1609–1648." *Heimat am Inn* 10 (1990): 157–200.
Wilfert, Johannes. *Emtmannsberg im Spiegel seiner Geschichte: Eine oberfränkische Gemeinde*. Bayreuth: Mühl, 1987.
Wilke, Jürgen. "Massenmedien als Quelle und Forschungsgegenstand der Kommunikationsgeschichte." In *Wege zur Kommunikationsgeschichte*, edited by Manfred Bobrowsky and Wolfgang R. Langenbucher, 697–711. Munich: Ölschläger, 1987.
Willax, Franz. "Die Befestigungsanlagen Gustav Adolfs von Schweden um Nürnberg 1632." *Mitteilungen des Vereins für Geschichte der Stadt Nürnberg* 82 (1995): 185–235.
Willax, Franz. "'Gefährliche Patrioten und schädliche Leuth': Antischwedischer Widerstand in Nürnberg 1631–1635." *Mitteilungen des Vereins für Geschichte der Stadt Nürnberg* 78 (1991): 123–73.

Williams, Gerhild Scholz. *Mediating Culture in the Seventeenth – Century German Novel: Eberhard Werner Happel, 1647–1690*. Ann Arbor: University of Michigan Press, 2014.

Wilson, Peter H. *The Holy Roman Empire: A Thousand Years of Europe's History*. London: Penguin Random House, 2017.

Wilson, Peter H. "On the Role of Religion in the Thirty Years War." *International Historical Review* 30 (2008): 473–514.

Wilson, Peter H. "Perceptions of Violence in the Early Modern Communications Revolution: The Case of the Thirty Years War 1618–1648." In *Violence and War in Culture and the Media: Five Disciplinary Lenses*, edited by Athina Karatzogianni, 13–29. London: Routledge, 2012.

Wilson, Peter H. *The Thirty Years War: Europe's Tragedy*. Cambridge, MA: Belknap/Harvard University Press, 2009.

Winkle, Stefan. *Geisseln der Menschheit: Kulturgeschichte der Seuchen*. Düsseldorf: Artemis & Winkler, 1997.

Winnige, Norbert. "Von der Kontribution zur Akzise: Militärfinanzierung als Movens staatlicher Steuerpolitik." In *Krieg und Frieden: Militär und Gesellschaft in der Frühen Neuzeit*, edited by Bernhard R. Kroener and Ralf Pröve, 59–83. Munich: Schöningh, 1996.

Wirt, Georg. "Die Kalender des Hochstifts Bamberg und ihre Entwicklung bis 1700." *Gutenberg Jahrbuch* 26 (1951): 87–93.

Wittmann, Pius. *Sophia Markgräfin von Brandenburg – Onolzbach, Herzogin in Preußen*. Munich: Ackermann, 1884.

Wolf, Thomas. *Reichsstädte in Kriegszeiten: Untersuchungen zur Verfassungs-, Wirtschafts- und Sozialgeschichte von Isny, Lindau, Memmingen und Ravensburg im 17. Jahrhundert*. Memmingen: Verlag Memminger Zeitung, 1991.

Wölfel, Dieter. *Salomon Lentz 1584–1647: Ein Beitrag zur Geschichte des orthodoxen Luthertums im Dreißigjährigen Krieg*. Gunzenhausen: Degener & Co., 1991.

Wolff, Reinhold. "Rezeptionsforschung und Contentanalyse." In *Internationales Archiv für Sozialgeschichte der deutschen Literatur*, vol. 3, edited by Georg Jäger et al., 208–219. Tübingen: Niemeyer, 1978.

Wolkan, Rudolf. "Politische Karikaturen aus der Zeit des dreissigjährigen Krieges." *Zeitschrift für Bücherfreunde* 2 (1899): 457–67.

Woodford, Charlotte. *Nuns as Historians in Early Modern Germany*. Oxford: Clarendon Press, 2002.

Worthington, David, ed. *British and Irish Emigrants and Exiles in Europe, 1603–1688*. Leiden: Brill, 2010.

Wunder, Gerd. "Georg Friedrich Seufferheld: Stättmeister der Reichsstaft Schwäbisch Hall, 1613–1686." In *Lebensbilder aus Schwaben und Franken*, vol. 9, edited by Max Miller and Robert Uhland, 56–68. Stuttgart: Kohlhammer, 1963.

Wunder, Gerd. "Johann Morhard: Arzt und Chronist 1554–1631." In *Lebensbilder aus Schwaben und Franken*, vol. 9, edited by Max Miller and Robert Uhland, 40–46. Stuttgart: Kohlhammer, 1963.

Wunder, Heide. "Überlegungen zum Wandel der Geschlechterbeziehungen im 15. und 16. Jahrhundert aus sozialgeschichtlicher Sicht." In *Wandel der Geschlechterbeziehungen zu Beginn der Neuzeit*, edited by Heide Wunder and Christina Vanja, 12–26. Frankfurt am Main: Surkamp, 1991.

Wüst, Wolfgang. *Reichskreis und Territorium: Die Herrschaft über die Herrschaft? Supraterritoriale Tendenzen in Politik, Kultur, Wirtschaft und Gesellschaft. Ein Vergleich süddeutscher Reichskreise*. Stuttgart: Thorbecke, 2000.

Wüst, Wolfgang, and Michael Müller, eds. *Reichskreise und Regionen im frühmodernen Europa – Horizonte und Grenzen im spacial turn*. Frankfurt am Main: Lang, 2011.

Zander-Seidel, Jutta. "Kleidergesetzgebung und städtische Ordnung: Inhalte, Überwachung und Akzeptanz frühneuzeitlicher Kleiderordnungen." *Anzeiger des Germanischen Nationalmuseums* (1993): 176–88.

Zeitelhack, Bärbel. "Untersuchungen zur Sozial- und Wirtschaftsgeschichte der Grafschaft Oettingen im 17. Jahrhundert: Die Entwicklung des Dorfes Hürnheim 1608–1660." *Zeitschrift für bayerische Landesgeschichte* 51 (1988): 411–46.

Zeller, Gaston. *Das Benediktinerkloster St. Emmeram zu Regensburg in der Reformationszeit*. Kallmünz: Lassleben, 1970.

Zeller, Gaston. "Le principe d'équilibre dans la politique internationale avant 1789." *Revue Historique* 225 (1956): 25–37.

Zimmermann, Gunter. "Territorium und Konfession am Beispiel Maximilians I. von Bayern." *Blätter für deutsche Landesgeschichte* 127 (1991): 211–33.

Zimmermann, Karl. "Segnitz und Umgebung im Dreißigjährigen Krieg (1)." *Alte Geschichten. Neues aus dem alten Segnitz* 9 (2008): 1–12.

Zinner, Ernst. *Geschichte und Bibliographie der astronomischen Literatur in Deutschland zur Zeit der Renaissance*. 2nd ed. Stuttgart: Hiersemann, [1941] 1964.

Zweig, Stefan. "Die Welt von Gestern. Erinnerungen eines Europäers." In *Gesammelte Werke*, vol. 6. 2nd ed. Frankfurt am Main: Fischer, [1944] 1982.

Index

abandonment/abandoned 44, 46, 51, 76–77, 85, 113, 121, 128, 144, 192–93, 195, 198–99
accord (military) 75, 128–29, 184, 201
  tenuousness of 30, 193, 206
action 5, 7–8, 21, 23, 61, 76–77, 83–84, 87, 96, 105, 115, 119, 123, 149, 162, 164, 167, 205, 210, 214, 216, 219, 226, 229, 232–33
  collective/group 157–58, 160–61, 164, 170–72, 181
  God's 203–4
  individual 160, 170, 197
  legal 158–59, 93
  military 5, 27, 35, 59, 73–75, 125
  official 80, 87, 89
  panicked 144
afterlife 194, 219–20
agency 7, 120
Aichach 95
aimlessness 44–46
air
  cleansing of 102, 107
  good air 107
Albrecht, margrave of Brandenburg-Ansbach (r. 1639–1667) 19
Albrecht, Dieter 21*n*.51
Aldringen, Johann von (1588–1634) 13, 147
Alte Veste (Old Fortress) 14, 72
Altenhohenau (Dominican convent) 48*n*.72
Altentrüdingen 172
Altmühl River 29, 53
Altomünster (Brigidine convent) 167
Altötting, Blessed Lady of 60
Amberg
  Rentamt 21, 78, 97*n*.76
Amelang, James S. 24*n*.2, 25*n*.7
Ammerndorf 173–74, 176–77
Ammersee 36 fig. 9, 36–37, 143, 161
Anastasia (Poor Clare nun, Angerkloster, Munich) 51–52, 56
Andechs (Benedictine abbey) 36–37, 54–55, 66, 68, 143, 149, 161, 221
Angerkloster (Poor Clares convent) 39*n*.43, 50, 52, 56–57, 60, 124, 130, 144, 222
Ansbach 18–19, 40
antagonism 147

religious/confessional 56–57, 123, 206, 234
  between soldiers and peasants 69
anxiety 30–33, 35, 37, 39, 45, 110, 169
  and daring 170
  see also dread; fear; fright; horror; terror; trauma
Apianus, Peter (1495–1552) 226
apocalyptic mode 192–93, 220
army/ies 10, 35, 42, 53–55, 67, 69, 77, 110, 112, 120, 134, 141, 145, 158, 179, 210
  allied 113, 159
  Bavaria's 66
  of Bernhard of Saxe-Weimar 58, 65, 147, 166, 199
  Catholic 49*n*.74
  composition of 42
  contributions for 94, 164*n*.139, 209
  and the countryside 39
  criticism of 147–48
  cruelty/brutality of 58, 91, 95, 159
  draft 78*n*.2
  feeding of 14, 61, 74–75, 81–82, 121
  Hessian 166
  imperial 13, 72
  imperial-Bavarian 137
  joining of 55
  lack of payment 162
  marauding 100, 218
  mercenary 77*n*.20, 78*n*.22
  passage 71, 194
  peasant resistance 157–58
  plundering 96
  Protestant Union 19
  and religion 56, 65*n*.129
  routes 27
  size 12, 14, 53
  Spanish 95, 106, 108
  standing 75
  starved 112
  Swedish 14, 65, 72, 76, 102, 204*n*.245
  Swedish-French 73, 96
  of Tilly 11
  of Wallenstein 11, 14
  wintering/quarters 71, 88–89, 194
  see also militias; troops

Artzt, Franciscus   172–73, 175
Asche, Matthias   4n.13, 43n.57
Astrologica   122n.174, 139
Au   45, 96
Augsburg   8, 14, 39n.43, 55–56, 71, 82, 88, 102n.95, 127–30, 136, 144–45, 178, 181, 183, 223
Augsburg Confession (1530)   19, 174, 188
Augsburg diocese   48n.72, 55, 125, 145
Augsburg Recess (1530)   18n.39
Auslauf (leaving)   205–7
Austrian Habsburgs   10
authorities *see* government
autobiographical accounts/narratives/texts/writings   8, 24–26, 28, 133, 160, 177, 180, 199, 202, 219, 222n.299
  communal dimension of   26
  see also ego-documents; (personal) narratives/accounts
autobiography   24–26
  characteristics of   26

Bachmann-Medick, Doris   4n.11, 52n.89
Bahlcke, Joachim   5n.17, 43n.57
Bamberg   13, 31 fig. 7, 32, 38, 57, 60–62, 71, 76, 121, 125–27, 131, 138, 141–42, 154–56, 160, 162–63, 168, 178, 183, 225–27, 229
  bishopric   16, 19
  leadership   154n.110, 156, 178, 180
  prince bishop of   125–27, 155, 185n.195
  and witchcraft   212
banishment   43–44, 58, 189
baptism(s)   110, 166, 206, 220
barbarity   58, 60, 67, 69, 158, 223
Barton, Walter   134n.36–37
Bauerreiss, Romuald   116n.153
Bavaria   5n.16, 7–10, 13–14, 16, 19, 20 fig. 5, 21–23, 27, 49n.78, 56, 58, 67, 70–73, 75–76, 78, 81, 84, 87–89, 91–94, 97, 100, 102, 113–16, 118–19, 121n.172, 125, 128, 132, 144–45, 147–48, 150, 157, 159, 161, 199, 207, 212–14, 225, 230, 233
  Bavarian army   *see* troops
  Bavarian circle   16
  Bavarian countryside   96, 107
  Bavarian Forest   44, 214–16
  invasion of   71

Lower Bavaria (Bavaria-Landshut)   20, 147
  and pestilence   102–9
  Rentämter   20 fig. 5, 21
  Bavarian Swabia   102n.95
  territorial estates   22
  Upper Bavaria (Bavaria-Munich)   20, 35
  witchcraft in   212–13
beggar(s)   72, 83, 91–94, 96, 99
  closet-poor   100
  employed in fortifications   92
  foreign   90–92, 94–96
  sturdy   92
  unworthy   99
begging   46, 54, 92, 97, 99, 150–51, 153, 173, 175
  abolition of   93
  expedition (*terminey*)   149–51, 153
  legitimate   92
  authorities attuned to local needs   100
  ordinances   91–94, 97, 99–100
  prohibition of   92
  regulation of   90, 94
Behringer, Wolfgang   6n.19, 53n.91, 133n.33, 134n.36, 212–13
Beineke, David   121–22
Benedictines   26, 37, 44–45, 49, 54–55, 58, 66, 68–69, 76, 125, 130, 132, 144–48, 151, 154, 161, 164, 179–80, 182, 185, 221, 223
Berlin-Hohenzollern line   19
Beyer-Fröhlich, Marianne   171n.158
Bireley, Robert   21–23
blasphemy   107, 115, 207, 215, 217 *see also* cursing
blessings (magic practice)   211, 214–15, 217
Blickle, Renate   159
Bog, Ingomar   16n.35
Bogen   33
Bohemia/Bohemian   9–10, 135, 214
  Bohemian War (1618–1620)   18
Book of Concord (1580)   19
booty   76, 121
Bötzinger, Martin   177
Bourdieu, Pierre   151n.103
Bouwsma, William J.   28n.13
Brady, Thomas A. Jr.   2n.6

INDEX

Brandenburg   12, 19
Brandenburg-Ansbach   7, 16, 18–19, 41, 46,
    83, 112, 114, 158, 166, 172, 204–5, 208–9
  consistory   172–73, 194, 201, 208
  political dynamics   119
Brandenburg-Bayreuth   126, 183
Brändle, Fabian   24n.1
Brandschatzung/Brandsteuer (fire tax)   75, 79
Braunau   73n.10, 104n.103, 132
bravery   77, 170–71
  see also courage
Brecht, Bertold (1898–1956)   236
Brednich, Rolf W.   135n.39
Breitenfeld   13, 71
  Battle at (17 Sep 1631)   13
Briegel, Manfred   43n.57
broadsheet(s)   8, 14, 133, 135
Brockdorff, Silvia Gräfin von   125n.6
Brownmiller, Susan   41n.49–50, 42n.55
Bücher, Karl   134n.37, 135n.39 and 41, 139n.60
Buchner, Franz X.   149n.95, 165n.145,
    168n.152, 171n.159, 207n.252
Bülow, Johann   61
Burghausen   159
  Rentamt   21, 97n.76, 159
Burke, Peter   217
Burkhardt, Johannes   3–4, 6, 9n.22, 12n.28,
    188n.200

Calvinist(s)/Calvinism   9, 12, 15, 19, 57, 61, 63,
    189n.202, 224, 228
  Lutheran-Calvinist divide   12
  recognition in Peace of Westphalia   15
cannibalism (reports/rumors)   53–54, 56
Capuchin(s)   63–65, 104n.102, 116, 130, 179,
    199–201, 216, 223–25
  Capuchin monastery (Landshut)   38n.41, 65
care   24, 39, 53, 58, 65, 92, 113, 124, 174, 223, 226
  healthcare   100–101, 104–5, 108, 113
  lack of   163
  spiritual care   104, 112, 176
  taking care of the poor   93–94, 96, 99–101
Carolina (1532 law code)   41n.51

catastrophe   1n.2, 109, 146
  see also disaster
catechism class   114–16, 176, 208, 214–15, 217
Catherine of Siena (1347–1380)   229
Catholic(s)/Catholicism   8–10, 12, 15, 18–19,
    22–23, 37–38, 46, 57–59, 61–62, 119,
    126–27, 129, 138, 140–41, 154–55, 158,
    162, 166, 171, 180n.182, 186–87, 195–97,
    201, 203n.243, 205–7, 211–13, 216,
    218–19, 223–26, 228, 230, 233–34
  alliance   13, 15, 225
  armies   49n.74, 147
  Church (Roman)   12, 171n.160, 225
  clergy   41, 46, 57, 176, 205, 216
  mass   168, 205
  newspapers   138, 140
  poor relief   90n.57
Catholic League   9–11, 18, 71, 204n.245
changeability of life   46–47
charity, Christian   94
cheerfulness   222
  see also humor; laughter
censorship   136n.47, 140
(Lake) Chiemsee   35
childbirth, rigors of   204
children   19, 33–34, 40–41, 46, 54, 56n.98,
    66–67, 74, 76, 88, 113, 115–16, 132–33,
    157, 161, 170–71, 181, 200, 202, 204, 215, 223
chores (daily)   26, 48, 51, 220
Chrisman, Miriam Usher   90n.56
Christian IV, king of Denmark (r. 1588–1648)   10–11
Christian, margrave of Brandenburg-
    Bayreuth (also Brandenburg-Kulmbach)
    (r. 1603–1655)   19
chronicle   8, 26, 35, 38–39, 46n.67, 48n.73,
    51n.81, 109n.123, 110n.129, 127n.11,
    134n.38, 160, 201, 205, 228
church
  use as stable   56, 58, 61, 64–65
citizen(s)/citizenry   30, 32n.26, 60–61, 76,
    85, 91, 96, 104, 106, 109, 115, 118, 125,
    156–57, 159, 185, 193, 220, 235
  criticism of their leaders' retreat   121
  and fortifications   72, 74
  and negotiations   80n.29

citizen(s)/citizenry (cont.)
    and protection   40, 75–76, 156
    resistance   67
    ruin/suffering of   56, 58, 62, 88, 108, 130, 193
    sense of abandonment/loss of trust   77, 121
city   12–13, 18, 30, 32, 61, 64–65, 72–76, 82–83, 88, 91–92, 124–30, 132, 140–41, 145, 154, 163, 165, 168–69, 171, 176, 178, 180–81, 184–85, 202, 210, 223–25, 233
    and countryside   8, 27, 91–92, 115, 190
    court city (Munich)   8, 23, 72–73, 96, 105, 109
    dangers of overcrowded cities   40
    defense of   76, 168
    devastation and plundering in and around/ threat of   56, 60, 62, 67, 204, 225
    fortifications   72–73
    expulsion   46
    flights into   39, 43, 48, 50, 63n.123, 76, 91, 95, 130, 144, 163, 185
    flight of leadership   121
    imperial city   16, 18, 21, 71, 85, 110–11, 160n.129, 177, 193
    occupation of   60, 63, 73, 75, 129–30
    and pestilence   92, 103–11
    and poor relief   95–96, 100
    university city   72
civilians   42, 65, 110
civility   156, 230
cleanliness   105, 107, 113
clergy   114, 123, 130, 132, 139, 143, 171, 199, 201, 205, 232
    destitution of   175
    discord between central authorities and local clergy   119
    and epidemics   132
    exploitation by   118
    and afterlife   220
    and catechism class   116
    negotiations of   80n.29
    in protective disguise   32n.23, 46, 165
    religious formation   216, 221
    rural   173
    sparing of   30
    spiritual aids   186, 194–95, 197, 199
    and superstition   214
    and acts of survival   233
Clever, Adolph   226
coexistence   5–6, 201, 206
comet   46n.67, 219
    comet of 1618   219
comfort   44, 67, 114, 125–26, 156, 169, 179, 186, 188–89, 193–95, 197n.224, 198–99, 204, 207, 210, 218, 220, 233
    see also consolation
communication(s)   128, 134, 139, 142, 146
    exchanges   87, 91, 104
    history of   5
    limits of   48
    oral networks   139, 141, 143
    revolution   133
    systems of   134, 139, 141, 148
    see also information; media; news
community   26, 74, 80, 82, 108, 120, 133, 140, 145, 167, 170–71, 178–79, 184, 186, 203, 210, 213, 219n.287, 233
    disruption of   179–80
    monastic/religious   27, 29, 34, 38n.41, 39, 47–48, 50–52, 67, 123–26, 130, 145, 153, 156, 178–81, 183, 189, 201, 207, 223
companionship   123, 179, 225
    see also fellowship
complexity
    of communications system   134, 141
    of dynamics and behaviors   5, 57, 84, 229, 233
    of experiences   27
    of the war's image   233, 235
    political   19–20
    of reality/people's situation   120, 126, 158, 177, 207
    of relationship between witchcraft and war   212
    religious   19, 199, 218
    of space   180
compromise   3, 6, 12,
    Augsburg (1555)   9
concern(s)
    care and concern   24, 47, 56, 58, 120, 127, 130, 153, 156, 187, 223, 226
    financial   96, 118, 132, 164
    health   96, 104, 121

INDEX

political 22, 77, 96, 119, 132, 157–60, 187, 209
practical/physical 2, 39, 72, 75, 77, 164–65
social 21, 89, 91–94, 96, 99–100, 117, 218
spiritual 30, 104, 114–15, 215
Conermann, Klaus 58n.106
confession 2, 5, 9, 40, 46, 56, 63, 65, 172, 186, 206, 210–11, 216, 219, 229
and armies 65n.129
navigation between different confessions 65
and politics 62–63
of sins 105, 112, 200
see also Augsburg Confession
confessional 10, 138, 216, 218–19, 234
antagonism 59, 123, 206, 234
bias/distortion 224, 227
boundaries 218
division 6, 191, 201, 225, 228
identity 188, 190, 210
language 2, 56, 187–88, 192, 229
music 230
trans– 234
violence 56–57
confessionalism 235
conflict, military 1–6, 8–9, 24, 39, 42, 61,70, 75, 102, 123, 143, 152, 186, 188, 190, 201, 215–16, 218, 223, 225, 233, 235–36
conditions of 2
origins of 2
unending 190, 192
victims of 63
views of 4–6, 218, 232
see also Thirty Years' War
confusion 79, 127, 145, 223, 225
connection(s) 62, 148, 154, 178, 185–86, 234
bond 151, 180, 226, 234
between witch hunts and war 212
consolation 119, 122, 186, 192–93, 195, 199, 217–20
see also comfort
contagion 104–8, 111n.134
control of 104, 113
theory 102
see also disease; illness; infection; pestilence

contribution(s) 27, 52–53, 74, 79–81, 88, 90, 94, 98, 118, 151, 154, 164n.139, 209
system 75
Contzen, Adam, S. J. (d. 1636) 22
cooperation 5, 74, 233
coping strategies 141, 232
Cossacks 109n.123
Council of Trent (1545–1563) 45, 171n.160
countryside 8, 27, 71, 89, 91–92, 105, 115, 190, 233
administrators 84
and blasphemy, swearing 115
compliance 209, 213–14, 218
dealing with violence, deprivation 160, 163–64
exhaustion/dearth/suffering 14, 54, 56, 72, 84, 87, 89, 94, 99, 161–62
flights from the 40, 45, 144–45, 185
ministers in 171, 208
and pestilence 104, 107–8, 110, 112–13
and the poor/poor relief 93–94, 97
protection of 163–64
troops marching through/quartering in 69, 83, 86, 88, 96
vulnerability of 72, 81, 93
Coupe, William A. 135n.39
courage 7, 129, 131, 150, 154, 157, 165–68, 170–71, 188, 204, 221
lack of 147–48
see also bravery
couriers (of news) 138, 140, 143
Creveld, Martin van 14n.31
Critchlow, Donald T. 90n.56
Croats 49, 66, 158, 161, 165
Cubero, José-Ramón 41n.49
cultural turns 4
Cunningham, Andrew 90n.56
curiosity 58, 181, 223, 225–26, 235
cursing 114–15, 208
see also blasphemy

Dachau 144
district 167
daily press/literature 32, 133, 136n.47, 137, 139, 146
dancing 114, 117, 208, 214
Dane, Gesa 41n.49
Davies, Mererid Puw 25n.8

Davis, Natalie Z.   90*n*.56
dearth   35, 52–55, 70, 118, 164, 167*n*.149, 221, 232
  see also poverty; scarcity
Defenestration of Prague (second, 23 May 1618)   9
Denmark   11
  intervention of   10
depletion, economic   56
deprivation   51, 53–55, 69, 88, 90, 106, 121, 129, 152, 160, 177, 204, 220
desertion/deserted   51, 98, 143, 168, 199
  of home   44, 98
  sense of   121, 164, 198
  villages   41
desolation   43, 56, 118, 140, 149, 180, 191, 221
  see also destruction; ruin
despair/desperate/desperation   5, 7, 27, 44, 89, 96, 121, 126, 132, 139, 158, 167*n*.149, 172, 174, 176–77, 180, 192, 198, 205, 233
despondency   82, 149, 193
destitution   53–54, 56, 100, 172
destruction   1, 5–6, 24, 27, 29, 32, 37, 47–48, 52–53, 56–57, 60–61, 64–65, 67, 91, 97*n*.76, 117–18, 125, 140, 154, 156, 160, 162, 175, 184, 187, 191–92, 199, 214–15, 218, 223
  narrative of   223, 234
  see also desolation; ruin
determination   78, 148*n*.94, 149, 152–53, 171, 222
devotion   22, 114, 199, 201, 203, 227
  devotional literature   220–21, 226
  devotional pictures   116
diaries   8, 24*n*.2, 25–26, 30, 35, 37*n*.33, 40, 42, 49*n*.77, 147
  diary–style   27, 29
Dienstorfer, Ursula   49–50
Dietwar, Bartolomæus   41, 46, 58, 112, 166–67, 172, 201–6
Dietwar, Regina   202–4
disaster   1, 5, 7, 35, 94, 179, 193, 212, 232–33, 236
  anticipation of   35
  making sense of   186
  natural   137
  see also catastrophe
disease   6, 14, 27, 69, 90–92, 94, 100–102, 105, 109–10, 112*n*.136, 113, 236

control   7, 70, 90, 105, 107, 109, 232
epidemic   5, 7, 40, 69, 100–101, 105–7, 109, 113, 120
  see also contagion; illness; infection; plague; pestilence
disguise   32, 46, 57, 123, 165, 168
disillusionment   67, 86, 121
dislocation   48
disorder   6, 92, 117, 220
disorientation/disoriented   40, 51–52, 234
displacement   6, 53, 232
disruption   6, 37, 50, 69, 98, 109, 140, 145, 180
  of categories   65
Dixon, Scott C.   171*n*.160
donations   99, 149–52, 178
Donaubauer, Stephan   70*n*.1
Donauwörth   14, 48*n*.72, 71, 145
dread   30, 33, 35, 39, 43, 148
  see also fear; fright; horror; terror; trauma
Dressel, Johann, abbot of the Cistercian abbey Ebrach   162–63
Duchy of Bavaria   *see* Bavaria
Duhr, Bernhard   216–17
dynastic
  claims   2
  goals and ambitions   10, 21
  quarreling   2
dysentery   101, 109*n*.125

Early Modern Europe   2, 3 fig.1, 4, 114
Early modern European studies   5
earthworks   91, 92*n*.64
Eberhardt, Otto   43*n*.58
Ebermeier, Werner   49*n*.74
Ebrach, Cistercian abbey   162
Eckert, Edward A.   101*n*.87–88, 102–3*n*.92–96, 109*n*.124
Edict of Restitution (1629)   12, 15, 192–93
education   116, 171, 221
  religious   115–16, 214–17
  educational spectrum   217
  lack of   215
ego–documents   24–25*n*.2, 26
  see also autobiographical accounts; personal accounts; narratives
Eichstätt   29 fig. 6, 29–30, 35, 71, 124–25, 149, 151, 167, 170–71, 178, 185, 196, 207
  bishopric of   16, 19, 71, 149–50, 165, 167–68

INDEX   295

Electoral Bavaria   *see* Bavaria
Electoral Saxony   12
Elend see exile
Elizabeth Stuart (1596–1662)   10*n*.24
Elsmann, Thomas   58*n*.106
emigration   43
emotions   5
   see also despair; dread; fear; fright
empire   *see* Holy Roman Empire
   visions of   3, 12*n*.28
empirical
   newspaper   134*n*.38
   data collection   105
enclosure   44, 125*n*.4, 145, 181–84
Enders, Christoph   86–87
Endres, Rudolf   71*n*.2
enemy   30, 33, 35, 37, 39–40, 42, 47, 49, 54,
   57–59, 62–67, 69, 71, 74, 76–77, 79, 92,
   124, 129, 138, 143, 147–48, 154, 156–57,
   160–63, 167–68, 171, 176, 180–81, 188,
   193, 195–96, 200, 212, 216, 222–23,
   227–28, 230, 235
   accord with the   75
   complex relationship to the   59, 62–63,
   65
   confusing dividing lines between enemy
      and friend   62–63, 65–66, 69, 225
   (religious) dominion over   65
   encounters beyond the friend-enemy
      constellation   66
   negotiations with   89, 154
   occupation   235
   positive aspect about the   59–62, 65–67,
      69, 86, 155, 174
   puzzlement about the   59, 200
   ruthless   58–59
   troops   10, 39, 53, 59, 65–67, 86, 121,
      147–48, 157, 159, 173–74, 180, 204
Engelsing, Rolf   139*n*.59
England   10, 224
epidemics   *see* disease; illness; infection;
   plague; pestilence
Erling   36, 54–55, 67, 144, 164
Europe, ruler of   3
European Order   4
European Powers   3
Evangelicals/evangelical   46, 58*n*.108, 166,
   181–82, 188, 193, 195, 205–6, 216, 230

attendance of sermons elsewhere   206
books   205
cause   158, 188
embattled church   188
position/teachings/truth   187–88, 192
Evelein, Johannes F.   43*n*.57
exile (*Elend*)   5–6, 41, 43–44, 46, 48, 50–52,
   56, 124, , 128, 131, 133, 144–45, 151, 172,
   176, 178, 180, 184–85, 189, 201, 204–5,
   207, 210, 220, 222–23, 236
   Exile of Christ   (*Exul Christi*)   175
   and separation   48
   temporary vs. permanent   43
experience(s)   6–7, 23–25, 28–29, 31–33, 37,
   43, 46, 52–53, 65, 69–70, 76, 80, 177, 185,
   194, 199, 201, 222, 232–33, 235
   access to   24
   brighter   235
   of cognitive dissonance (*Stör-Erfahrung*)
      67
   communal   25, 30, 38*n*.41, 39
   complexity/diversity of   1, 5–6, 27–28,
      228, 234
   of concern and care   24, 223
   everyday   4
   expressing experiences and its limits   28,
      33
   of fear   30, 33, 35, 37, 70, 185
   homogenous   27
   horrific/negative/traumatic/violent   24,
      27–28, 30, 42, 44, 46–50, 53, 55, 57–59,
      67, 70, 167, 170, 180, 185, 188–89, 194,
      198, 201, 203, 212, 232, 235
   inconsistency of   24
   and observation   102
   personal   29–31, 39
   of plundering   86, 185
   processing of   179–80
   of vulnerability   6, 39, 70, 185, 232
   of war   4, 70
extortion(s)   53, 55, 75*n*.16, 183, 232

fairness   21, 100, 117–18
famine   6, 27, 47, 52–53, 55
   see also hunger
fatherland   76–77, 79, 157, 187, 191
fear   6, 28, 30–39, 42–43, 45, 47–48, 50–51,
   57, 69–70, 81, 109–10, 113, 125–29, 143,

fear (cont.)
    155, 163, 165, 168–70, 176, 178, 193, 198, 200, 215, 218, 221–22, 228, 232
    as anticipation   35, 43, 45
    and audacity   170, 221
    as cause for contagion   106
    communal   30, 34, 39
    in communities off the beaten track   35
    depersonalized   39
    effects of   48
    fearless comportment   170, 224
    and flights   124
    of God   28n.13, 38–39n.41
    inability to express fear   30, 51, 169
    individual   30, 33, 35, 38–39
    of peasant uprisings   159
    of rape   42, 127–28
    real or a figure of speech   33
    see also dread; fright; horror; terror; trauma
Fehler, Timothy   90n.56
fellowship   179–80
    see also companionship
Ferdinand (1578–1637)
    archduke   9
    and the Edict of Restitution   12
    emperor (Ferdinand II, r. 1620–1637)   12, 15, 22n.54, 71
Ferdinand (1608–1657)
    king of Hungary (from 1625)   53
    emperor (Ferdinand III, r. 1637–1657)   53
Feuerstein-Herz, Petra   101n.87
Fischer, Helmut   135n.39
Fischer, Michael M. J.   222n.298
Fisher, Alexander   230
Fisher, Jaimey   52n.89
flight(s)/fleeing   7, 35, 37, 39–40, 43–45, 47–48, 66, 76, 78, 81, 85, 94, 96–97, 110, 119, 122–25, 128, 131–33, 144, 157, 164, 179–80, 184–85, 202, 233
    decision for or against   85
    diverse impact   45
    of leaders/administrators   132
    mental and physical suffering during   48
foraging   81, 86, 162, 167
    see also looting; plundering
Forchheim (fortress)   71, 77, 121, 125–26, 160, 174, 185n.195

fortification(s)   40, 70–74, 80, 91–92, 118, 143, 168, 232
    limited resources for   73
    people's unwillingness to build   73
    unfit workers for   74
Fracastoro, Girolamo (c. 1467/78–1553)   102
Franciscans (Reformed/Observant)   63–64, 179, 225
François, Etienne   5n.17
Franconia(n)   7–8, 14, 16, 17 fig. 4, 18–20, 41, 46, 56, 58n.106, 60, 70–72, 76, 81, 89, 91, 94, 100, 102, 109, 113, 138, 150n.99, 155n.113, 160n.129, 170, 177, 193, 217, 233
Franconian circle   16, 19
    political and religious complexity   19
Franz, Günther   6
Frauenholz, Eugen von   14n.29, 77, 78–79n.22-26
Frauenwörth/Frauenchiemsee (Benedictine abbey)   35, 125
Frederick V (elector of the Palatinate, the "Winter King"; 1596–1632)   9–10
Freising   50, 78
    bishopric of   21
(the) French   10, 143
    Catholic side   62
    Swedish/French armies   67, 73, 96
    troops   168, 199
    vision of empire   3
Friedberg(ers)   95, 145
Friedensreiter (heralds of peace)   15, 235
Friesenegger, Maurus   26, 36–37, 53–56, 66–69, 76, 132–33, 143–45, 148, 154, 161, 164, 168n.151, 185, 221–22
fright   30, 32–33, 35, 37–40, 48–50, 77, 106, 124, 126, 128n.19, 129, 163, 166–67, 169, 172, 217, 228
    see also dread; fear; horror; terror; trauma
Frölich, Anna Catharina   51, 60, 145, 147
Fruchtbringende Gesellschaft   58n.106, 121, 234
Frühwald, Wolfgang   43n.57
Fuchs von Dornheim, Johann Georg (r. 1623–1633)   126
Fulbrook, Mary   26n.9–10
fumigate/fumigation   104–5, 113

INDEX   297

funerals 114, 220
    funeral procession 221
Fürleger, Magdalena 49
future 1–2, 74, 77, 203, 210, 236
    belief in a better future 177, 221, 223, 231
    in the beyond 199
    creating a more promising future 40, 185
    here on earth 220
    hope for a brighter future 222, 231
    ruined hopes for the future 55, 68, 210

Gehm, Britta 212
gender 25, 27, 39, 67, 156, 185
gentleness 156
Georg Friedrich, margrave (r. 1556–1603) 19
Germany's political path 4
Gerstenberger, Erhard S. 172n.161
gift/gifting 61, 65, 81, 151–53, 200, 226
Ginzburg, Carlo 210n.262
Glaser, Hubert 21n.51
Glaser, Rüdiger 53n.91
Gleichgewichtsstörung (disequilibrium) 52
Glockenschlag/Feuerzeichen 157
Goethe, Johann Wolfgang 25
(Swedish) Gothic Empire 3, 12n.28
government(al) 7, 16, 21, 23, 27, 70–72, 74, 77–81, 86–87, 90–91, 93–94, 97n.76, 99–104, 106, 108–9, 112–15, 117–22, 127, 132, 134, 139–40, 143, 154–59, 162, 166–67, 171, 175, 187, 206–9, 211, 213, 215, 218, 220, 232–33, 235
    action 7, 69, 70, 77, 80, 87, 94, 121
    breakdown of lord-subject relationship 159, 164
    dynamics between levels of government 84, 87–89, 96, 100, 107
    dynamics between levels of government and subjects 7, 70, 80, 93, 119, 159, 164–65, 209–10, 213
    inability/failure 7, 76, 80, 82–83, 87, 89, 120, 155, 160, 183
    lack of trust in 77, 83, 86–87, 121–23
    lack of understanding between government and subjects 209
    limits of 96, 113
    local/regional 94, 108, 116–18, 142, 157, 160, 213, 233

    protection of 69, 85
Gräfenberg, district 82, 86, 164
Graff, Catharina Bernardina 39n.43
Grass, Günther (1927–2015) 236
gray zones 5
Grel, Colonel 168–70, 226–27
Grell, Ole Peter 90n.56
Greyerz, Kaspar von 5n.17, 24n.1–2, 25n.4, 26
Grimmelshausen, Hans J. C. von (1621–1676) 236
Grindl, Constantia 51, 222
Großhabersdorf 173
Großner, Rudolf 166n.146
Groth, Otto 135n.39
Grotius, Hugo (1583–1645) 41n.50
Grünbaum, Max 134n.36
guidance 80, 82, 89, 117–18, 121, 128–29, 201, 204
    spiritual 175, 178, 201, 204
Gustavus Adolphus, king of Sweden (r. 1611–1632) 12–14, 18, 27, 52, 56n.100, 70–73, 75, 86, 88, 126–28, 130n.24, 137, 167, 193, 212
    admiration of 66
    civilized behavior of 60, 67, 167, 230
    motives for entering the war 12
    and news/papers 135, 140
    path of his army 13 fig. 3, 14
    as religious hero 14

Habersdorf 177
Habsburg(s) 2, 9, 75
    Austrian Habsburgs 10
    Spanish Habsburgs 10
    vision of empire 3
Hacke, Daniela 25n.8
Hagendorf, Peter 42, 47
Haidenbucher, Maria Magdalena 35, 48
Haidhausen 96
Haller, Bertolds Freiherr von 166n.146
Hambrecht, Rainer 220n.294
Hamburg 5, 140n.64
Harms, Wolfgang 135n.39
harvest(ing) 55, 164, 201, 208–10
    bad harvests 52, 90, 211
    plentiful harvests 55, 222
    and weather patterns 53n.91
    without equipment 55

Haude, Sigrun   21*n*.51, 117*n*.157, 142*n*.69
healthcare   101
    system   100
Heberle, Hans   40
Head, Randolph C.   134*n*.35
head– or Hungarian sickness   110
Heidelberg   10
Heiliggrab/Heiligengrab (Dominican convent)   31, 60, 125–27, 154–56, 168, 170, 178, 180–81, 183–85, 228–30
Heimat   44–45, 145, 180, 185–86
Heimatprinzip   92
Heimbucher, Max   63*n*.121
Heimers, Manfred   103*n*.97
helpless(ness)   7, 46, 83, 87, 121
Hengsberger, Walburgia   222
Herlicius, David   101*n*.89
Hersbruck, district   86–87
Herz, Andreas   121*n*.173
Heydenreuter, Reinhard   21*n*.48 and 51, 23, 75*n*.15, 97*n*.76, 213–14
Heymach, F.   41*n*.47
Hirschmann, Gerhard   214*n*.271
historical anthropology   4
history of everyday life   4
Hitzigrath, Heinrich   134*n*.36
Hofmann, Hanns H.   72*n*.4–5
Hohenwart (Benedictine convent)   48–50, 80, 143
Holy Roman Empire   6, 8–10, 11 fig. 2, 12, 15–16, 18, 21–22, 88, 111, 190
    coexistence in   5
    destruction of   191
    fragmentation of   2
    future of   1–2
    the war's impact on   6
Holzen (Benedictine convent)   48*n*.72, 125, 145, 182, 223
Holzfurtner, Ludwig   162*n*.135
home(s)   5, 33, 43–46, 49–52, 55, 78–79, 81, 88, 92, 117, 119, 124–25, 131, 144–45, 150, 152–53, 159, 161, 166, 170, 174, 176, 180–81, 184–86, 205, 207, 222, 230
homelessness   6, 44, 91–92, 232
homesickness   43*n*.58
honor   30, 41–42, 58, 67, 77, 127–28, 138, 170, 181, 195–96

honorable rules of engagement   65
    see also rape; violence, sexual
hope   43, 66–67, 70, 81, 83, 85, 114–15, 117, 126, 128–29, 133, 139, 173–76, 185, 188, 190, 193, 196, 199–200, 221–23, 231, 233
    despair/loss of   44, 180
    for the future   210
    in God   153, 199, 223
    thwarted/vain   37, 67
    for peace   89, 190, 222–23
Hörger, Hermann   217*n*.284
Horn, Gustav, count (1592–1657)   13, 15
horror   1, 28, 30, 34–35, 125, 217
    see also anxiety; fear; fright; terror; trauma
horse(s)   52–56, 62, 106, 144, 160–61, 163–65, 183
Höser, Veit (Vitus)   26, 33–35, 37–38, 44–46, 54, 57–60, 66, 69, 76, 130–32, 144, 146–47, 179–80, 221
hospital   99
    pest hospital   105
hostage, taking of   40, 73, 108, 123, 127, 131, 173, 224
humanist(s)   58, 234
Hümmer, Friedrich K.   32*n*.22 and 24–26, 42*n*.56, 61*n*.112–13, 126*n*.8–9, 127*n*.10–12, 142*n*.67–68, 154–56*n*.111–17, 160–61*n*.130–31, 163*n*.138, 169–70*n*.153–57, 181*n*.184, 183–84*n*.189–91, 223*n*.301, 227–30*n*.311–17 and 320
humor(ous)   37, 221–22, 231
    see also cheerful(ness); laugh(ter)
humors (of the body)   101–2*n*.90
Hungarian (head–) sickness   110
hunger   6, 15, 40, 52, 54–56, 68–69, 100, 101*n*.89, 107, 110, 112, 129, 140, 202, 204
    see also famine
Hutcheon, Linda   222*n*.298
Hüttner, Franz   162–63*n*.136–37

identity   52, 165, 180–81
    confessional/religious   188, 190, 210
ignorance   216–17
    of commoners   216
    feigning   107
illness   78, 100, 101, 103, 106, 210–11
    see also contagion; disease; infection; pestilence; plague

INDEX

Imhof, Arthur E.   30*n*.21
Imhoff, Christoph von   91*n*.62, 193*n*.216
Immler, Gerd   21*n*.50–51
imperial circles   16
individual   25, 27–28, 39, 56, 81, 102, 157, 160, 170, 178, 180, 199, 214, 217, 222, 225, 234
   attention to the   99–100
infant mortality   202
infantry (of lansquenets)   75
infection   95, 100–106, 108–10
   see also contagion; disease; pestilence; plague
inflation   6, 10, 27, 52–53, 91, 93, 100, 101*n*.89, 170, 204
   hyper– (*Kipper– und Wipperzeit*, Tipper and See-Saw period) 10, 53*n*.90, 93
   see also price increase
informants, system of   105
information/informed   84, 103, 105, 106*n*.109, 107, 119*n*.168, 133–46, 148–49, 177, 179, 201, 208*n*.256, 225
   uncertainty of   142
   psychological importance   146
   reliable   133, 142, 144, 148
   transmission of   135, 139
   see also communication
ingenuity   5, 82, 150–51, 153–54, 165, 170–71, 233
Ingolstadt   14, 30, 48, 71–72, 124, 150–51, 180
   fortification of   71–72
   University of   213, 226*n*.309
(River) Inn   73*n*.10, 88, 159
Inn Viertel   20
Innsbruck   150
instability   6, 43, 46, 70, 232
   see also uncertainty
(River) Isar   67, 159

James I, King of England (r. 1603–1625)   10*n*.24
Jancke, Gabriele   25–26*n*.8–9
Jarzebowski, Claudia   33
Jeremiah (prophet)   194
Jesuit(s)   22*n*.54, 38, 57–58, 61–63, 104*n*.102, 116, 121, 150, 216–17, 225–26, 228
   confessor   22
   prejudice against   57

Jesuit College (Bamberg)   38, 57, 61, 76, 131, 225, 228
Jew   219
   Jewish school   227
Joachim Ernst, margrave of Brandenburg-Ansbach (r. 1603–1625)   19
Joachim Friedrich, elector of Brandenburg (r. 1598–1608)   19
Johann Sigismund, elector of Brandenburg (r. 1608–1619 and duke of Prussia from 1618)   19
John George I, elector of Saxony (r. 1611–1656)   15
jubilee
   celebration   9, 188*n*.200
   sermon   188, 190
judgment   58, 68, 146–47, 149
   God's   132, 192, 194, 196–98
Junius, Johannes   32
Junius, Maria Anna   26, 31–33, 38, 42, 60–61, 80, 125–27, 141, 154–56, 163, 168–70, 183, 225–30
justice   80, 117–18
   administration of   21, 97*n*.76, 187
   local   21, 117
   mercy before divine justice   192
   sense/understanding of   116
   social   21
Jütte, Robert   90*n*.56–58

Kaiser, Michael   70*n*.1
Kaplan, Benjamin J.   5*n*.17
Kästner, Alexander   30*n*.20
Kitzingen   19*n*.43, 41, 46, 47 fig. 10, 59*n*.108, 112, 166, 172, 201–2, 204–6
Knauer, Martin   5*n*.15
Koopmann, Helmut   43*n*.57
Kormann, Eva   25*n*.8, 171*n*.158
Kratz, Wilhelm   226*n*.310
Kraus, Andreas   21*n*.51, 70*n*.1
Krauss, Marita   43*n*.57
Kreitzer, Beth   195*n*.219
Kronach (fortress)   71, 141
Kroner, Michael   41*n*.46, 143*n*.73
Krug, Tobias   173–77
Krusenstjern, Benigna von   4–5, 25*n*.2, 27*n*.12, 220*n*.293

299

Kurz, Maria, prioress of Augsburg's Dominican Katharinenkloster   127–29, 181–83

Labouvie, Eva   211n.263, 216n.279
laity
   and afterlife   220
   reliance on religion   199, 205
   spiritual aids for   186, 195, 199
Landesdefension (territorial defense system)   77–79
Landshut   38n.41, 48, 59, 63, 65, 125, 130–31, 147, 179, 199, 223–25
   Rentamt   21, 97n.76
   War of Succession (1504–1505)   20
language   33, 37, 58n.106, 137, 234
   confessional   2
   language society (German)   58n.106, 234
   limits of   28
   mystical   198–99
   power of   28
Lauf, district   85–86
laughter   221–22, 227, 231
   see also cheerful(ness); humor
law(s)   83, 187, 221, 234
   Carolina   41n.51
   international   4
   law and order   21, 97n.76
   natural law   236
   re. poor relief   94, 100
   sumptuary   118
   re. superstition   213
   of war   86, 162
(River) Lech   14, 20, 67, 71
Lehmann, Hartmut   53n.91
Liebhart, Wilhelm   167n.149
Lindberg, Carter   90n.56
Lindemann, Margot   135n.42, 136n.44, 138n.57, 140–41n.62–65
Lindemann, Mary   5n.17
literacy   27, 139n.59
"Little Ice Age"   53, 91, 212
Loetz, Francisca   41n.49
Lohausen, Wilhelm von (Wilhelm von Kalcheim/Kalkum)   57–58, 61, 154–55, 225–26, 229, 234
looting   35, 148, 165
   see also foraging; plundering

loss   6, 14, 27, 89, 103, 130, 149, 153, 194, 212, 221, 231–32
   of children   204
   of confidence/trust   7, 77, 86–87, 89, 122, 233
   of honor (rape)   41, 127
   of life   43, 112
   material   7, 41, 69, 194, 232
   of sanity   30
   military loss   15
   see also population loss
Louthan, Howard   5n.17
Lower Saxony   10, 137
Luebke, David   5n.17, 206
Lüdtke, Alf   4n.11
Luria, Keith P.   5n.17
Luther, Martin (1483–1546)   9n.22, 132n.30, 147n.86, 188–89, 192, 196
Lutheran(s)/Lutheranism   9, 12, 15, 18–19, 46, 129, 141, 162, 175n.169, 186n.196, 189, 192, 195–96, 201, 204–7, 226–27, 230
   clergy   41, 46, 58n.108, 201
   jubilee celebration   9
   Lutheran–Calvinist divide   12
   see also Protestants
Lützen
   Batlle of (16 Nov 1632)   14–15

Magdeburg
   destruction of   12, 48
magic   211, 213–15, 217–19
   power   120
   practice/rituals   186, 207, 211–13, 215–18
   reliance on   218
   spectrum of   211, 215
   and witchcraft   211
Mandlmayr, Martin   75n.14
manliness   156
marauder(s)   39, 66, 80, 160–62, 164–65, 170, 210
Mariastein (Augustinian convent)   29, 31, 35, 47, 54, 126, 130, 149, 151–53, 167–68, 178, 196–97, 200, 220
Marie von Brandenburg-Bayreuth, margravine (1579–1649)   126, 183
Marschke, Benjamin   2n.6
Mary Magdalene   197n.224
material culture and religion   210

INDEX

Mathäser, Willibald   37n.33
Maximilian of Bavaria (duke 1598–1623;
    elector 1623–1651)   10, 13–14, 16, 21–23,
    71–76, 78–79, 87–89, 92–97, 99–100,
    104–9, 114–18, 120–21, 128, 132, 142,
    144–45, 147–48, 150n.99, 154, 157, 159,
    162n.135, 167n.149, 185, 207, 213, 215–17,
    225, 233
  objectives   22
  privy council   159, 213
  relationship with Munich's councilors
    74, 95–96, 105
  relationship with territorial administrators
    88, 116
  relocation   132
  role as *Landesvater*   21
  system of informants   105
  and Wallenstein   147
Mayer, M. Stephan   41
media   5, 133–35, 139–40
  see also communication; information;
    news; newspaper
mediator(s)/mediating   81, 84, 197, 210
  Christ   187
  Mary (mediatrix)   196
Medick, Hans   2n.6, 4–5
melancholy   30, 41
Melanchthon, Philip (1497–1560)   19
Melchior von Straubing   38n.41, 63–65, 130,
    179, 200–201, 223–25, 229
memory
  body's   33
  German   1
Mennel, Barbara   52n.89
Menocchio   210
mental
  boundaries   234
  comfort   233
  preparation/resources/strategies   123,
    141, 146, 186, 194, 207, 221
  consequences/costs/suffering   48, 153,
    236
  world   204
merchants   16, 30n.16, 82, 135, 139–40, 143,
    154, 234
mercy, divine   41, 125–27, 174, 187, 191–92,
    194–95, 197, 199, 203–4

Mercy, Franz von   84
  regiment   83
Meßrelationen (reports ahead of fairs)
    135n.42, 146–47
Metzger, Amrosius   193
Meumann, Markus   219n.291
miasma theory   101–102
micro history   4
Midelfort, H. C. Erik   212
migration   1, 43n.57, 90, 94, 100
military leaders   4, 61, 75–76, 80, 121, 146–47,
    192, 225, 229
  comments on   59, 146–49
military strategies   4
militia   77–79
  civic/town   77–79, 157
  rural/country   37, 75, 77–79, 157, 163
minister(s)   27, 40–41, 46, 50, 57, 58n.108,
    97n.76, 111–16, 118–19, 143, 166, 171–78,
    185–86, 194–95, 201, 204–5, 208–10, 214,
    216, 218, 223
  and their congregations   171–72
  as hostages   40
  lot of ministers   40
  petitions/supplications of   172–77
  protective measures during plague   113
  serving several parishes   173–77
  solitary figures   171–72
  superiors' expectations of   40
  treatment of   41
  see also pastor(s)
misery   4, 32, 35, 37, 40, 43–44, 46, 52, 56,
    68–69, 95, 106, 128n.19, 129, 132, 146,
    170, 174, 179, 191–93, 195–96, 198–99,
    205, 209, 219–20, 222
  going into misery (*ins Elend gehen*)
    43–44, 180
mockery   83
  religious   64
Modern Europe
  evolution of   1
monks   27–28, 36–37, 39, 43, 50, 54, 62, 123,
    145–46, 152, 161n.134, 165, 221, 225
  see also (the) religious/*religiosi*
mortality   102, 109–10
  crisis   102–3, 108
  infant   202

Mortimer, Geoff   2*n*.5, 4
movement
   religious   142*n*.69, 197
   of people   6–7, 48, 185, 206, 223, 225, 234–35
   see also troop movement
Mummenhoff, Ernst   14*n*.30, 74*n*.12, 110*n*.131
Münch, Paul   24*n*.1
Munich   8, 14, 20, 23, 36–37, 39*n*.43, 48–52, 54–57, 60, 65, 71–75, 88, 94–98, 95 fig. 12, 106–9, 117, 120–21, 124–25, 128, 132–33, 140–42, 144–45, 147, 154, 167, 185, 213, 215, 222, 230
   city council   23, 72–73, 92–93, 95, 105, 107, 132
   city councilors' relationship to Maximilian   74, 95–96, 105
   countryside   56
   court officers   87
   fortifications   72–74
   hostages   73
   and poverty   97
   and pestilence   103–9
   population   103
   Rentamt   21, 97–98
Münster   15
   bishopric of   137
   Treaty of Münster (1648)   4, 15
music   221
   as common denominator   230
   religious   229–31
   secular   114
mystical/mysticism
   bridal   198
   language   198–99
   literature   221
   resources   197

Naphy, William G.   28*n*.13
narrative(s)   27–28, 33, 38–39, 43, 46, 51, 54, 56, 59, 65–66, 126, 130, 143, 148–49, 162, 177, 204–5, 223, 225–26, 232
   and collective experiences   39
   of conflict   5, 59, 223
   disruption of neat categories   65, 223
   historical   193
   personal   24–26, 39
neediness   172, 177
   spectrum of   96

needs   22, 69, 93–94, 112, 120, 148, 175, 220, 232
   spiritual   104*n*.102, 112, 177, 210
negotiation(s)   6–7, 14, 30, 70, 80, 89, 153, 156, 165, 178, 181, 190, 224, 233–34
   peace   15, 37, 190, 192, 235
networks   27, 135–36, 143, 151, 178, 178, 186, 233–34
   monastic   123, 151, 178
   oral   139, 141, 143
Neuegg, Agnes von (abbess of Holzen)   48*n*.72, 223
neutrality   12, 15*n*.33, 18*n*.40
Newe Zeitungen   32, 135
news   32, 35, 37, 42, 50, 53, 126, 128, 133–49, 179, 214
   agents   140
   confirmation of   144
   couriers   138, 140, 143
   psychological importance of   145–46
   scouts   143–44
   uncertainty of   142–43, 145
newspaper   8, 133–41, 146
   foundations (Swedish)   140
   handwritten   134–36, 139–41
   international reach   136
   printed 133–41, 146
   weekly   133–38, 140–41, 146
   writers (*Novellanten*)   135, 137–38, 141
Niederschönenfeld, Cistercian convent   125
Niefanger, Dirk   219*n*.291
Nolting, Uta   30*n*.16, 32*n*.22
Nördlingen   13
   battle of (1634)   15, 19*n*.45, 53
normative year (*Normaljahr*)   12, 15
nun(s)   26–30, 32–33, 35, 39, 42–43, 47–54, 57, 60–62, 80, 123–30, 141, 145, 149–56, 167–71, 178, 180–85, 197–99, 220, 226–30
   see also (the) religious/*religiosi*
Nuremberg   7–8, 13–14, 16, 18, 29, 31, 33, 40, 46, 71–73, 75, 81–83, 85 fig. 11, 86–87, 89, 91–92, 94, 104, 109–112, 114–15, 120, 128, 132, 140, 143, 157–58, 160*n*.129, 165, 172, 176–77, 187, 190, 193, 208, 219–20, 235
   authorities of   16, 72–73, 82–83, 85–87, 89, 91–92, 109, 114–15, 157–58, 164–65, 190, 208

INDEX 303

deaths and births   111 fig. 13
finances   82
fortifications of   40, 71–72
governing body   16
neutrality   18
population   18n.37
territory of   16, 18–19, 75n.13, 81, 85, 88, 91, 164, 208, 213, 214n.271, 216, 218

Oberalteich (Benedictine abbey)   33, 44, 54, 76, 131, 149, 179
Oettinger, Rebecca Wagner   230
officer(s)
  civic   91, 93, 97n.76, 132, 164
  establishment of new administrative officers   90
  central administrators   87, 105
  local administrators   21, 98–99, 116, 120
  military   53–54, 60–63, 66, 68, 77, 80–81, 106, 141–42, 154–55, 157–58, 183, 221, 223–30
Old Bavaria *see* Bavaria
Opel, Julius O.   136n.43 and 45–46, 137n.48, 138n.54, 141n.65
(feeling) orphaned   51, 125–26
Ortenburg, county of   21
Osnabrück   15
  Treaty of Osnabrück   4, 15
"the other"   231
  curiosity about   225
  as human being   225
  greater knowledge and appreciation of   223, 225, 229 235
Otto, Elias   176–77
Ottoman Empire   75n.15
Oxenstierna, Axel (1583–1654)   14

Paas, John R.   135n.39
the Palatinate (Rhenish or Lower)   9–10, 140, 212
pamphlets   8, 133, 135
  health   111n.134
panic(ked)   35, 39, 85, 96, 101, 103, 110, 120, 144, 144
parishes
  combining of   173–77
Parker, Charles H.   90n.56
Parker, Geoffrey   53n.91

Parrott, David   14n.31, 77n.20
Pastenaci, Stephan   25n.6
pastor(s)   40–41, 46, 55, 57–58, 112, 166, 171–72, 175, 186, 194, 204, 208, 210, 214–16
  dearth of   55
  see also minister(s)
patience   89, 222
  advice to be patient   80, 83, 121
  calls for   87
  lack of   108, 195–96, 223
  patient in faith   189, 193
peace   4, 16, 22, 63, 89, 187, 190–92, 212, 222–23, 228–29, 234
  of the dead   58
  heralds of peace   15, 235
  peace negotiations   15, 37, 190, 192, 235
  quiet/tranquility   185, 191, 35, 44–45, 130, 156, 174, 203
Peace of Augsburg (1555)   2, 9, 12, 15
  and the Reformed   189n.202
  relationship to Thirty Years' War   2, 15
Peace of Lübeck (1629)   11
Peace of Passau (1552)   12
Peace of Prague (1635)   12, 15, 27, 122, 223
Peace of Westphalia (1648)   1–4, 10n.25, 15–16, 235–36
  assessment and significance   3–4
  legal dimensions   4
  negotiations   15
peasant(s)   30, 37, 40, 47, 53–56, 68–69, 78–81, 83, 86, 91, 95–97, 134, 145, 157–65, 171–72, 177, 186, 208–10, 215, 232
  aids for   81
  antagonism between peasants and soldiers   69, 160
  and territorial defense   77–79
  destitution among   53–56, 68, 95, 106, 108
  dynamics within peasant communities   164–65
  fear of peasant uprising   159
  exposed/vulnerable   40, 55
  and flights   39–40, 81, 96–97, 108, 123, 133, 144, 157, 161, 185
  and fortifications   72, 74
  life and work situation   208–10
  loss of faith in authorities' protection   87

peasant(s) (cont.)
  negotiations with authorities   164–65, 210
  pooling resources   40, 164
  peasant rebellion (1625–26 in Upper Austria/Bavaria)   159
  peasant rebellion (1633–34 in Bavaria)   159
  Peasants' War (1524–1526)   159
  resisting mandates   120, 210
  striking back/resistance   157–63
perseverance   40, 131, 149, 179
personal accounts   24–27
  communal context/dimension of   25–27
  see also autobiographical accounts/writings; ego–documents; (personal) narratives
personality   21, 25, 80, 88, 177, 221, 233–34
  role of   16, 27, 62
  and structures   2
personnel   104, 109, 111–13, 217
  reliable   91, 94
pestilence   5n.16, 27, 40, 55, 73n.10, 90, 101–5, 109–12, 120, 132, 197, 202, 220
  causes   101
  control of   101, 103
  theories   101–2
  see also contagion; disease; illness; infection
Peters, Jan   42n.54, 47n.69
petition(s)   80, 88, 151, 172–73, 176–77, 191
  see also supplication(s)
Pfeffer, Maria   135n.40
Pfister, Christian   6n.19, 21n.51
Philip II, king of Spain (r. 1556–1598)   21
Piccolomini, Octavio, regiment   82
Pietsch, Andreas   5n.17
pietism   235
piety   37, 114, 120, 217n.284, 230
plague (epidemics)   15, 101–2, 104–5, 107, 109, 112–13, 118, 121, 167, 171, 220
  activity   102
  Black Death (Great Plague, 1348–1350)   102
  common perceptions of   109
  economic impact   110
  origin   106
  resistance to   103
  zones   102
plundering   27, 35, 46, 48, 58, 73, 80–82, 85–86, 96, 158–62, 164, 166–67, 172, 176, 183, 190, 193, 204, 232
  see also looting; foraging
Poles (also *Polacken*, derogatory)   66, 143
Polish–Swedish War (1626–1629)   12n.28
political dynamics
  between government and subjects   7
  between levels of government   7
politics   18n.40, 134n.38
  confessional identity politics   190
  discourses on   225, 228, 230
  dynastic   2, 10, 21
  and religion/confession   2, 62
Pollizeywesen (local economy)   21, 97n.76, 117–18
Pomerania   12, 102
Poor Clares (Munich)   39n.43, 50, 56, 124, 125n.4, 130, 144–45, 147, 222
poor relief   5, 7, 69–70, 91–94, 97, 100, 176, 232
  history of   90
  legislation   94, 100
  limits of   96
  system   91, 94, 177
Popkin, Jeremy D.   146n.84
Poppenreuth   164, 204
population loss   1, 71, 110–12
Porzelt, Carolin   16–18n.35–37, 101n.90, 109n.124–25, 111–12n.132–36
positive
  aspects of the enemy   58–60, 183n.190
  assessment of Germany's development   4
  encounters   5, 7, 59, 221, 223, 234–35
  energy/thinking   221, 231
  results (tenuous)   153
Roßtal   176
postal system/courier   136, 138
poverty   5, 7, 52–53, 55, 68–70, 90–94, 100, 106, 113, 120–21, 177, 185, 204, 232, 236
  cyclical factors   53
  driven by war   53
  see also dearth; scarcity
practical
  concerns   2, 56, 91, 99, 107, 113–14, 119, 140, 145, 148, 165, 235
  decisions   141, 233

INDEX

resources 7, 64, 105, 194, 226
measures/strategies 123, 186, 221
practice(s) 75n.16, 77, 120, 139n.60, 151, 164, 186
   chivalric 65
   Christian 192–93
   common 64, 92, 106, 137
   around the dead/burial 110, 112
   of *Auslauf* 206–7
   of gifting 151–52
   magic 186, 207, 211–18
   orthodox 211
   religious 114, 120, 209, 218, 220
   social 114, 218
   traditional 116
   uniform 209
pragmatism 5, 149, 153–54, 233
Prague 10, 23, 201
   castle 9
   Defenestration of 9
   Peace of (30 May 1635) 12, 15, 27, 122, 223
Prak, Maarten 90n.56
prayer 22, 45, 52, 107, 112–14, 119, 186–87, 189–93, 196–98, 200, 209, 218, 220
   books, Catholic 196, 197n.224
   days of 219
   emotional 192
   hours 114, 119, 168, 207–9, 218
   meetings 119
   political 187, 190–91
pre-Reformation era 218, 229
price increase 40, 52
see also inflation
procession(s) 107
   funeral 110, 112, 221
propaganda 2, 12, 65, 134, 140, 230
protection 49, 57, 62, 69–71, 74–75, 79–80, 84–87, 100, 119, 128, 155–61, 165, 211, 218–19
   of enclosure 183–84
   God's 129, 193, 224
   governmental 7, 69–70, 85–87, 89, 121, 157, 159–60, 183, 232–33
   lack of 6–7, 31, 41, 51, 69, 76–77, 101, 121, 147, 159–60, 167
   military 63, 74–75, 79, 84, 147, 163
   physical 7, 31, 40, 69, 71, 73, 121, 144

   of sacred objects 120, 219
   spiritual 70, 218–19
   task of government 70
   of women 41, 51, 123–24, 183–84
Protestant(s)/Protestantism 8, 10, 12–15, 18–19, 22–23, 37, 41, 57n.106, 61–62, 71, 75, 90, 126–27, 138, 140, 147, 154–55, 166–67, 171, 183, 187, 193, 196–97, 206–8, 211, 213, 216, 218–19, 225–26, 228, 230, 233–34
   clergy 166, 171, 216, 230
   coalition 15, 49n.74
   estates 12
   Union 9–10, 15, 18–19, 126
   see also Lutherans; Reformed
providence 62
Pullan, Brian 90n.56
punishment 87, 94, 96, 115, 117, 166–67, 206, 213
   the war as God's punishment 38n.41, 112, 114–15, 117, 187, 190, 192, 195–96, 199, 201, 204, 207–10
   of women 141–42
Püttrich convent (tertiary, Munich) 49n.76, 124, 125n.4
puzzlement 59, 61, 64, 200, 224

quarantine 104, 108, 112, 233
   violation of 107–8, 110, 113, 120, 233

Rain am Lech 71
   Battle of (1632) 14
rape 41–43, 127–28
   trauma of 42
   and virginity 42
   see also honor; violence, sexual
readership 134, 136–41, 146
reading
   circles 139
   the situation 62, 154, 165
realism 83, 131, 146, 149, 182, 208
Rebdorf
   Augustinian canons of 29, 124
Redlich, Fritz 75n.16
Rebel, Hermann 159n.125
Reformation 1, 9, 18, 181, 206
   centennial 9n.22
   corps of ministers 216

Reformation (cont.)
　　and communications revolution　133,
　　　135, 140
　　and music　230
　　and poor relief　90–91
　　Counter Reformation　21, 230
　　and superstition　211
Reformed (Religion) *see* Calvinist(s)/
　　Calvinism
refuge　30, 38, 40, 47–48, 54, 63, 81, 96,
　　124–26, 128, 155, 161, 178–79, 182,
　　185n.195, 188, 230
refugee(s)　35, 40, 45, 48, 50, 58, 68, 96–97,
　　99, 103n.97, 106, 111, 113, 125, 131–33, 145,
　　180
Regen　215
Regensburg　21, 45, 138, 146–47, 150
　　bishop of　216–17
　　bishopric of　21
　　diocese　33, 34 fig. 8, 37, 54, 125
Reicke, Emil　16n.35, 18n.40, 71n.2, 72n.5,
　　82n.41
Reischl, Georg A.　48n.73
religion　21, 46, 114, 206, 208, 218, 221, 226
　　(religious/confessional) antagonism
　　　56–57, 123, 206, 234
　　as consolation　220
　　cuius regio eius religio　9
　　discourse on　228, 230
　　importance/strength of　152, 207
　　Lutheran　9
　　material culture and religion　210
　　multi-faceted landscape of　186, 201, 218
　　official/orthodox religion　210, 218–19
　　people's attitudes toward　208
　　and politics　2
　　Reformed/Calvinist　9
　　role in coping with the war　186, 199, 205,
　　　207, 218–19, 233
　　Roman Catholic　9, 76, 216
　　and superstition　217
　　teaching the right kind of　216
　　and the war　2, 63, 186, 235
religious objects
　　violence against　56, 58
religious orders, members of　27, 43, 57, 63,
　　80n.29, 139, 143, 155, 178, 196, 225, 232
　　assessing military leaders　146–49
　　dissolution　224
　　networks　178
　　question of flight　123
　　role in Bavaria under Maximilian　116
　　The religious/*religiosi*　27, 31, 35, 38–39,
　　　45–47, 57–58, 63, 123–24, 129, 131,
　　　143–46, 154, 160, 163, 169, 178, 180, 200,
　　　224–25, 228, 232
Rentmeister　21, 78, 97–100, 117–18
　　responsibilities　21
repentance　107, 112, 114, 187, 191, 197n.224,
　　208, 210, 219
　　lack of　190
resilience　5, 9, 149, 171, 234, 236
resistance　172, 184
　　to government initiatives　115, 120, 209
　　peasant　158
　　to plague　103
　　to providing information　119n.168
resourcefulness　62, 150, 153, 170
resources　6, 123, 232–33
　　financial　35, 73–74, 123, 133, 149, 178
　　lack of　71, 82–83, 91, 93
　　mental　186, 221
　　mystical　197
　　pooling resources　40
　　practical　7
　　religious/spiritual/theological　7, 186,
　　　199–200, 211, 217
restlessness　34, 45, 130
rhetoric(al)　9, 126
　　skill　26, 33, 59
Richelieu, Armand-Jean du Plessis de
　　(1585–1642)　15
riders/horsemen/cavalry(men)　44, 49n.74,
　　50, 61, 66–67, 75, 77–78, 81, 83, 144, 158,
　　160–61, 165, 184
Ridler convent (tertiary, Munich)　124,
　　125n.4
rituals
　　religious　26
　　mundane chores　26
robbery/robbed　38, 40, 45–46, 66–67, 76,
　　81, 83, 129, 154, 161–62, 166, 170, 190–91,
　　202
　　riders as robbers　66
Roberts, Penny　28n.13
Roeck, Bernd　70n.1, 127n.13, 128n.15

INDEX

Rothenburg (ob der Tauber) 16, 193–94
Rublack, Ulinka 26n.9–10
Rudersdorf, Manfred 19n.42–44
Ruff, Julius R. 41n.49
Rüger, Willi 91n.60
ruin 1, 5, 24, 27, 37, 49, 56, 64–65, 82, 86–88, 94–95, 97, 99, 106, 118, 138n.55, 144, 148, 149, 167, 173, 175–77, 207, 210, 212, 234
  see also desolation; destruction
Rystad, Göran 134n.36

Sachße, Christoph 90n.56–57, 91n.59
sacred objects/treasure 58, 119, 128n.18
  protective powers of 119–20, 219
sacrilege 66
safety 7, 31, 35, 40, 45, 49–50, 62–63, 65, 70, 72, 74–75, 77, 121–22, 124, 126, 131, 133, 164, 167, 184–85, 201
Safley, Thomas M. 6n.17, 90n.56
St. Augustine (354–430) 196
St. Katharina (Dominican convent, Augsburg) 39n.43, 127, 129–30, 178, 181
St. Mary 60, 195
St. Walburg (Benedictine convent, Eichstätt) 30, 151, 220
St. Willibaldsburg (St. Willibald's Castle) 30, 47, 124, 168, 185
Salva Guardia 50, 63, 68, 79–80, 86, 126, 154, 161, 163–64, 182, 184
Salzburg 37n.33, 150, 223
sanity 30
  place of 156
savagery 66
Saxe-Weimar, Bernhard of, duke (1604–1639) 15, 58, 60, 76, 130, 154–55, 200, 224, 226, 228, 229–30
  army of (*Weimarers*) 44, 58, 65, 66, 147, 166, 199
scarcity 53, 165, 207
  see also dearth; poverty
Schanzgeld 74
Scheibelberger von Wielbronn, Johann 60–61, 155n.113
Schiewek, Ingrid 25n.5
Schiller, Johann (1759–1805) 236
Schilling, Michael 135n.40
Schindling, Anton 4n.13
Schlögel, Karl 52n.89

Schmalkaldic League 18
Schmalkaldic War (1546–1547) 212
Schmidt, Jürgen 212, 213n.268
Schock, Flemming 134n.35
Schönauer, Tobias 72n.6
Schorn-Schütte, Luise 171n.160
Schreibkalender (recording calendar) 101n.89, 122n.174, 133, 140, 219
Schröder, Thomas 134n.38, 138n.56
Schultheiss, Werner 82n.40
Schweinfurt 16
Schwerhoff, Gerd 115n.148
science/scientific 59, 226, 234, 236
Scottish 62
Scott, Joan 24n.1, 33
secularization 235
security 12, 43–44
seeds (for harvest) 40, 55, 68,165–66, 210
  mustard seed (simile, Matthew 13:31) 188
Seligenthal, Cistercian convent 125
separation
  from Christ 189
  of a community 43, 48, 50, 59, 145–46, 179–80, 223
  from a place 59, 180
  of the sick 102, 105, 107
  of state and church 235n.1
siege(s)/besieged 8, 12, 30, 72, 75, 146–47, 160, 168
Sigl, Rupert 33–35n.29–30, 38n.36 and 38, 44–46n.60–66, 54n.95, 57n.105, 58–60n.107–10, 76n.17, 131n.26–28, 146–47n.85–87, 179–80n.178–81
sign(s)
  heavenly 132, 219
  wearing of visible signs 90n.58, 93
skepticism 59n.108
  religious 235
Sloterdijk, Peter 67
smallpox 101n.88
smell 104
  foul 101, 104
  see also stench
social discipline 114, 207–8
social mobility, rejected 118
Soden, Franz Freiherr von 70n.1, 114n.144, 158n.122, 220–21n.294–95

Soergel, Philip M.   119*n*.170
soldier(s)   12, 30, 32*n*.26, 37, 40–42, 44, 47,
    53–60, 62–69, 75, 77, 79–84, 86–88, 101,
    106, 110–11, 118, 121,124, 147–48, 150, 156–
    68, 173–74, 181–84, 195–96, 199, 204–5,
    209, 221, 223–24, 227, 230, 234–35
  and civilians   42
  and diary-style account   27, 42, 47
  and disease   101
  exploitation of   47, 68
  payment of   47
  and rape   41–42
  see also army
Solms–Laubach, Heinrich Wilhelm von,
    count (1583–1632)   75*n*.13
Solms–Rödelheim, Friedrich von, count
    (1574–1649)   19
song(s)   1, 8, 137, 186, 188, 192–93, 195–96,
    219, 230
  see also music
Sophia, margravine of Brandenburg–
    Ansbach (1594–1651)   19
space   5, 33, 48, 50, 52, 62, 157, 178, 180–81,
    184–86, 229, 235
  enclosed   44, 181–83
  hierarchy of   185
  religious/sacred   56–57, 59, 64, 66, 181–83
spacial turn   52*n*.89
(the) Spanish
  army/troops   66*n*.137, 68, 95, 104, 106, 108
Spanish Habsburgs   10
Spicer, Andrew   90*n*.56
spies   92, 141
Spindler, Max   18*n*.38, 19
Spohnholz, Jesse   6*n*.17
Sporhan–Krempel, Lore   141*n*.65
Stahleder, Helmuth   23*n*.56, 72*n*.7, 73*n*.9 and
    11, 75*n*.15, 92–93*n*.65–66, 96*n*.72
Staiger, Clara   26, 29–33, 35, 39*n*.43, 47–49,
    53–54, 80, 124, 147–53, 167–68, 180,
    185, 220
Stalla, Gerhard   125*n*.5
Steiger, Heinhard   4
stench   106
  see also smell
stigma   42
stigmatization   90*n*.58
Stollberg-Rilinger, Barbara   5*n*.17

Stolleis, Michael   235*n*.1
Stör–Erfahrung (experiences of cognitive
    dissonance)   67
Strasser, Ulrike   44*n*.59
Straubing   33, 66, 76, 146–48
  Rentamt   21, 97*n*.76
Stromer, Wolff Friedrich   91–92
structures
  and personalities   2
  physical   89
suffering   6, 24, 28, 43, 45, 48, 54, 89, 100,
    112, 135, 149, 157, 186, 198, 200, 204, 209,
    220, 235
  of Christ   192
  limits of   167
  meaning of   219
suicide   30, 167
superstition   211, 213–19
  prosecution of   213
supplication(s) /supplicant   172–75, 177,
    187, 190–92, 196–98
  see also petition(s)
Swabia(n)   14, 19, 53, 107*n*.111, 125
  Bavarian Swabia   102*n*.95
Sweden   10, 15, 137
  entry into the war   8
  intervention   12, 27, 41, 53, 71, 141
Swedes   22, 29*n*.15, 30, 32, 34, 38, 45–46,
    48–50, 52, 56–58, 61–62, 66–67, 69–71,
    73, 78, 104*n*.103, 110*n*.129, 121*n*.172,
    124*n*.2, 125–31, 140, 143–44, 148, 154–57,
    160–62, 166–68, 171, 178, 180*n*.182,
    182–83, 204, 227–30

Tallett, Frank   42*n*.52
Taupadel, Georg Christoph von (ca. 1600–
    1647)   62, 168
tax(es)   21, 79, 97*n*.76, 108
  contribution   75
  "fire tax"   75, 79
  lists   18*n*.37
  special tax for fortifications   73
teachings
  condemnation of religious
    teachings   188–89
  theological differences of   196
  of witchcraft   211
Tegernsee   37, 133

Tennstedt, Florian   90*n*.56–57, 91*n*.59
territorial defense system   77–79
terror   32–35, 37–38, 43, 45, 200
    effects of   34
    see also anxiety; dread; fear; fright; horror; trauma
Theatrum Europaeum   133
Theibault, John   6*n*.19
theology
    differences between Catholic and Protestant teachings   196
Thieser, Bernd   212, 213*n*.268
Thirty Years' War   4–8, 16, 70, 75, 82, 155, 223, 232
    and Augsburg   128*n*.15
    broader political significance   3
    complex dynamics of interaction   5
    composition of armies   42
    and contemporary Europe   1
    and contribution (war tax)   75
    conventional assumptions/image   60
    and destruction   5
    and disease/pestilence   100, 102
    end of   235
    war as equalizer   46
    evaluation of   3–4
    experiences   24–69
    and fortifications   71
    as God's punishment   114, 187
    image of   5, 24, 221, 223, 232, 234, 236
    involvement of other European powers   3
    and jubilee celebrations   188
    local dimension   4, 7, 77, 233
    making sense of the war   6, 24
    and mercenary armies   77*n*.20
    and movement of people   6–7
    outbreak of   1, 18
    and magic practices   211, 214
    and Maximilian of Bavaria   21–23
    and media   133–41
    panoramic view of   4
    and patterns of coexistence and cooperation   5
    and Peace of Augsburg   2
    and positive encounters   5
    and poverty   90–91
    psychologically debilitating power of war   50
    and readership   139
    in Reformation history   1
    and religion   207
    and superstition   215
    and survival   170
    theological interpretation   186–87
    up close   5, 24
    violence of   7
    and witchcraft   212–13
    see also conflict
Thuringia   14
Thuringian–Franconian borderland   177
Tilly, Johann Tserclaes, Count of (1559–1632)   10–11, 13–14, 138, 140, 162*n*.135
time, its importance for finding common ground   227–29
Tode, Sven   5*n*.15
tradition   91, 116, 120, 218, 221
trauma(tic)   5, 7, 35, 41–42, 44, 47, 185, 232, 236
    see also anxiety; dread; fear; fright; horror; terror
traumatization   30*n*.21
treason   92
troop movement   27, 70, 81, 85, 90, 190, 233
    corridor/line of   5, 13 fig. 3, 27–28, 31, 35, 54, 71, 80, 125, 130
troops   6, 29–30, 53, 55–56, 62, 66–67, 69, 74–76, 80–82, 86–89, 93–95, 100, 104, 108–9, 119, 121, 144, 147, 150, 160–62, 167, 172, 176, 180, 232
    auxiliary   66, 79
    Bavarian   13–14, 22, 66, 69, 76, 84, 148
    behavior   7
    and their demands   53
    enemy   10, 39, 59, 65–66, 86, 121, 144, 148, 159, 180
    French   15*n*.32, 168, 199
    "friendly"   39, 59, 62, 65–66, 77, 86, 159, 161, 166, 204, 234
    imperial   14, 85, 143, 148
    imperial–Bavarian   137
    Ligistic   71, 204
    Polish   143
    quartering of   46, 55, 68, 70, 81, 84, 88, 106, 108–9, 117–18, 121, 159, 210

troops (cont.)
    relief troops (*Entsatztruppen*)   75
    rescue troops   75
    Swedish   13 fig. 3, 45, 73, 204
    starving   68
    and their train   53
    withdrawal of   16, 77
    see also armies; soldiers
Truchseß, Wolf Dietrich   162–63
trust(ed)   50, 76–77, 87, 121–22, 127, 132, 146, 182, 236
    lack of   59n.108, 67, 69, 77, 121–22, 143, 215–26, 227, 233
    in Christ's mercy/aid   125, 127, 192
    in God/His mercy/aid   41, 76, 125–26, 188, 193–95, 201, 204
    trustworthy news   142, 144, 148
Tuan, Yi-fu   28n.13
Turk(s)   75
    as bogeyman   75n.15
    Long Turkish War (1593–1606)   9–10, 75
typhus   101, 110
Tyrol   49n.76, 52, 55, 107n.111, 124, 125n.4, 128, 150, 222

Ulbrich, Claudia   25n.8, 26n.9
Ulbricht, Otto   101n.87
Ulm   40
uncertainty   6, 46, 120, 127
    of roads   35, 82
    see also instability
unity   187, 192
    jurisdictional   16
    religious   9, 180, 228–29
unpredictability   44, 46
Untergiesing   96
upbringing   27, 221
(the) Upper Palatinate   8, 10, 73, 77, 150n.99, 212
Upper Saxony   14

Vervaux, Johannes S. J. (1586–1661)   22
Vetter, Anna   170, 171n.158
Vienna   140n.64, 150–51
Vigarello, George   41n.49–50
Vinzensbronn   173
violence   6, 24, 27, 33, 39, 42–43, 47, 48, 53, 56–58, 62, 65, 70, 80, 83, 86–88, 110, 121, 123–26, 150, 157–58, 160–61, 163–64, 190, 193, 202, 223, 231–32, 234, 236
    against women   41
    anticipation of   33
    fear of   69
    protection against   70, 89, 101, 232
    religious   56–57, 64–65, 184, 228
    sexual violence   42
    threat of   37, 43, 157
    see also rape
virginity   42
Vogelka, Karl G.   75n.14
volatility   12, 39, 44, 47–48, 69–70, 224, 232
vulnerability   6, 24, 39, 43, 46, 55, 69, 70, 76, 81, 91, 93, 100, 129, 232

Wagentroz, David   208
Walker, Garthine   41n.49 and 51, 42n.53
Wallenstein, Albrecht Wenzel Eusebius von (Waldstein, 1583–1634)   13–15, 76, 86, 140, 147
    army of   11, 14
    dismissal of   12
Wallner, Ida   29n.14, 30n.16
Walter, François   1n.2
Wang, Andreas   135n.39
war
    see Thirty Years' War
Wasserburg   48n.72
Weber, Heinrich   38n.39–40, 39n.42, 56n.101, 57n.103–4 and 106, 61–63n.114–20, 76–77n.18–19, 125n.7, 132n.29, 225–26n.307–9
weddings   114, 166, 220
Wedgwood, Cicely V.   2n.4
Weimar army/horsemen (*Weimarers*)   44, 58, 65–66, 131, 147, 166, 199
Weißenburg   16, 71, 170
Werder, Paris von dem   121n.173
werewolves   214–16
Werve, Hermann de   140
White Mountain, Battle (8 November 1620)   10, 23, 72, 212
Wicht, Ambrosius   59–60
Wildenstein, Georg Wolf von   61, 228
Willax, Franz   72n.5
Williams, Gerhild Scholz   133n.34

Wilson, Peter H.   2*n*.6–7, 6, 8*n*.20, 9, 10*n*.23
  and 26, 15*n*.33, 70*n*.1, 71*n*.3, 75*n*.15
Windsheim   16, 160
Winter King *see* Frederick V
Wirth, Volkmar   46*n*.67
witchcraft   32, 211–13
Wittmann, Pius   19*n*.45, 175*n*.170
Wolff, Heinrich   219
Wolkan, Rudolf   134*n*.36
wolves   214–15
women   33–34, 42, 66–67, 68, 151, 161, 170, 181, 185–86, 205, 214, 221–22, 233–34
  as commentators   146
  defending a city   160, 168
  and fortification work   72, 74
  leaders   39
  as messengers   141–42
  of a religious community   29–30, 32–33, 42–43, 48, 53, 57, 123, 125, 127*n*.13, 128, 146, 150, 152, 156, 185, 200, 226–29
  scholars   25
  unprotected   41
  rape/violation of   41–42
Württemberg   42*n*.53
Würzburg   32, 46, 71, 127–28, 141, 162–63, 182
  bishopric of   16, 19
  bishop of   46, 166, 201, 206
  witch hunts in   212

Zillhardt, Gerd   40*n*.45
Zweig, Stefan   52
Zwingler, Irmgard E.   39*n*.43, 51–52*n*.81–87, 56*n*.99–100, 57*n*.102, 60*n*.111, 124–25*n*.2–4, 144*n*.78, 145*n*.83, 148*n*.91, 222*n*.297

Printed in the United States
by Baker & Taylor Publisher Services